The Patriarchal Political Order

Women across the Global South, and particularly in India, turn out to vote on election days but are noticeably absent from politics year-round. Why? In *The Patriarchal Political Order*, Soledad Artiz Prillaman combines descriptive and causal analysis of qualitative and quantitative data from more than 9,000 women and men in India to expose how coercive power structures diminish political participation for women. Prillaman unpacks how dominant men, imbued with authority from patriarchal institutions and norms, benefit from institutionalizing the household as a unitary political actor. Women vote because it serves the interests of men but stay out of politics more generally because it threatens male authority. Yet, when women come together collectively to demand access to political spaces, they become a formidable foe to the patriarchal political order. Eye-opening and inspiring, this book serves to deepen our understanding of what it means to create an inclusive democracy for all.

SOLEDAD ARTIZ PRILLAMAN is an assistant professor of Political Science at Stanford University. She is also the faculty director of the Inclusive Democracy and Development Lab at Stanford. Prillaman specializes in comparative political economy, development, and gender, with a focus in South Asia.

Cambridge Studies in Comparative Politics

General Editor

Kathleen Thelen, *Massachusetts Institute of Technology*

Associate Editors

Lisa Blaydes, *Stanford University*
Catherine Boone, *London School of Economics*
Thad Dunning, *University of California, Berkeley*
Anna Grzymala-Busse, *Stanford University*
Torben Iversen, *Harvard University*
Stathis Kalyvas, *University of Oxford*
Melanie Manion, *Duke University*
Prerna Singh, *Brown University*
Dan Slater, *University of Michigan*
Susan Stokes, *Yale University*
Tariq Thachil, *University of Pennsylvania*
Erik Wibbels, *University of Pennsylvania*

Series Founder

Peter Lange, *Duke University*

Editor Emeritus

Margaret Levi, *Stanford University*

Other Books in the Series

(continued after the index)

The Patriarchal Political Order

The Making and Unraveling of the Gendered Participation Gap in India

SOLEDAD ARTIZ PRILLAMAN

Stanford University

CAMBRIDGE
UNIVERSITY PRESS

CAMBRIDGE
UNIVERSITY PRESS

Shaftesbury Road, Cambridge CB2 8EA, United Kingdom

One Liberty Plaza, 20th Floor, New York, NY 10006, USA

477 Williamstown Road, Port Melbourne, VIC 3207, Australia

314–321, 3rd Floor, Plot 3, Splendor Forum, Jasola District Centre, New Delhi – 110025, India

103 Penang Road, #05-06/07, Visioncrest Commercial, Singapore 238467

Cambridge University Press is part of Cambridge University Press & Assessment, a department of the University of Cambridge.

We share the University's mission to contribute to society through the pursuit of education, learning and research at the highest international levels of excellence.

www.cambridge.org
Information on this title: www.cambridge.org/9781009355759

DOI: 10.1017/9781009355797

© Soledad Artiz Prillaman 2024

First published 2024

A catalogue record for this publication is available from the British Library

A Cataloging-in-Publication data record for this book is available from the Library of Congress

ISBN 978-1-009-35575-9 Hardback
ISBN 978-1-009-35580-3 Paperback

For Cammy, Kim, and Ami, the most powerful
women I know

Contents

Contents

Figures

Tables

Acknowledgments

After every focus group I conducted with women, I asked them whether they had any questions for me. The most commonly asked question (well, actually the second most common after one about farming) was about my women's group and from where I derived support. Like the women in this book, my success in completing this manuscript was only possible with the support of awe-inspiring mentors and incredible friends.

I owe a great debt, intellectually and personally, to my early advisors who have inspired me, taught me, and encouraged me, and without whom I would not be where I am today. Torben Iversen has been an intellectual role model and ardent supporter throughout this process. He believed in this project since its inception and pushed me to unlock its full potential. Knowingly or unknowingly, his insightful and candid feedback forced me to reevaluate all prior assumptions and challenged me to become a better thinker and scholar. I am forever grateful to have walked into Rohini Pande's office in 2014. Rohini has shown me how to get to the core of questions and arguments, and in doing so, how to learn about our social world. Her ability to combine a focus on social impact with academic rigor is unrivaled and empowered me to think big. She has supported and guided me through every detail of this project, and her influence is embedded on each page. Gwyneth McClendon has served as an example of the kind of academic I desire to be. She has filled pages with her comments on this work and provided continual encouragement in the moments of doubt.

My time at Harvard was filled with informal mentorship and support from more people than I can name. James Robinson nurtured this project in its early stages and provided invaluable feedback at a critical juncture. I am grateful for the support of Jim Alt, who opened his door on my first day of graduate school and helped me to weather the transition into academia. Gary King helped show me how to capture and convey the big idea, and I am thankful to have benefited from his guidance and support. I have also benefited from the example and support of many others, including Fran Hagopian, Steve Levitsky, Bob Bates, Melani Cammett, and Jeff Frieden.

My academic journey began as an undergraduate at Texas A&M. This book and much more was made possible by Ken Meier's willingness to take a chance on me as a research assistant. Ken taught me what academic research is and showed me that you can make a profession of your passions. He has continued to be an unparalleled mentor, and I endeavor to honor his example.

I had the immense privilege of spending two years at Nuffield College as a postdoctoral fellow. It was there that this book really took shape. I am grateful to David Rueda for many lunches filled with advice and political economy debate. I also want to thank Ben Ansell, Ray Duch, Des King, Alex Kuo, and Ezequiel Gonzalez-Ocantos for their encouragement during this time.

I was once told that the best way to make use of time at Stanford is to allow it to breathe into you and fill you with ideas. I am grateful to be full of breath. In their never-failing pursuit of the big question and important discovery, the mentors I have benefited from at Stanford have pushed me to uncover and communicate the core truths with the biggest social impact. I owe deep thanks to all of my colleagues for this mentorship and especially to Lisa Blaydes, Anna Grzymala-Busse, David Laitin, Beatriz Magaloni, and Paul Sniderman, who read and provided critical feedback on early drafts of this manuscript. To my fellow junior colleagues, I am thankful for your camaraderie and solidarity. To the incredible department staff, thank you for making this work possible.

While in the thick of pandemic lockdowns, several people gave their time to share feedback at a book workshop for this manuscript. That feedback led me to reframe the book and consider new angles for analysis. I owe the deepest debt of gratitude to Mala Htun, Tariq Thachil, Steven Wilkinson, and the late Frances Rosenbluth. This book is undeniably improved from their wisdom.

Without the support of PRADAN, this project would not have been possible. Nivedita Narain has championed me from the beginning, shared her wisdom, provided deep friendship, and enabled my achievements. Her limitless enthusiasm and energy are infectious, and she is a source of daily inspiration. Her impact on this book is immeasurable. I am exceedingly thankful to Madhu Khetan for supporting and feeding into this work for the past seven years. I have learned more from her than I can express. I am honored to know these very powerful women. To Archana Singh, Sundandita Banerjee, Irfan Ahmad, and all of the team members who have given their time to support this research, I am deeply grateful. Your desire to learn and your deep wisdom are inspiring.

I have also had the exceptional support of many research assistants, for whom much of this work is indebted. This project would not have been possible nor successful without their commitment to and passion for this work. I do not have enough words to show my gratitude. Jasleen Kaur joined me while I was still a graduate student and was tireless in her efforts to capture the stories of women across Madhya Pradesh. She led the data collection that fills these pages. Sayanti Sur has, for the past four years, carried out this work with compassion and tenacity and oversaw the challenging task of censusing whole villages. Gurjot Singh spent three years resiliently analyzing data and providing critical support. Somer Khambu Bryant spent most of her years at Stanford working closely with me on questionnaire design, data coding, and analysis. Her commitment to women's empowerment and support of this research agenda have supported my success. I am also grateful to Maya Bedge and Nina Ramachandani. To all of the interviewers and enumerators who traversed challenging geographies to capture the data shown here, I owe deep thanks.

The voices of women in India have often been muted because of limited data. I am indebted to the funders who made it possible to make women the centerpiece of this study. The Abdul Latif Jameel Poverty Action Lab Governance Initiative, the National Science Foundation, the Evidence-based Measures of Empowerment for Research on Gender Equality Initiative, the Center for Effective Global Action and Oxford Policy Management, and the Stanford University Lancet group provided financial support for data collection. The Weatherhead Center for International Affairs, the Multidisciplinary Program in Inequality and Social Policy, the South Asia Institute, and the Institute for Quantitative Social Sciences all provided financial support for fieldwork as well as a broader intellectual community at Harvard.

Rachel Blaifeder has been a wonderful editor and champion at Cambridge University Press. I am grateful to the anonymous reviewers for incisive feedback that has significantly improved this manuscript. Kelley Friel provided masterful copyediting. Japani Shyam Dhurve designed and painted the cover art. She is one of the most prominent and acclaimed Gond artists and her art brings together the power of nature and the experiences of modern life. I had the immense privilege of meeting with her in Bhopal and sharing stories. Her work and story are inspiring, and I am in awe of how she captured the life of this book.

Parts of this book appeared in "Strength in numbers: how women's groups close India's political gender gap," *American Journal of Political Science* (2021). I thank the publishers for permission to use these materials.

Over the years I have benefited from a range of solidarity groups. These groups provided me with energy, motivation, and sanity. My words will never be enough to say thank you. Rakeen Mabud and Jonathan Phillips have journeyed with me in this endeavor since day one. They celebrated every victory and carried me through every low and showed me the value of smart critique in a warm environment. Zeynep Pamuk and Ranjit Lall spent every Tuesday afternoon and many more evenings in Cambridge (and later Oxford) brightening my week, providing lively debate, and stretching my mind. Their continued friendship provides immeasurable comfort and constant intellectual invigoration. While in the United Kingdom, I benefited enormously from the feedback and support of Rachel Bernhard, Ana Catalano Weeks, and Mona Morgan-Collins. I have enjoyed countless dinners with Andreas Wiedemann roasting the endeavor that is book writing. Charity Troyer Moore taught me how to do fieldwork while sitting in an office in Shahpur Jat. Her guidance and friendship enabled this work. I have been invigorated by the energy and wisdom of Julia Lowe and Nivedita Narain on several continents. I have treasured getting to know and learn from the group of women studying gender in South Asia, including Rachel Brulé, Sarah Khan, Bhumi Purohit, Rashi Sabherwal, Tanushree Goyal, Rithika Kumar, and Shandana Khan Mohmand. The EGEN community helped me find an academic home and has provided feedback and friendship ever since. I am especially grateful to Tiffany Barnes, Amanda Clayton, Diana O'Brien, and Dawn Teele. Saad Gulzar and the entire ID2 lab have modeled the unique combination of compassion and critique and provided me with an intellectual home.

To everyone else who has provided comments on papers and talks, conversed over coffee about ideas and challenges, and supported me in this process, I am eternally grateful. I would especially like to thank Antonia Peacocke, Wendy Salkin, Shane Taylor, Brandon de la Cuesta, Amanda Kennard, Hakeem Jefferson, Yiqing Xu, Vicky Fouka, Ali Cheema, Emmerich Davies, Rikhil Bhavnani, Alex Lee, Mike Callen, Deepak Singhania, Adam Auerbach, Aluma Dembo, Asli Cansunar, Barbara Piotrowska, Jakob Schneebacher, Lucia Kalousova, Lorena Barberia, Tsin Yen Koh, Stephen Pettigrew, Melissa Sands, Aytug Sasmez, Julie Weaver, Liz Davis, John Marshall, Sara Lowes, Shelby Grossman, Molly Roberts, Alicia Harley, Emily Clough, and Gabe Koehler-Derrick. I also want to say thank you to Brittney Fleming for her friendship and never-ceasing support for more than two decades.

I owe the greatest gratitude to my family, who has stood by my side with unfailing optimism and encouragement. To my mom, Cammy Shay, an incredible woman with fierce convictions, who taught me to question assumptions, think deeply, and dream big, I dedicate this endeavor. To my dad, Ernest Artiz, I owe my strength, resilience, and drive. My sister, Ami Artiz, embodies what it means to be empowered and provides daily inspiration (and Marco Polo messages of encouragement). My brother, Ernie Artiz, inculcated my fighting spirit from a young age and journeyed with me to India to fight for this wonderful adventure. The powerful women in my life are numerous and have undoubtedly inspired the ideas that fill these pages. Kim Shay, Shirley Miller, Norma Artiz, Algene Artiz, Tammy Prillaman, and Jessika Carter have all modeled how to be both powerful and kind, and I have learned who I want to be simply by watching them. And I would not be where I am without the support of John Shay, Jim Miller, Ernest Artiz, and Walter Prillaman. While our time together was brief, Ted Shay's legacy is evidenced on these pages. To Ridge Prillaman, who has moved continents, traversed monkey-laden fields, and learned to scrape data all in support of my ambitions, I am eternally grateful. My work is only possible because of his devotion.

I am beholden to the women featured in this project. These women inspire me daily and have affected me more than I can say. It is my honor to share a piece of their stories.

PART I

THE PUZZLE OF WOMEN'S POLITICAL PARTICIPATION

I

Introduction

On a hot summer day in 2015, I sat down alongside Sushila, a middle-aged woman who is the leader of her village's women's movement.[1] We sat on a woven cotton blanket on her front porch sipping chai while she recounted her transformation from being a woman constrained to the domestic sphere and forbidden to leave her house without permission into being a woman with power and voice in village politics today. Sushila's personal transformation mirrored a transformation in her village, where historically women were not even political outsiders, but seen as apolitical, and now are a political force to be reckoned with.

Reflecting on years past, Sushila shared that she was married at the age of twenty to a man she had met only once. As is customary in much of India, she moved in with her husband and his parents just after they got married. This left Sushila more than 100 kilometers from her family and the friendships she had developed throughout childhood and adolescence. In her new village, her only ties were through her husband. She grew nostalgic as she reflected on her life before marriage, stating simply that during that time, "she was free." Her prior freedom stood in stark contrast to her life after marriage, where Sushila fulfilled the set of obligations expected of her as caretaker of the house despite her own desire to work. Instead, she was expected to cook and clean so that her husband could tend to the small plot of land that was their primary source of income.

---

[1] This recounting constitutes my recollection and interpretation of a day spent with Sushila (pseudonym). While I have attempted to tell her story, to the best of my ability, as she shared it with me, I have inevitably imposed my experience and position onto this account. It is also important to acknowledge that even what Sushila shared with me that day is undoubtedly a function of my position as a non-Indian foreigner. For these reasons, I share women's own words to describe their lived experiences from their perspectives as much as possible throughout this book.

Sushila also helped harvest the crops and tend to the soil, but her family (like most official definitions) did not consider this work. The customary assumption is that *he* who plows the fields reaps the financial rewards from the crops. Yet plowing is the exclusive purview of men. And so, despite putting in much of the work to harvest and produce the crops sold at the market, Sushila received no credit for her family's earnings from the land.

Like most of the women I spoke to over six years of fieldwork in rural India,[2] Sushila's life revolved around her domain: the household. She fetched the water, prepared the meals, and cared for her children, spending the majority of her day inside the house. The presiding norms – the invisible rules arbitrating which behaviors were deemed possible and permissible and which merited social sanction – defined the division of labor in Sushila's house as well as where she was allowed to travel, to whom she could speak, and how she was expected to spend her time. Sushila's husband, Nandkishor, spent the majority of his days outside the house. He would leave in the morning to work in their fields or take their crops to market. When he completed his business, he would often spend time in the village center, chatting with other men before returning home. Nandkishor, like most men, did not need to ask permission to leave the village, go to the market, or socialize with others in the community.

Even as I spoke with Sushila, a cluster of men sat together huddled around a deck of cards a few hundred yards away. Sushila said it was common for men in the village to sit together to drink and gamble. To Sushila, these activities were not merely reflective of the differences in the social lives of men and women, but tied to more insidious challenges faced by women in her village. She shared that alcoholism was a challenge in their village and that many women lived in fear of male aggression. She told me about a woman in a nearby village who had approached the local elected official to help her file a legal claim against her husband for regularly assaulting her while intoxicated. The official suggested adjudicating the matter informally rather than taking it to the courts. He convened a meeting of the family, at which he chastised her husband for the violence he perpetrated. He told the woman that she need not approach the police, as the matter was now resolved.[3] This story had convinced Sushila that her local institutions would not protect her from men's violence and power.

Sushila, like women in much of the world, is subject to a political order rooted in patriarchy, the de facto allocation of power to elder males. This

---

[2] While the vast majority of the fieldwork I conducted was in Madhya Pradesh, I spent long periods of time in rural Bihar and Odisha, which also inform my analysis.

[3] This recounting reflects the importance of informal institutions in adjudicating conflict in rural India. More than 85 percent of village disputes are handled by customary (often caste-based) village councils, which are almost exclusively run by men (Krishna 2002a).

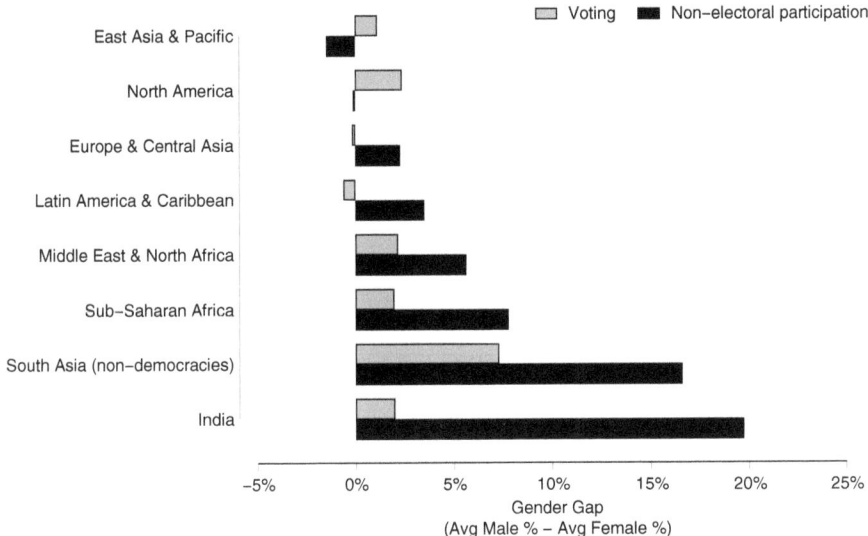

FIGURE 1.1 Gender gaps in political participation in democracies across the globe
Note: Data are from the World Values Survey, Waves 5–7, representing 2005–2022 (Inglehart et al. 2014). Except where noted, data are for democratic countries only, as defined by an average polity score from 2005 to 2018 of greater than 6 (polity V data documented by Marshall and Gurr 2021). In total, the data represent ninety-one democracies and two non-democracies in South Asia (Pakistan and Bangladesh). Voting is measured as those that report turning out to vote in the most recent national election (wave 6) or that they usually or always vote in national elections (waves 5 and 7). Non-electoral participation includes respondents who reported protesting, petitioning, striking, political occupation, or other political action. "Don't knows" are coded as not participating. Responses are weighted by the population survey weight provided.

political order is marked by the absence of women and the centrality of men in most domains of politics and the devaluation of women's voices in political decision-making. This book exposes the patriarchal political order and documents its tangled relationship with many structures of political power.

Many have called attention to the persistent and prevalent gender inequalities in politics, noting women's underrepresentation in electoral office, at the ballot box, and in other interactions with the state. Such inequalities are most prevalent in the Global South: World Values Survey data (2005–2022) reveal in Figure 1.1 that men participate in politics in these countries at substantially higher rates than women (reflected in the positive gender gaps). These inequalities have largely been attributed to characteristics that men have but women lack: money, time, skills, social status, inclinations, and opportunities. According to these arguments, women could enter politics if only they had what men have; their level of engagement in politics is their (often rational) response under these constraints.

Yet there is an important and unexplained puzzle in women's political participation: while women are markedly less politically present than men between elections, women vote at high rates, almost equal to those of men (see Figure 1.1).[4] This pattern of substantially larger gender gaps in non-electoral political participation is present across democracies in the Global South, but nowhere is it more acute than in India, where the gender gap is roughly 2 percentage points for voting, but nearly 20 percentage points for non-electoral political participation.[5] More than half of the women who voted on election day were absent from politics afterward. In fact, India has the lowest level of women's non-electoral political participation of the ninety-one democratic countries surveyed.

Why do women vote but not participate in politics between elections? Prior explanations of gendered political behavior fail to explain this puzzling pattern of participation, rarely distinguishing between the drivers of electoral and non-electoral political behavior. Yet they provide two foundational explanations of gendered political behavior: women's relatively lower levels of political participation are due to resource inequalities (lack of money, time, and skills) and social inequalities (lack of social status and inclination). Access to resources lowers the costs of political participation by facilitating the accumulation of relevant information and easing the financial and procedural barriers to participation.[6] Social inequalities, largely seen as the product of norms that socialize women into domestic and docile roles and sanction those who deviate from these prescribed roles, also condition the costs and perceived benefits of political participation.[7]

---

[4] The Middle East and North Africa are exceptions regarding electoral gender gaps; on average, 20 percentage points fewer women report voting than men.

[5] The World Values Survey only captures forms of political participation that can be consistently and reliably measured across countries and time. As a result, many of the more nuanced and context-specific forms of political participation, most of which occur between elections, are not represented. Chapter 2 presents evidence from an original survey in India that the patterns presented in Figure 1.1 replicate when accounting for a more comprehensive and contextual understanding of political behavior.

[6] Iversen and Rosenbluth (2010) posit that male dominance and, more specifically, gendered differences in political preferences derive from inequalities in bargaining power rooted in women's lack of resources and opportunities. Schlozman, Burns, and Verba (1994) and Burns, Schlozman, and Verba (2001) explain women's lower levels of political participation as resulting, in part, from a lack of resources (money, skills, and networks). Similarly, Carpena and Jensenius (2021) find that delayed marriage – which leads women to have more education and more free time after marriage – is associated with higher levels of political participation. Brulé and Gaikwad (2021) also find that a lack of economic resources, principally control over land, explains lower levels of political participation in patrilineal societies compared to matrilineal societies.

[7] Karpowitz and Mendelberg (2014) suggest that women's lesser authority in political deliberation is the result of a lack of opportunity (driven by institutional characteristics) and inclination (driven by socialization). Similarly, Burns, Schlozman, and Verba (2001) highlight the role of socialization in limiting women's political interest and, in turn, participation. Focusing on inclination, Barnes and Burchard (2013) show that having more women in elite positions of political power who can act as

Both explanations yield an expectation that development, and its consequent economic growth and norm renegotiation, will improve women's political participation. Economic growth is assumed to generate political inclusion, and accordingly, the gendered lag in access to economic prosperity perpetuates women's exclusion.[8] Economic growth increases incomes, expands job opportunities, and improves state capacity and, as a result, service provision. Such economic gains enable households to invest more evenly in both genders; therefore, economic growth ensures more gender-equal access to the constituents of development: health, education, and earning opportunities.[9] Women's greater access to economic resources increases their bargaining power within the household and provides easier access to information, broader networks outside the household, and incentives to invest in young girls' education.[10] Even cultural- or norm-based explanations of women's exclusion suggest that the norms constraining women's behavior are most likely to erode when they gain economic power.[11] As the value of women's production rises (as opposed to their value in reproduction), norms related to which behaviors are considered acceptable for women tend to shift.[12] Girls are then socialized alongside boys into roles associated with economic productivity.

But these economic and social inequalities are only half of the story. Many of these models treat women as atomized individuals endowed with resources and

---

symbols of possibility and acceptability translates into greater female political participation (see also Desposato and Norrander (2009)). Robinson and Gottlieb (2019) suggest that cultural norms shape political behavior by facilitating coordination around gender roles and acceptable behaviors and, in turn, privileging certain strategy sets and equilibria.

[8] These ideas were originally touted in modernization theory (for example in Lipset (1959) and Inkeles (1969)), which suggested that democratic values of inclusion follow industrialization. While modernization theory has been widely contested and discredited, the idea that inclusion often follows growth (albeit for different reasons than modernization theory posits) has remained (Jayachandran (2015)). Norris and Inglehart (2001), for example, suggest that growth and industrialization often bring more women into the workforce, therefore creating a larger pool of qualified women as potential political candidates, which yields equalizing changes in gender norms (see also Reynolds (1999)).

[9] Goldin (2006); Duflo (2012).

[10] Bargaining models of the household attribute exit options and bargaining power to women's economic opportunities, particularly labor force participation and income (Manser and Brown 1980; McElroy and Horney 1981; Lundberg and Pollak 1994; Agarwal 1997; Pollak 2005; Iversen and Rosenbluth 2010). Additionally, studies have shown that changes in the structure of the economy that increase women's earning potential vis-à-vis men yield increased investment in young girls (Qian 2008; Doepke and Tertilt 2009; Pitt, Rosenzweig, and Hassan 2012; Carranza 2014).

[11] Brulé and Gaikwad (2021); Karpowitz and Mendelberg (2014).

[12] Iversen and Rosenbluth (2010) most notably define norms as a *product* of the structure of the economy and the legal institutions regulating marriages, in the same way that political preferences and behavior are a product of the same structures.

constraints that either facilitate or hinder their political action.[13] But they fail to identify how physical and psychological coercion constrain women's political agency and action. Feminist theorists and scholars of empowerment (who largely emanate from the Global South and South Asia in particular) have long drawn attention to the coercive structures that control women's behavior.[14] They focus on the concepts of freedom and agency, or the ability to act in line with one's strategic life goals, as pivotal to our understanding of gender inequities. In the domain of politics, feminist theorists have honed in on the household as a locus of disempowerment for women.[15] More recent research, also largely rooted in South Asia, has empirically shown how household members manipulate and constrain women's political behavior.[16]

I combine these two paradigms – rational and coercive explanations of women's political behavior - and proffer a strategic answer to the puzzle of women's political participation: many women participate in politics only when it serves the interests of men. Women's voting is of benefit to men in systems of clientelist mobilization (where electoral support is exchanged for private benefits), while their more general political participation threatens male authority without reaping rewards for men.

While it is true that many women lack the resources that incline and support men's political action, these resources alone do not explain the variance in women's political participation. In addition, we must ask: who benefits from women's political exclusion? On close inspection, it is the men in Sushila's community, including those in her household and the elites who run village

---

[13] Past research has highlighted how social and normative institutions shape women's behavior, but mostly still presumes that women rationally respond to this set of institutional circumstances (Inglehart and Norris (2000); Iversen and Rosenbluth (2001); Burns, Schlozman, and Verba (2001); Robinson and Gottlieb (2019); Brulé and Gaikwad (2021)).

[14] As I describe in greater detail in Chapter 3, see the works of Sen (1985, 1995, 1999), Batliwala (1993), Kabeer (1999), and Nussbaum (2000) for an understanding of the empowerment (also known as capabilities) approach. This approach highlights the importance of individual agency as an indicator of welfare, as opposed to more traditional economic models of welfare maximization. Taking agency as the key subject of analysis forces a consideration of the factors (and actors) that inhibit agency. See also Folbre (2021).

[15] See, for example, Okin (1989) and Pateman (1988), though even in the nineteenth century theorists recognized the role of the household as a coercive actor in women's political behavior (Mill (2018)). For a less coercive account, see Glaser (1959).

[16] Analyzing a get-out-the-vote experiment, Cheema et al. (2021) show that women in Pakistan are more likely to vote if their husbands receive information about the value of women's vote. (The same is not true when only women receive this information.) Chhibber (2002) suggests that autonomy from the household is the most important correlate of women's political participation in India. Khan (2021) demonstrates in Pakistan that women defer political authority to their husbands by elevating their husbands' political preferences over their own even under inducement, especially when the former are most distinct. Afzal et al. (2016) show that women's influence in household decision-making decreases with the importance of the decision. Less coercive work demonstrating intra-household political influence includes Stoker and Jennings (1995) and Foos and Rooij (2017).

politics, who gain from her submission to the political order and who have the power to (often violently) enforce this submission. Gendered patterns of social and economic inequalities and the capacity for coercion rooted in patriarchal norms and permissive legal structures delineate de facto authority and power and generate incentives to build and maintain a political order that maximizes men's welfare – the patriarchal political order.[17]

The patriarchal political order is thus defined not only by women's limited political participation but also by their political disempowerment – their inability to exercise free choice. For many women, men are the strategic actors deciding their political behavior. Or, more accurately, women are the pawns in men's political games, enabling men to extract greater spoils.

At the center of these political games is the household. Patriarchy is fundamentally based on the allocation of power within the household to elder men. The household has long been considered a critical unit of analysis. It was once treated as a cohesive and aligned unit,[18] but later revealed to be a space for bargaining and negotiation as household members navigate distinct preferences but joint decisions.[19] In addition to being spaces of collective decision-making, households are domains of coercion. One in three women around the world reports violence at the hands of a male household member.[20]

In the patriarchal political order, the household is the fundamental unit of political organization. Thus, when men dominate the household, they dominate politics. In close-knit political communities like the thousands of villages in India, in which electoral patronage and clientelistic exchange are commonplace,[21] political entrepreneurs benefit from organizing politics around households.[22] By treating the household, the fundamental organizing social structure, as a political unit, the costs of political mobilization, particularly with patronage, are lower. But households are also the principal domain of patriarchy, where patriarchal hierarchies are most explicitly defined. Those with power, both legitimate and coercive, within the household, namely elder men, have

---

[17] Similarly, Folbre (2021) provides a theory of gender inequality explained by the synergies of political, cultural, and economic institutions that unite to elevate male authority. Patriarchy, in her conception, is a structure of collective power built on interlocking institutions that circumscribe the opportunities available to people. Folbre (2021: 11) similarly argues that once these institutions are in place, they create incentives for those with power to maintain them: "strong groups often find ways to exploit weak groups and institutionalize their gain in ways that perpetuate their advantage."

[18] Becker (1981) most notably defined the household as a unitary actor with common preferences.

[19] Manser and Brown (1980); McElroy and Horney (1981); Lundberg and Pollack (1994); Agarwal (1997); Pollak (2005); Iversen and Rosenbluth (2010).

[20] World Health Organization (2021).

[21] Anderson, Francois, and Kotwal (2015); Bardhan and Mookherjee (2012); Auerbach (2016); Auerbach and Thachil (2018); Lehne, Shapiro, and Eynde (2018); Asher and Novosad (2017); Wilkinson (2006); Kitschelt and Wilkinson (2007); Berenschot (2010).

[22] Ronconi and Zarazaga (2019) show that clientelist brokers consider household size when making political offers.

incentives to maximize their personal gains from politics by subordinating other household members. Such systems of political mobilization and exchange under patriarchy thus benefit from the alignment of households (and the subordination of the women within them).[23]

In this book, I will show that households in rural India behave as a unit in political decision-making but that women's agency is often subordinated by strategic and powerful men.[24] The coercive unitary household enforces women's voting and restricts women's non-electoral participation because these responses align with the incentives of those with bargaining and coercive power in the household. The institutionalization of the coercive unitary household yields a structure of politics organized around identities shared within households (namely caste) and where men inhabit the center of village politics and women exist on the periphery. These facts align with a political order strategically built on women's political exclusion and explain the puzzle of women's political participation.

Women's political exclusion therefore persists because it benefits those with economic, normative, and coercive power. No amount of money, education, social status, inclination, or opportunity will enable women's political empowerment unless it also allows them to contest male coercion. Yet women can challenge this political order even where patriarchal norms remain strong, and without changes in their stocks of the resources thought to facilitate political action.

How is the patriarchal political order unraveled? Returning to my day with Sushila and her experiences at present, Sushila discussed a recent village assembly meeting, where she sat among a mass of women at the front. She described speaking up at the meeting as a representative of her women's group and articulating their concerns – a lack of water, an absent teacher, and the prevalence of domestic violence at the hands of inebriated husbands – demanding responsiveness from local politicians. She also documented how this political action was met with challenges: her husband's disapproval of her newfound political voice and the experience of being forcibly removed alongside other women from an earlier village meeting, as it "was not their place." Yet she remained strident in her desire for women to politically mobilize.

Sushila's public presence and informal community leadership mark a drastic shift from her life right after marriage. She attributes this change to her joining a women-only credit group, known in India as a self-help group (SHG), seven years prior. She joined this group so that she and her family could access

<hr/>

[23] Isaksson, Kotsadam, and Nerman (2014) also document a link between the prevalence of clientelism and women's political participation in Africa, showing that gender gaps are larger when clientelism is more prevalent.

[24] Mohmand (2019) documents how powerful men (landlords) can also suppress the political agency of socioeconomically lower status men (the landless). She, too, suggests that clientelism structures the way that collectives of the subordinate must navigate and sometimes defer to those with power to access the state.

cheaper credit and learn about new farming techniques. But when asked what has changed most in her life since joining the SHG, she replied decisively that it was the depth of her connection with other women in the community. She stated, "We overcame our fear when we met together. Alone, we were very frightened. We took each other's support when we were together. With the support of our sisters, our fear disappeared gradually."

I will show that women can gain autonomy from the household and challenge the patriarchal political order through collective action. This collective action is made possible by strong political ties, a common gender consciousness, and social solidarity among women. Sushila's experiences reflect the power generated by women's collective action. A credit group may seem an unlikely place for political empowerment. Yet, as I will causally demonstrate, such institutions enable women's autonomy from the household and can in some cases build women's social solidarity around a shared gender identity.[25] In turn, this social solidarity can foster collective action to demand political agency and representation. Dense and solidaristic ties among women, built on norms of reciprocity and trust, channeled toward demands for political representation, are effective at increasing women's political participation and countering subsequent male backlash.

This book documents the patriarchal political order and then unravels it by demonstrating the power of public policy and women's action to reshape Indian women's political lives. At its core, this book is about the nature of governance in Indian villages, and how existing governance structures, including those of clientelism, are built on the sustained political exclusion of women. It accounts for an entire gender system that subordinates women – the patriarchal political order – highlighting the complexity of their political inclusion and the ways in which identity can shape power in democratic systems. It sheds light on the political worlds and networks in which women reside and illustrates how women's most intimate network, the household, shapes their political behavior. It highlights the central role of violence and coercion in suppressing women's political voices, but also demonstrates how (and when) policies can give women the tools to overcome this subordination. This book is also about development and the unconventional and unanticipated ways it is tied to women's political representation in modern democracies. It examines cases of women, like Sushila, who have found their voice in politics, and unearths the process and instruments of their political empowerment.

In this endeavor, I analyze a variety of novel data sources, including surveys and interviews, and multiple methodologies, such as natural experiments and network analysis, to explore the experiences of women across villages in one state of India, Madhya Pradesh, that are in most ways indistinguishable but

---

[25] Feigenberg, Field, and Pande (2010) document how regular microfinance group meetings can stimulate social capital among group members.

where women's political lives differ in important ways. I analyze data on women's and men's political networks from an original census of all adult residents of six Indian villages and reveal the substantial gender inequalities in political ties and influence as well as the particular importance of extra-household political relationships for women's political behavior. It is abundantly apparent that village political networks center on men. These data, alongside data from several hundred qualitative interviews in the same communities, also demonstrate how households and communities jointly constitute women's political behavior, often through the deployment of fear and violence. I then wield the tools of causal inference to evaluate the unintended consequences of a series of public policies designed to increase women's financial inclusion through microcredit groups (SHGs) for women's political empowerment. I find that bringing women together outside of their homes can foster a collective identity, generate collective action, and ultimately increase political agency and participation.

THE PUZZLE OF WOMEN'S POLITICAL PARTICIPATION IN INDIA

As India is the world's largest democracy and the home of the world's most expansive political gender equality policy,[26] we would expect the political lives of Indian women to be flourishing. Multiple studies have documented the immense gains in women's representation generated by an electoral quota policy that ensures that more than 1.3 million women hold elected office in local governments.[27] This policy has enabled women to gain access to previously exclusionary political institutions and to accumulate power to achieve their unique demands.[28] As expected by those who tout institutional solutions to political gender gaps, this quota policy has also been shown to raise women's political participation[29] and shift attitudes about the acceptability and

---

[26] In 1992, the 73rd and 74th Amendments to India's Constitution established the current structure of local government and mandated reservations for women and ethnic minority groups, including members of the historically marginalized Scheduled Castes (SC), Scheduled Tribes (ST), and Other Backward Classes (OBCs). These amendments require reserving one-third of all elected seats and chairpersonships in Gram Panchayats (village councils) for women. The amendments also reserved elected seats for SC and ST members in proportion to their population shares. Implementing these reservations was left to the states; since 1992, twenty out of twenty-nine states have extended this gender reservation to 50 percent, including Madhya Pradesh.

[27] Bhatnagar (2019).

[28] Chattopadhyay and Duflo (2004); Beaman et al. (2009); Bhavnani (2009); Goyal (2020); Karekurve-Ramachandra (2021); Goyal (2019).

[29] A large literature on gender quotas suggests that these policies can help rectify gender gaps driven by social inequalities. The core of these arguments is that women's descriptive representation provides information about their capacity as leaders and their acceptability in leadership positions. Chattopadhyay and Duflo (2004) show that women citizen's political participation is higher in Indian villages randomly allocated to female reservation for the village chairperson.

competence of women's political leadership.[30] India's most recent national election had the highest turnout of women in history, where more women turned out than men in many parts of the country.

However, the cascade of gender equality envisioned with the widespread imposition of electoral quotas appears to have left the majority of India's women behind. World Values Survey data (2005–2022) show that only one in five women in India reported having engaged in any of the measured political actions other than voting (i.e., protesting, petitioning, striking, political occupation, and other political action). Yet nearly half of Indian men reported engaging in politics outside elections, ranking alongside countries lauded for political representation, such as Finland, the Netherlands, Japan, and Germany. Women in India ranked alongside those in Russia, South Africa, and Mexico, countries known for political inequality. Representative data from the Indian Human Development Survey, shown in Figure 1.2, corroborates women's low levels of non-electoral political participation: fewer than 10 percent of women reported attending village assembly meetings, the cornerstone of village government, in a majority of Indian states, which is all the more puzzling given their high (and rising) voter turnout.

Local gender quotas have also failed to transform women's political representation outside of reserved seats in local offices. Data from four state election commissions reveal that women win only around 10 percent of seats not reserved for them in local elections.[31] Furthermore, as of 2019, only 14 percent of members of parliament and 7 percent of members of state legislative assemblies were women (see Figure 1.3). Panel A of Figure 1.3 demonstrates that women's representation in the national parliament has improved only marginally over the past six decades and remains steadily below the global average for democracies. In 2019, India ranked among the ten democracies with the lowest national parliamentary representation of women.[32] Panel A of

---

Barnes and Burchard (2013) document an uptick in female citizens' political participation in twenty African countries when there were more women in national legislatures. Desposato and Norrander (2009) present correlational evidence that the share of women in the visible elite is positively correlated with women's reported political participation in Latin America. Karpowitz and Mendelberg (2014) experimentally show that the more women involved in (lab-based) deliberation, the greater women's perceived and realized authority. However, Clayton (2015) instead finds that a subnational gender quota policy in Lesotho led to a reduction in self-reported political engagement of female citizens. She suggests this is a function of women's heightened suspicion of affirmative action measures in response to the quota.

[30] Beaman et al. (2009) find that residents, particularly male residents, of villages randomly reserved to have a female chairperson reported less implicit and explicit bias against women in leadership positions in India. Like with political participation, Clayton (2014) finds the reverse in Lesotho: Women's attitudes become more regressive in response to a subnational quota policy.

[31] Specifically, data from the 2016 (2015) [2019] and {2015} local elections in Haryana (Rajasthan) [Telangana] and {Uttar Pradesh} show that women won 11.4 percent (5.4 percent) [10.4 percent] and {16.1 percent} of non-reserved seats.

[32] Inter-Parliamentary Union (2022).

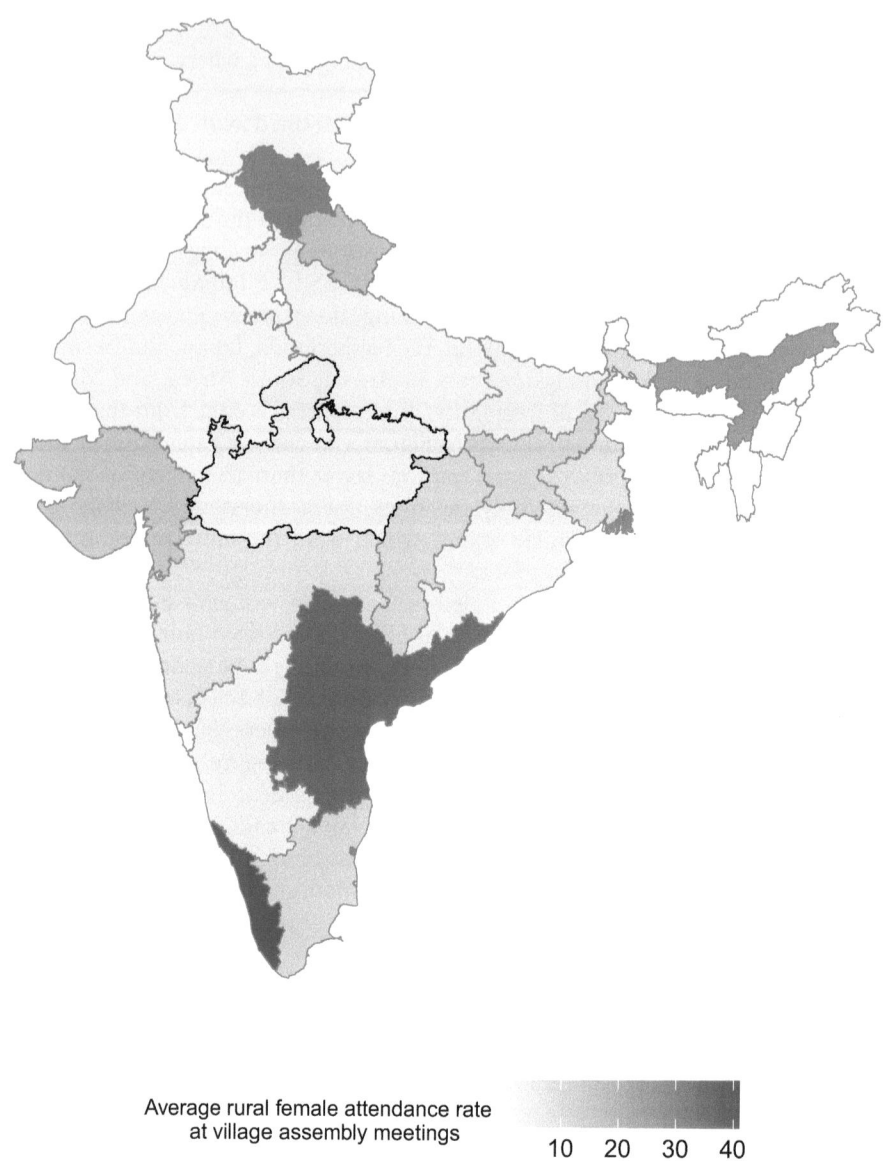

Average rural female attendance rate
at village assembly meetings

10   20   30   40

FIGURE 1.2 Map of India depicting state averages of women's attendance rate at village
assembly meetings
Note: Data are from the eligible women survey conducted as part of the Indian Human
Development Survey in 2011–2012 (Desai and Vanneman 2015). Madhya Pradesh is outlined in
black. Only rural respondents are retained and states with fewer than 200 respondents are excluded.

(a) Female share of Members of Parliament (MPs) in the National Assembly

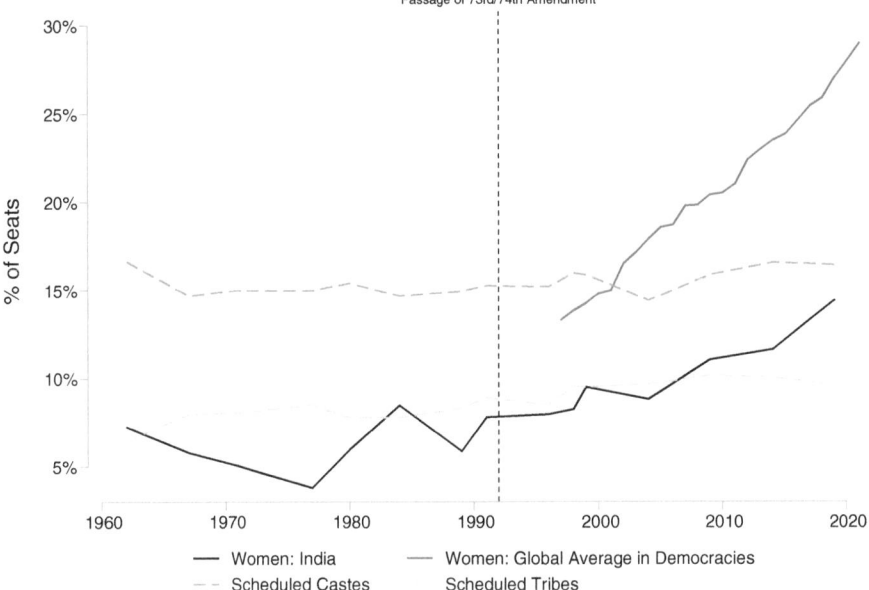

FIGURE 1.3 Women's electoral representation in national and state assemblies in India
Note: Data for both panels are from the Indian Elections Data repository at the Trivedi Centre for Political Data (TCPD 2021). Global data on women's parliamentary representation in Panel A are from the Inter-Parliamentary Union women in national parliaments database (Inter-Parliamentary Union 2022). Global average is for democracies, as defined by an average polity score from 2005 to 2018 of greater than 6 (polity V data documented by Marshall and Gurr 2021).

Figure 1.3 also shows that women's electoral representation in India is markedly below that of Scheduled Castes (SCs) and similar to that of Scheduled Tribes (STs), even though women make up roughly 48 percent of the population as compared to 17 percent and 9 percent for SCs and STs, respectively.[33] Women's representation in state assemblies is even worse than in the national parliament: in no state do women account for more than 15 percent of state legislative assembly members (see Panel B of Figure 1.3). Clearly, widespread descriptive representation driven by a quota policy, even one as expansive as India's, neither explains nor closes the bulk of the gender gap in political participation and representation.

---

[33] There are quotas for SCs and STs in higher level office that enable their greater representation (Jensenius 2017), but local election data reveals that SCs and STs win in unreserved seats at significantly higher rates than women.

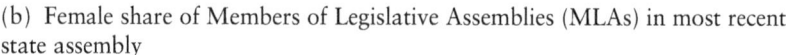

(b) Female share of Members of Legislative Assemblies (MLAs) in most recent state assembly

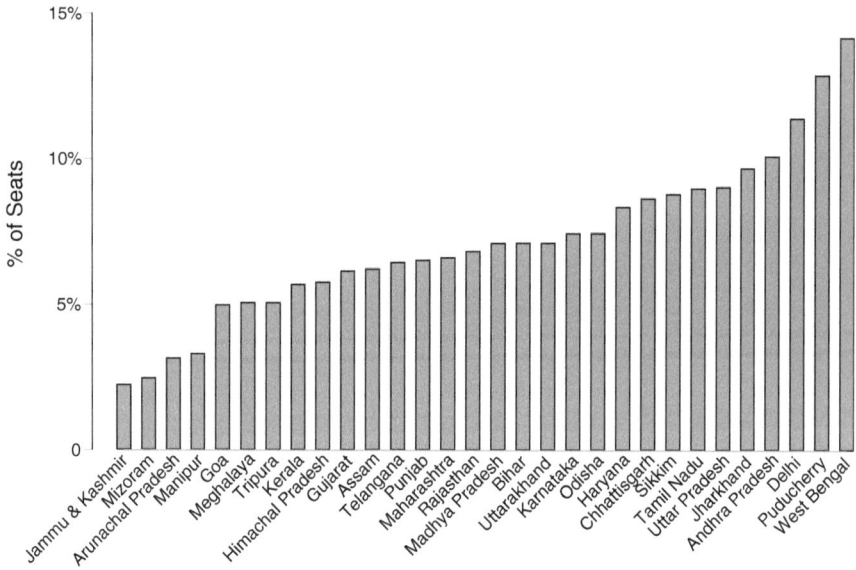

FIGURE 1.3 *(cont.)*

Scholars of norms would suggest that these persistent and stark gender gaps are rooted in deeply entrenched patriarchal norms.[34] India is indeed an extreme example with respect to the strength of its patriarchal attitudes. As Figure 1.4 demonstrates, more than 50 percent of women and 65 percent of men in India state that they believe men make better political leaders than women, and this is representative of general patterns in South Asia. While such patriarchal attitudes are common across the globe, they are particularly

---

[34] The most definitive evidence linking normative institutions with gendered political participation comes from comparing matrilineal and patrilineal societies. (In matrilineal [patrilineal] communities, inheritance and ancestral wealth are passed through the matriline [patriline].) Both Brulé and Gaikwad (2021) and Robinson and Gottlieb (2019) show that women's political participation is significantly higher in communities where inheritance is passed through women in northeast India and sub-Saharan Africa, respectively. Brulé and Gaikwad (2021) suggest that inheritance norms structure access to resources, which in turn shapes political behavior. Robinson and Gottlieb (2019) instead argue that cultural norms shape political behavior by setting expectations regarding what behaviors are socially accepted. (See Bursztyn González, and Yanagizawa-Drott (2020) for a similar explication of the role of social norms in shaping women's labor market behavior.) They suggest that cultural norms create community-based coordination around how identity, namely gender, translates into political behavior. Empirically, they document how it is not land ownership per se but rules of land inheritance that drive women's political participation.

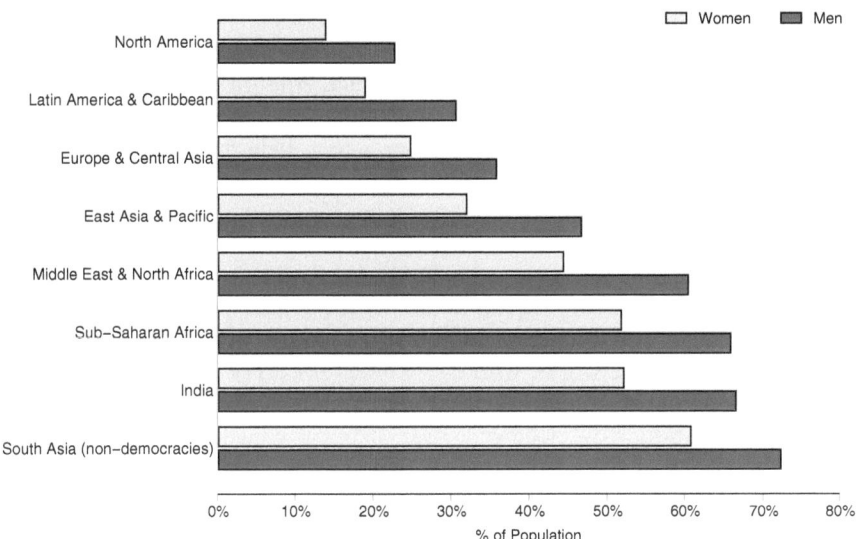

FIGURE 1.4 Share of men and women reporting that men make better political leaders than women in democracies across the globe

Note: Data are from the World Values Survey, Waves 5–7, representing 2005–2022 (Inglehart et al. 2014). Except where noted, data are for democratic countries only, as defined by an average polity score from 2005 to 2018 of greater than 6 (polity V data documented by Marshall and Gurr 2021). In total, data represent ninety-one democracies and two non-democracies in South Asia (Pakistan and Bangladesh). Responses of either "agree" or "strongly agree" are coded as affirmative, and "disagree," "strongly disagree," and "neither agree nor disagree" are coded as negative. "Don't knows" are coded to missing. Responses are weighted by the population survey weight provided.

acute in Africa, the Middle East, and South Asia. The extent of these beliefs among both women and men makes India a hard case in which to observe instances of women's political empowerment, for if a majority of people do not believe women can be competent political actors, why would they support their political inclusion?

Yet there are important cases of women challenging these norms and actively engaging in politics. For example, the Gulabi Gang is an informal group of women in north India known for their pink saris who have fought to reduce domestic violence and improve women's political representation. Sushila's story is another example of empowerment where women in the same community and without a shift in patriarchal norms (as evidenced by the resistance they faced) became politically active. Furthermore, norms alone do not explain the patterns of political participation displayed in Figure 1.1. A 2022 report produced by the Pew Research Center using novel survey data found substantial variation across Indian states with respect to the belief that men make better political leaders than women.[35] Strikingly, the states with the highest rates of women's political participation (see Figure 1.2) are those with the strongest patriarchal attitudes. Himachal Pradesh, Kerala, Andhra Pradesh, and Assam (the four states with the highest reported village assembly participation by women) ranked in the top half with respect to beliefs that men make better political leaders; and Odisha, Delhi, and Punjab (three of the four states with the lowest women's village assembly participation) ranked in the bottom half, with the vast majority reporting beliefs of gender equality.

The last common alternative explanation for women's low political participation centers on resource inequalities across the genders. And, here too, stark inequality persists in India. Most notably, the sex ratio in India remains one of the most skewed in the world, with 877 women for every 1,000 men.[36] As Sen first noted, millions of women are missing in India.[37] And while girls have made strides in education, now achieving near-identical educational attainment as boys, women's labor force participation remains one-third that of men's and is the lowest in the G-20 with the exception of Saudi Arabia. And, as in much of the world, gender wage gaps persist: women in India earn 28 percent less than men on average.[38]

However, these economic and resource inequalities imperfectly explain women's non-electoral political participation in India. All three panels of Figure 1.5 – which uses World Values Survey data to illustrate the relationship between education, income, caste category, and non-electoral political participation – show that resources have only a limited ability to predict non-electoral participation. Panel A, for example, shows that the gender gap in non-electoral political participation is greatest when comparing women and men with no formal, middle, or secondary education. The gender gap disappears only for those who have completed a university degree. Similarly, Panel B documents that the gender gap in non-electoral participation *increases* with household income. While surprising, this pattern mirrors that found with respect to female labor force participation, where labor force participation is largely uncorrelated with educational attainment in India.[39] Furthermore, my analysis of survey data from men and women in Madhya Pradesh reveals that 78 percent of the variation in men's and women's political participation is unexplained by differences in educational attainment, labor market participation, income, land ownership, and free time.[40] This corroborates studies from the Global South

---

[35] Pew Research Center (2022). The levels reporting agreement with the statement that men make better political leaders vary between the World Values Survey and the Pew report likely because of difference in the response options allowed. The Pew report allowed for the response that men and women make equally good leaders, while the World Values Survey did not.

[36] Kulkarni (2020).   [37] Sen (1990).

[38] Labor force survey from the National Sample Survey Office from 2018 to 2019.

[39] Chaudhary (2021).   [40] This is estimated using a Blinder–Oaxaca decomposition.

(a) By education

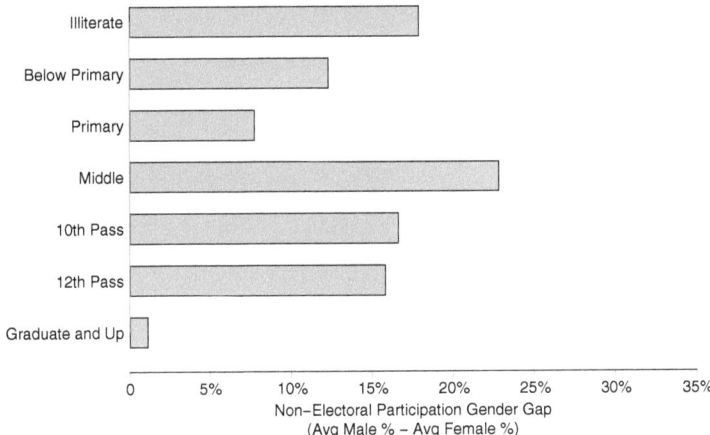

(b) By income decile

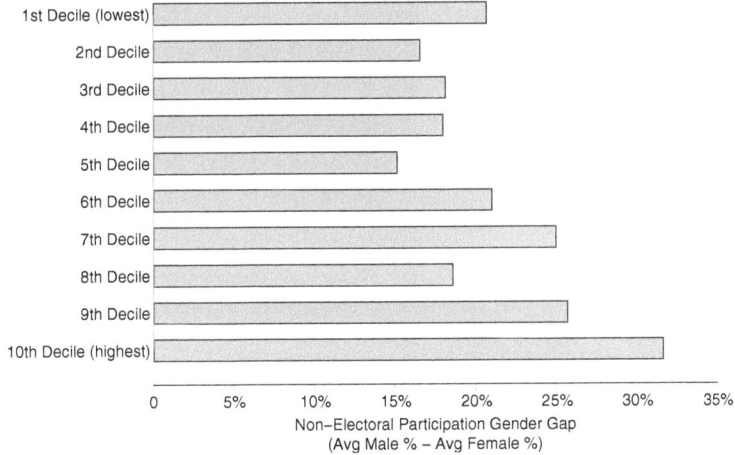

FIGURE 1.5 The gender gap in non-electoral political participation is not fully explained by education, income, or caste category

Note: Data are from the World Values Survey, Waves 5–7, representing 2005–2022 (Inglehart et al. 2014). Data are for India only. Non-electoral participation includes respondents who reported protesting, petitioning, striking, political occupation, or other political action. "Don't knows" are coded as not participating. Responses are weighted by the population survey weight provided.

(c) By caste category

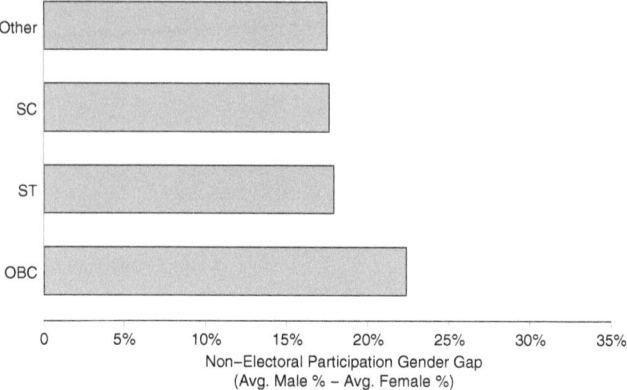

FIGURE 1.5 (*cont.*)

that find little or no evidence of a link between economic development and women's political participation.[41]

These patterns reveal that women's political participation is puzzling both because of the way participation is distributed across voting and non-electoral participation and because of the limited predictive power of institutions, norms, and resources alone. This book provides an alternative explanation of broader patterns of politics in rural India that explains women's continued absence from politics.

THE POLITICAL LIVES OF INDIAN WOMEN: ARGUMENT IN BRIEF

The Patriarchal Political Order

Women's lives are shaped by the institutions in which they operate, starting at the most micro level, the household.[42] Households are also the ascribed domain of women in societies that adhere to patriarchal norms.[43] While men are expected to provide economically for their families, women are expected to handle the domestic responsibilities. Men, particularly elder men, exercise de facto authority in household decisions under patriarchy. Patriarchal authority in the household is upheld by a broader social system that elevates and

---

[41] Desposato and Norrander (2009) show this in a study of seventeen countries in Latin America.
[42] Okin (1989).
[43] Kandiyoti (1988); Folbre (1994); Johnson (1997); Braunstein and Folbre (2001); Lowes (2017).

institutionalizes men's authority and power. Patriarchal norms are deployed to constrain women's autonomy from the household by, for example, limiting their labor force participation, mobility, and social interactions.[44]

I argue that in rural India, women's political lives revolve around their household, and that many women lack complete agency over their political decision-making. Instead, households make political decisions jointly, and because of intra-household inequalities and the potential for socially sanctioned and legally tolerated coercion by men, women often concede political authority and representation to the men in their families. Men, as a result, generally act as their households' political representatives, which enables them to drive household behavior, advocate for their specific interests, and build political capital.

This pattern – what I call the institution of household political cooperation – yields high rates of electoral participation from both men and women in the household, because all-household voting is strategically valuable for those with power in the household. The more household representatives who show up to vote, the greater the likelihood of achieving the household's preferred electoral outcome, and the greater the likelihood of patronage and clientelistic benefits for its political representatives. Women's voting therefore serves the interests of the men in their household.

However, women (and younger men) are not expected to participate in non-electoral politics, because it has little strategic value for those with power in the household. Since the marginal return of an additional household representative participating in these spaces is low, women's non-electoral participation does not improve the outcomes for household members who have bargaining and coercive power over women's political behavior. In fact, women's non-electoral participation is likely to incur social costs for both women and the men in their household, as such norm-deviant behavior will be sanctioned to ensure the continuation of patriarchal dominance.

Household political cooperation therefore implies the appearance of equality in voting but limited autonomy over vote choice in practice and the persistence of gender-based political inequalities in non-electoral political institutions. Further, men's preferences dominate demand-making, and women's distinct interests remain underrepresented.

Household cooperation can be both a rational response to a service delivery system that privileges households as an institution and the irrational consequence of within-household patterns of coercion and inequality. Given a political system in which many goods are either privately or locally distributed, and where patronage is a common means of service delivery, households – and, particularly, household members who have power – benefit from mutual cooperation. Households have a shared set of interests rooted in common

---

[44] Lowes (2017); Kumar et al. (2019); Anukriti, Herrera-Almanza, and Pathak (2019); Jayachandran (2020).

household identities, though women also have a set of unique demands separate from those of the men in their household.[45] Yet, given intra-household power hierarchies and the potential for coercion, households can also be wielded as a tool for the benefit of the powerful. The promise of an entire household's electoral and political support increases the expected likelihood of political returns for the political head of the household who brokers these relationships. And with the potential for coercion, household cooperation is not efficient, especially given the likelihood that women will internalize the preferences of men as a self-protection mechanism. As Sen powerfully suggests, "the family identity may exert such a strong influence on our perceptions that we may not find it easy to formulate any clear notion of our own individual welfare."[46]

Household political cooperation incentivizes strategic politicians to court the household vote and lessens their costs to electoral mobilization. Patronage and responsiveness are easier to deliver to households than to individuals. And if household behavior is aligned, there is no electoral loss associated with mobilizing only those with power.[47] Those in dominant positions within the household therefore have incentives to subordinate others in the household and ensure joint household political cooperation. Political elites too, have incentives to maintain a political system centered on the household and to challenge contestation to it.

Men's participation in politics becomes self-perpetuating as they accumulate political skills, capital, and networks. Ties between politicians and male household heads deepen, cementing the link between political institutions and household institutions. The institution of household political cooperation becomes socially upheld as it facilitates and sustains patriarchal dominance and the prevailing (clientelist) political system. Those with power in the system – dominant men and political elites – have a stake in maintaining this institution and are expected to resist attempts to dismantle it. Backlash against attempts to renegotiate these norms or threats to men's political authority is enabled by male coercive power;[48] broader patterns of inequality give men the resources and networks to organize and maintain a system in which they are dominant. This political system – what I term the patriarchal political order – yields a politics centered on the household and around men.

The Power of Women's Collective Action

When patriarchal norms and gender-based inequalities enable men to strategically uphold a political order that elevates their political authority in both the household and the community, the key to women's political inclusion is

---

[45] Sapiro (1981); Molyneux (1985).   [46] Sen (1987: 6).   [47] Rosenstone and Hansen (1993).
[48] Clayton (2015); Gottlieb (2016b); Brulé (2020a).

autonomy from the household, but only when it enables women to credibly challenge the likely resistance from those benefitting from the patriarchal political order. Autonomy from the household promises women both material benefits from the greater representation of their distinct interests and psychological benefits from the ability to voice these interests freely. But autonomy challenges the patriarchal political order. Those with power in this order are likely to resist giving up that power and therefore women's autonomy. Backlash is to be expected from those with the greatest stake in the patriarchal order and to those challenges that most threaten their power.[49]

How do women gain autonomy from the household and the freedom to make their own political decisions? Shifts in women's individual endowments are unlikely to overcome the coercive structures of the patriarchal political order.[50] Instead, I argue that women's collective action is a successful response to male power and coercion, even without a priori structural change.[51] Autonomy from the household and collective action alongside other women enables women to credibly contest these household and societal patterns of male political dominance, including coercive backlash.

Organizing collectively, however, bears high transaction costs: women must have sufficient information about their interests and who would share these interests (informational costs), women must be able to negotiate as a group about their priorities and strategies (bargaining costs), and women must be able to enforce sustained collective action (enforcement costs).[52] Given these transaction costs, I argue that collective action is most likely when women are connected to each other and their relationships involve political discussion, when they have a common framework of interests rooted in a shared identity, a recognition of shared injustice, and the belief that their action could address those injustices,[53] and when they have high levels of social solidarity built on trust and norms of reciprocity.[54]

Given these high transaction costs and a dominant political order centering women's political lives on the household, solidaristic collective action of this nature is unlikely to emerge endogenously. External intervention is often needed to disrupt self-perpetuating power structures and facilitate social change. As Batliwala, a leading theorist of and activist for women's empowerment in India, argued, "the process of demanding justice does not necessarily begin spontaneously, or arise automatically from the very conditions of subjugation. The process of empowerment must therefore be induced or stimulated by external forces."[55]

---

[49] Mansbridge and Shames (2008: 626).
[50] Roychowdhury (2020). Cools and Kotsadam (2017) show that economic resources are uncorrelated with the experience of domestic violence.
[51] Dahlerup (1988); Htun and Weldon (2012).   [52] Coase (1960); Ostrom (1994).
[53] Klein (1986); Van Zomeren, Postmes, and Spears (2008).
[54] Putnam, Leonardi, and Lanetti (1994); Singh (2015).   [55] Batliwala (1993: 49).

I, therefore, consider the role of public policies, specifically the creation of economically oriented women's groups (SHGs), in creating autonomy from the household and expanding and deepening women's political relationships. SHGs are the largest policy intervention aimed at women's empowerment both globally and within India. SHGs are principally economic institutions that offer microcredit to poor women, but they also bring together women with shared interests, provide an institutionalized space for discussion and to explore gendered interests, and foster the development of civic skills through deliberation and information sharing.[56] SHGs thus create the conditions for collective action.

While many have highlighted the tenuous benefits of SHGs for women's economic empowerment,[57] I argue that if (and when) these groups yield solidarity among women, their political participation is likely to rise. By engaging in group-based collective action, women can jointly challenge political power structures and demand political representation. As a result, membership in SHGs can increase women's political participation even when social norms and household dynamics continue to reinforce their exclusion from politics.

I study a snapshot of the lives of women in the thick of attempting to renegotiate gender-biased norms and generate social change. When successful, I suggest that this will not only yield a renegotiation of power through women's presence but also a likely restructuring of politics. Collective action among women is expected to center on their distinct and underrepresented interests, including gender equality and public goods provision.[58] However, the strategies that women can deploy to navigate the complex structures of coercion are numerous. Yet it is this coercion that creates the conditions that unite women in solidarity against their continued oppression.

Collective action by women, therefore, has the potential to corrode the patriarchal political order. The process of change will not be linear, as many will contest this transformation, but if successful, it can cascade into more inclusive and representative politics and even broader improvements in governance and development.

THE STAKES

Many historical legal institutions and even major academic models have not treated women's limited political participation as a problem. The argument is generally that men and women share the same preferences, so it does not matter who participates; the outcome will be the same. This is particularly true under household-based political decision-making. Legal institutions such as coverture, which gave men legal authority over their wives, were designed with this

---

[56] Sanyal (2009, 2014).   [57] Banerjee (2013); Brody et al. (2015).   [58] Clayton (2021).

assumption in mind. Unitary models of the household also assume that since the household has common preferences, it may even be efficient (household welfare maximizing) for women not to participate in politics.[59]

Like these models, I also suggest that the household often behaves as a unit. But unlike these models, I show that women are first and foremost *subjects* – not citizens – of their households. In this book, I demonstrate that intra-household preferences are diverse, and that women and men have distinct desires related to the functioning of government. Importantly, as I will show with evidence from women's collective action across India, when women do politically act, they do so in accordance with these interests. My analysis builds on a large literature that has demonstrated the substantial differences in political preferences between women and men across the globe[60] and work that documents the specific demands raised by women's movements.[61] Recent empirical work from Khan in Pakistan reveals that not only do such preference gaps exist but also women are more likely than men to subvert their preferences in favor of those of their spouses.[62] Strikingly, this is most likely when the preference differentials are largest. So, while households may act as a unit, there is little evidence that doing so maximizes the welfare of the household; instead, it is most likely to maximize the welfare of those with power in the household.

This book, therefore, has implications for democracy: What is democracy with limited agency and unequal representation? Sen questioned whether growth without freedom can really be considered development.[63] The same can be asked of democracy; even if men perfectly represent women's demands (although abundant evidence suggests this is unlikely), what is lost for democracy from women's lack of freedom and representation?[64] Dahl explicitly argued the need for inclusivity, in addition to electoral contestation, for

---

[59] This was most notably detailed in Becker (1985).

[60] See, for example, Beckwith (2011) and Molyneux (1985) for a theoretical conceptualization of why men and women might have different preferences. Molyneux, for example, describes how women's preferences may differ from men's both as a result of the gendered economic division of labor under a patriarchal gender system and because of the existence of a patriarchal gender system itself, which women may more acutely prefer to contest. Others, such as Edlund and Pande (2002), Iversen and Rosenbluth (2006), Inglehart and Norris (2000), and Shapiro and Mahajan (1986), empirically document these gender gaps and demonstrate how changes in women's autonomy from, and bargaining power within, the household yield larger gendered differences in political demand-making.

[61] See, for example, Alvarez (1990), Molyneux (1998), Ray (2000), Baldez (2002), Weldon (2002), Tripp (2008), and Htun and Weldon (2018). Ray, for example, documents how women's movements in India take two different forms: sometimes organizing around service provision that benefits women, and at other times, organizing around protection from violence and gender inequities.

[62] Khan (2021).   [63] Sen (1999).

[64] Teele (2018) asks a similar question with respect to voting, considering how our understanding of democratic formation was limited by a lack of focus on the enfranchisement of women.

democratic functioning.[65] Mansbridge reflected on the many impacts of inclusion and representation in democracies, suggesting that inclusion matters not only because of the differences in outcomes that may be expected from representing distinct interests, but also because political inclusion creates social meaning for underrepresented communities and bestows legitimacy on democratic institutions.[66] Understanding the underrepresentation of women, and particularly the limits of their political agency, will enable a deeper appreciation of the limits and possibilities of democracy and its institutions.

The state of Indian democracy has received substantial academic attention in recent years, and new evidence has challenged conventional wisdoms.[67] As in many of the political debates in India since independence, this work has focused on the representation of the marginalized. Since it is one of the most ethnically diverse countries in the world, understanding how (and when) democratic institutions reflect and represent such diversity is critically important. A long history of work, largely centered on caste, has explored the nature of political mobilization in India and the conditions under which identities become politically salient.[68] Past research has also considered how the design of political institutions, particularly the implementation of electoral quotas, creates a politics of identity and enables more inclusive elite political institutions.[69] Others have focused on the substantial heterogeneity in the functioning of Indian

---

[65] Dahl (1971). See also Urbinati and Warren (2008) for a summary of the vast literature that also takes seriously the need for representation in democratic theory.

[66] Mansbridge (1999).

[67] Auerbach et al. (2022) provides a summary of how recent evidence from India updates three conventional wisdoms: India is a clientelist democracy marked by substantial vote buying, caste is the most important domain of political mobilization, and parties are weakly institutionalized.

[68] See, for example, Kothari (1964). Chandra (2007) notably drew attention to the prevalence of ethnic head counting in electoral mobilization and identity-based representation in India, especially in the presence of strong institutions of patronage exchange. Ahuja (2019) and Lee (2020) both consider the role of caste mobilization and activism outside politics in shaping the political organization of castes.

[69] Jensenius (2017) documents how state-level quotas for SCs increased political representation and participation, shaped policy outcomes, and created a politics of recognition for these marginalized communities. Chauchard (2017) provides similar evidence for local-level quotas for historically marginalized caste groups (see also Pande (2003), Dunning and Nilekani (2013), and Gulzar, Haas, and Pasquale (2020) for further evidence). A wide range of scholars have considered the representational, material, and psychological impacts of local-level quotas for women in India, including Chattopadhyay and Duflo (2004), Ban and Rao (2008), Beaman et al. (2009, 2012), Bhavnani (2009), Iyer et al. (2012), Palaniswamy, Parthasarathy, and Rao (2019), Goyal (2019, 2020), Karekurve-Ramachandra (2021), and Karekurve-Ramachandra and Lee (2021). Pande and Ford (2012) provide a useful summary of the broader evidence on the impact of gender quotas. Clots-Figueras (2011) considers similar questions in the context of the state-level representation of women absent quotas. Brulé (2021) critically revealed how women's local-level representation via quotas enabled them to contest the backlash against changes to norms of gendered economic distribution, namely the distribution of land. Chhibber and Verma (2018) more explicitly consider variation in citizen beliefs about the state's role in addressing the needs of various marginalized identity groups.

democracy and considered the role of identity and diversity in explaining the outcomes of governance.[70] Exploring inclusion in institutions of patronage and clientelism, which are most prevalent in the Global South, has been particularly important. Chandra revealed the strong link between ethnicity and patronage in Indian politics.[71] Current research explores how patronage networks operate on the ground and how they contribute to larger patterns of political organization.[72] Like these studies, this book centers on the link between political institutions and identity, bringing the attention to gender and, more specifically, women citizens. It introduces new insights into the study of clientelism and identity by exposing how the structure of gender relations and the primacy of the household as a political unit perpetuate and enable clientelist machines. Accordingly, this book also has implications for governance.

The way in which women are incorporated into politics has important implications for policy and development. I show in this book that women's political empowerment may itself drive both women's economic empowerment and broader development. I document how women deploy their newfound political voices to demand gender equality and equal and programmatic access to public services for all. Having spent decades as political outsiders who have limited access to the spoils of politics, women recognize the importance of and demand high-quality governance.[73] Ample evidence from around the world suggests that policy outcomes shift in line with women's preferences when they gain the right to vote or are elected to office. In their seminal study,

---

[70] Singh (2015) demonstrates how ethnic solidarity in only some Indian states created conditions that led to more equal governance in the long run and, as a result, improved social development. See also Kapur (2020) for an exposition of how social cleavages and democratic institutions shape development outcomes in India today. Huber and Suryanarayan (2016) demonstrate how caste-based voting varies at the state level based on the level of within-caste economic inequality. Thachil (2014) explores variation in support for the Bharatiya Janata Party by low-caste voters and highlights the role of party-led but non-state service provision as an alternative mechanism of generating a vote base. More classic work has considered variation in the prevalence of ethnic conflict in India (see Wilkinson (2006) and Varshney (2009)).

[71] Chandra (2004, 2007).

[72] Berenschot (2010) shows how political mediation is an entrenched component of the Indian state. Bohlken (2016) examines how extending democratic institutions at the local level gives parties deeper control of diverse geographies. Ziegfeld (2016) highlights how clientelist institutions support the perpetuation of regional political parties. Auerbach (2019) documents how party workers in slums condition citizens' access to development. Bussell (2019) studies the prevalence of constituency service as a non-exchange-based relationship between politicians and citizens.

[73] In Argentina, Daby (2021) shows that because women's networks are smaller than men's, they are less able to mobilize votes via clientelist offers. Wantchekon (2003: 401) argues that "younger voters or rural women might be systematically excluded from the most common forms of clientelist redistribution, and those groups might therefore be more responsive to a platform of public goods. This would imply that initiatives to promote women's participation in the political process at all levels of government are likely to help improve the provision of public goods." See also Vicente and Wantchekon (2009).

Chattopadhyay and Duflo show that village chairpersons in rural India invest "more in infrastructure that is directly relevant to the needs of their own genders."[74] Others have shown that women's political representation has led to an overall rise in expenditures[75] as well as increased spending on public health[76] and education.[77] Women's political inclusion can also lead to the enactment of policies that institutionalize gender equality and outlaw gendered coercion.[78] And autonomous women's movements have been shown to precede and precipitate government action, particularly on issues pertinent to women.[79]

Given the high stakes of women's political inclusion for democratic functioning, governance, and development, a thorough understanding of the mechanisms of women's exclusion and empowerment can improve the design of public policies aimed at empowerment. Policy attention to date has largely focused on the economic roots of women's disempowerment; policies have mostly sought to increase women's economic agency through financial inclusion, access to education and jobs, and protection of inheritance rights.[80] India's largest policy aimed at empowering women, which has touched the lives of more than 75 million women, is the promotion of SHGs – small, women-only microcredit groups designed to improve livelihoods through financial inclusion. These policies assume there is a link between women's economic empowerment and broader development and inclusion. Yet, as I will show, mobilizing women into SHGs has a much larger impact on their political behavior than on their economic well-being. Most policies that seek to address gender inequality in politics have concentrated on women's electoral representation; the cornerstone of policymaking to increase women's political inclusion

---

[74] Chattopadhyay and Duflo (2004: 1409).   [75] Lott and Kenny (1999); Aidt and Dallal (2008).
[76] Miller (2008); Clots-Figueras (2011); Clayton and Zetterberg (2018)
[77] Carruthers and Wannamaker (2014); Clots-Figueras (2011).
[78] In her study of village-level women's collective action in rural West Bengal, Sanyal (2009) shows that women mobilized around domestic violence against women, men's sexually permissive behavior, and anti-liquor campaigns. Htun and Weldon (2018) demonstrate that policies aimed at combatting violence against women only emerge as the result of sustained women's movements. Iyer et al. (2012) show that female electoral representation in local governments in India led to a substantial rise in claims filed due to gender-based violence but argue that indicates greater trust in the legal system and, therefore, greater reporting as opposed to actual increases in experiences of violence. Clots-Figueras (2011) demonstrated that female state legislators in India were more supportive of "female-friendly" laws, including the Hindu Succession Act, which protects women's property rights. Brulé (2020) shows that female electoral representation directly affects women's property ownership and property rights in rural India. Weeks (2019) provides evidence that parties with greater female representation pay more attention to social justice issues. Greater institutionalized protections for women are likely only when they are represented in politics and, as Htun and Weldon (2012) point out, only when a critical mass of women organize to demand such protections.
[79] Alvarez (1990); Gelb and Palley (1996); Molyneux (1998); Randall and Waylen (1998); Hassim (2006); Tripp and Kang (2008); Htun and Weldon (2012, 2018).
[80] Batliwala (1993); Sen (1997); Kabeer (1999); Banerjee (2013); Brody et al. (2015); Jayachandran (2020).

is the use of electoral quotas. A total of 130 countries, including all countries in South Asia, have introduced some form of quota to ensure the representation of women in political office.[81] And while these policies have made important headway in women's political inclusion, I have already demonstrated how they have only a limited capacity to fundamentally transform outcomes for ordinary women. A key observable implication of this book is that even the most expansive gender equality policies will imperfectly achieve their goals unless they support women's counter-resistance to coercion. A surprising finding of this book is that some of the most successful public policies for women's political empowerment never intended such an outcome, which highlights the need to reevaluate our approaches to political empowerment.

EMPIRICAL STRATEGY

Case Selection

The evidence I bring to bear in this book combines first-person narratives and extensive data analysis. Gathering a compelling body of evidence to prove the existence of a patriarchal political order required directly communicating with more than 9,000 rural Indian citizens. The paucity of data on women's political behavior, particularly outside of voting, necessitated large-scale original data collection to draw more general inferences. This process generated a depth of understanding of the political lives of these citizens and allowed me to draw comparisons from a wide range of lived experiences. I concentrated on a limited geographic area to enable a causal research design, but I broaden the scope of analysis to the entire country where available data permits.

The majority of the book is based on original research conducted over six years in five districts in the Indian state of Madhya Pradesh (outlined in black in Figure 1.2): Balaghat, Betul, Dindori, Hoshangabad, and Mandla. Madhya Pradesh is the second-largest state in India and has a population of more than eighty-five million, approximately the same as that of Germany or Turkey. It is located in the poorer central belt of the country, and has historically had worse outcomes for women and stronger patriarchal norms. One in three residents of the state lives in poverty, and more than three-quarters reside in rural areas. As in much of India, women are particularly economically disadvantaged. In 2018, women in the state had an average rural labor force participation rate of 17 percent (55 percent for men) and average wages of INR 726, or $10.60, per week (INR 1,831, or $26.73, for men).[82] These statistics reflect slightly higher female labor force participation than the national average but substantially lower female wages than the national average of INR 1,296, or $18.92.

---

[81] International Institute for Democracy and Electoral Assistance Gender Quotas Database.
[82] All statistics are based on author's calculations from the Periodic Labour Force Survey from 2017 to 2018.

Importantly, Madhya Pradesh is a richly diverse state. While the official language is Hindi and more than 90 percent of its population is Hindu, it was once a center of Muslim rule. Bhopal, the present-day capital of Madhya Pradesh, was India's second-largest Muslim state during British colonial rule; it was ruled by four Muslim women from 1819 to 1926 (the Begums of Bhopal). Furthermore, Madhya Pradesh has the largest tribal population in the country; more than forty tribal communities comprise roughly 27 percent of its rural population (see Table A1.1). Tribal populations, also known as Adivasis, are economically worse off than most other ethnic groups in India. On average, they have lower incomes, lower literacy rates, higher rates of maternal and child mortality, and own less land.[83] Due to their historical exclusion and continued inequality, tribal populations as a group have received formal protections under the law, including through reservations in various domains and limited rights to self-governance. Yet, despite ST numerical dominance in many of the villages studied in this book, Chapter 6 shows that political influence and power is often concentrated in OBC and General Category (GC or upper caste) communities.

The distinct and rich ethnic diversity prevalent in Madhya Pradesh makes this state a valuable place for inquiry and provides an opportunity to explore how gender operates across these intersecting identities. Norms and practices vary in important ways across the many cultures within India and even within villages. The villages I study exhibit substantial ethnic diversity, largely divided among Hindu caste groups and indigenous tribes. This diversity is important to our understanding of how the gender system operates. Tribal populations are often assumed to have much more gender-equal norms, as evidenced through higher female labor force participation and higher sex ratios. Yet evidence abounds that patriarchal norms dominate these communities.[84] According to their codified norms and rules, women face harsher sanctions for deviating from marriage and birth norms. I show in Chapter 2 that attitudes toward gender equality in these villages vary little across caste groups. In most tribal cultures, men retain rights over children and property and are the de facto household heads, while women have little authority within the household. In this regard, women find common ground across their intersecting identities. Throughout this book, I evaluate the experiences of women from a variety of backgrounds, all of whom are subject to patriarchal norms in their households and communities.[85] I pay close attention to how caste and gender dynamics intersect but also reveal the depth of commonality in women's experiences across the country.

---

[83] Guha (2007).   [84] Kabeer et al. (2019).

[85] By focusing on the experiences of rural women, this study does not speak to the varying experiences of women residing in urban cities, who navigate very different social and economic worlds.

Similarly, while socioeconomics and ethnic diversity may vary across states and districts in India, women's underrepresentation in politics does not. Figure 1.2 demonstrates that, in the domain of non-electoral political participation, the highest rate of reported participation in village assembly meetings by women was 41% (Kerala), and women's participation in these meetings topped 15% in only four states (Assam, Himachal Pradesh, Andhra Pradesh, and Kerala). Compared to the rest of India, Madhya Pradesh reports relatively low rates of female non-electoral political participation (3%), although these rates are similar to those in neighboring states. Only 27 of its 230 state representatives are women, and female voter turnout was 68 percent in the 2019 parliamentary elections, which was just above the national average of 67 percent.

I situated this study in India (and, more specifically, in Madhya Pradesh) for three reasons. First, it represents a conservative and challenging case in which to identify positive effects on women's political empowerment given its particularly low levels of women's political participation and representation. Yet women vote at high rates. The strength of this puzzle of participation opens up opportunities for inquiry, which allow us to observe more clearly what dynamics explain these patterns and to hold constant many of the factors historically attributed to women's political subordination, such as their relative economic position and gender norms. Second, India and Madhya Pradesh more specifically are domains of policy experimentation. In the regions I study, I observe substantial variation in women's political participation. Much of this variation, as I will show in the second half of the book, is driven by the large body of governmental and nongovernmental actors working to identify policy levers for women's empowerment. My decision to focus on the six aforementioned districts was rooted in a series of policy experiments run in these districts by one such nongovernmental organization (NGO). And given the depth of patriarchal norms in this region, the identified solutions will provide strong evidence of what is likely to work even under challenging conditions. Finally, I chose to center this book on India as it is a diverse and consequential subcontinent with 665 million women, representing 17 percent of the global female population. The large majority of empirical research on gendered political behavior has been concentrated in the Global North, primarily in the United States. There remains much to be learned from taking an expanded geographic scope, and India is a clearly important case. Beyond its importance as the world's largest democracy, conclusions from India can help identify more general patterns of gendered exclusion that are often masked in contexts where norms are harder to observe.[86]

---

[86] While I expect many of the patterns documented in this book to be relevant to other democracies, some characteristics may differentiate India, and Madhya Pradesh more specifically. India as a whole, and the five districts in Madhya Pradesh where this research was conducted, is largely rural; over 60 percent of the population and 69 percent of women live in rural villages. State

Mixed Methods and Causal Identification

I test these arguments in rural India using a diverse set of data sources and empirical methods. Six years of research, including more than a year spent in India, inform the research design and data collection. A key challenge associated with examining relational theories and identifying the causal effects of social relations for behavior is differentiating the effect of social ties from the rest of the social system. Furthermore, a principal reason why we have such a poor understanding of women's political behavior in India is a lack of data from women. Rural public opinion polls rarely stratify their samples based on gender due to the difficulty of speaking with women away from their husbands; those who do focus mostly on voting, which, due to household coercion, may not be an informative measure of women's political agency.

This book overcomes these methodological challenges by analyzing observational qualitative and quantitative data alongside a series of natural experiments that manipulated theoretically important variables. Combined, these data and methodologies generate a preponderance of evidence that supports the existence of household political cooperation, the patriarchal political order, and the value of household autonomy and women's social solidarity for women's political behavior. I draw on three principal data sources, which I describe in greater detail in the subsequent chapters.

First, I utilize data from an original survey conducted in 2016 in rural Madhya Pradesh of more than 5,000 women and 2,500 of their husbands across 376 villages. In each village, fifteen women and eight of their husbands were asked a series of questions about their political behaviors and attitudes. Second, I draw on data from a second original survey in 2019 that randomly sampled 6 villages from the 2016 sample of villages and censused all 3,565 adult residents of those villages. This census survey sought to measure political network characteristics and employed a series of name-generator questions to map respondents' networks. In both surveys, data were collected in person by trained surveyors. Given the sensitive nature of the questions and concerns about social desirability bias, respondents were gender matched to surveyors, and all surveys were conducted in complete privacy. Third, I analyze data from semi-structured, qualitative interviews with 120 randomly sampled women and 80 of their husbands across a second random subsample of twenty villages.

---

building and political participation are of heightened importance in this setting. State capacity is often lower in rural areas, generating weaker political institutions (Herbst 2014; Bates 2000), though recent work suggests the opposite is true in India (Auerbach and Kruks-Wisner 2020). Women's social isolation is potentially more acute in rural villages, which are characterized by a strong gender-based division of labor (Agarwal 1994). Patriarchy in India takes a particular form as a result of the persistence of the joint family, where sons reside with their parents even after marriage (Kandiyoti 1988). While such patterns of women's social exclusion and patriarchal norms may set India apart, they also permit a clearer evaluation of how social relations shape women's political behavior.

These interviews sought to understand *how* women make political decisions and to capture how women understand their own political agency and participation. I additionally pair these three original data sets with nationally representative survey data from the Indian Human Development Survey (IHDS)[87] and data on all reported instances of women's collective action from the Armed Conflict Location & Event Data Project (ACLED)[88] to demonstrate the generalizability of my argument across India.

I analyze these data using a combination of analytic description and causal inference methodologies. To document the existence of household political cooperation, the nature of women's political participation conditional on a norm of such cooperation, a broader political order built around women's exclusion, and the role of political ties in each, I use observational methods to describe the wealth of data provided in my original surveys. I also deploy network analysis tools to map and document the gendered nature of political connections in rural Indian villages. I use both qualitative reporting and quantitative coding of interview transcripts to add richness to this description and better examine the harder-to-observe mechanisms of women's political subordination.

To more precisely estimate whether particular factors drive women's political behavior, I examine a series of natural experiments that shocked women's access to two NGO empowerment interventions. The two interventions I study sought to increase women's autonomy from the household and solidarity with other women. The first mobilized women into SHGs, the women-only microcredit groups described earlier. The second intervention applied a gender consciousness-raising program within SHGs to build solidarity and trust among women. Since only some villages were eligible for these interventions – eligibility was arbitrarily determined – I can causally estimate their impact on women's political behavior. The samples for both surveys and the qualitative interviews included villages that did and did not receive these interventions, so the survey and interview data are used to estimate the causal effects of these programs.

The 376 villages in Madhya Pradesh in which data were collected were sampled with these two sets of analyses in mind. As a result, the villages fall into three categories: (1) those that have not received any SHG-related NGO program, (2) those that have received only the SHG program, and (3) those that have received both the SHG and gender consciousness-raising programs. Respondents were sampled in two ways for the 2016 Madhya Pradesh sample survey. In the first set of villages with no SHG programs, women were randomly sampled from census lists subsetting to adult, ever-married women. In the second and third sets of villages, where the SHG program had been implemented, women were randomly sampled from lists of SHG members.

---

[87] Desai and Vanneman (2015).   [88] Raleigh et al. (2010).

TABLE 1.1 *Village samples and data sources across chapters*

	No SHG Program	SHG Program	SHG Program + Gender Consciousness-Raising Program
MP Sample Survey	76 villages	226 villages	74 villages
MP Census Survey	2 villages	4 villages	
MP Interviews		10 villages	10 villages
Sample analyzed by chapter			
Chapters 4, 5, 6	X		
Chapter 7	Control (76 villages)	Treatment (76 villages)	
Chapter 8		Control (74 villages)	Treatment (74 villages)

These sampling strategies and their implications for the research design are described in the relevant chapters. As I describe in Chapter 7, a supplemental survey in 2016 revisited some SHG villages and surveyed a sample of women who had been randomly chosen from census rosters to ensure comparability with non-SHG villages. Table 1.1 describes the mapping of the survey samples with the samples used in each set of analyses.

OVERVIEW OF THE BOOK

This book presents a theory of coercive political power with four core arguments: (1) The household is the primary unit of political decision-making in rural India, (2) women's political participation aligns with the strategic interests of the men in their household given inequalities in bargaining and coercive power, (3) this yields a larger political system sustained by women's political subordination, and (4) autonomy – or freedom to make political decisions distinct from the household – and solidaristic collective action among women enable women's greater political participation.

The first part of the book (Chapters 2 and 3) describes the conditions surrounding women's political lives and develops a theory of their political exclusion as rooted in power relations. Chapter 2 sets the stage by defining and describing the manifestations of patriarchy and inequality in India that serve as the backdrop for theorizing. I describe the system of patriarchy in rural India and how widespread and entrenched patriarchal norms generate a patriarchal social order that centers women in the household. I demonstrate how patriarchal norms have enabled the use of violence to control and dominate women, including by internalizing the acceptability of this means of coercion. I further highlight the role of legal and political institutions in perpetuating this social order. I additionally document the state of women's and men's political participation in rural India, revealing substantial disparities in political participation between men and women and, even more strikingly, between different forms of participation within women.

In Chapter 3, I build a theory of women's political behavior under these conditions. I argue for the defining role of the household in women's political lives. I describe the conditions that would lead to household political cooperation – joint household political decision-making – and hypothesize its implications for individual women's political behavior and the structure of political organization more broadly. I then develop a series of expectations about how and when women will become active political citizens, arguing for the importance of women's autonomy from the household, their social solidarity with each other, and the potential for women's collective action to transform their political lives.

The second part of the book (Chapters 4–6) empirically proves the existence of household political cooperation, demonstrates how it relates to women's political participation, and documents the patriarchal political order. Chapter 4 brings the household into focus and demonstrates how it denies women political agency and constrains their political participation. Drawing on the census survey and interview data, I document the alignment of the household in political decision-making and the authority of elder men in these decisions. I show that women lack autonomy in their vote choice and are often coerced into compliance with the wishes of the heads of household. I further document the inefficiency of household cooperation for women and demonstrate its perpetuation as rooted in coercion and strategic political mobilization.

In Chapter 5, I show that power *within* the household and autonomy *from* the household most strongly predict women's political participation. Using the census data, I estimate the determinants of women's (and men's) political participation. Comparing within households, bargaining power is associated with women's non-electoral political participation, though not their voting. Comparing within villages, autonomy from the household is a clear predictor of women's political participation. In fact, the behavior of women who enjoy a high degree of autonomy from the household mirrors that of men. I also provide suggestive evidence that intra-household coercion plays a role in women's political participation by showing a lack of correlation between political interest and participation in the household for women but not men and a negative correlation between regressive gender attitudes of the dominant male household member and women's political participation.

Building on this, Chapter 6 illustrates that household political cooperation begets a system of political organization that centers on men. Using network data from the census survey, I describe the structure of the overall village political network, including gender homophily of political ties, centrality in the entire network, and the average degree of connectivity between individuals and political elites. I show that village political networks are structured such that men comprise the center of the network, while women remain on the periphery. As a result, influence is concentrated among men, and village politics is structured around men's other intersecting identities, namely caste. I then compare the size and composition of women's and men's political networks and show that women are connected to village politics largely through the men in their household. For men, women do not register as political actors. Household political cooperation thus implies strong limits on women's access to power, influence, and information and yields a broader gender and political system that perpetuates male dominance.

The third part of the book (Chapters 7–8) generates causal evidence showing that autonomy from the household and collective action among women increase women's non-electoral political participation. Chapter 7 provides cause for optimism: women's participation in apolitical women's groups enhances their political agency and doubles their political participation. Leveraging a natural experiment to identify the impact of access to SHGs, I show that access to spaces outside of the household with other women generates solidaristic collective action oriented toward women's political participation that succeeds in changing women's political behavior: SHG members were significantly and substantially more likely to participate in politics than nonmembers. Further, this impact is evident in the larger village political network; women are more densely politically connected, and gender emerges as a more salient political cleavage. This positive impact of SHGs occurs despite no change in women's economic resources.

Chapter 8 demonstrates that such effects can be augmented by stimulating solidarity among women with a focus on gender consciousness-raising, but that such actions generate backlash. I test the importance of social solidarity in stimulating women's collective action by exploiting arbitrary variation in the delivery of a gender consciousness-raising program to SHGs. I show that women are more likely to undertake collective action after identifying shared experiences of deprivation and forming a bond based on their gender identity. This collective action is also more likely to be aimed at women's strategic interests[89] – their interests rooted in their patriarchal suppression – and therefore garners more resistance from men in the community, including through increased experiences of (public) violence and harassment. I show that women navigate this resistance through their collective strength and solidarity.

In the final part of the book (Chapters 9 and 10), I explore my argument's implications for (and generalizability to) broader patterns of women's political representation and governance in India. Chapter 9 reveals that the circular patterns of norm renegotiation manifest at the national level in India's broader women's movement. I describe the history of this movement and then use ACLED data on all women-led protest events in India from 2016 to 2021 to

---

[89] Molyneux (1985).

illustrate the breadth of women's collective mobilization and the range of demands raised. Women most often come together to protest more explicitly gendered issues, such as gender-based violence. However, many women-led protests focus on other demands, including improved government accountability and service delivery. The nature of women's demand-making suggests possibilities for both gender equality and improved governance with their political inclusion. Finally, I document broader patterns of resistance to women's collective action at the national scale, documenting a range of explicit instances of violent backlash and summarizing the rise of the men's rights movement in India. This provides further evidence of male coercion and suggests conditions under which women's collective action can succeed.

I conclude in Chapter 10 by taking stock of the evidence and looking ahead at the long-run implications of women's political inclusion for broader processes of development and social change. I argue that women's political inclusion hinges on their ability to navigate resistance and co-optation. If they are able to achieve real political representation, I suggest it is likely to yield important changes to governance and development more broadly.

2

Patriarchy, Inequality, and the Political Lives of Rural Indian Women

Patriarchy, or norms of male dominance and de facto authority, is widespread and deeply rooted in rural India. Elder men with submissive and secluded wives are accorded the highest social status in a system that generates large gender inequalities in access to social, economic, and political institutions. The specific role allocated to women in society and within the household restricts their lived experiences and choice sets. Gender disparities in political participation thus do not exist in a vacuum; they are just one manifestation of a broader social equilibrium.

In this chapter, I describe how widespread and entrenched norms generate a patriarchal social order in rural India that elevates men and subordinates women. This social order is rooted in the Hindu notion of 'joint family' and norms of patrilocality, which oblige sons to reside with their parents throughout their lifetime and to provide care and protection in old age. Sons are thus the key to comfort later in life. Women also have a stake in this social hierarchy, which gives them power over their daughters-in-law. The patriarchal system is upheld by deeply internalized beliefs regarding male superiority and acceptance of their dominance. At its most extreme, this manifests in women accepting men's use of violent punishments against women in their household.

Male dominance is further enshrined in the Indian legal system, which has historically upheld men's status through discriminatory personal and family laws and weakly enforcing policies designed to prevent violence against women. The patriarchal social order is further perpetuated through gender inequalities in access to valuable resources such as education and jobs. These inequalities begin at birth (with male-skewed sex ratios), are deepened in marriage (nearly half of all women are married by the time they reach adulthood), and are sustained by limits on women's earning power (women's labor force participation is one-third that of men's).

How can women overcome such norms and institutions that curtail their productivity and independence to become active political citizens? Until now, we have lacked the basic data needed to answer such a question and understand where gendered inequalities in political behavior persist. To the best of my knowledge, this book presents one of the most comprehensive accounts of non-electoral political participation in its many forms in India for both women and men. The original data I collected for this study from women and men across five districts in the state of Madhya Pradesh permit a more in-depth examination of the nature of men's and women's political participation than previously explored.

I examine gendered patterns of political behavior in rural Madhya Pradesh, and show that, relative to men, women are substantially underrepresented in political spaces. However, an unexplained puzzle emerges: while women are largely absent from politics between elections, they are almost as likely to vote as men, even after accounting for caste category, education, and employment status. It is clear that gender is more likely to influence rural Indian citizens' political participation than other intersecting identities such as caste, tribe, class, and education level.[1] The presumption that these patterns of women's political participation result from gendered inequalities in resources fails to account for the multiple interrelated features of the patriarchal social equilibrium that shape both women's political behavior and societal inequalities. Understanding women's puzzling political behavior first requires exploring the broader social equilibrium in which they live.

THE PATRIARCHAL SOCIAL ORDER IN RURAL INDIA

Patriarchy is a social order that elevates the status of men as dominant to women.[2] Following Bicchieri's[3] definition of a social norm as "a rule of behavior such that individuals prefer to conform to it on condition that they believe that (a) most people in their reference network conform to it (empirical expectation), and (b) that most people in their reference network believe they ought to conform to it (normative expectation)," under patriarchal norms, male dominance is both widely assumed[4] and normatively valued. These norms reinforce (and are reinforced by) societies' elevation of men in most domains and the gender inequalities this generates in social, market, and political institutions.

Most, if not all, countries around the world operate under some form of patriarchy that allocates de facto authority to men: men are the presumed heads

---

[1] I cannot distinguish between religions, except insofar as they intersect with tribal identity, as nearly all residents in the study villages identify as Hindu.

[2] Hunnicutt (2009).   [3] Bicchieri (2016: 35).

[4] Iversen and Rosenbluth (2010) define this wide assumption as common knowledge; therefore, patriarchy influences expectations of how power across systems and structures will be allocated across genders.

of household, attributes traditionally associated with masculinity are socially desirable, and men fill most positions of authority and status in markets and politics. Johnson argues that a society is patriarchal if it is male *dominated* (men fill positions of authority), male *identified* (ideas about what is good/preferable are associated with norms of masculinity), and male *centered* (attention is focused on men and their actions).[5] But forms of patriarchy vary across societies and regions. Women have substantial autonomy in some regions and regularly engage in productive activity even though power is still associated with maleness. In others, including South Asia, patriarchal norms more strictly limit women's mobility and productivity.

India is what Kandiyoti[6] would classify as a "classic patriarchy," the strictest and most restricting form. At its core, classic patriarchy gives a household's senior male authority over both its women and its younger men. It is most commonly found in South Asia, North Africa, the Middle East, and East Asia. As Kandiyoti explains, the patriarchal bargain in such areas constitutes "protection in exchange for submissiveness and propriety."[7] Under this system, men control the economic, social, and political spaces and are expected to protect women from both financial destitution and social disrepute. Women, in return, manage and care for the household and children and embody the socially desirable attributes of subservience and seclusion to ensure a higher social status for their household.

The highest social status is bestowed upon households with (1) high-earning men who can provide for their family without help from women and (2) secluded women who remain in the household and are therefore pure. The ideal woman does not work, cares for the household and children, does not interact with other men except with the permission or presence of men from her household, defers to the authority of her husband and male elders, and elevates household needs above her own. In striving for this ideal, women often have restricted mobility within the community and access to independent networks outside the household except insofar as they serve the household's needs. For example, according to data from the Indian Human Development Survey, 86 percent of rural women report that they must ask permission to travel a short distance by train or bus, and only 50 percent stated that they would be able to do so alone.[8]

Such norms in India derive in part from Brahmanical, or upper-caste, belief systems, which suggest that being born a woman is evidence of having sinned in previous lives.[9] Elite castes that have been elevated in economic and social institutions have the economic power to ensure strict obedience to these social dictates and have set the standards for the normatively desired behaviors of women and men.[10] In need of a higher income, lower-caste men generally

---

[5] Johnson (1997).   [6] Kandiyoti (1988).   [7] Kandiyoti (1988: 283).   [8] Desai (2015).
[9] Kapadia (1994).   [10] Kapadia (1995).

exercise less control over women, as their work is required for economic survival. Women in lower-caste communities therefore often enjoy greater freedoms, albeit still within a system that privileges men.

However, as numerous studies of class mobility in India have demonstrated, as lower-caste households improve their financial position, women become more socially secluded and controlled in an attempt to mirror the behavior of upper-caste households.[11] Upper-caste behavior typically dictates what is considered normatively good and proper for women. As Kapadia notes, "it is among [the upwardly mobile groups] that 'appropriate' female behavior suddenly becomes the coin of new social status for men."[12] She observes the irony that women's status is "steadily falling" among those who are "economically bettering themselves."[13] Under this pattern, as a household's economic position improves, women enjoy less autonomy and authority – particularly in rural villages, where networks are insular and norm-violating behavior is easy to observe. Therefore, patriarchal norms and the gendered power systems they are associated with are fundamentally intertwined with caste and class power structures.[14]

Marriage and the Joint Family

Male dominance within classic patriarchy is perpetuated through two institutions. The first is the joint family, in which multiple generations reside together and constitute a household. The second is patrilocality, in which newly married couples live with the man's family. Sons are expected to live with their parents along with their wives and children and to ensure their parents are cared for in old age. The joint family therefore acts as a form of social insurance in old age, which makes sons particularly valuable to parents in securing care and protection later in life.

Under classic patriarchy, upon marriage a woman is dispossessed from her natal family: her family transfers her share of the inheritance to the groom's family in the form of a dowry payment, thus shedding (financial) responsibility for her.[15] The degree of a woman's ties to her natal family varies across India: in some regions, families retain some responsibility for their daughters after marriage. In much of India, however, women are largely considered the responsibility of their husband's family following marriage, and the dowry releases natal families from their economic obligation to daughters. These norms contribute to skewed sex ratios from prenatal sex selection[16] and general son preference;[17] parents have greater incentives to invest in male children because

---

[11] Kapadia (1995); Hunnicutt (2009); Heyer (1992).   [12] Kapadia (1995: 169–170).
[13] Kapadia (1995: 253).
[14] See Folbre (2021) for a thorough exploration of the links between intersecting power structures.
[15] Bloch and Rao (2002).   [16] Sen (1990).   [17] Jayachandran and Pande (2017).

they will remain in the household after marriage.[18] Indeed there is a saying in India that "raising a daughter is like watering your neighbors' garden."[19] When Ramji, an Adivasi man in Madhya Pradesh, was asked in an interview why he had educated his sons but not his daughters, he highlighted the explicit inter-generational transmission of these norms by stating that "my father taught me that daughters wouldn't stay in our house lifelong. We need to give her away to some other house. That's why I didn't educate them."[20]

Young women relocate to their husbands' communities and become subor-dinate members of their new households. In a joint family, new daughters-in-law are subject to the authority of senior men in the household, their husbands, and their mother-in-law.[21] Women's greatest value in this system is the pro-duction of sons, as only they provide financial security in old age by remaining in the household after marriage.[22] Sons further establish women's place within the patriline; under norms of patrilineality, land and inheritance pass through male heirs. Evidence from India and China suggests that women's bargaining power in the household increases with the birth of sons.[23]

Women's economic autonomy is suppressed by a well-defined division of labor that leaves women responsible for caring for children and the household and men responsible for providing financially for the family.[24] A woman's skill in caring for her family and her willingness to abide by the division of labor are key determinants of her success in the marriage market. Since women are discouraged from working outside of the home, brides are selected in arranged marriages based on their domestic work skills and social purity. Investment in young girls seeks to build these domestic skills to ensure their competitiveness in the marriage market, as unmarried daughters are a financial burden to their families. Recent evidence from online marraige matching sites demonstrates that employed women are roughly 15 percent less likely to receive male interest in India.[25] Investment in young boys' human capital, by contrast, ensures their ability to provide for their parents in old age. Of course, not all house-holds can afford to limit women's economic productivity. Poorer households, historically those in lower-caste communities, have yielded "worse" outcomes in the marriage market because women have been forced to work. Because women's work is devalued in the marriage market, and since their greatest protection comes through marriage, women have a stake in perpetuating patriarchal norms.

---

[18] Braunstein and Folbre (2001).   [19] Jayachandran (2015).
[20] Ramji (pseudonym), male, 45 years old, Scheduled Tribe (ST).   [21] Jayachandran (2020).
[22] Braunstein and Folbre (2001).   [23] Li and Wu (2011); Zimmerman (2018).
[24] Iversen and Rosenbluth (2010); Alesina, Giuliano, and Nunn (2013).   [25] Afridi et al. (2023).

Internalized Patriarchal Norms

Socialization into patriarchal norms begins at a young age. Households and communities demonstrate the appropriate gender roles to young girls and boys. As they enter adulthood, these roles are reinforced by social, economic, and political institutions that define the valued attributes of femininity and masculinity. Social status is conferred on those who conform to these roles, and role violations are socially sanctioned.[26] Male dominance within the household is perpetuated by the high social status associated with having compliant wives. Restrictive practices such as purdah (according to which women cover their face and body in the presence of men outside their family) signal women's subservience to men and compliance with patriarchal norms. Norms of social exclusion, which limit women's mobility and ties outside the household, further perpetuate men's dominance. Men benefit socially from women's subordination and are punished if women meant to be under their control violate these norms. Men therefore have incentives to establish their authority within the household and to enforce these gender roles.

When a woman's financial security is rooted in her marriageability, parents are incentivized to socialize their daughters to pro-male norms in hopes of improving her prospects in the marriage market.[27] Drawing on data from across India in the World Values Survey, Figure 2.1 reports men's and women's average responses to a set of statements regarding gender attitudes and explicit gender biases. A majority of women reported pro-male gender-biased attitudes across all measures except one: 66 percent of Indian women agreed that men make better political leaders than women, 69 percent responded that men make better business executives, 75 percent stated that it is a problem if women earn more than men, and 63 percent agreed that university education is more important for boys. The prevalence of pro-male attitudes held by women indicates the extent of internalized patriarchal social norms.[28] Men, on average, reported roughly similar rates of agreement with these attitudes; marginally fewer men highlighted male superiority in leadership roles. The only attitude that generated significant disagreement is employment: women were less likely to agree that men had more rights to jobs than women (47 percent of women versus 53 percent of men). These gender-biased attitudes are also prevalent in and consistent with the results of the survey I conducted in rural Madhya Pradesh, which suggests that gender attitudes in these communities are representative of India more broadly (see Figure A2.1).

Strikingly, these gendered attitudes do not differ substantially across caste categories or age groups (see Figure 2.2). A majority of men and women from nearly all caste categories agree that men make better political leaders and

---

[26] Sapiro (1983).   [27] Jayachandran (2020).   [28] Diekman and Schneider (2010).

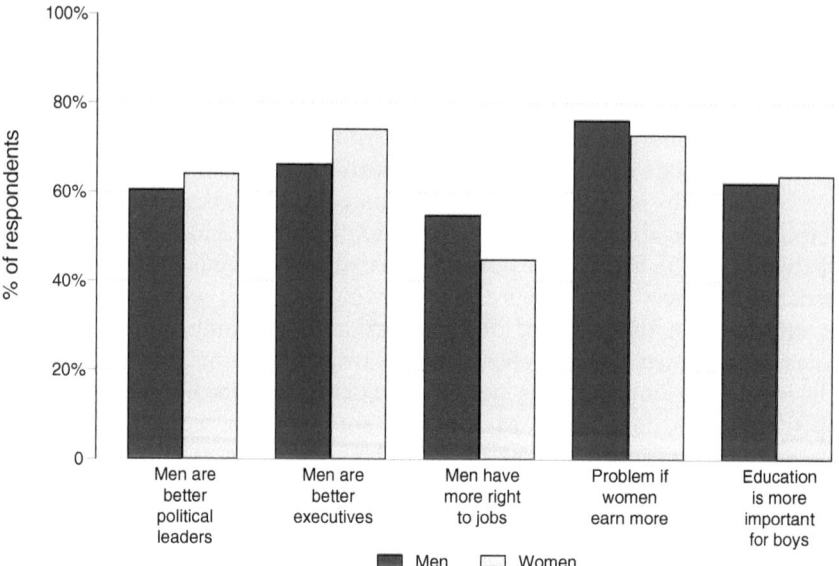

FIGURE 2.1 Most women and men report pro-male gender attitudes in India
Note: The figure plots the average share of men and women that report agreement with a series of
statements about attitudes toward gender. Data are from the World Values Survey Wave
6 conducted from 2010 to 2014, subset to only India (Inglehart et al. 2014). Responses of agree
or strongly agree are coded as affirmative, and disagree, strongly disagree, and neither agree nor
disagree are coded as negative. The sample includes 985 men and 596 women.

executives than women, it is a problem if women earn more than men, and
education is more important for boys than for girls. Average affirmative
responses to all gender attitudes are remarkably similar for women across
caste categories, particularly Other Backward Class (OBC), Scheduled Caste
(SC), and Scheduled Tribe (ST) women, and women from most caste categories are on average more likely to report pro-male attitudes than men. It is
striking that Muslim women report similar attitudes to most Hindu and ST
women, given they are often presumed to be the most strictly bound by
patriarchal norms. Scheduled Tribe women, too, are often presumed to hold
more gender progressive attitudes, which are not evidenced here. The one
notable difference relates to the behavior of upper or General Category (GC)
castes. Upper-caste women were less likely to report gender-biased attitudes,
which is at odds with common conceptions that upper-caste households more
strictly adhere to patriarchal norms. High rates of reported gender-biased
attitudes among SC and ST men and women demonstrate that even those
from historically economically deprived caste groups have internalized norms
of women's inferiority.

Since the sample sizes within each gender–caste pairing are small, particularly among women, these averages should be interpreted with caution. Figure A2.2 replicates these figures using my survey data from Madhya Pradesh, which included a substantially larger sample but excluded both upper castes (GC) and Muslims due to the low representation of these groups in the areas surveyed. In this larger sample, gender attitudes are even more similar across caste categories.

Figure 2.2 also demonstrates a remarkable similarity in gender attitudes by age. Men and women of all ages report near-identical beliefs regarding male dominance. This finding is at odds with arguments that older men and women have a greater stake in the patriarchal order and therefore may have internalized such norms to a greater extent. It instead suggests that men and women of all ages have internalized patriarchal norms, which I also find in the data from Madhya Pradesh (see Figure A2.2). However, in the Madhya Pradesh

(a) By caste category

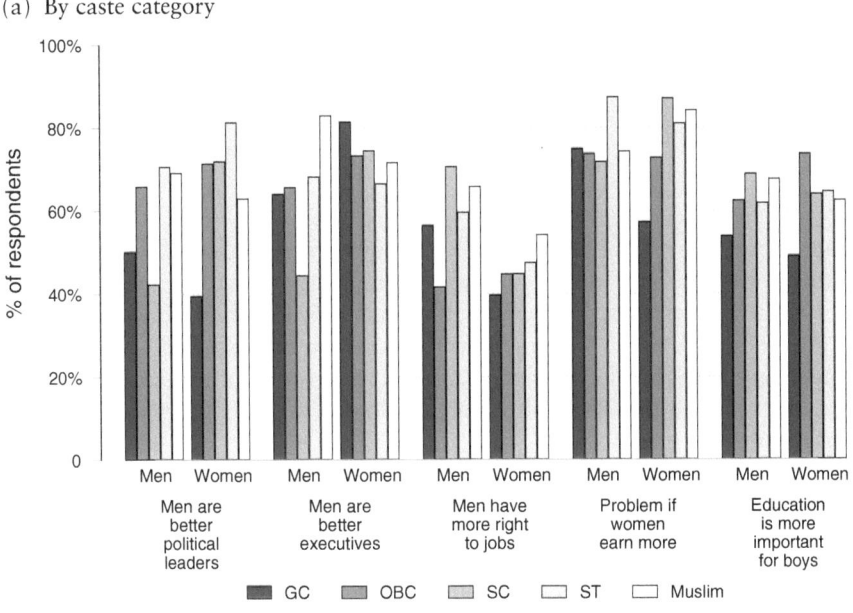

FIGURE 2.2 Reported gender attitudes in India do not vary by caste category and age group

Note: The figure plots the average share of men and women, by caste category and age group, that report agreement with a series of statements about attitudes toward gender. Data are from the World Values Survey Wave 6 conducted from 2010 to 2014, subset to only India (Inglehart et al. 2014). Responses of agree or strongly agree are coded as affirmative, and disagree, strongly disagree, and neither agree nor disagree are coded as negative. The sample includes 985 men and 596 women.

(b) By age group

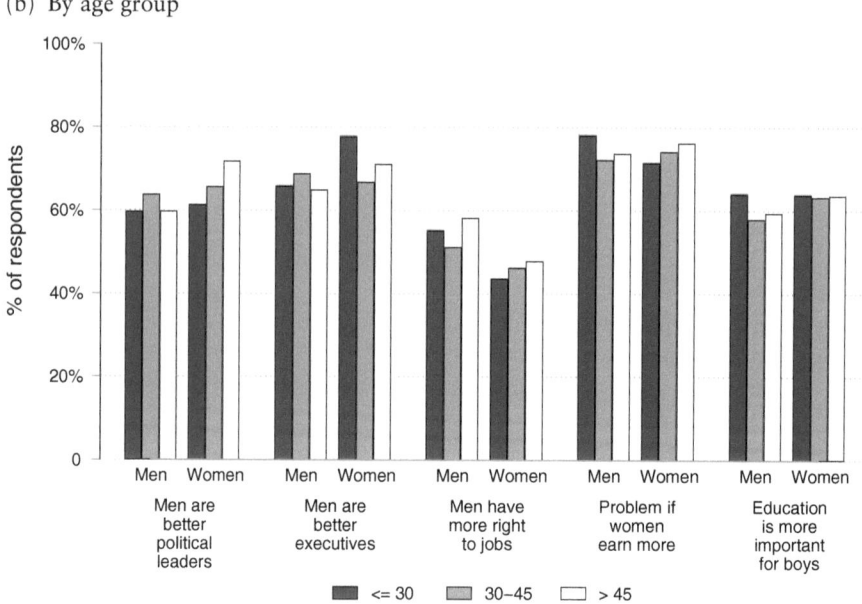

FIGURE 2.2 (*cont.*)

sample, I find that men under thirty are the most likely to agree with pro-male attitudes. Others have noted that young men often have the most gender-discriminatory attitudes,[29] suggesting that such attitudes may temper following the birth of daughters.[30] These sentiments may also be attributed to the greater competition between younger men and women for opportunities and jobs; young men in Madhya Pradesh report the lowest support for women's equal right to jobs.

Overall, data from across India demonstrate that a large share of both men and women continue to believe that men should – and do – dominate economic and political institutions. Women hold even more pro-male attitudes in most domains than men, which demonstrates how deeply women have internalized patriarchal norms. These attitudes are also shared across caste categories and age groups, highlighting the pervasiveness of these beliefs.

Patriarchy and Power in the Household

Patriarchy structures household power relations both between men and women and between women. Within patriarchal households, all men hold de facto

[29] Prillaman et al. (2017).   [30] Washington (2008); Glynn and Sen (2015).

authority over women; older men dominate younger men, as older women outrank younger women. Male status in the household is codified within many bureaucratic systems in India, where women's identity is defined by the men they are attached to. For example, to register to vote or contest office, men and unmarried women are uniquely identified using their name and their father's name, while married women are uniquely identified using their name and their husband's name.

Male power in the housoehold is presumed under patriarchy, and this power is sustained through women's internalization of inferior status and through the explicit use of psychological and physical coercion as punishment for deviation from patriarchal norms. Numerous studies across the globe have demonstrated that men whose authority is threatened within the house or the community engage in domestic violence to demonstrate and retain their authority under patriarchal norms.[31] Drawing on data from the National Family Health Survey, Figure 2.3 reports the share of women across India that report having been controlled or emotionally or physically abused by their husbands. The use of violence against women in the household is pervasive: 31 percent of all women (and nearly 40 percent of SC women) report being physically abused by their husbands. Appendix Figure A2.3 illustrates a similar prevalence among women in Madhya Pradesh. Additionally, the National Family Health Survey data indicate that roughly 15 percent of women report being emotionally abused by their husbands through humiliation, threats, or insults, and more than 50 percent of women state that their husbands had attempted to control their behavior. While SC women do report higher rates of physical abuse, women from all caste categories report high rates of violence and abuse.

While explicit psychological and physical abuse is widely prevalent, rates of domestic violence likely underreport the extent of intra-household coercion. Because women internalize the normative value structure imposed by patriarchy, explicit coercion to sanction norm violation should be limited. As a result, measuring intra-household coercion is challenging, as explicit evidence of this coercion only manifests when norms are violated. To understand the extent of internalized acceptance of coercion, Figure 2.4 reports men's and women's beliefs about the acceptability of domestic violence under five conditions: when a woman goes out without her husband, neglects her children, argues with her husband, refuses sex with her husband, or cooks poorly. Across the board, women are more likely than men to say that the use of violence is justified against women. Nearly half of the women surveyed (45 percent), but only 32 percent of the men, stated that a husband is justified

---

[31] Hunnicutt (2009).

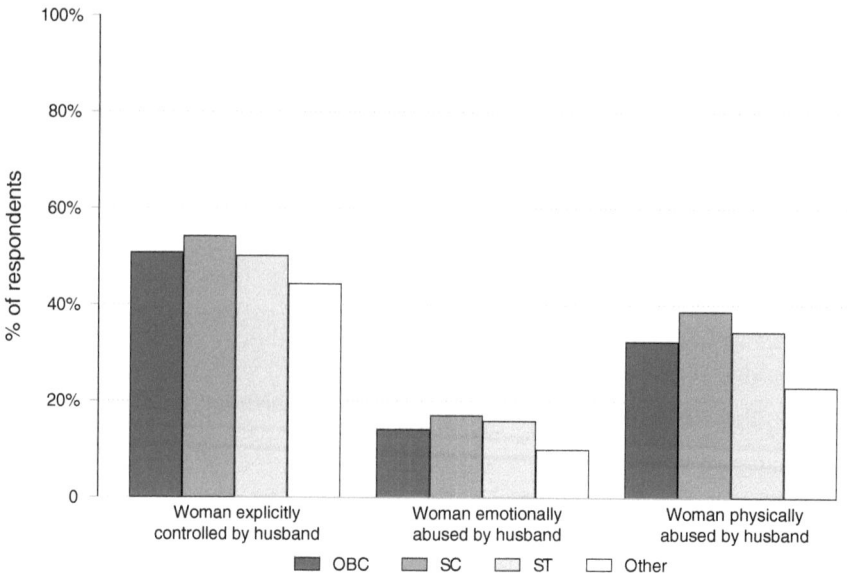

FIGURE 2.3 One-third of women report experiences of domestic violence, and one-half report being controlled by their husbands

Note: The figure plots the average share of women, by caste category, that report having experienced any of three indicators of intimate partner violence. Data are from the 2015–2016 National Family Health Survey (IIPS 2017). Experience of explicit control is determined by affirmative responses to any of the following statements: he (is/was) jealous or angry if you (talk/talked) to other men, he frequently (accuses/accused) you of being unfaithful, he (does/did) not permit you to meet your female friends, he (tries/tried) to limit your contact with your family, he (insists/insisted) on knowing where you (are/were) at all times, or he (does/did) not trust you with any money. Experience of emotional abuse is determined by affirmative responses to any of the following questions: Does your husband ever say or do something to humiliate you in front of others? Does your husband ever threaten to hurt or harm you or someone close to you? Does your husband ever insult you or make you feel bad about yourself? Experience of physical abuse is determined by affirmative statements that the respondent's husband had done any of the following: push you, shake you, or throw something at you; twist your arm or pull your hair; slap you; punch you with his fist or something that could hurt you; kick you, drag you, or beat you up; try to choke you or burn you on purpose; threaten or attack you with a knife, gun, or any other weapon; physically force you to have sexual intercourse with him even when you did not want to; physically force you to perform any other sexual acts you did not want to; force you with threats or in any other way to perform sexual acts you did not want to. Responses are weighted by the survey weight provided. The sample includes 66,013 women.

in beating his wife under some circumstances.[32] The prevalence and gender differences of these beliefs hold across caste categories and age groups,

---

[32] It is important to note that men's reported acceptability of violence perpetration is below the rates of reported violence perpetration, signaling that these estimates are likely downward biased due to social desirability concerns.

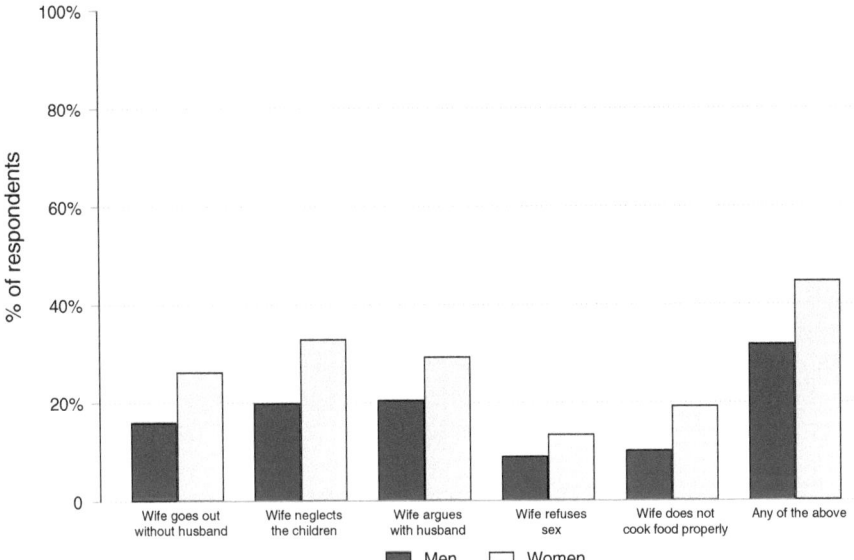

FIGURE 2.4 More than one-third of men and women state that domestic violence is acceptable under some conditions

Note: The figure plots the average share of men and women that state that a husband beating his wife is acceptable under each of five conditions. Data are from the 2015–2016 National Family Health Survey (IIPS 2017). Average responses to the question "In your opinion, is a husband justified in hitting or beating his wife in the following situations?" are reported, with responses of "don't know" coded as missing. Responses are weighted by the survey weight provided. The sample includes 111,188 men and 121,651 women.

although they are marginally more likely as men and women age (see Figure A2.4).

The social acceptability (and credible threat) of violence against women sustains male household power. Cools and Kotsadam importantly show that paid employment does not protect women from the experience of domestic violence, and may even worsen it, in communities with greater social acceptance of domestic violence.[33] Women come to expect violence as a mechanism of intra-household punishment and understand and accept its use as part of the patriarchal social order. Coercion is part and parcel of the patriarchal system and women's subordination. Women arguably abide by and even perpetuate norms of classic patriarchy because of how these norms structure women's

---

[33] Cools and Kotsadam (2017).

power throughout the lifecycle.[34] Mothers-in-law control the functioning of the house and have authority over the behavior of their daughters-in-law. Recent evidence suggests that abuse perpetrated by mothers-in-law against daughters-in-law in India is nearly as common as intimate partner abuse, though these data are limited in scope.[35] Young brides occupy the lowest position in the household hierarchy and must survive subordination and deprivation. They do so in the expectation that, one day, they will be mothers-in-law themselves. The prospect of power in old age incentivizes women to prize sons, who are the vehicle of the joint family and through which women can have daughters-in-law and, therefore, power. The prospect of this authority in old age gives women a stake in the patriarchal social order: as women age, they benefit less from renegotiating patriarchal norms.[36] By creating enemies or at least adversaries among women, patriarchy divides women and potentially inhibits their collective resistance to their subordination.

Family Law and the Institutionalization of Male Dominance

Why might domestic violence and the oppression of women persist at such high rates in India? In addition to these being socially accepted (as shown in Figure 2.4), personal and family laws in India have historically upheld the subordination of women and provided legal grounds for men's dominance and authority. Personal and family laws govern rights related to property ownership, inheritance, marriage, divorce, and child custody and therefore set the stage for legal equality or inequality in family negotiations.

In India, family law is anchored in religion. In the late eighteenth century, colonial rule explicitly separated family law into three distinct streams of jurisprudence: Hindu, Muslim, and Christian. Each religious community was governed by separate personal and family laws rooted in their religious laws and customs.[37] While religious-based family law seeks inclusion and sensitivity to group rights, its primacy has often legalized women's subordinate status. For example, the Hindu Succession Act of 1956 states that while the property of a man who dies intestate goes first to his children and widow and second to his family's heirs, the property of a woman who dies intestate goes first to her children and husband and second to the heirs of her husband's family. A woman's dispossession from her natal family is therefore enshrined in the legal patterns of inheritance. In addition, the Hindu Minority and Guardianship Act of 1956 establishes the father as the primary legal guardian of children over five, and the mother as secondary. A key exception is when a

---

[34] Kandiyoti (1988). While much (if not all) of India operates under patriarchy, there is variation in the specific manifestations of patriarchy. Most notably some cultures in south and northeast India practice matrilineality, where inheritance passes through the mother instead of the father (Brulé and Gaikwad 2021).

[35] Ragavan and Iyengar (2020).   [36] Blaydes and Linzer (2008).

[37] De Alwis and Jaising (2015).

woman is married while still a minor: her guardianship is passed to her husband. In this way, Hindu law designates men as both the head of the household and the guardians of women.

Indian family law has also historically made it difficult for women to leave marriages, thus incentivizing their allegiance to the household. One of the most notable challenges to the discriminatory practices enshrined in Indian family law relates to the practice of triple *talaq*, which allows a Muslim man to divorce his wife simply by repeating *talaq* (Arabic for "divorce") three times. In 1978, Shah Bano, a Muslim woman, filed a petition against her husband after he divorced her in this way.[38] She petitioned the court for alimony, which, under Muslim Personal Law, is provided for roughly three months after a divorce. In 1985, the Supreme Court of India ruled in her favor. Due to rising pressure from Muslim groups claiming that this ruling infringed on their right to govern according to Muslim Law, the Muslim Women (Protection of Rights on Divorce) Act of 1986 was passed, which overturned the Supreme Court's judgment and reestablished the dominance of Muslim Law. In 2016, Shayara Bano demanded that her husband's triple *talaq* be voided on the grounds that it violated Muslim women's rights. In 2017, the Supreme Court of India ruled in her favor and declared the practice unconstitutional. The Muslim Women (Protection of Rights on Marriage) Act of 2019 made triple *talaq* illegal; however, many dissented and some argued that this insufficiently addressed the difficulties associated with legally obtaining a divorce. For example, the Dissolution of Muslim Marriages Act of 1939 places a more stringent burden of proof on women seeking divorce than on men.

In addition to historically discriminatory family laws, violence against women, while illegal, has seen limited adjudication. While rape and other forms of violence against women have been criminalized in the Indian Penal Code, it was only in 2005 that the Parliament passed the Protection of Women from Domestic Violence Act and legally defined domestic violence. Before 2005, numerous rulings in favor of women were overturned due to the exceedingly high burden of proof demanded from them.[39] The 2005 law made major strides in protecting women from physical, sexual, verbal, emotional, and economic abuse. It has since led to further amendments to the Penal Code to protect women from additional forms of abuse and increase the punishment for rape. However, marital rape is still not considered a crime under Indian law unless the wife is under fifteen years of age.[40]

---

[38] De Alwis and Jaising (2015).

[39] See, for example, *Pratap Misra and Others v. the State of Orissa, Smt. Harvinder Kaur v. Harmimder Singh Choudhary*, and the High Court ruling in the Sudha Goel case (Calman 1992).

[40] Rape is prohibited by Section 375 of the Indian Penal Code, which includes an exception for marital rape, stating that "sexual intercourse or sexual acts by a man with his own wife, the wife not being under fifteen years of age, is not rape."

The legal framework of religiously based family law has institutionalized discrimination against women in India. Women have faced a high burden of proof when demanding both freedom from marriages and protection against violence.[41] While courts and judges have recently used flexibility in the laws to secure more equal rights for women and amendments to many laws have sought to redress the most grievous of inequities, the existence of a legal-institutional framework that has historically protected the status of men and subordinated the status of women institutionalizes male dominance and control. For many decades, the laws' presumption that families are religious, largely immutable, and headed by men supports the patriarchal social order.

GENDER INEQUALITY IN INDIA

The preference for males is expressed from sex selection at birth to investments in children's education and life opportunities, which generates pervasive gender inequalities in access to education, markets, and other social institutions. These inequalities are both the product of patriarchal norms that incentivize investments in sons and institutions that privilege men for many reasons, including explicit discrimination. Understanding the lives of women therefore requires investigating the manifestation of gender inequality. Table 2.1 documents average gendered outcomes across India from the early 2000s to the late 2010s. It demonstrates that 886 women were born for every 1,000 men in 2000, and this sex ratio has worsened over the past two decades: only 877 women were born for every 1,000 men in 2016. India is thus missing sixty-three million women.[42] These sex ratios can only be attributed to sex-selective abortions.[43]

Limited family resources are much more likely to be used to educate sons rather than daughters. While the literacy gap between men and women has narrowed since the early 2000s, women continue to lag. As of 2018, girls completed primary and lower secondary school at a higher rate than boys, although girls still lagged 7 percentage points behind boys in completing upper secondary education, and only two-thirds of Indian women were literate. While education inequalities persist, particularly in the highest realms of education, Table 2.1 signals a trend of equalizing education among girls and boys.

Despite reductions in educational inequalities, the gender gap in labor force participation is widening, and women's labor force participation has markedly declined to only one-fifth that of men.[44] As of 2019, only 22 percent of women participated in the labor force, compared to 74 percent of men. Despite the recent increases in women's educational attainment, it is often India's most

---

[41] Roychowdhury (2020).   [42] Sen (1990).   [43] Madan and Breuning (2014).
[44] Fletcher, Pande, and Moore (2017).

TABLE 2.1 *Gender inequality persists in multiple domains but has improved in recent decades*

	Early 2000s		Late 2010s	
	Male	Female	Male	Female
Sex Ratio at Birth (per 1,000 male births)		886		877
Literacy Rate	73%	48%	82%	66%
Primary Education Completion Rate	59%	59%	86%	87%
Lower Secondary Education Completion Rate[4]	60%	46%	81%	85%
Upper Secondary Education Completion Rate[5]	26%	19%	46%	40%
Labor Force Participation Rate, Age 15+[6]	83%	31%	74%	22%
Percent First Married by Age 18[7]	~14%	50%	4%	27%

Note: This table expands on Table 1 in Duflo (2012). Sex ratio data are reported for the years 2000 and 2016 from Kulkarni (2020). These data are from the Civil Registration System. The 2001 census data suggest a sex ratio of 933, and Sample Registration System data suggest the sex ratio was 894 in 2000. Literacy data are reported for the years 2001 and 2018 from UNESCO (2020). Primary education data are reported for the years 2000 and 2018 from UNESCO (2020). Lower secondary education data are reported for the years 2002 and 2019 from UNESCO (2020). Upper secondary education data are reported for the years 2005 and 2016 from UNESCO (2020). Labor force participation data are reported for the years 2000 and 2019 from the International Labour Organization (2021). Age of marriage data are reported for the years 2000 and 2015 from UNESCO (2020).

educated women who do not engage in paid employment.[45] This trend has largely been attributed to rising household incomes that have allowed patriarchal norms to be more strongly enforced.[46]

Gender inequalities are particularly acute after marriage: 27 percent of women were married by age eighteen in 2015 (down from roughly 50 percent in the early 2000s), compared to only 4 percent of men. These high rates of adolescent marriage are particularly striking given that husbands attain guardianship over minor spouses.

Table 2.1 demonstrates that while women have made important strides in education, gender inequalities in access to economic resources and institutions persist. These inequalities manifest in precisely the ways that dominant patriarchal norms would suggest: pro-male sex selection at birth, girls marrying at a young age, and limited economic autonomy thereafter. Ultimately, India's normative, legal, and economic systems are skewed toward men.

---

[45] See Moore, Pande, and Prillaman (2021) for evidence of even lower labor force participation rates among the most educated women.
[46] Klasen and Pieters (2015).

THE POLITICAL LIVES OF RURAL INDIAN WOMEN

Where norms and institutions devalue women's productivity and social participation, why would we expect women to be active political citizens? And how (if
at all) do they navigate political spaces in such contexts? Based on the degree of
social exclusion and inequality across economic and educational institutions,
we would expect women to be distinctly absent from political institutions.
Indeed they are, but they vote at rates nearly equal to those of men.
Discrimination and inequality caused by patriarchal norms and access to
economic resources alone cannot explain this dichotomy of women's political
behavior.

Political Participation in Rural India

This book broadly explores how citizens interact with and express their
voices to the state. This, of course, includes the most basic and studied form
of political expression – the vote. But voter turnout is not always a good
measure of political engagement, particularly when it is linked to threats or
inducements.[47] As I will show, women's voting does not guarantee their
political agency; their high turnout may even be a direct byproduct
of coercion.

Between elections, there are myriad ways in which citizens interact with the
state that have as great (or greater) impact on their daily lives. These include
participation in deliberative spaces such as community assembly meetings,
contact with elected officials, claims-making for goods and services from political officials and the bureaucracy, participation in electoral campaigns as
mobilizers or attending campaign events, and resisting the state through activities such as protesting.[48] Some forms of participation may be more relevant in
some settings in rural India than others. For example, financial contributions to
campaigns are largely irrelevant in this setting. I focus on how women engage
with formal government institutions and express their voice directly to the state,
largely in day-to-day interactions. I do not study the many informal ways in
which women may contest or subvert political authority (such as through
engagement with civil society) except insofar as such actions facilitate interaction with the state and formal political participation. I focus on formal
political spaces because these are the spaces most often denied to women and
the spaces with the legitimate authority to respond to women's political
demands.

An amendment to India's 1992 Constitution enshrined the central importance of citizen participation in democratic institutions by creating a three-tier

---

[47] Verba, Schlozman, and Brady (1995); Krishna (2002b).
[48] Verba, Nie, and Kim (1978); Kruks-Wisner (2018).

structure of local governance in rural areas. Each state has governing bodies at the district (the Zilla Parishad), block (Panchayat Samiti), and village (Gram Panchayat) levels. This entailed the creation of more than 250,000 local government bodies and devolved power to allocate development and public works projects, establish schools and health centers, and determine eligibility for government schemes.

As the lowest level of government in India, each Gram Panchayat represents a population of 1,000–25,000. Prior to the constitutional amendment in 1992, Gram Panchayats existed across India but were not institutions of democracy. They were instead led by village headmen, usually upper-caste men in the village. These headmen moderated citizen's relationship with the state and parties used them to mobilize voters. Today, the Gram Panchayat is governed by a body of 7–17 elected ward members, one of whom is selected as the chairperson. Gram Panchayat officials in each state are elected at the same time and serve five-year terms.

The Constitution mandates each Gram Panchayat to hold a Gram Sabha (village assembly meeting) at least four times a year to convene eligible voters and make decisions on issues related to local governance. These meetings were intended to represent self-rule and direct democracy, and all eligible voters are permitted to attend and participate.[49] The Gram Sabha is thus a key institution for citizens to raise their demands on the state. Yet it has historically been reserved for men, both explicitly and implicitly. Throughout this book, women's political inclusion will be benchmarked by their attendance and participation in these village assembly meetings and through their claims-making to the state for benefits or services.[50]

The Political Behavior of Women and Men

How do men and women engage with the state? Figure 2.5 documents the percentage of men and women who report having participated in politics in each of seven ways over the past year, including voting in the most recent local (Panchayat) and state-level (MLA) elections, attending village assembly

---

[49] The Gram Panchayat mirrors the set of customary institutions that have historically dominated local governance. In these customary institutions, often known as Jati Panchayats (aka caste Panchayats), caste-based leaders adjudicated local disputes and served as gatekeepers to state resources. Historically, Jati Panchayats were primarily the domain of men. Today they largely resolve social disputes in villages, such as disagreements over marriage decisions or intra-household disputes. Women often refer to them as the council of male elders who shape community discussions about who each caste group will vote for.

[50] Kruks-Wisner (2018); Auerbach and Kruks-Wisner (2020).

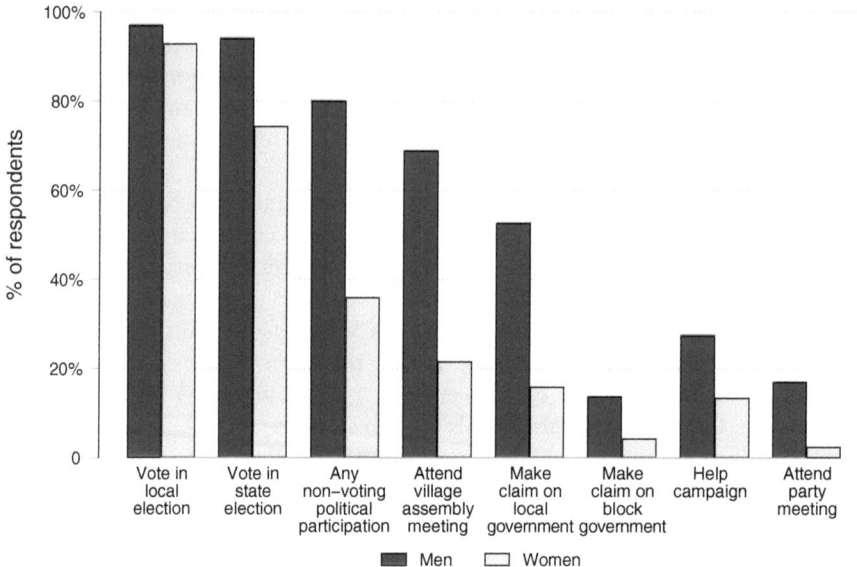

FIGURE 2.5 Men participate in non-electoral politics substantially more than women in rural Madhya Pradesh

Note: The figure plots the average share of men and women who have participated in each of eight forms of political participation. Data are from the 2016 sample survey administered in seventy-six villages in five districts of Madhya Pradesh. The sample of villages includes only those who did not have access to the self-help group (SHG) intervention studied later in the book. This includes data from 1,106 women and 512 men, all of whom are spouses.

meetings (Gram Sabhas), making claims on Panchayat or Block officials, campaigning at rallies or directly through door-to-door mobilization, and attending political party meetings.

Men participate substantially more in politics than women between elections. The most striking difference is in reported attendance at village assembly meetings: only 20 percent of women had been to a village assembly meeting in the past year, compared to 68 percent of men. The village assembly is the backbone of the local governance system in India (Panchayati Raj System), as voters come together to collectively decide on village issues. It is therefore revealing that these meetings appear to substantially underrepresent women. Women are also significantly less likely to attend political party meetings. In addition, they are underrepresented in customary institutions: 37 percent of men stated that they had participated in a Jati Panchayat meeting, or traditional caste association, compared to only 5 percent of women. Altogether, Figure 2.5 provides strong evidence that men dominate community forums.

Fewer men and women had made a claim for government services than had participated in community meetings.[51] However, women were still significantly less likely than men to have contacted elected representatives: 53 percent of men, but only 16 percent of women, had made a claim to a Panchayat official in the last year. At the Block level, the percentage of men and women who had been in contact about a government benefit was 14 percent and 4 percent, respectively. In the Panchayat and the Block, roughly four times more men than women spoke with elected officials.

The gender gap in non-electoral political participation is summarized as the share of men and women who had participated in at least one way in the previous election. Excluding voting, 36 percent of women (vs. 80 percent of men) reported having participated in politics in at least one of the six forms presented in Figure 2.5. Thus, twice as many men as women raised their demands in political spaces outside the ballot box.

Yet women vote in local elections at rates almost equal to those of men (97 percent vs. 93 percent of men), and while there is a gender gap in voting in state elections, more than 75 percent of women turn out for these as well. Even in state elections, women vote at more than twice the rate that they participate in any form of politics between elections. In other words, half of the women who vote in elections did not formally interact with the state between elections. Herein lies the fundamental puzzle of this book: Why do the majority of women vote but few participate in other forms of political participation?

Over the past decade, the gender gap in voter turnout has narrowed substantially across India, all but closing in the 2019 parliamentary elections.[52] While many have argued that this trend signals broader changes in women's political empowerment, the rise in women's turnout in 2019 did not correspond to a similar increase in women's candidacy or election.[53] Thus, it is unclear whether these recent changes will substantively improve women's representation in politics.

Table 2.2 more closely examines how men's and women's political behavior varies based on education, caste category, age, and employment. Since substantial inequalities in access to (and participation in) education and economic institutions persist in India, it is important to consider how these experiences interact with women's political behavior. Does women's unequal access to education and employment explain their political behavior? Four key observations emerge.

First, education is positively correlated with political participation for both women and men. While the percentage of women reporting that they had voted, attended a village assembly meeting, or engaged in any form of non-electoral political participation increases with education level, there is a distinct

---

[51] Kruks-Wisner (2018).   [52] Vaishnav and Hintston (2018); Spary (2020).
[53] Vaishnav and Hintston (2018); Spary (2020).

TABLE 2.2 *Large differences in political participation between women and men exist even considering education, caste category, age, employment, income source, and poverty status*

		Vote in State Election		Attend Village Assembly Meeting		Any Non-Voting Participation	
		Men	Women	Men	Women	Men	Women
Education Level	Illiterate	91%	74%	59%	18%	68%	30%
	Below 5th	94%	76%	77%	14%	88%	31%
	5th Pass	95%	79%	70%	24%	81%	42%
	8th Pass	95%	66%	75%	22%	86%	35%
	Secondary (12th Pass)	99%	82%	66%	33%	82%	49%
Caste Category	Other Backward Class	95%	73%	69%	15%	81%	31%
	Scheduled Caste	95%	83%	70%	19%	80%	36%
	Scheduled Tribe	94%	73%	68%	23%	79%	34%
Age Decile	20–29	88%	63%	55%	12%	73%	23%
	30–39	97%	82%	72%	24%	85%	39%
	40–49	94%	78%	74%	20%	79%	36%
	50–59	93%	75%	66%	28%	76%	41%
	60–69	98%	71%	71%	17%	86%	29%
	70–79	94%	73%	61%	14%	61%	18%
Employment	Not Employed	95%	72%	61%	16%	73%	28%
	Employed	94%	77%	71%	24%	82%	40%
Source of Income	Agricultural Wage Labor	88%	84%	69%	21%	81%	34%
	Agriculture Own-Fields	95%	72%	72%	19%	83%	32%
	Non-Agricultural Wage Labor	94%	72%	69%	23%	78%	39%
Poverty Status	Below Poverty Line	95%	73%	70%	26%	83%	40%
	Above Poverty Line	94%	75%	69%	19%	79%	33%

Note: The table shows the share of men and women – by education, caste category, age, employment, income source, and poverty status – who have participated in each of three forms of political participation. Data are from the 2016 sample survey administered in seventy-six villages in five districts of Madhya Pradesh. The sample of villages includes only those who did not have access to the SHG intervention studied later in the book. In total, this includes data from 1,106 women and 512 men. Some age, caste category, and economic groups were excluded due to small sample sizes. Employment status refers to whether the respondent had worked for pay at any point over the past year, whereas the source of income refers to the household's primary source of income.

positive jump for women who had completed secondary education. Yet for men, this positive association is mostly driven by differences between illiterate and literate men. For example, men who had below fifth-pass education (primary school) reported having participated in politics at a rate of 20 percentage points greater than illiterate men. Furthermore, at every level of education – even completion of secondary – men participated in politics at significantly higher rates than women.

Second, the gender gap in political participation is orders of magnitude larger than the caste gap. While caste has been argued to form the basis of political organization in India,[54] on its own, it appears to have little explanatory power for women's low political participation. There is a striking similarity in patterns of political participation across caste categories, suggesting a set of shared experiences among women across caste groups.

Third, employed men and women reported higher rates of political participation than unemployed men and women. For example, 40 percent of employed women had participated in politics other than voting, compared to only 28 percent of unemployed women. This positive relationship is also evident for men, suggesting a similar gender gap across levels of labor force participation. Within women, the gap between voting and non-electoral political participation persists across levels of labor force participation, but the higher rates of non-electoral political participation among working women are not met by similar rises in turnout rates. This provides further suggestive evidence that turnout in elections reflects different patterns of behavior than other forms of political participation. Additionally, the household's primary source of income is largely unrelated to rates of political participation. There is also little variance in men's political participation by poverty status, though women below the poverty line participated in politics more than those above the poverty line.

Finally, men and women aged 30–60 reported the highest political participation, and those aged 20–29 the lowest. This is surprising, given that young people and the elderly are more likely to have free time to participate politically. For women, this may be indicative of norms within the joint family: 51 percent of respondents aged 20–29 lived with their mother-in-law, declining to 29 percent of those aged 30–39 and only 13 percent of respondents aged 40–49. Women's position in the household hierarchy – and, in turn, their autonomy – increases with age and as women evolve from being the daughter-in-law in a household to being the mother-in-law.

What is most striking is the lack of substantial variation across these intersecting identities. While other attributes appear to correlate with men's and women's political participation, none eradicates or even markedly closes the gender gap in non-electoral political participation. Caste, tribe, poverty status,

---

[54] Chhibber (2001).

and education level are each individually far less predictive of political participation than gender. In many respects, women appear to have much more in
common with each other than they do with men from their intersectional
identities, even after accounting for these social and economic inequalities.

Equally striking is that for all education levels, caste groups, ages, and
employment status, women vote at substantially higher rates than they participate between elections. And the difference between women's electoral and non-
electoral political participation is substantially greater than the same difference
for men. Institutional inequalities and demographics have little predictive
power in explaining the puzzle of women's participation. Thus, there appears
to be more to the story of women's political participation than their historical
exclusion from social and economic institutions.

DISCUSSION

This chapter highlights the background conditions that characterize women's
lives. Power and authority in rural India are rooted in a patriarchal social order
that incentivizes male dominance through norms of inheritance and elder care
and perpetuates this dominance through the common acceptance of male
superiority and authority. When investments in sons rather than daughters
are life determining, resources are channeled to men. This creates large inequalities in access to productive institutions.

Women in rural India largely live under strict patriarchal norms sustained
through discriminatory social and legal institutions and in a society where
gender inequalities dominate most social and economic institutions. With such
discriminatory formal and normative institutions, how and when do women
engage politically?

While patriarchy in rural India marks an extreme system of male dominance,
by understanding the roots of women's political participation in such severe
conditions, we can unravel how societal relations – and the resulting patterns of
distribution – shape political behavior. Identifying and documenting how
women demand and achieve political representation amid social seclusion
and economic deprivation allows us to better isolate the mechanisms of actual-
izing a more inclusive society.

3

A Relational Theory of Women's Political Participation

Women were long deemed incapable of reason and rational thought. Political theorists, including Rousseau, Kant, and Hegel, reconciled gender inequality in the household and the subordination of women by characterizing women as sentimental rather than rational.[1] Women's political participation, in their view, was unnecessary because men acted as women's agents, perfectly representing their interests. More recent economic models have espoused a similar logic by assuming a unitary and efficient household. Becker most notably modeled the household as a unit of economic decision-making with an efficient division of labor such that men represented the household's interests in public domains and women managed internal household affairs.[2] The key assumption of this model is that men and women in the same household share identical preferences.

Most current theories of political behavior treat women as rational and independent, and treat their behavior as a function of the costs and benefits associated with political participation. Individual attributes shape these costs and benefits, specifically women's resources and environment, which are influenced by both normative and political institutions.[3] Women's political behavior is a rational response to their choice set and their circumstances.

Modern feminist and social theorists diverge from both characterizations by questioning the capacity for women's rationality not on the grounds of their

---

[1] Okin (1982) discusses in depth the gendered philosophies of these and other theorists. She documents the inconsistencies of these theories of the equality of men vis-à-vis the state with the unequal treatment of women in the household. In most cases, she argues that the authors justify these inconsistencies by calling on "the sentimental household," where relegation of domestic responsibilities leave women without sufficient reason to be treated as equals, but the altruism of men for their wives leads to a more efficient and moral household politics.

[2] Becker (1981).   [3] Inglehart and Norris (2000); Burns, Schlozman, and Verba (2001).

incapacity but because of the prevalence of oppression and coercion. According to these theories, male dominance precludes female agency. The regular use of violence against women, principally within the household, is argued to limit women's autonomy and agency as individuals. Liberal feminist thought suggests that freedom and autonomy are individual attributes that can be achieved when women are able to gain freedom from male dominance.[4] Radical feminist thought, instead, maintains that because male dominance is enshrined in patriarchal norms and societal structures, women's equality can only be obtained via societal upheaval.[5] In both models, empowerment requires the agency to act according to one's own interests and the freedom from coercion and resistance to execute those actions.[6] In these accounts, political participation is an outcome of a broader process of empowerment – the process by which those who have been denied the ability to make strategic life choices acquire such an ability[7] – and the struggle for power and agency.

Why do women in rural India remain underrepresented in political spaces in between elections but turn out to vote at high rates almost equal to those of men? To answer this question, we must first ask: Is it fair to assume women have agency over their political behavior? Given the pervasiveness of gender inequality and the use of coercion to uphold male authority, I argue that women are often subjects, principally of their households, rather than agents. To explain the puzzle of women's political behavior, we must first understand the conditions under which women act as autonomous agents to advance their own interests.

I reconcile the rational choice and feminist approaches to political behavior by (1) identifying the set of strategic actors that makes decisions about women's political behavior and (2) outlining the conditions under which women maximize their own welfare in political decision-making. My argument builds on an emerging literature seeking to incorporate coercion into household bargaining and decision-making models,[8] and builds on existing arguments that draw attention to the role of resources, norms, and institutions in shaping women's political behavior by better defining the role of power in political decisions.[9]

---

[4] See Okin (1989); Pateman (1988).

[5] Folbre (2021) argues for the way that political, economic, and cultural institutions interact to perpetuate male authority and inhibit coalitions of the disempowered.

[6] Sen (1985).

[7] Kabeer (1999: 435). See also Batliwala (1993, 1994); Kabeer (1994); Sen (1997); Cornwall (2016).

[8] See, for example, Bloch and Rao (2002); Anderberg and Rainer (2013); Lowes (2017). Afzal et al. (2016), Khan (2021), Cheema et al. (2021), and Kumar (2022) also explore the role of men in the household in women's decision-making.

[9] Schlozman, Burns, and Verba (1994); Burns, Schlozman, and Verba (2001); Desposato and Norrander (2009); Barnes and Burchard (2013); Isaksson, Kotsadam, and Nerman (2014); Karpowitz and Mendelberg (2014); Gottlieb (2016b); Brulé and Gaikwad (2021); Prillaman (2021); Skorge (2021).

I explain how these attributes confer power, both legitimate and coercive, in women's relationships and how this power is deployed to shape their political behavior. We cannot assume a woman has free choice where she is under threat of coercion, for what is freedom when one has a gun to their head? But that does not mean we cannot understand women's political behavior as a rational response to the structures she inhabits. It may simply be a rational choice by those with power over her, maximizing their own welfare.

I build a conceptual model of women's political behavior that does not presume individual agency; it instead models the conditions under which agency exists. I make three core arguments. First, I argue that the household is the primary unit of political decision-making in rural India. Second, households bargain to reach political decisions, but dominant household members determine the political decisions (and behavior) of subordinate household members when they hold coercive authority. In such cases, the household decision maximizes the welfare of the dominant members. Third, autonomy – or freedom to make political decisions distinct from the coercive household – enables subordinate household members' (i.e., women's) agentic political decision-making and political participation.

What is at stake in this endeavor is not only an understanding of the nature of women's political participation, which democratic theorists argue is important in its own right,[10] but also an insight into the nature of power relations in rural Indian communities and the mechanisms used to sustain these hierarchies. By highlighting the vested interests of those who hold political power over women, I argue for the existence of a patriarchal political order where gender defines the structure of political power, participation, and even political organization, including those of clientelism and identity politics. Ultimately, the patriarchal political order is marked by two key characteristics: the primacy of male-led households and the dominance of men in larger political networks. Women's political autonomy can challenge this political order built on their disempowerment.

These arguments and their subsequent empirical evaluation are grounded in fieldwork conducted in rural India over a period of six years, largely concentrated in the central state of Madhya Pradesh (and to a lesser extent, Odisha, Bihar, and Delhi). This field research included interviews with male and female citizens and elites as well as ethnographic observation. This region, like much of India and the rest of the world, is marked by deeply rooted patriarchal norms that reinforce male dominance in political, economic, and social arenas. It also features substantial inequalities in access to human capital resources: women have less education, higher poverty rates, and significantly lower labor force participation than men. And, like elsewhere in India, local politics in these

---

[10] Dahl (1971); Mansbridge (1999).

regions operates through patronage, personalistic relationships, and clientelist exchange.[11]

These circumstances, described in greater detail in Chapter 2, are the background conditions that structure political decision-making, including the incentives and choice sets of actors. I will first conceptualize the patriarchal political order and examine how it incentivizes and enacts women's political exclusion. I then consider how shifts in the characteristics of this political order, and particularly shifts in women's political attachment to the household, create conditions for women's political empowerment.

THE PRIVATE ROOTS OF POLITICAL EXCLUSION

The Coercive Unitary Household

The most fundamental social relationships are those shared within families; households are the primary unit of social organization and have long been considered the nucleus of economic decision-making. Economic models of the household developed in response to the observation that the assumption of single-agent decision-making over consumer demand and labor supply is untenable given a social structure centered on households. They therefore focus on how households jointly allocate income given shared expenses and public goods (e.g., children).

The first of these models – Becker's efficiency model – assumes households behave as a unit in order to benefit from gains from trade in both household work and income-generating work. In this model, spouses divide roles such that one specializes in paid work and the other in domestic work to take advantage of the increasing marginal returns to human capital in both domains. Women are assumed to take the role of domestic work because of a marginal advantage in childcare and corresponding socialization into caretaker roles. This model predicts a perfect gendered division between productive and reproductive responsibilities in aggregate. To explain why women would accept this role, Becker assumes common preferences (a single household utility function) and income pooling (a single household budget constraint).[12] Under these assumptions, this economic division of labor (and women's relegation to domestic

---

[11] I take my definition of patronage democracies from Chandra as democracies "in which the state monopolizes access to jobs and services, and in which elected officials have discretion in the implementation of laws allocating the jobs and services at the disposal of the state" (Chandra 2007: 86). Clientelism is the use of this discretion in exchange for electoral support. While India, in general, may be moving toward programmatic politics, rural areas remain heavily reliant on the public sector, and local politics is still dominated by patronage networks (Wilkinson 2006; Kitschelt and Wilkinson 2007; Berenschot 2010; Besley, Pande, and Rao 2012; Piliavsky 2014; Anderson, Francois, and Kotwal 2015; Bardhan and Mookherjee 2012; Auerbach 2016; Asher and Novosad 2017; Auerbach and Thachil 2018; Lehne, Shapiro, and Eynde 2018).

[12] Becker (1974, 1981, 1985); Samuelson (1956).

work) is efficient, meaning that it maximizes both individual and household welfare.

Contesting the idea that all household members have identical preferences, bargaining models of household behavior introduced bargaining into the process of household allocation.[13] Individuals with distinct preference cooperate with others in their household so long as the outcome of doing so is better than the outcome of household exit. Again, gains to trade and shared responsibilities in the household (e.g., children and chores) motivate household cooperation. A person's willingness to exit the household defines their power in the bargain,[14] as determined by an individual's outside options which are a function of individual resources such as access to employment, income, assets, or social support systems,[15] legal institutions such as rules governing divorce,[16] and cultural institutions such as social norms around marriage exit.[17] The more bargaining power an individual has, the more the household decision will reflect their preferences. Bargaining is expected to yield an imperfect household economic division of labor with an individual's level of domestic work decreasing in their bargaining power.

While most economic models of the household presume that all household members have agency, meaning they make decisions that maximize their welfare, a few recent studies have begun to question this assumption, especially in the presence of domestic violence. In these coercive models, men instrumentally deploy violence against women in the household to achieve their preferred economic allocation and to extract rents from women. Lowes sets this up as a principal–agent model in which husbands are the principals and wives are the agents: the principal employs domestic violence to coerce the behavior of the agent. In her model, a wife's "cooperation" increases with the husband's ability to use coercion, which is a function of the cost of domestic violence and the woman's outside options.[18] Anderberg and Rainer model the use of violence by men in a household to enforce their desired level of women's contribution to the

---

[13] Manser and Brown (1980); McElroy and Horney (1981); Lundberg and Pollak (1993); Browning and Chiappori (1998).

[14] Cooperative bargaining models assume that exit from the household manifests as divorce. Noncooperative bargaining models assume that exit from the household manifests as the occupation of separate spheres or retreat into separate domains (see, for example, Lundberg and Pollak 1994, Doepke and Tertilt 2011, Malapit 2012, and Ziparo 2014). The key difference between cooperative and noncooperative bargaining models is the income pooling assumption, with spouses in noncooperative models allocating some chosen amount of their income to household public goods and retaining the rest for themselves .

[15] McElroy and Horney (1981); Pollack (2005).

[16] Gray (1998); Stevenson and Wolfers (2006); Iversen and Rosenbluth (2010).

[17] Agarwal (1997); Bittman et al. (2003).

[18] Lowes (2017). This model builds on Acemoglu and Wolitzky (2011) who consider the case of coercive labor practices.

household public good. They show that the use of violence generates a noncooperative equilibrium.[19]

In political science, most models of political behavior assume an individual agent choosing political actions that maximize their welfare. Rational models of voting – and, by extension, other forms of political participation – treat individuals as independent strategic actors who weigh the costs and potential benefits of political engagement.[20] These include *informational costs* – that is, the costs to acquire information relevant for participation (how political structures work, what are the policy options, where and when are political opportunities); *resource costs* – that is, the financial (transportation, leave from work, childcare) and opportunity costs of political participation; and *social costs* – that is, the cost of social sanctioning that would come from engaging in norm-violating behavior. The benefits are the utility a person derives from their preferred political outcome if it is achieved and the psychic value of participation (performing one's civic duty).

Explanations of the gender gap in participation largely focus on gendered differences in the costs and benefits of participation. *Resource-based theories* suggest that inequalities in political participation result from gender inequalities in access to the resources, such as education, income, and free time, that lower the informational and resource costs to participation.[21] *Cultural theories* focus on the role of social norms, attitudes, and beliefs in defining the allocation of social costs to political participation for violating prescribed roles.[22] Given patriarchal norms, which relegate women to domestic responsibilities, women face steeper social costs to political participation.[23] *Institutional theories* focus

---

[19] Anderberg and Rainer (2013).

[20] See Blais (2000) and Feddersen (2004) for a summary of this literature.

[21] Schlozman, Burns, and Verba (1994); Brady, Verba, and Schlozman (1995); Burns, Schlozman, and Verba (2001); Gleason (2001); Iversen and Rosenbluth (2006); Karpowitz and Mendelberg (2014); Carpena and Jensenius (2021). For a similar argument told at a national level, see also Inglehart and Norris (2000).

[22] Braunstein and Folbre (2001); Kandiyoti (1988); Iversen and Rosenbluth (2010); Alesina, Giuliano, and Nunn (2013); Blaydes and Linzer (2008); Beaman et al. (2009); Bursztyn, González, and Yanagizawa-Drott (2020). Cross-national studies have also revealed a larger correlation between cultural norms (rather than resources) and the gender gap in political participation (See Inglehart and Norris 2000; Desposato and Norrander 2009).

[23] Robinson and Gottlieb (2019) compare patrilineal and matrilineal communities in sub-Saharan Africa, and argue instead that cultural norms shape political behavior by setting expectations regarding whose behavior will be socially accepted. They suggest that cultural norms create community-based coordination around how identity, namely gender, translates into political behavior. They empirically document how it is not land ownership per se, but rules of land inheritance that drive women's political participation. Even women who have more economic resources will be unlikely to participate in politics if there is a norm against doing so. Brulé and Gaikwad (2021) instead argue that norms shape women's behavior not through differences in social costs but through differences in material costs given the way that norms allocate resources disproportionately to men. They study variation in matrilineal and patrilineal communities in northeast India and show that women's political participation is significantly higher in

on the ways in which political institutions, and women's representation in them, affect the benefits to political participation by shaping women's perceptions of their own political efficacy based on the incentives they provide for female candidates to emerge and parties to court the female vote as a bloc.[24] If women are more likely than men to believe that parties and institutions will not represent their interests, their expected benefits from political engagement will be lower.

A diverse literature has called for greater attention on the household as the locus of political decision-making.[25] In the nineteenth century, many countries legally defined the household as a joint *political* unit. In England, the institution of coverture assumed a husband and wife were one person with identical interests, and therefore a woman's legal rights were subsumed by those of her husband. Coverture was used to justify women's disenfranchisement as women were presumed to have identical political demands to their husbands and so their enfranchisement would bear no impact[26] (though this has since been shown to be incorrect).[27] As early as 1959, scholars argued that households were central in decisions over vote choice even after these legal institutions were removed.[28] More recent models of political decision-making have maintained that women's and men's political preferences are a function of their labor force participation and negotiated role in the household.[29] While these models do not propose a household bargain over political decisions, they do suggest that the household economic division of labor shapes demands for public policies. Feminist political theorists have theorized how households influence political behavior but drawn attention to households as unjust and unfair institutions.[30] A nascent literature in South Asia has begun to empirically evaluate whether the household is a constraining force in women's political lives.[31]

---

communities where inheritance is passed through women. They argue that this is rooted in the way that norms of matrilineality shape economic resources. According to their account, resources are still the principal driver of political behavior, but norms importantly determine the nature of resource allocations.

[24] Iversen and Rosenbluth (2008); Pankaj and Tankha (2010); Brulé (2020a); Schwindt-Bayer and Mishler (2005); Corder and Wolbrecht (2016); Kittilson and Schwindt-Bayer 2010; Kittilson and Schwindt-Bayer 2012; Atkeson 2003; Morgan-Collins (2021); Skorge (2021); Clayton (2015). See also Karpowitz, Mendelberg, and Shaker (2012) and Karim, Maries, and Singh (2018). Parthasarathy, Rao, and Palaniswamy (2019) demonstrate that reserving elected seats for women in local governments in India made women more likely to make demands in public fora.

[25] See Glaser (1959) for an early example.   [26] Teele (2018).

[27] Lott and Kenny (1999); Miller (2008); Aidt and Dallal (2008); Carruthers and Wanamaker (2014); Morgan-Collines (2021).

[28] Glaser (1959). See also Stoker and Jennings (1995) and Foos and Rooij (2017).

[29] Iversen and Rosenbluth (2010).   [30] Okin (1982); Pateman (1988); Okin (1989).

[31] Chhibber (2002); Khan (2021); Afzal et al. (2016); Gine and Mansuri (2011); Cheema et al. (2021); Kumar (2022).

I build on the bargaining models of household economic decision-making to propose a conceptual model of household political decision-making, including decisions over which political demands to articulate and who will articulate them in political spaces. Drawing on the recent insights from coercive models of the household, as well as an emerging literature on coercion and backlash in political science,[32] I conceptualize joint household decision-making as being determined by both bargaining and coercion. Household members will cooperate with the household if it serves their interests – that is, so long as the outcome of doing so is better than not doing so. Additionally, dominant household members – those with coercive power – will instrumentally deploy coercion to force subordinate members to cooperate[33] with the household around their preferred outcome if the benefits to them of household cooperation outweigh the costs of coercion.

Coercion within the household can constitute indirect pressure and persuasion as well as explicit constraints on behavior through threats, intimidation, or violent force.[34] Coercion can also be latent and obscured and entail the tacit acceptance and internalization of subordination resulting from a lifetime of enforced compliance with gender roles.[35] Coercion therefore constrains the acceptable choices (enforced via sanctioning) and limits the imagined options (restricted via socialization). Under coercion, subordinate household members do not have political agency – that is, freedom of choice to maximize their own welfare.[36]

Coercive power is an individual's capacity to force other people to bend to their preferences, for example, by using (or threatening to use) violence. The distribution of coercive power, or the ability to engage in coercion, within the household is not random: it is determined in aggregate by social norms. In contexts characterized by patriarchal norms, where elder male dominance is socially valued, coercive power is unequally distributed across gender and

---

[32] Mansbridge and Shames (2008); Brulé (2020b).

[33] Throughout, I use the word "cooperate" to imply aligned household behavior. Cooperation, however, does not imply agency.

[34] This aligns with the conception of norms as shaping which equilibria will be selected by making coordination around norm-deviant equilibria inefficient. See, for example, Milgrom, North, and Weingast (1990).

[35] This aligns with the conception of norms as internalized restrictions on behavior. In this conception, norms shape an individual's choice set and what is within the imagined set of options. Given socialization under patriarchy, women may not imagine an option of noncooperation with the household. See, for example, Akerlof (1976) and Sen (1987).

[36] A synonymous way of defining agency in this framework is having a choice set greater than one. If an individual has a choice set of only one, either because they will face severe sanctioning from any alternative choice or because their imagined options are constrained to only one, then they would not be considered to have agency over that choice.

age; elder men retain coercive power over younger men and women, though men of all ages generally retain power over women.[37]

Bargaining power measures an individual's influence within the household, defined as the individual's willingness to exit the bargain. In household economic decision-making, exit from the bargain generally means exit from the household and bargaining power is determined by the costs to exiting the household, typically assumed to be a function of income-generating capacities. In household political decision-making, exit from the bargain is exit from household cooperation or a shift to individual political decision-making, and bargaining power is determined by an individual's costs to political participation and the strength of their preferences for participation (i.e., their political interest and expected benefits from participation). I have documented that resource, informational, and social costs to participation are a function of education, networks (which help transmit information),[38] economic resources, and social norms. Bargaining power is thus also a function of these factors. Social norms further shape bargaining power through their impact on the strength of preferences, which are a function of socialization into political interest.

Like with economic decisions, there can be benefits to household cooperation in political decision-making. Household political cooperation can improve individual welfare by (1) pooling the costs of political action and (2) increasing the probability of political success. First, under household cooperation, the costs of political participation can be shared by household members. Resource costs benefit from income pooling and informational costs benefit from intra-household information-sharing. Social costs are also assumed to be shared by the household, meaning norm-deviant behavior by one will generate social sanctions for all.[39] Second, the probability of a desired political outcome rises with the number of people organized around it; household cooperation thus increases the probability of political success.[40] The more aligned household preferences are, the more likely household cooperation will yield a higher payoff as compared to individual political decision-making. Additionally, in patronage democracies, the probability of a clientelist offer increases with the number of people cooperating to provide electoral support. Resource-constrained clientelist brokers maximize their returns by prioritizing higher-value

---

[37] Anukriti, Herrera-Almanza, and Pathak (2019) highlight the use of coercion by mothers-in-law against daughters-in-law.

[38] Abrams, Iversen, and Soskice (2011) and Sinclair (2012) demonstrate how networks can shape the costs to participation via information-sharing.

[39] Household sharing of social costs may be unavoidable even with individual political decision-making if social norms are structured around the household as in the case of patriarchy.

[40] This logic is similar to that of Uhlaner's (1989) and Morton's (1991) group mobilization theories, which posit that group rationality and coordination can explain positive turnout in elections.

(larger) groups.[41] Clientelist offers can benefit the household equally (as with the promise of a desired club good such as a proximate road) or they can disproportionately benefit household members approached by brokers (as with direct vote buying or the promise of public employment). Those believed to have more political power in the household are more likely to be targeted by mobilizers and therefore are more likely to benefit from household cooperation.

An individual will cooperate with the household when their individual welfare under household cooperation is greater than their welfare in individual decision-making or when they are coerced into participation (i.e., when their cooperation is in others' interests). Both suggest that dominant household members – those who have power over subordinate members – will disproportionately benefit from household cooperation as the household decision will more closely resemble their preferences and competition in the political marketplace is reduced.

When will it be in an individual's interests to cooperate with the household? Absent coercion, the cost of household cooperation is the policy loss if the household's negotiated preference deviates from an individual's preference. Since the household's policy choice is the result of a bargaining process, the household policy outcome is the average of all household members' individual policy preferences weighted by their relative bargaining power (unless coercion dictates the bargain). I expect rational household cooperation when, for all members of the household, the benefits outweigh these costs, which is most likely when household preferences are closely aligned and the costs to political participation are high.

When will coercion be deployed to enforce household cooperation? Coercion is likely when the benefits to coercion are high and the costs to coercion are low. Under coercion, the united household decision will strongly reflect the preferences of dominant household members. As a result, their benefits to coercion are the higher probability of achieving their desired political outcome. The costs to coercion are determined by the social and legal acceptability of coercion – that is, the likelihood that coercion will be sanctioned, and the ability of subordinate members to exit the household (e.g., through divorce or moving away). Coercion is less costly when social norms make shaming and violence within the household acceptable as well as when legal institutions to protect those subjected to violence or in need of a divorce/household exit are weak. Coercion is also more likely when subordinate members have fewer exit options from the household, such as income-generating opportunities. Cools and Kotsadam demonstrate that employment, however, is uncorrelated with women's experiences of domestic violence when

---

[41] Ronconi and Zarazaga (2019). Even in non-patronage systems, high mobilization costs imply that larger groups are more likely to be politically targeted. This logic is outlined in the case of the United States in Rosenstone and Hansen (1993).

they live in communities where such violence is seen as socially acceptable.[42] This suggests that norms may be a stronger determinant of coercion than exit options. In India, weak legal institutions, permissive social norms, and large gender inequalities in paid work make coercion against women less costly.

Coerced household cooperation cannot efficiently represent subordinate members' interests. Coercion implies that subordinate members' political behavior is decided by and maximizes the welfare of dominant household members. In fact, under conditions of coercion, subordinate members may internalize the preferences of dominant members as a self-protection mechanism. Women's subordination under patriarchy often involves the slow and steady suppression of their autonomous interests in the process of elevating household interests. Over time, the central importance placed on the household ties women's identity to it. It restricts the scope of possibilities and interests under consideration and limits women's access and desire to seek information on other ways of existing.

It is, therefore, difficult to disentangle coerced cooperation from rational cooperation and therefore to assume household efficiency. Sen argues that the suppression of individual welfare does not preclude the existence of personal welfare. He articulates this in his description of the role of the household in India:

Insofar as intrafamily divisions involve significant inequalities...the lack of perception of personal interest combined with a great concern for family welfare is, of course, just the kind of attitude that helps to sustain traditional inequalities. There is much evidence in history that acute inequalities often survive precisely by making allies out of the deprived. The underdog comes to accept the legitimacy of the unequal order and becomes an implicit accomplice. It can be a serious error to take the absence of protests and questioning of inequality as evidence of the absence of that inequality.[43]

Three implications emerge when evaluating the trade-offs of household versus individual decision-making. First, (rational) household cooperation is more likely within households that have more closely aligned preferences. Second, household cooperation benefits most those with more power in the household; those with more coercive power thus have incentives to force those with less to cooperate. Household cooperation is more likely when the costs to coercion are low, though it is unlikely to be efficient. As a result, coerced household cooperation is expected to be uncorrelated with the distribution of preferences and the strength of those preferences (political interest) in the household. Finally, household cooperation benefits political entrepreneurs by reducing their mobilization costs, thus incentivizing an entire system to be organized around households as opposed to individuals. The benefits to household cooperation for individuals are expected to increase as direct electoral mobilization is more valuable, such as given the exchange of patronage.

[42] Cools and Kotsadam (2017).   [43] Sen (1987: 7).

I argue that, given these trade-offs, the coerced unitary household dominates political organization in rural India due to the unequal distribution of bargaining and coercive power within households (due to patriarchal norms and large gender inequalities in resources) and the positive political returns associated with household cooperation under clientelism. The benefits of household cooperation are significant: easier and more likely access to the spoils of politics. These benefits incentivize coercion within the household, which bears minimal cost for elder men under strong patriarchy and weak institutions governing household violence. This makes the costs of autonomous action by the subordinate exceedingly high and suppresses their political agency.

Political Participation under Household Cooperation

Access to politics brings power. Political participation, particularly between elections, determines whose voices are heard and which demands have the possibility of being met.[44] It builds social and human capital by facilitating information acquisition and the development of ties to other community members and powerful elites.[45] In patronage democracies, it also determines who receives access to goods and services offered in exchange for political support.[46] In rural India, the benefits of local political participation are direct and observable; the decentralization of authority over the delivery of goods and services to the village level institutionalized the value of regular political participation, as was intended when the 73rd Amendment to the Indian Constitution enshrined village governments. Most goods and services are allocated as a direct result of citizen engagement in political spaces, either through attending public meetings or registering requests directly with locally elected officials.[47]

How will the unitary household allocate political participation? For some activities, like voting, the success of political action is conditional on high household participation. Voting is a low-cost political act that yields direct benefits in patronage democracies. When patronage is an important component of the vote calculus, and electoral mobilization occurs through local networks, there are increasing marginal returns to each additional household member showing up at the ballot box. The notion of "vote-bank politics" refers to the common practice of electoral candidates securing entire groups of voters through conditional exchange.[48] The value of creating (and potentially trading)

---

[44] Mansbridge (1999).　　[45] Putnam, Leonardi, and Nanetti (1992).
[46] Kitschelt and Wilkinson (2007).　　[47] Kruks-Wisner (2018).
[48] Srinivas (1960) originally coined the term "vote-bank politics," which Breeding (2011) describes in greater detail. Auerbach (2016) also highlights the ways that politicians respond to aggregate groups of voters as opposed to individual voters. This concept is connected to models of group-based mobilization in political economy as principally developed by Uhlaner (1989) and Morton (1991).

a household vote bank generates incentives to ensure all in the household turn out.[49] Other forms of participation with increasing marginal returns to additional household participation include protesting and petitioning; for both actions, more representation improves the probability of successful demand-making. In such instances, the expected benefits to the household (or the dominant member of the household) increase as more members participate.

In other forms of participation, including most non-electoral types of formal political participation, the marginal additional probability of success in advocating for the group's preferred outcome decreases with additional group participants. These actions often entail higher costs, and little is gained from having another person participate in these activities when someone is already representing the household. For example, attending a village assembly meeting requires time and money to cover the costs of transportation or childcare. If a household wanted to raise a political demand at a meeting, the attendance of all household members would be at best only marginally more likely to yield the desired outcome than if just one household member went,[50] whereas the costs of attendance increase with household participation. In such forms of participation, a political division of labor is likely to minimize household costs while maximizing household welfare (or the welfare of dominant household members).

Bargaining and coercive power determine who participates when there are diminishing marginal returns to additional household participation under household cooperation. I assume that individuals desire political participation given the political capital generated through participation. This is similar to the assumption in economic bargaining models that household members prefer paid work over unpaid work as it expands outside options. As a result, those with and willing to deploy coercive power are expected to participate in politics and act as the representative of the household in political acts where a division of labor is more efficient. Absent coercion, bargaining power determines who will serve as the household representative, which, as discussed earlier, will privilege members with the lowest individual costs to participation and strongest preferences for participation.

Given the way that social norms enable coercion by men, socialize them into stronger preferences for participation, and increase women's social costs and the way resource inequalities enable men's lower costs to participation, I expect that men, especially elder men, will predominantly act as the representative of the household even absent the deployment of coercion. Subordinate household members are expected to participate in politics when there is a benefit to high household turnout, such as in voting, and not when their participation is costly

---

[49] Similar dynamics have been described in Argentina (Ronconi and Zarazaga 2019) and the Philippines (Cruz 2019).

[50] This is, in part, due to the fact that, under household cooperation, politicians will know that those in attendance are acting as representatives of their household.

for the household. As a result, this model predicts a gender gap in political activities with diminishing marginal returns to greater household participation (e.g., most non-electoral politics) and no gender gap in actions with increasing marginal returns to greater household participation (e.g., voting).

Household political cooperation, and women's subordinate position in household political decision-making, is likely to become a norm itself. Women will be socialized into the expectation of cooperating with the household and deferring to male political authority. Men will further entrench their dominance through the creation of strong political ties and capital outside of the household. Politicians will observe men's political dominance and reinforce it in their political behavior. Over time, household political cooperation will become an established rule – an informal institution – dictating political behavior. Deviation from this rule is expected to be challenged. As Folbre argues, "The intergenerational transmission of group advantage requires more than mere transfer of time and money...it requires the establishment and maintenance of social institutions that organize and internalize norms of behavior."[51]

According to this conceptualization, resource inequalities and patriarchal norms shape women's political behavior in two ways. First, they generate the incentives for women to cooperate, by choice or force, with the household. Second, they structure within-household negotiation in favor of men. This conceptual model of political behavior therefore helps to explain *how* and *when* norms and resources lead to gender gaps in political participation. But it also demonstrates that women's political participation under patriarchy is most likely to increase with their ability to exit household cooperation – that is, their autonomy from the household. Women's autonomy from the household raises the costs to coercion, and, thus, affords women greater agency in the household bargain and over their level of political participation inside and outside the household.

The Patriarchal Political Order

Examining how the dynamics of household political cooperation operate in aggregate reveals a broader patriarchal political order (diagrammatically depicted in Figure 3.1). The unitary household, and elder men's dominance within it, become self-perpetuating as men's continued political participation leads to their entrenchment in political networks and accumulation of valuable resources that in turn reduce the costs of political participation and elevate their bargaining power.[52] And when men act as the household representative, this affirms their dominant position and reinforces the patriarchal norms enabling coercion. Women's position within the household also becomes reinforced,

---

[51] Folbre (2021: 33).
[52] Cruz and Tolentino (2019) show the dominance of men among the politically influential.

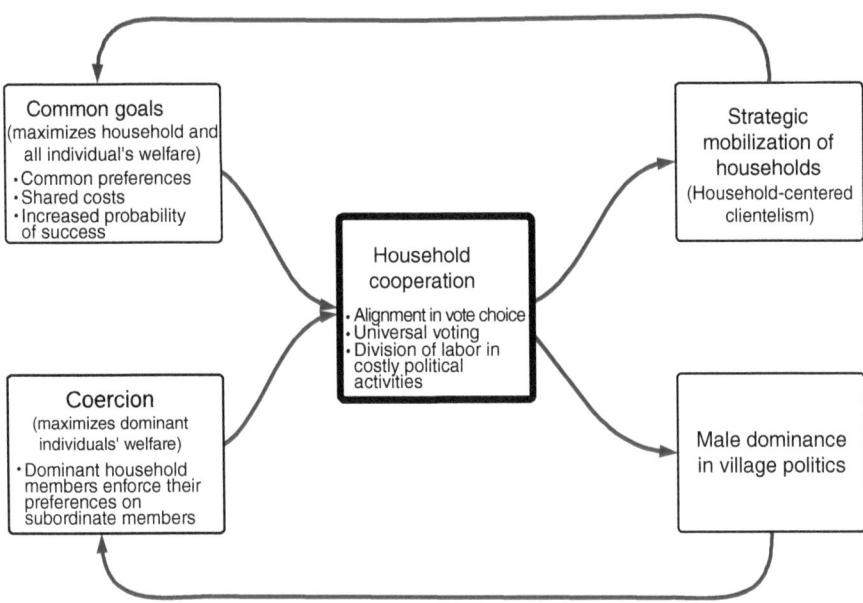

FIGURE 3.1 Diagram of the patriarchal political order

inhibiting their autonomy and therefore their political agency. Sen coins a similar concept, the "feedback transmission," in which typical patterns of employment and education solidify men's position relative to women.[53] Via the political feedback loop, village politics becomes centered on the household – and on men.

What sustains the patriarchal political order? Ostrom argues that once a collective institution is established, there are incentives for those who designed the institution (and for elites) to sustain it.[54] The patriarchal political order maximizes the welfare of dominant members of the household, generally not the household as a whole. This incentivizes dominant men to ensure the persistence of the patriarchal political order. Enforcing the institution of household political cooperation requires collective coordination, which men have greater capacity for given their higher levels of social and political capital.[55] Men can deploy this capital to establish and maintain this institution and further their common interests, including by socially sanctioning both men who fail to impose it in their own households and women who seek to contest it.[56] Household political cooperation thus becomes a socially upheld political system.

[53] Sen (1987).   [54] Ostrom (1994).   [55] Knight and Ensminger (1998).
[56] Coleman (1986); Ostrom (1994).

Household political cooperation is further sustained by strategic political elites who benefit from the lower costs of household-based mobilization. Household cooperation facilitates the targeting of patronage to critical citizens – male heads of household – who in turn deliver large vote blocs from their households.[57] Politicians observe women's cooperation with the household and respond strategically by minimizing their mobilization costs and efficiently targeting critical and politically well-connected nodes within households: men.[58] By defining the set of clients, household cooperation provides the structure to establish and sustain political elites' power. This creates a system of local political organization characterized by household-centered clientelism, in which households become the engine of clientelist mobilization.[59]

Although political participation is highly gendered, the patriarchal political order is not organized around gender but around other intersecting identities that generate coalitions *between* men. Women are attached to politics largely by the men in their household and so inhabit the periphery. The identities that define political organization are instead intersecting identities shared within the household, preserving and incentivizing the united household.[60] Many scholars have studied which identities are salient to the structure of political organization, including in India.[61] Little of this research considers gender as a politically salient identity; I argue here that this is because gender rarely becomes an organizing identity, particularly when households structure politics. Because politics centers on men, cleavages are most likely to manifest *within*, as opposed to across, genders. In rural India, this helps to explain why politics is largely organized around caste and increasingly around religion.[62] Thus, while gender – and, more specifically, women's subordination – enable the patriarchal political order, women fade into the background as largely nonstrategic pawns in men's political games.

CONTESTING THE PATRIARCHAL POLITICAL ORDER

The relational account of women's political exclusion provides an explanation of how women's political participation affects the welfare of those around them: it benefits men and sustains male dominance. How, then, is women's

---

[57] Benstead (2016) demonstrates that in clientelist systems of mobilization, it is easier to mobilize male votes than female votes.

[58] Kitschelt and Wilkinson (2007); Cox, Rosenbluth, and Thies (1998); Huckfeldt and Sprague (1992).

[59] Mohmand (2020) documents a similar pattern in rural Pakistan with respect to landholding identity. She shows that landless collectives often act as a unit when negotiating their vote in the clientelist exchange. Landlords also have incentives, in this context, to perpetuate this collective clientelism.

[60] Htun and Weldon (2018).

[61] See Laitin and Watkins (1998); Posner (2005); Chandra (2007).

[62] Kothari (1964); Chandra (2007); Ahuja (2019); Lee (2020); Allie (2023).

political empowerment achieved? And how can women become the agents of their own political decisions when men have a stake in their subordination?

The patriarchal political order suggests three possible pathways to political agency. First, if male coercive power declines, women will have more agency over both whether to cooperate with the household in political decision-making and their ultimate political behavior. This suggests a path to inclusion through the erosion of patriarchal norms that condone male coercion and maintain women's relegation to domestic spheres. Second, if the incentives to deploy coercive power decline, similarly, women's agency over political decisions is expected to increase. Coercion is less likely when legal and social institutions more severely punish it. Additionally, coercion is expected to decrease as the private benefits to political participation decline, as with a decline in clientelist politics, and as women's capacity to completely exit the household increases. Finally, women can demand agency in political decision-making if they can credibly challenge male coercion.[63]

These pathways to agency make clear that women's exclusion is rooted in patriarchy and politics. Yet changes to both are slow moving at best. The renegotiation of social norms and political systems is as likely to be the product of women's political mobilization as it is to be the cause.[64] As Ray notes, "political culture becomes both a constraint and an enabler of social movements, something that limits the possibilities of discourse and action and is itself a target for change and, at times, rupture."[65]

In the presence of patriarchy and extractive systems of governance, I argue the most likely path to agency lies in autonomy from the household – noncooperation with the household – and the ability to credibly challenge male resistance.[66] Most simply, autonomy from the household means the freedom to make choices independent of the household, including freedom from household coercion. Autonomy allows women to determine their own political behavior and make political demands in line with their interests. This most closely relates to the philosophical conception of autonomy as freedom of choice and freedom from oppression, insofar as we focus on the household as the site of oppression.[67]

---

[63] Women's ability to challenge coercion should, under perfect information, eliminate the use of coercion in the first place. However, given the entrenchment of patriarchal norms and limited experience of challenges to male authority, uncertainty around women's capacity to challenge coercion is expected to be high. This would lead to the deployment of coercion even when women have the capacity to contest this coercion.

[64] Sapiro (1981).   [65] Ray (2000: 8).

[66] Chhibber (2002) similarly argues that autonomy from the household is the critical variable determining women's political participation in rural India. What I add to this argument is an explanation of why autonomy is critical and a theory about how it can be achieved.

[67] Philosophers often define agency as freedom of choice within a social context and autonomy as freedom of choice outside of the social context. In the realm of gender, the distinction is often based on oppression: an agentic women has freedom of choice even under a set of oppressive social norms that may shape her choice, while an autonomous woman's freedom of choice is

It also reflects the economic conception of agency in that it implies personal welfare maximization, as opposed to women's behavior maximizing the welfare of those dominant in the household. Autonomy from the household includes but does not require household exit.

Household autonomy directly challenges the coercive unitary household. As a result, attempts to gain autonomy and separate from the household will likely engender resistance.[68] Male power holders, both within the household and in the community more broadly, are likely to view such attempts as both a threat to their authority and interests and a violation of norms. Coercion will be deployed to suppress attempts to change the status quo and enforce household political cooperation.

For women to autonomously act, they must be able to credibly contest this coercion, which requires the belief that autonomy will improve their personal welfare enough to outweigh the costs of challenging resistance. Autonomy from the household can manifest for many reasons, including typical explanations for household exit (e.g., divorce, earning opportunities, etc.), but not all provide tools or resources to challenge backlash. I argue that one pathway to autonomy that enables the credible contestation of resistence is solidaritistic collective action among women.

The Benefits to Women's Political Autonomy

Women have much to gain from their political empowerment. Household political cooperation is inefficient under coercion. Women's preferences are underrepresented, women reap few of the spoils of politics, and many women live under the threat of coercion. They also live in an ideological order that diminishes their value.[69] Political empowerment is likely to yield both material and psychological benefits.

The material gains associated with political autonomy derive from the underrepresentation of women's interests under household political cooperation. Inequalities in coercive and bargaining power mean that the household

---

unshaped by oppression or the social context (Sherwin 1998). Here, I define the social context as the household to invoke autonomy in this way. Philosophically women have agency under the extreme oppression of the household and have autonomy only when they can make decisions absent that oppression. I do not suggest, however, that such autonomy implies that women have freedom from oppression more generally. See, for example, Bevir (1999) for a discussion of Foucault's conceptions of agency and autonomy in this vein.

[68] Krook (2020) provides a comprehensive account of the pervasiveness of violence against female politicians and argues that such violence is used to undermine women's political authority explicitly. Brulé (2020) documents substantial evidence of resistance to women's electoral representation in rural India.

[69] Knight and Ensminger (1998).

decision more closely aligns with dominant men's interests than subordinate women's interests. Thus, the larger the difference between men's and women's interests, the more women stand to gain from autonomy.

Prior research has demonstrated that women's political preferences systematically differ from those of men, particularly where women have been excluded from formal politics.[70] Molyneux theorizes that these gendered differences fall along two axes – practical interests and strategic interests.[71] *Practical interests* are born out of the economic division of labor and each gender's different needs given this division.[72] For example, in rural villages in India, women are responsible for domestic work, which includes caring for children and collecting water and fuel. Women have been shown to prefer allocations toward these public goods, such as water improvement projects.[73] Women's practical interests are thus those that exist because of the existing gender order.

Strategic interests are born out of the existing gender order and women's position in the larger social system. According to this logic, women have different interests from men due to their subordinate position. Strategic interests can include demands for agency, representation, and protection from coercion.[74] Afzal et al. show that a non-trivial share of women were willing to pay for agency in household decisions even after being informed that their spouse's choice matched their preference.[75] The representation of women's strategic interests therefore stands to bring both material benefits (such as protection) and psychological benefits (such as legitimacy).

Autonomy from the household is expected to benefit women when it enables them to articulate these distinct interests. These benefits derive from the psychological value in articulation itself and the material value in the greater chance of these interests being represented in politics.

---

[70] Khan (2021); Inglehart and Norris (2003); Gottlieb, Grossman, and Robinson (2016); Sapiro (1981); Shapiro and Mahajan (1986); Liaqat (2019); Chattopadhyay and Duflo (2004); Lott and Kenny (1999); Aidt and Dallal (2008); Carruthers and Wanamaker (2014); Miller (2008).

[71] Molyneux (1998). [72] Iversen and Rosenbluth (2006); Edlund and Pande (2002).

[73] Chattopadhyay and Duflo (2004). As another example, Weeks (2022) documents women's greater general preference for policies that protect women's ability to simultaneously work and care for the family and shows that quota policies increase gender equalizing work–family policies. Clayton (2021) provides a thorough review of the literature on the policy impacts of gender quota policies.

[74] The most common demand from women's movements across the globe is a reduction in violence against women (Htun and Weldon 2012; Htun and Weldon 2018). In rural India, the fight against gender-based violence is intimately linked to demands for alcohol prohibition; prohibition in at least one state has been attributed to women's mobilization. Other commonly articulated strategic interests are demands for descriptive representation, which is valuable because it establishes the legitimacy of historically excluded groups (Mansbridge 1999).

[75] Afzal et al. (2022)

The Costs to Women's Political Autonomy

If women seek to contest and negotiate for power, those with power – for whom women's subordination maximizes their welfare – are likely to resist giving up that power. Social change that seeks to expand women's orbit outside the household threatens the very conception of the family and the patriarchal political order and has historically led to the rise of countermovements.[76] Having political power creates a set of vested interests in the maintainenance of status and power. Challenges to that status and power constitute challenges to those interests and are therefore expected to be socially sanctioned and resisted.

Such social sanctioning and resistance are often termed "backlash," or what Mansbridge and Shames call "the use of coercive power to regain lost power."[77] Backlash can be insidious (e.g., withholding pertinent information), coercive (e.g., public shaming or threats), or even violent; it is expected from those with the greatest stake in the prevailing power structure.[78] The direct loss to these constituencies from successful power renegotiation is increased competition in the political marketplace. The indirect loss is a new set of social norms that redefine de facto authority as being more equally distributed across genders.[79]

Women's autonomy will pose the greatest threat to male dominance when it accompanies demands for women's strategic interests. Such demands directly challenge male authority and threaten the tools that men use to enforce that authority. Demands in support of women's practical interests are less threatening to men's welfare as their cost is in skewing the outcomes of politics away from dominant men's preferences as opposed to eroding male authority altogether. Resistance to women's autonomy is expected to be higher when it leads to demands around strategic interests.

Dominant household members and powerful political elites have a greater stake in the patriarchal political order and thus have more to lose from

---

[76] Conover and Gray (1983).   [77] Mansbridge and Shames (2008: 626).

[78] For example, Suryanarayan and White (2021) demonstrate that white resistance was greatest post-Reconstruction in the regions of the US South where slavery was strongest, which suggests that, where power structures are the most unequal, challenges to those structures yield the greatest backlash.

[79] It is important to highlight that women also have a stake in the persistence of patriarchy, particularly as they begin to benefit from it as they age (Kandiyoti 1988; Narayan 1997). Women have invested substantial resources in conforming to patriarchal norms to maximize their chance of one day holding status in the system. This implies that women can also resist changes in patriarchal norms. Similarly, men can also be rationally supportive of women's autonomy. While patriarchy creates incentives for men to sanction women stepping outside their normatively defined roles, for some men, the benefits they would reap from supporting women's goals will outweigh the costs of changes in social norms. Poor and marginalized men are likely to support women's empowerment when it is seen as bringing resources and development to their households and communities or when it challenges power structures that have devalued them personally (Batliwala 1993).

women's autonomy from the household. Additionally, when the locus of clientelist exchange is the household, those with a stake in clientelism stand to lose from women's autonomy from the household.[80] These actors are likely to use their power and their control of political institutions to suppress women's autonomy, such as by not responding to legitimate demands for goods and services or obstructing access to political institutions. Those, however, with less stake in the status quo will see women's autonomy as an opportunity, such as to expand their electoral support base.[81]

The costs of political autonomy, thus, come from backlash and resistance in three primary domains – the household, the community, and political institutions. This resistance is rooted in both a normative desire to sustain the patriarchal order and a material desire to sustain the political system. This resistance can be mitigated if powerful actors, including political elites and constituencies of men, stand to benefit from women's political inclusion. Backlash will therefore be most likely, and the costs to autonomy highest, under three conditions. The first is when women's autonomy and mobilization around their strategic interests are perceived to directly threaten male power. Such political participation by women is, by definition, norm-deviant. Mobilization around more practical interests will be less threatening, as it conforms to the prevailing gender order, especially if it can be framed as norm-abiding and in service to the household.[82] Second, backlash is more likely where power structures across genders are more unequal, such as where patriarchal norms are more strictly enforced and gender inequalities starker. Here, those with power have more power to protect. Finally, backlash is more likely when there is cohesion among the powerful, and power is more evenly shared within dominant groups, such as when there are small inequalities between men. In such instances, fewer men will be willing to deviate from the status quo to support women's autonomy and political inclusion.

Challenging Coercion through Collective Action

When autonomy is welfare-enhancing for women, how do women credibly challenge backlash and resistance from both the household and the community in response to their demands for political representation? When women seek to

---

[80] Wantchekon (2003); Cruz and Tolentino (2019). Lizzeri and Persico (2004) demonstrate that extensions of the franchise led to a redistribution of benefits to those politically incorporated.

[81] Skorge (2021); Weeks et al. (2023); Mohmand (2019).

[82] Baldez (2002) shows that women's movements in Chile were only successful when framed around women's exclusion from politics, not around women's interests. Baldez argues that while women have a wide range of interests, what unites women is their assumed position in the household and not in politics, which is rooted in cultural norms. Chowdhury (2023) shows that the BJP has mobilized women to vote and serve as party workers through the frame of seva, or highlighting how their political participation is in line with Hindu (and gendered) norms of service.

contest a collectively upheld social institution (household political cooperation), given limited institutional mechanisms to protect from coercion,[83] I argue that collective action among women can enable them to challenge backlash.[84] As Batliwala argues, "the process of empowerment must take place collectively…When one or two women try to break free of tradition, the power structure is easily able to isolate and ostracize them – sometimes by deifications, more often by vilification. But if whole group of women begin to demand change, this is much more constructive."[85] If enough women mobilize to demand political autonomy from the household and access to political institutions collectively, women's political participation can increase even without a priori structural change.[86]

Organizing collectively, however, bears high transaction costs: women must have sufficient information about their interests and who would share these interests (informational costs), women must be able to negotiate as a group about their priorities and strategies (bargaining costs), and women must be able to enforce sustained collective action (enforcement costs).[87] Given these costs, I argue that collective action is most likely when women are densely connected to each other and these connections entail political discussion, when they have a common framework of interests rooted in a gender consciousness, and when they have solidarity with each other such that there is sufficient trust to enforce collective action.

Overcoming the informational costs to collective action requires women to collectively engage in political discussion. For political discussion to occur, women must first be connected to each other. When ties outside of the household are limited, this implies the need for expanded or strengthened networks. For these network ties to provide information about political interests, they must entail political discussion; purely social connections (such as those with whom you gossip) may not provide the information needed to organize collective action. Through political dialogue, women can explore their preferences, practice deliberation, develop confidence and authority, and accumulate information about the political process. Network theorists have documented the value of network ties in transferring information and the denser the network (the more ties between people in the network), the better information will flow. This suggests that the better connected women are with each other and the

---

[83] See Chapter 2 for documentation of the limitations of legal institutions as enforcement mechanisms.

[84] Kanter (1977); Dahlerup (1988); Knight (1992); Ostrom (1994); Knight and Ensminger (1998); Htun and Weldon (2012).

[85] Batliwala (1993: 50–51).

[86] The suffrage movements of the early twentieth century are clear examples of the coordination of women to demand representation. See Teele (2018); Morgan-Collins (2021).

[87] Coase (1960); Ostrom (1994).

more their connections involve political discussion, the lower the informational costs to collective action.

Collective action also entails bargaining costs – that is, the costs of reaching a collectively agreed set of priorities and strategies. Agreement will be easier when women have a common framework of interests. Yet women have diverse interests that span multiple intersecting identities. Patriarchy itself inculcates different interests within genders: older women have a different stake in the prevailing social order than younger women. Common priorities are more likely when women have a strong gender consciousness – a shared identity – that motivates them to collectively demand political inclusion.[88] Without such a consciousness, women may remain inured to their subordination and unable to reach agreement about why they would bear the costs of collective action. Feminist theorists have long highlighted the importance of gender consciousness and group identity for changes in women's political situations.[89] Cornwall makes clear the intersecting value of discussion among women and gender consciousness-raising:

It is [the] process of changing the way people see and experience their worlds that can raise awareness of inequalities, stimulate indignation about injustice and generate the impetus to act together to change society...A focus on enhancing women's assets and resources alone misses a crucial dimension of the process of empowerment in feminist economic empowerment initiatives: that which is wrought out of coming together with and spending time with others, in breaking with isolation, and in contesting the beliefs and expectations that perpetuate the injustice suffered by women living in poverty and working in low-income jobs.[90]

Collective action is therefore more likely when there is a shared identity, a recognition of shared injustice, and the belief that group mobilization could address those injustices, as similarly articulated in the social identity model of collective action.[91]

The final transaction cost to collective action pertains to the enforcement of the agreed-upon strategy. A fundamental challenge to collective action is free riding. Olson famously argued that free riding is solved through the provision of selective incentives, or private benefits (material, solidary, or psychic) received for engaging in collective action.[92] Alternatively, social theorists have suggested that social solidarity within the collective, often defined as "social capital" or the "features of social organization such as networks, norms, and social trust that facilitate coordination and cooperation for mutual benefit,"[93] can indirectly enforce collective action. Social capital can be conceptualized at the micro, meso, or macro level.[94] My focus on social solidarity brings

---

[88] Sapiro (1983); Klein (1986); Dahlerup (1988).
[89] Klein (1986); Batliwala (1993); Kabeer (1994).   [90] Cornwall (2016: 344, 350).
[91] Van Zomeren, Postmes, and Spears (2008).   [92] Olson (1965).
[93] Putnam (2000, 67). See also Coleman (1988) and Krishna (2002a).   [94] Krishna (2002a).

attention to the meso level – the strength of social ties and the presence of norms of reciprocity and trust within networks and groups. Social solidarity is expected to enforce collective action by generating a strong expectation that other women will act according to the negotiated strategies.[95] For collective action in the face of resistance, women's ties to each other cannot be superficial; they must be deep enough for women to be compelled to contest their household, the most intimate of all social structures, and bear the risk of resistance.

Given these high transaction costs and a dominant political order centering women's political lives on the household, solidaristic collective action of this nature is unlikely to emerge endogenously. External intervention is often needed to disrupt self-perpetuating power structures and facilitate social change.[96] As Sharma notes, "even though [nongovernmental organizations] and state-partnered empowerment-based development interventions have the potential to deradicalize empowerment, depoliticize inequality, and reproduce power hierarchies, they also spawn subaltern political activism centered on redistribution and justice."[97] External interventions that create the conditions for women to collectively challenge the power hierarchies that keep them confined to the household can foster their empowerment – and, ultimately, social and political change.[98]

In this book, I examine whether a nongovernmental welfare program that mobilized women into microcredit groups can enable women's political autonomy by creating the conditions for gender-based collective action. My arguments suggest that this program is likely to generate collective action among women oriented toward political inclusion when these groups entail political discussion, particularly around women's shared identity, and develop social solidarity among women. Under such conditions, even though unintended, programs, like microcredit groups, are expected to yield an organized group of women pursuing a shared agenda of inclusion and representation, mobilized to command access to political institutions, demand change in both political outcomes and in who has the power to decide those outcomes, and contest those with a stake in perpetuating the prevailing political order.

DISCUSSION

In this chapter, I have developed a theory of gendered political behavior rooted in village and household social relations. I have argued that women's political participation in patriarchal societies is a function of the way that norms tie women to the household and convey bargaining and coercive authority within the household. The structure of power and influence in patriarchal societies constrains and coerces many women's behavior to align with that of their

---

[95] Ostrom (1994).   [96] Batliwala (1993).   [97] Sharma (2008: xxi).
[98] Sanyal, Rao, and Majumdar (2015).

household and inhibits their ability to contest this cooperation alone. The explanation for the puzzle of women's political participation thus lies in the interests of the dominant men in their household: women participate when it is strategically valuable to those dominant men (voting) and remain home when it is not (non-electoral politics).

Autonomy from the household is therefore key to women's political participation. Yet demanding autonomy is likely to trigger backlash from the very power structures from which women seek freedom. When power disproportionately favors men in the household and in society, women are best able to challenge male dominance through gender-based collective action. Through the collective action of a critical mass, mobilized around a shared gender consciousness and identity, women can contest their subordination and credibly challenge men's resistance. Social solidarity among women and a strong gender consciousness are important in reducing the transaction costs associated with collective action. Women thus have the capacity to challenge their political subordination and demand political agency if they can leverage their collective strength.

These arguments describe alternative pathways for the ways in which resources, bargaining power, and norms shape women's political behavior by highlighting the central roles of agency and autonomy. No single explanation is sufficient to explain women's political behavior; resources, norms, and institutions interact to create the conditions to enforce women's political exclusion. Shifts in any of these are only likely to yield change for women if they reduce men's coercive power and enable women's autonomy from the household.

In the remainder of this book, I test the hypotheses generated from these arguments. I will evaluate whether the household acts as a unitary political actor and whether women's agency is subordinated by powerful men. I will test the observable implications of coercion, such as the lack of correlation between intra-household preference differentials and household cooperation and between political interest and costly political participation. I examine whether indicators of bargaining power and autonomy from the household correlate with men's and women's political participation, with sharp predictions for differential relationships across the genders. To test the existence of a patriarchal political order, I consider the distribution of political ties and power in a village by gender and caste category. I then examine whether the aforementioned microcredit program disrupts political dynamics and shifts women's political participation. The evaluation of a supplemental gender consciousness-raising program given to these groups enables me to parse out the importance of social solidarity from household autonomy. Finally, I examine whether backlash is greater when women demand more disruptive political change.

One possible interpretation of the arguments I have presented is that they describe a particular set of conditions that are unique to India, which include a gender gap in political participation and the confluence of inequality, patriarchal norms, and permissive institutions. Under these conditions, the household emerges as a central actor in politics. As these parameters change, so too will the manifestation of patriarchal political dominance. However, my arguments more generally highlight the need to understand the conditions of women's agency and coercion and the incentives of those with political power to suppress women's political identities. My focus on coercion, and the institutions with the greatest ease of coercion (i.e., households), introduces a distinct conceptualization of gendered political behavior from existing political economy models and provides a conceptual framework for a more general understanding of the conditions of women's empowerment.

PART II

THE PATRIARCHAL POLITICAL ORDER

4

The Patriarchal Political Household

Once the wedding is celebrated and the newly married bride has moved to her husband's home, she is not only a bride but also a potential hostage.[1]

To understand the political behavior of women, we must consider the contexts in which they live. Yashoda appears to be a paragon of women's political empowerment. She served as an elected local ward member for three years before leaving to take up what she felt was a more prestigious position as an Anganwadi worker, a village bureaucratic position caring for young children's nutrition and early education. As she explained, "the Anganwadi job is for a lifetime, whereas the ward member position is for five years. So it is better to work for a lifetime." Yet even the Anganwadi position is seen as a politically important post, since the responsibilities include maintaining village registers and conducting local surveys. These positions are almost exclusively held by women; Anganwadi workers are often the most visible women in their village.

While we know that men participate in village politics much more often than women, we would expect Yashoda, and women like her, to be the exception to this pattern. If not the formerly elected, then who? Her ward member position was reserved for a Scheduled Tribe (ST) woman. No other ST woman in her ward wanted to challenge the seat, so she and her family decided she would run. This reservation gave her the opportunity to enter into politics. But even serving as an elected official did not solidify her regular political participation.

In speaking with Yashoda, it was indisputable that she cares about politics and is well informed about local village issues. She articulated that the core issue facing her village was the lack of work from the government's large workfare program. She blamed the Panchayat chairperson and secretary for

---

[1] Bloch and Rao (2002: 1030).

failing in their responsibilities to bring this work to the village, highlighting that they did not file applications for more work to the Block government.

Yet since she left her elected post, Yashoda has not attended a single village assembly meeting. "Now that I have joined Anganwadi, I don't get to go. My children are small, and then I have to do housework also. So I don't go." But her husband attends every meeting.

Yashoda describes her lack of autonomy even in the most private act of political participation – voting. When discussing how she decided whom to vote for in the recent election, she described a system of communal voting, concentrated in the household but radiating through her hamlet:[2]

A meeting was conducted in every hamlet. [The men] all discussed who to cast the vote for, whom to elect and whom to reject. They gather at one place, such as someone's house, and then decide whom to vote for. They discuss this topic and vote accordingly... Men take this decision, and women don't. Women only go to cast their vote...The same thing happens in every family. Husband takes the decision, and then they tell their family to vote for this candidate.

Women's ability to freely move within political spaces in Yashoda's village in Madhya Pradesh remains heavily contested. Yashoda describes how women are treated in village assembly meetings when they raise an issue:

YASHODA: [When women speak up in Gram Sabha], men get annoyed, asking, "Why are you raising issues? You should only listen to the discussion." So women don't raise issues. We just go and come back. They call us to come, we go, we sign the register, and then we come back.

INTERVIEWER: Has any such incident [where a woman was silenced in a meeting] happened with any woman that you remember?

YASHODA: Ramli bai. A Gram Sabha was going on at the Anganwadi. She stated that a school needs to be constructed in the village or make an Anganwadi for children and give some facilities for them, as they are not getting a good meal. One woman, Gomti bai, was there and supported Ramli. This annoyed the men. They didn't say anything, but they stood up and beat [Ramli's and Gomti's] husbands.

INTERVIEWER: Why?

YASHODA: They said that why you are telling such things here. They said that we are providing a good meal. [Ramli] had to hear so many men ask why she raised the issue. Whenever we say anything, they get annoyed.

INTERVIEWER: So you also didn't say anything in the meeting?

YASHODA: Yes. I had raised my point when my children were small. But they told you don't try to be smart. Have we grown our hairs since we have been running the school, and you are becoming smart in two days? So now I don't say anything.

INTERVIEWER: And it happens here in Gram Sabha.

[2] Villages in India are informally divided into hamlets, which are usually organized around jati and tribe.

YASHODA: Such a thing happens there. [Gram Sabha] is in name only.

INTERVIEWER: Women who go to Gram Sabha, what do men of the village think about them?

YASHODA: They think that women should not go there. They say that women don't have the right to speak among men. When women come back home, their husbands get angry and ask them why they were speaking in the meeting. So no one raises an issue, because men speak badly about them.

Women are expected to be subjects of their household, not citizens of their village. I have argued that households define women's political lives and constrain their political choices under what I call the institution of household political cooperation. Demanding access to political spaces challenges this institution as well as the pre-negotiated roles for men and women. As Yashoda later shared, her "husband always says that 'you are a woman and so live within your limits.'" The sanctioning of Ramli, the woman from Yashoda's story, began with punishing her husband. This sanctioning of men is then transferred to the offending women in the household, where their behavior is censured and condemned. And, such sanctions were applied when a woman demanded better meals and education for her children.

The answer to the puzzle of women's political participation begins in the household. This chapter evaluates the institution of household political cooperation and the argument that women coordinate their political behavior and interests with the household, by choice or by force. Measuring household cooperation is associated with many of the same challenges as measuring other dynamic power relationships. These dynamics often lie under the surface and are not explicitly contested or negotiated within households; nor are they the consequence of conscious deliberation. Even if cooperation can be observed and measured, it would be difficult to know whether such cooperation is the result of free will or coercion. I, thus, focus on the decision-making process.[3]

In this chapter, I test two hypotheses: First, I evaluate whether households align their political behavior. I begin by highlighting the patterns of within-household behavior we should expect to observe if the institution of household political cooperation is operational. Under such an institution, we would expect households to ensure the participation of all household members in the particular forms of political participation for which there are increasing marginal returns of additional household participation, and to devise a political division of labor for the forms of political participation that have diminishing marginal returns to additional household participation. I provide evidence in line with these expectations. I then more explicitly demonstrate the control that elder men have over women's (and younger men's) political decisions through an

---

[3] Using decision-making patterns as an indicator of agency has a long history in the study of women's empowerment (Kabeer 1999).

exploration of vote choice. I show that while most household members vote, vote choice is unified across the household and at the determination of elder men.

Second, I consider what might explain the perpetuation of household political cooperation and evaluate three possibilities: shared preferences within the household, intra-household coercion, and household-based electoral mobilization. I find that intra-spousal and intra-household preferences are quite distinct; the average distance between spouses' preferences over ten government services is closer to the maximum difference than the minimum difference. More generally, men and women want different things from their local governments and prioritize issues distinctly. I take this as evidence that shared preferences alone do not sustain household political cooperation. Instead, I use qualitative evidence from interviews to document the presence of fear for many women in stepping beyond the household in political spaces. I further show that neither political interest nor an index of bargaining power nor intra-spousal preference differences are correlated with women's vote autonomy, providing suggestive evidence of coercion. I also show that political entrepreneurs strategically target households as their unit of electoral mobilization. These results suggest that household political cooperation is upheld by coercion, both within the household and in the community more broadly, and by a system of political mobilization that reinforces the household as a political unit.

Ultimately, this chapter provides evidence in support of the argument that households are unitary political actors but demonstrates that this aligned political behavior is not efficient. The most powerful in the household have control over vote choice and are seen by the community as the political authority of the household. Those with political power also benefit from household cooperation and so reaffirm this institution. Understanding these power dynamics and the centrality of the household provides an answer to the puzzle of women's political participation.

DATA AND METHOD

In this chapter, I evaluate the role of the household in shaping women's political behavior. Patriarchal norms prescribe an economic division of labor such that women's economic lives center on the household, but the ways that these norms contribute to and translate into women's limited participation remain unclear. To examine this relationship, I draw on two principal sources of data. First, I utilize survey data I collected from a complete census of adults in two villages.[4] This survey, by capturing data on all members of each household in

---

[4] This survey was conducted in a total of six villages in Madhya Pradesh. However, villages were sampled from three "types" of villages: those without PRADAN's SHGs, those with PRADAN's SHGs, and those with PRADAN's SHGs plus gender consciousness-raising trainings. To provide an accurate picture of "status quo" networks and avoid conflating the impact of SHGs, this

two villages, allows me to compare relations and experiences *within* households, which I define as all persons residing in the same shelter and using the same kitchen (households may contain multiple families). I supplement this survey evidence with data from semi-structured interviews with a random sample of men and women in twenty villages in Madhya Pradesh. While the survey data enable a more general understanding of household behavior, the interviews provide an in-depth understanding of how such behaviors manifest and are negotiated.

Network Data

To capture the complexity of women's political ties, and to understand how gender operates within household networks, this chapter draws on data from my survey of all adults in two villages in Madhya Pradesh in 2019. To ensure that all residents of a village were surveyed, members of the research team visited each village one to two weeks prior to the start of survey data collection. Beginning with a census conducted by the state of Madhya Pradesh in 2015 (Samagra census), the research team created a list of all households and individuals in the village by speaking with key informants such as the Anganwadi and ward representatives and by conducting focus groups with members of each village hamlet. This process also allowed the research team to introduce the survey to key community members and build support and gain permission to conduct the survey, which was critical for ensuring mass participation in the survey. In total, 93.3 percent of all adults in both villages completed the survey (see Table A4.2 for a complete breakdown of response rates). The majority of those who did not complete the survey were either sick and unable to participate or had temporarily migrated for work. Table A4.1 reports the general descriptive characteristics of the two villages surveyed.

The survey captured data on a small number of village-level networks from a large number of individuals, herein referred to as nodes. Unlike network data collected from only a few nodes per network, these data allow me to map the villages' entire networks and compare women's positions across them. These data also permit within-network comparisons of men and women based on the size and nature of their ties, as well as mapping intra- and extra-household ties. I acknowledge that surveying all adults limits my ability to make comparisons across villages but, since the most relevant dimension of variance for this study is across genders, my theory is best tested by making comparisons within, rather than across, networks.

Sinclair defines a citizen's social network as the "collection of individuals tied to them by social connections, such as friendships, family relationships, or

chapter subsets to only the two villages without SHGs, Villages A and B, pseudonymized for respondent anonymity. The other villages will be explored in Chapters 7 and 8.

work colleagues" and their political network as the "subset of these social peers with whom [they] discuss politics, elections, or government."[5] While most research on the role of networks in political behavior focuses on broader social networks,[6] I show that it is important to distinguish between social and political ties and that poltical ties do not necessarily nest within social ties. Most men and women report discussing politics with a distinct set of individuals than those with whom they spend time and socialize. Distinguishing between social and political ties thus allows me to evaluate not only how the size of an individual's network affects their participation, but also how the nature of their ties matters.

I define an individual's social network as the set of people with whom they socialize and spend their free time, and their political network as the set of people with whom they discuss politics. I do not contest the general definition of a social network as the complete collection of individuals with whom an individual is tied; I simply differentiate the *nature* of the tie from within this broader social network and show that this is important for understanding how ties shape individual behavior. To measure these networks, residents of the two villages were asked to name up to five people from their village, including those in their household, with whom they spend free time (their social ties) and discuss politics (their political ties).

How do men and women conceptualize their social and political ties? The interviews highlighted that, while both men and women consider their social ties to be the set of people they see on a regular basis for informal communication and socializing, men and women conceptualize the set of people with whom they discuss politics quite differently, largely due to differences in their definitions of politics more generally. Political discussion for men and women was more specific and often more pragmatic than social exchanges. Men defined politics as centering on contestation for political power. They often referred to parties and coalitions and saw politics as the arena for these contentious deliberations. For men, politics spanned beyond the village and inhabited spaces in broader political arenas. As a result, men saw political discussion as involving these broader dynamics of partisan and contentious politics. Women, by contrast, defined politics as local. To them, politics was about their immediate everyday needs and largely focused on the local provision of services. For women, political discussion was therefore more pragmatic; it focused on their expectations and needs from the local government. These distinctions are important for contextualizing and interpreting gendered differences in networks.

---

[5] Sinclair (2012).

[6] Leighley (1990). For example, Larson and Lewis (2017) define an individual's network as the union of several types of networks, including both social and political networks.

Interview Data

I analyze data from 200 semi-structured interviews conducted in twenty study villages in Madhya Pradesh in 2018. These interviews provide rich and contextual insight into the lived experiences of women, like Yashoda, in rural India. In this chapter, I draw on the interviews conducted in four villages that involved more extensive qualitative data collection. In these villages, interviews were conducted with husbands and wives, including women who were members of self-help groups (SHGs) and those who were not, along with political elites.[7] The results presented in this chapter draw on interviews conducted with the sample of women who were not in SHGs and their husbands. Five women of this category and five men (their husbands) were interviewed in each village, yielding a total sample of forty interviews, plus interviews with five political elites in each village. In subsequent chapters, I explore data from those belonging to SHGs.

Respondents were randomly sampled from census rosters,[8] stratifying on SHG membership. Elite respondents included the village ward member, the Panchayat chairperson and their spouse, and a random sample of known informal (largely caste and tribe) customary leaders. The women interviewed for this chapter represent a range of ethnic and socioeconomic backgrounds of all ages.

Citizen interviews ranged from sixty to ninety minutes and focused on the respondent's political participation and political decision-making, particularly within the household. Elite interviews additionally focused on broader participatory and gender norms within the village as well as elite perspectives on influential political actors and communities in the village.

While I was present for the process of questionnaire development and testing and in close proximity throughout the interviews, the interviews were conducted by a small team of research assistants who were trained in both interviewing methods and the research aims of these interviews. Utilizing research assistants to conduct interviews allowed for gender matching of interviewer and interviewee, which was particularly important given the need to ensure complete privacy when asking about household relations.[9] Interviews were recorded with consent, and interviewers also took field notes that they summarized at the end of each day. The entire research team, including myself, debriefed regularly about the interviews conducted to ensure the quality of interview data collection.

---

[7] The remaining sixteen villages only included interviews with SHG women and so were not analyzed for this chapter.

[8] Respondents were sampled from the Samagra census data collected in 2015 by the state of Madhya Pradesh.

[9] Cammett (2013).

Interview recordings were transcribed and translated by a professional transcription firm in India that was provided with a glossary of common local words to ensure correct translation. The research team validated 20 percent of the transcriptions. Transcripts were then coded by the author and two undergraduate research assistants who had not been involved in the interview process. The coding scheme was developed iteratively using 10 percent of the study interviews. I, alongside the two research assistants, read through the interviews and applied a preliminary coding scheme and then met to reconcile any discrepancies and further refine the coding scheme.[10] This process was repeated until almost no discrepancies were found. The undergraduate research assistants then applied the coding scheme, which was designed to capture core themes in each section delimited by the interview guide, to the remainder of the interviews.

Where useful throughout this chapter, I present quantified results from these qualitative interviews based on the coding process, which demonstrate the representativeness of patterns across all interviews. In addition, I share quotes from a large range of these interviews to demonstrate the experiences and beliefs of women and men in their own words and to facilitate a deeper understanding of these dynamic processes. When paired with the network data, a clear picture of the household's centrality in political decision-making and its role in constituting women's political participation emerges.

HOUSEHOLD POLITICAL COOPERATION

An implication of household political cooperation is that costly political participation should be distributed across as opposed to within households. If these arguments are correct, we would expect to see high rates of electoral participation within the household given the numerical benefit of greater participation, and low rates of non-electoral participation where there are lower marginal returns to additional household participation; in the latter case, a single household member is expected to act as the household's political representative. The census data enable an evaluation of within-household patterns of political participation. Figure 4.1 utilizes these data in Villages A and B to test this hypothesis by plotting the average number of household members that engaged in each of seven forms of formal political participation over the past year (for households in which at least one member participated).

The patterns depicted in Figure 4.1 align with the hypothesized patterns of political behavior. First, on average, approximately five people voted per household, out of an average household size of 5.5 people. Second, for most non-electoral forms of political participation, the average household participa-

---

[10] Weston et al. (2001).

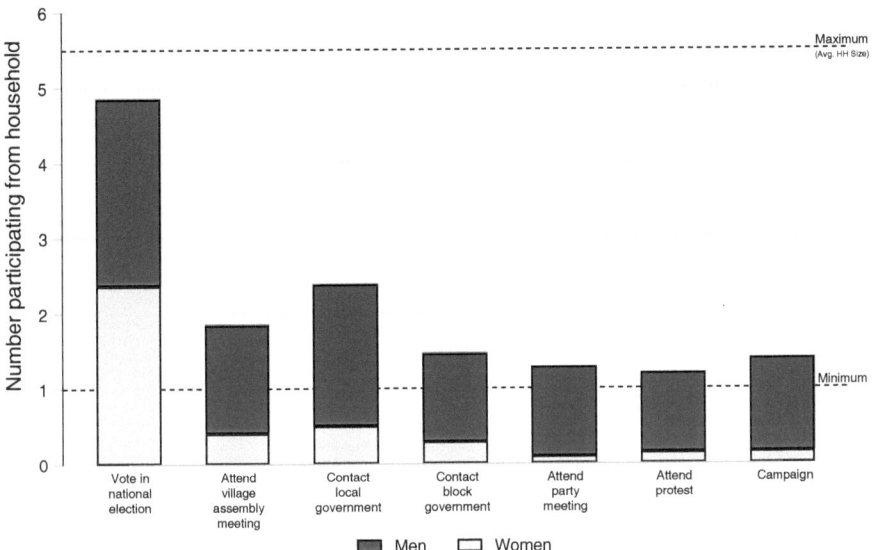

FIGURE 4.1 Everyone in the average household votes, while only a few (mostly men) participate in politics otherwise

Note: The figure plots the average number of household members, by gender, who participated in each political activity conditional on at least one person from the household having participated in that activity. Data are from the census survey conducted in Villages A and B. Data on non-electoral participation are from responses to survey questions asking whether the respondent had participated in each activity at some point in the past one year. The survey question on voting asked explicitly about the most recent national election. Each bar subsets to households where at least one member from the household had participated in that activity.

tion is one to two members. While not a perfect division of labor (which would look like only one household member participating in these activities), this low level of within-household participation is strong evidence for a household political division of labor since the survey measured any participation over the past one year. An average of one (the lowest possible value since this analysis is restricted to households in which at least one person participated) would mean that all households in these villages had only one person participate in each type of activity for an entire year. Given the many opportunities to engage in politics, it striking that fewer than two household members on average participate in most forms of non-electoral politics. Figure 4.1, therefore, documents how nearly all adults in the household typically vote, while only 20–30 percent (1–2) of household members participate in costlier political activities.

Importantly, 71% of households had at least one person who reported attending a village assembly meeting and 82% had at least one person who

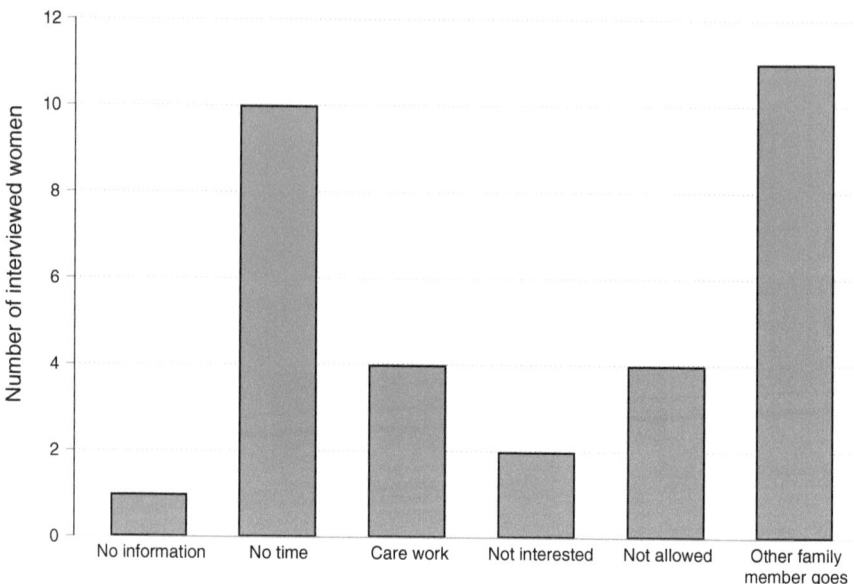

FIGURE 4.2 Women report not attending village assembly meetings because they are not allowed or someone else from their household is already going

Note: The figure plots the number of interviewees that provided each type of explanation for why they did not attend the village assembly meeting. Data are from qualitative interviews with twenty-two women.

reported contacting the local government. This suggests that low rates of political participation within households do not coincide with low rates of households engaging in politics. While a large majority of households participate in all forms of politics, only a minority of household members participate in costlier political activities.

Women's political participation appears to be related to this household political division of labor. Intra-household gender gaps in political participation mirror aggregate gender gaps with near equal rates of voting but unequal rates of non-electoral participation in the household. Additionally, the few women who do participate in non-electoral politics are distributed across, as opposed to within, households: only 4 percent of households had more than one woman attend a village assembly meeting, while 20 percent of households had exactly one woman attend.

When women were asked in interviews why they did not attend village assembly meetings, the most common response provided was that someone from their household was already attending (see Figure 4.2). Other common explanations were because women did not have time, had care work, or because they were explicitly not allowed to attend. Nearly two-thirds (64 percent) of women, or fourteen out of twenty-two, stated that they were either not allowed to attend the meetings or did not attend because someone else from their household was already attending. Men echo the creation of a household political division of labor. When asked why he does not go to the village assembly meeting, Thakur said, "We don't go as mostly my elder brother's son goes and only he talks to [the elected ward members]."[11] Mahesh describes the political division of labor more explicitly; in reply to a question on whether women should attend village assembly meetings, he said, "In Gram Sabha, if one man had gone from their house, then they don't need to go."[12]

Autonomy and Agency in Voting

Voting represents a clear point at which political decisions can be negotiated, therefore, studying voting patterns is an effective way to observe the decision-making process and manifestations of political agency. I have argued that women's turnout during elections is a poor measure of their political empowerment if they lack agency over political decisions. In relationships of dominance, in which some have undue influence over others, there are clear incentives to exercise that influence when it comes to voting. Even absent coercion, household political cooperation may manifest in voting behavior if households optimize their likelihood of electoral success or benefit.

When asked about electoral mobilization and voting behavior in interviews, many men explicitly conceptualized their household's votes as a currency that could be traded: "[In our household] we both give our vote. My son went to Gujarat for work, and so his name was not on the register, so he didn't vote. Two votes go from my house."[13] In many of these conversations, men articulated the number of votes they had (and ostensibly controlled) in their house. Interview respondents explicitly described the extent to which their families aligned their vote choices: A large majority, 67 percent of men and 75 percent of women, reported that their family always votes as a unit, suggesting a high degree of political cooperation among households in voting decisions.

Does this household-based vote coordination impede women's political agency? To evaluate whether men influence and coerce women's voting behavior, Figure 4.3 examines reported autonomy in voting decisions, or the freedom to make voting decisions independently, for men and women by age. The survey asked respondents to name all household members who help decide whom they will vote for, and then asked them to identify which of these people, including themselves, has the most say over their vote choice.

---

[11] Thakur (pseudonym), male, 52 years old, ST.
[12] Mahesh (pseudonym), male, 36 years old, OBC.
[13] Prabhu (pseudonym), male, 36 years old, ST.

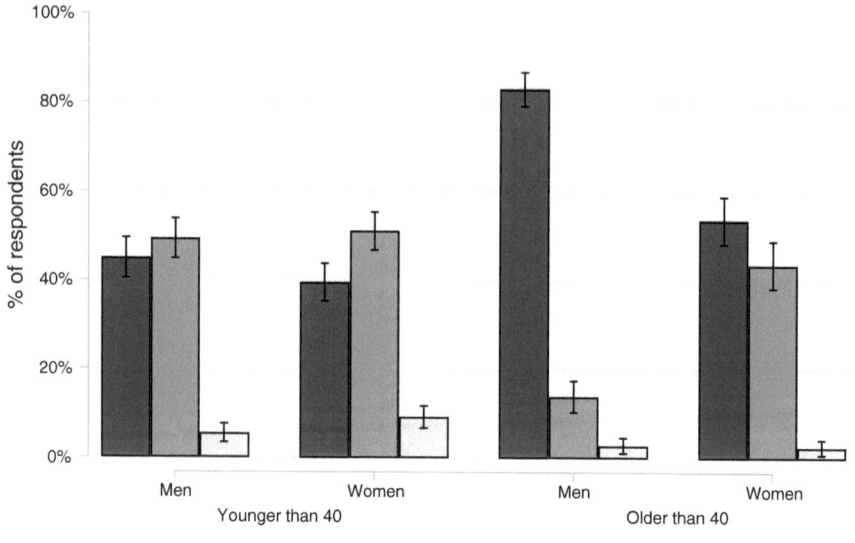

FIGURE 4.3 Women and young men report significantly less vote autonomy than elder men

Note: The figure plots the share of men and women, by age category, who report having the most say over their voting decision, who report a male family member having the most say, and who report a female family member having the most say. Data are from the census survey conducted in Villages A and B. Error bars denote 95 percent confidence intervals around the reported means.

It is difficult to measure coercion directly as successful coercion results in the desired behavior and visible coercion (the actual use of sanctions or violence) only occurs when the coerced challenge what is desired of them. This figure allows me to gain traction on this by measuring direct *control* of women's political behavior by others in her household. I assume that individuals who do not report that they have the most say over their own vote do not have complete agency in their vote choice. Differences by age are used to understand how normative authority – which is allocated to elder men under patriarchy – interacts with vote autonomy.

Men over the age of forty report significantly greater autonomy over their vote choice than women of all ages. Importantly, these patterns of vote autonomy are statistically identical across caste categories (see Figure A4.1): fewer than 50 percent of Other Backward Class (OBC), General Category (GC), and ST women stated that they had the most say over their own vote choice. Women's vote autonomy increases with age and with the death of a husband, though the gender gap in autonomy persists at all ages: 59 percent of women over 55 and 74 percent of widows state that they have the most say over their vote choice, as compared to less than 40 percent of married women under forty.

Kamla bai,[14] a thirty-three-year-old OBC woman, recounts the process of deferring to the family when voting in the following exchange:

INTERVIEWER: We want to understand how you make a decision in this regard in your family. We don't want to know who you cast your vote for; rather, we want to know how you make the decision.

KAMLA BAI: We decide to vote for one person altogether, and if we decide to vote for Congress, then all of us will vote for Congress only.

INTERVIEWER: So has it ever happened that there was a disagreement? Like your mother-in-law says that she wants to vote for someone, while your father-in-law wants to vote for some other person.

KAMLA BAI: No, it has never happened.

INTERVIEWER: So who decides for whom you will vote?

KAMLA BAI: Father-in-law.

INTERVIEWER: Suppose a very good friend of yours is contesting the election and you want to vote for her. But your husband may want to vote for someone else. Then what will you do in this situation?

KAMLA BAI: I will listen to my husband.

INTERVIEWER: What is the reason? Can you explain it?

KAMLA BAI: I will accept whatever my husband will say. My friend is only a friend. But my husband is my family.

While ballot secrecy should arguably provide some protection of an individual's agency when voting, a lifetime of subordination can inhibit a woman's understanding of her rights and possibilities. It can also obstruct the realization and contestation of practices that contradict her personal interests. In fact, 32 percent of women surveyed in the 2016 survey across seventy-six villages stated that they believed neighbors or friends can find out how you voted even if you do not tell them. I consider household cooperation to be an institution, meaning that it structures the rules of political participation. Once these rules are in place, abiding by them is likely to become second nature. Kamla bai's quick reply that her father-in-law decides her vote and her inclination to privilege her family above her own wishes are likely evidence of the internalization of these rules.

Additionally, young men have as little autonomy over their vote choice as women, which aligns with patriarchal power structures within joint families in India. Young men, like women, state that (older) male family members most often have the greatest say over their vote choice. Yet older men have near-complete autonomy in voting: more than 80 percent of men over the age of forty stated that they had the most say over their vote, compared to roughly

---

[14] Kamla bai (pseudonym), female, 33 years old, OBC, December 4, 2018.

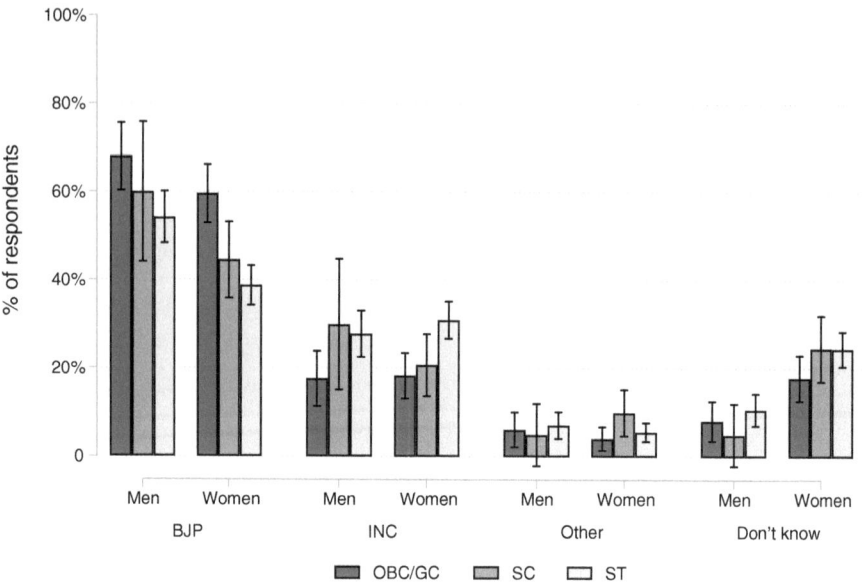

FIGURE 4.4 Women and men vote similarly, but women often don't know for whom they voted

Note: The figure plots the share of men and women, by caste category, who report having voted for various political parties. Data are from the 2016 survey administered in seventy-six villages in five districts of Madhya Pradesh but include only those who voted. The sample of villages includes only those who did not have PRADAN SHGs. In total, this includes data from 813 women and 467 men who reported voting in the most recent state election.

45 percent of those under forty. Harilal,[15] a fifty-year-old ST man, explained, "When it is the sarpanch election, then my elder brother would suggest that we need to make sure this sarpanch wins the election, so my dad and my uncles, they were eight to nine brothers, and all of us would vote for this candidate only."

One implication of household cooperation in voting is that men and women's actual voting behavior should be largely similar. Figure 4.4 plots the reported vote choice in the most recent state election from my survey in seventy-six villages in Madhya Pradesh for only those men and women who said they voted. To minimize concerns of social desirability bias, respondents were handed the tablet used for data collection and shown a sample ballot (including party symbols identical to those on the official ballot). They were then asked to replicate their most recent vote choice by indicating the symbol they chose when voting in the last election. They were informed that the enumerator

---

[15] Harilal, male (pseudonym), 50 years old, ST.

would not know which one they selected. Figure 4.4 demonstrates little difference in vote choice between men and women.

Men and women were statistically equally likely to have voted for the Indian National Congress Party (INC) in the most recent state elections across all caste groups. However, women, particularly ST women, were less likely to report voting for the Bharatiya Janata Party (BJP) than [ST] men. This is traded off with women saying they did not know whom they voted for rather than voting for another party. If "don't know" responses are removed, the distribution of vote choice for men and women is statistically identical. This is particularly striking given that men vote in state elections at marginally higher rates than women (94 percent as compared to 74 percent). The fact that nearly one in four women voters did not know how they had voted (23 percent as compared to 9 percent for men) is also an important indicator of women's more limited vote agency. As further evidence of coordinated voting, we can compare within spouse vote similarity, since these survey data were collected with spouse pairs. Removing spouses where one spouse reported that they did not know whom they voted for, 63 percent of spouses reported voting for the same party, almost perfectly mirroring the share of women who say that they do not have the most say over their vote choice. (This share jumps to 73% if we assume that spouses who reported not knowing who they voted for voted the same.) Finally, caste-based differences in voting are apparent, with OBC men and women supporting the BJP at significantly higher rates than ST men and women, suggesting that caste category more than gender structures vote choice.

The prevalence of explicit household cooperation in voting was undeniable from the in-depth interviews conducted with twenty-one men and twenty women[16] in four villages. Respondents were read a scenario about a campaign official coming to a house and sharing information about a candidate. They were then encouraged to think about the last election in their community and were asked a series of questions about how they, as individuals, decided whom to vote for. Respondents were then told to consider a scenario in which a friend of theirs was running for office, and they wanted to vote for them but their spouse did not. They were then asked whether they would vote for their preferred candidate or the candidate their spouse supported.

Men reported substantially more agency over their vote choice than women: 95 percent of men (20 out of 21) reported that their preferences for their friend would prevail when deciding for whom to vote, compared to only 55 percent of women (11 out of 20). Not a single man mentioned that his wife, or any other woman for that matter, was involved in his decision about whom to vote for, though many men shared that they would more generally discuss the election with their "family."

---

[16] Information was not reported for one of the original twenty-one women because she was 19 and had never been involved in any voting decision and was reluctant to share information.

This evidence makes clear that households are central actors in voting decisions; the observed alignment of household vote choices is not simply an indication of homogamy but the result of explicit deliberation and cooperation among household members. This process of household cooperation, however, regularly suppresses women's agency over their vote choice by excluding them from decision-making processes and diminishing their ability to act according to their own desires if they deviate from those of the household. Despite women turning out to vote at near-equal rates to men, this evidence suggests that this is not an indication of women's broader political empowerment. While more than 50 percent of women report deference to men in their vote choice, it is important to note, however, that there is substantial variation in the degree of women's reported vote agency and intra-spousal vote alignment, suggesting women's political empowerment is not precluded in the domain of voting even when households coordinate in voting decisions.

WHAT SUSTAINS HOUSEHOLD POLITICAL COOPERATION?

Why and when would women align their behavior with the household? Efficient models of the unitary household would suggest that women align their behavior with the household because maximizing household welfare is analogous to maximizing personal welfare.[17] Feminist theorists would instead question whether this alignment is the result of coercion.[18] Finally, such a system of household cooperation might be sustained and even rooted in broader patterns of strategic political mobilization.[19] The remainder of this chapter explores these mechanisms. I document the *inefficiency* of household cooperation and instead demonstrate its roots in broader patterns of coercion and mobilization.

Shared Household Preferences

Do households share a common preference function that would lead them to all behave in the same way? The answer to this question has far-reaching implications for our understanding of women's political participation. If it is true that household members share a common set of interests, then household cooperation may be deemed an efficient way to maximize both household and individual welfare. It would further imply that women's relative absence from political spaces has few consequences for political outcomes. If, however, men and women within the household have distinct political interests – as a substantial body of literature has shown – then household cooperation, and its attendant elevation of men in political participation, would amount to the

---

[17] Becker (1981).

[18] Sen (1987); Okin (1989); Agarwal (1997); Kabeer (1999); Chhibber (2002).

[19] Rosenstone and Hansen (1993). See also Posner (2004) and Chandra (2007) for arguments about the strategic use of identity to mobilize for political gain.

suppression and underrepresentation of women's interests.[20] Studies from around the globe, but particularly South Asia, have demonstrated both marked differences in men's and women's political preferences[21] and substantial changes in policy as a result of women's electoral representation.[22] Recent work by Sarah Khan shows that women are more likely to prioritize their husband's preferences when the intra-household preference differential is large – even if there are financial incentives against doing so.[23]

To examine whether women's cooperation of their political behavior with the household is driven by a common set of household preferences, census survey respondents were asked to rank ten local government responsibilities – road construction and maintenance, water provision, schools and education, health and health centers, toilet construction, housing construction, the provision of ration cards (BPL cards), reducing alcoholism, fighting violence against women, and providing Anganwadi (nutritional and educational services to young children) and ASHA (prenatal) services – from most to least important. I included alcoholism and violence against women as both have been objectives of broader women's movements in India.[24] Given high rates of illiteracy, respondents were shown ten picture cards, each representing one of the aforementioned responsibilities, and were asked to physically order the cards in their rank preference.

The availability of data for all members of all households allows me to estimate the difference in the ranking of preferences within households. Following Khan, I focus on spouse pairs and estimate the difference in each husband's and wife's preferences using a Euclidean distance measure for the ten ranks.[25] Figure 4.5 plots the distribution of these within spouse preference differentials, denoting the smallest and largest possible distance given the Euclidean metric.

If all spouses were perfectly aligned in their political preferences, we would expect a distribution clustered at zero. The result displayed in Figure 4.5 is far from that distribution. The distribution of preference differences is, in fact, centered closer to the maximum possible distance as opposed to the minimum possible distance. This demonstrates that there are nontrivial differences between the ordered preferences of spouses. The distribution also reveals that there is substantial variance across spouse pairs with respect to preference differentials, but none of the spouse pairs in the survey had identical preferences (although a few had almost completely oppositional preferences).

To understand whether these preference differentials are rooted in systemic differences in interests across genders, as opposed to idiosyncratic spousal

[20] Sapiro (1981).
[21] Edlund and Pande (2002); Iversen and Rosenbluth (2006); Gottlieb, Grossman, and Robinson (2016); Khan (2021); Weeks (2022).
[22] Lott and Kenny (1999); Chattopadhyay and Duflo (2004); Miller (2008); Clayton and Zetterberg (2018); Weeks (2019); Brulé (2020b).
[23] Khan (2021).   [24] Ray (2000).   [25] Khan (2021).

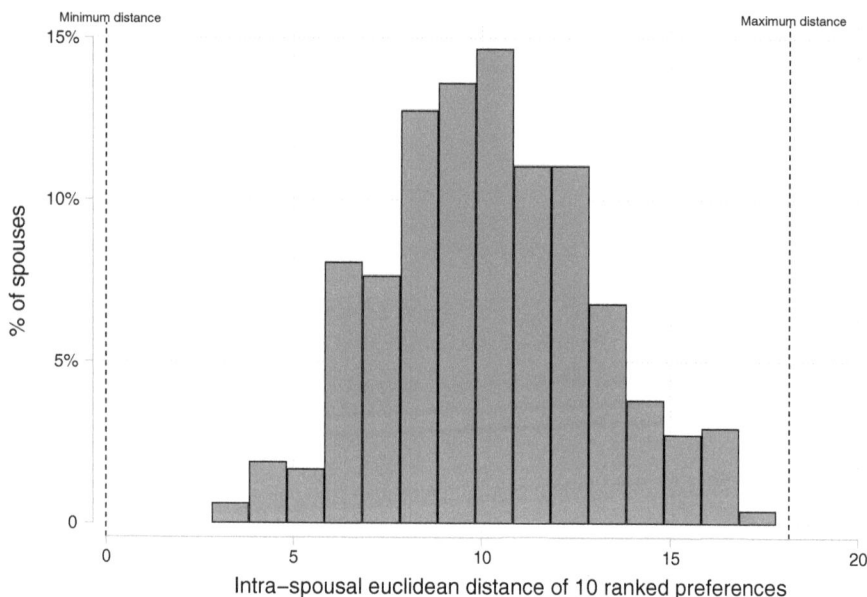

FIGURE 4.5 Husbands and wives report widely varying and distinct preferences over ten government services/issues

Note: The figure plots the distribution of the Euclidean distance between spouse's rankings of ten government issues. The minimum distance of zero would suggest spousal preferences are perfectly aligned. The maximum distance of roughly eighteen would suggest spousal preferences are completely misaligned. Data are from the census survey conducted in Villages A and B.

differences, Figure 4.6 plots the share of all men and women who named each policy issue as being the single most important. While men and women concentrated their responses in similar domains, there are significant gender differences in top priorities. Women were significantly more likely than men to name water and toilet provision and, to a less significant extent, housing as the most important responsibilities of local government, while men were substantially more likely to name schools and health as the most important responsibilities.

In sum, Figures 4.5 and 4.6 provide clear evidence that individual preferences within the household regarding local government responsibilities are far from interchangeable and differ in important ways. This implies that women's exclusion from political spaces likely underrepresents their distinct interests.

Intra-household Coercion

Strong patriarchal norms and the resultant inequalities in coercive power within the household may impede women's free agency over political decisions and force women into household cooperation. Dominant household members have strong incentives to maintain the hierarchal structures of patriarchy within

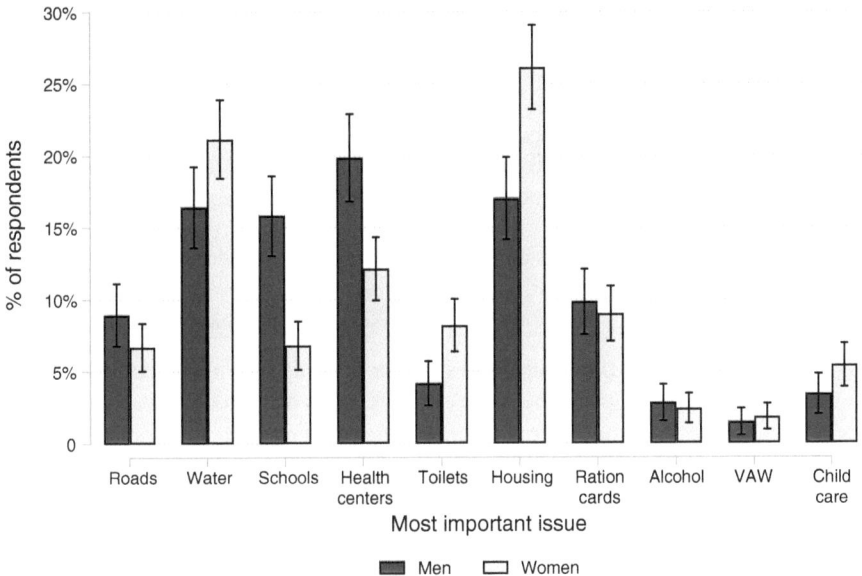

FIGURE 4.6 Men and women report significantly different views on the most important problem in their village

Note: The figure plots the share of men and women who report each of ten government issues as being the most important problem in their village. Data are from the census survey conducted in Villages A and B. Error bars denote 95 percent confidence intervals around the reported means.

the household. Since women's engagement in political spaces violates prevailing norms, it would likely entail social costs for both the woman seeking political access and the men in her household for allowing it, incentivizing men to curtail women's political participation.

As highlighted in Figure 4.2, a nontrivial share of women openly stated that they were not allowed to participate in politics. An exchange with Maya[26] about her participation in village assembly meetings (Gram Sabha) highlights the central role of fear in driving her behavior and suppressing the expression of her wishes and aspirations:

INTERVIEWER: Have you ever attended the Gram Sabha meeting?

MAYA: No.

INTERVIEWER: Can you tell me why you don't attend the Gram Sabha meeting?

MAYA: My husband and other family members go to the Gram Sabha, so we women don't go, and as my husband goes out for work, I cannot attend, as I have to take care of kids.

INTERVIEWER: And are you scared of your husband?

MAYA: Yes, fear is there.

[26] Maya (pseudonym), female, 23 years old, OBC, December 4, 2018.

INTERVIEWER: Why do you fear him?

MAYA: At home, there is no one else, only my husband. So for me, a husband is everything; therefore, I have to be scared, and I have to ask him before anything can be done.

INTERVIEWER: You are the youngest in your natal home, and here also you are the youngest, so how do you feel about it? Do you feel that others listen to your wishes?

MAYA: No, I don't feel that anyone knows my wishes. I just have to accept the decision taken by others.

INTERVIEWER: And when no one understands you, and you have to accept their decision, then how do you feel?

MAYA: I feel that maybe I am making some mistake; therefore, I have to listen to others.

While coercion within the household can manifest as fear and intimidation, as in the case with Maya, or in the most extreme cases as violence, it can also take the form of the gradual suppression of women's will to contest their own subordinate position. Coercion, therefore, will not always be overt and directly tied to specific political behaviors.

For example, coercion can manifest as learned reticence. Rajkumari[27] was married at the age of seventeen and moved from one household marked by male dominance to another. She shared in an interview that she wanted to continue studying but only got married because her elder brother "was too dominating at home, and no one could stand against his decisions." Rajkumari stated, "I would have felt so bad if someone were to get in trouble due to me, so I was 17 years old, and I got married." Rajkumari made the decision to marry, an incredibly consequential decision, out of fear that she would upset others. She submitted to both the wishes of her elder brother and the protection of others in the household. After marriage, Rajkumari found herself under the thumb of an abusive father-in-law and, after his passing, an abusive husband. She justified her receipt of "scolding" as being because she is "too simple" and stated that she tries to not "speak much to anyone" to avoid such confrontations. The many experiences during Rajkumari's life where she had been subtly coerced into behaviors against her preference taught her that the easiest way to avoid sanctioning is simply to stay quiet.

Gilasha bai echoed this sentiment when describing her response to years of abuse from her alcoholic mother-in-law, stating:

With whom will I talk? I used just to listen quietly. I used to console my mind in some way. Whom will I tell if I have a problem? I keep my problem with myself. Whom will I tell my problem? I didn't even tell my parents about my problem. I didn't tell anybody. I didn't tell my husband also. I used to keep my problem with myself. Why give them tension? I have never told anybody about my problems.[28]

---

[27] Rajkumari (pseudonym), female, 27 years old, OBC.
[28] Gilasha bai (pseudonym), female, 40 years old, ST.

Constraining women's mobility is a common way to signal their subordinate position. Sulochna[29] shared, "If my husband and in-laws are at home, then I ask them [to go out of the house]." And if she were to go without asking, then "he will scold me, asking, 'Whom did you ask before you went?' He scolds; therefore, I have to ask him. My husband will not ask me, as he can go anywhere." Such constraints on women's physical mobility directly translate into restrictions on their political participation.[30] When asked where women can go to raise any issues they may have, Halku replied, "They don't go anywhere. If there is any program of the MLA or program of the MP in our village itself, then they can go there to raise their issue. But they can't go anywhere else like Betul [the nearest urban city] or to the district collector to file a complaint."[31]

Women's lives are filled with instances of deference to male authority. Contesting this authority within the household is costly, particularly as it is supported by broader community norms that endorse men's authority in the household and in political spaces. Men in the broader community ensure the suppression of women's voice within their households by imposing strong sanctions on women and their households when they seek to raise their voices outside the household. Yashoda, in her experiences shared at the start of this chapter, highlighted men's annoyance at women's participation in political spaces. When asked whether women can participate in public meetings, Pushpa, a middle-aged man, replied, "They can, but men make fun. They say that the husband hasn't come and she has come."[32] His reply shows both the use of shame and verbal harassment to enforce political gender norms, and that such sanctioning is born by both the woman and the men in her household.

Interview respondents were read a scenario in which a woman, Bundo Bai, went to the village assembly meeting and raised an issue. In the scenario, several men in the meeting began shouting at her and demanding that she sit and stay quiet. Vinod's reaction to this hypothetical incident highlights the reality of such social sanctioning:[33]

VINOD: An incident just like this happened when a woman put forward her issues.
INTERVIEWER: So what do you think about this incident?
VINOD: She has done right. When we go to Gram Panchayat, we should put forward our issues in the same way. She did not do anything wrong. We don't go there only to hear the sarpanch and secretary. We go there to make them hear about whatever work is

---

[29] Sulochna (pseudonym), female, 35 years old, ST.
[30] Kumar (2022) shows that women whose husbands have migrated for work experience substantially greater mobility and political freedom and, ultimately, participate in politics at a higher rate than women with present husbands.
[31] Halku (pseudonym), male, 35 years old, OBC.
[32] Lakhan (pseudonym), male, 45 years old, OBC.
[33] Vinod (pseudonym), male, 26 years old, OBC.

not getting done in reality. So she did right. This thinking of people is wrong that she should not speak. If we won't speak, then our work would not get done ever.

INTERVIEWER: What happened when the woman raised her issue?

VINOD: It was like a woman was trying to speak, but others stopped her and said, "Don't say anything, because they could not get this thing done."

INTERVIEWER: And who stood against her?

VINOD: People of the village. They said that the Panchayat is not capable of doing anything, so it's useless to say anything to them. So it's better to talk to some higher official. There is no courage in the Panchayat.

INTERVIEWER: According to you, what should Bundo Bai have done?

VINOD: She should have sat quietly at her place. Or she should have complained to some higher official.

INTERVIEWER: If it had been a man who had raised his issue instead of Bundo Bai, would people have shouted at him?

VINOD: If a good man were to speak, then they would not have done anything. Since a woman stood, maybe that is why people did that. However, they should not have done anything like that.

INTERVIEWER: Is a woman able to speak up in Gram Sabha without any hesitation?

VINOD: They do speak up, but they feel scared also.

In another village, Pushpa shares a similar response but attributes the behavior to the assumption that Bundo Bai must be from a tribal (Adivasi) background. He highlights how women are not expected to be in the village assembly meeting (Gram Sabha) and would be chastised for raising an issue there instead of dealing with it on their own:[34]

INTERVIEWER: Has such an incident ever happened here?

PUSHPA: It happens many times. Sometimes two to four women will sit in our Gram Sabha, but mostly women don't go there. Women don't go there; only men go there in Gram Sabha.

INTERVIEWER: If, instead of Bundo Bai, a man had raised the issue, then would people have reacted in the same way?

PUSHPA: They should speak up. There is no problem in it. Women too should speak up. But people with low mind would say such things to women, like: "You are from a women's group, and get your work done in that group only; why you are raising the issue in the Gram Sabha?" They say such type of things.

INTERVIEWER: Do you think women should go to Gram Sabha?

PUSHPA: They should go, but no one will listen to them. As you said, they told Bundo Bai to sit down. Such types of things happen because Adivasi have [less education], and it's a community of Adivasis. Bundo Bai must be an Adivasi.

These lived experiences of coercion and sanctioning in the home and in public, which represent only a small sample of the many similar experiences relayed by

---

[34] Pushpa (pseudonym), male, 45 years old, OBC.

women in interviews and over years of fieldwork, demonstrate the real barriers to women's ability to freely move and act as political citizens. To provide evidence in support of coercion more generally, I test three observable implications of my argument: If women had freedom of choice, we would expect women with greater interest in politics, more bargaining power, and more distinct preferences from the men in their household to benefit less from household cooperation and instead exert greater autonomy over their vote. Figure 4.7 shows that political interest, bargaining power, and intra-spousal

(a) By political interest

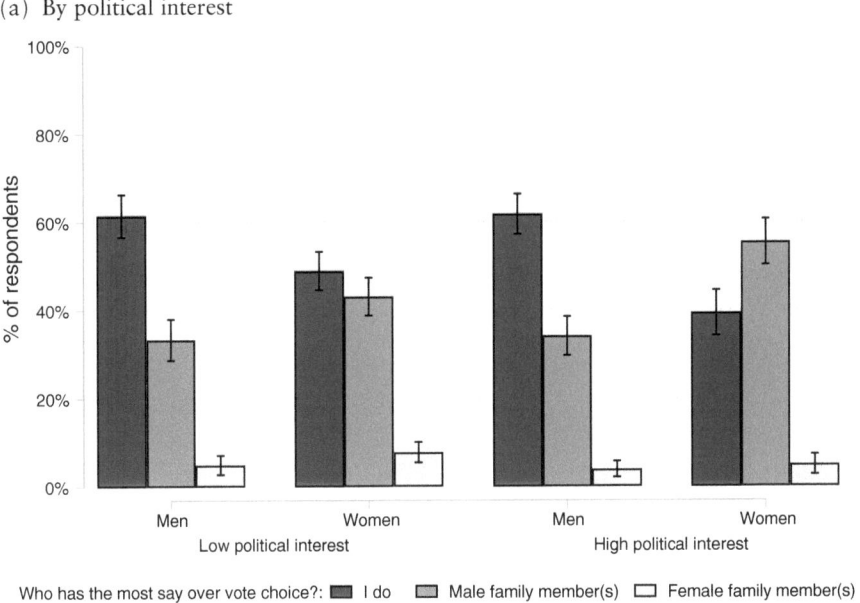

FIGURE 4.7 Women's vote autonomy is uncorrelated with their political interest, their bargaining power, and intra-spousal preferences differences
Note: The figure plots the share of men and women, by each category, who report having the most say over their voting decision, who report a male family member having the most say, and who report a female family member having the most say. Political interest is a binary indicator, with respondents reporting some or a lot of interest being categorized as high interest. Bargaining power is measured as the sum of indicators regarding whether the respondent personally owns land or livestock (an indicator of control over commonly assumed joint assets), whether they worked for pay in the past year, and whether the respondent was the highest earner in their household. High bargaining power respondents include those with a value of at least two. Intra-spousal preference differences are measured as the Euclidean distance between spouse's rankings of ten government issues. High difference is indicated by a distance value greater than the median. The sample in this panel is smaller as it subsets to only those respondents with surveyed spouses. Data are from the census survey conducted in Villages A and B. Error bars denote 95 percent confidence intervals around the reported means.

(b) By bargaining power

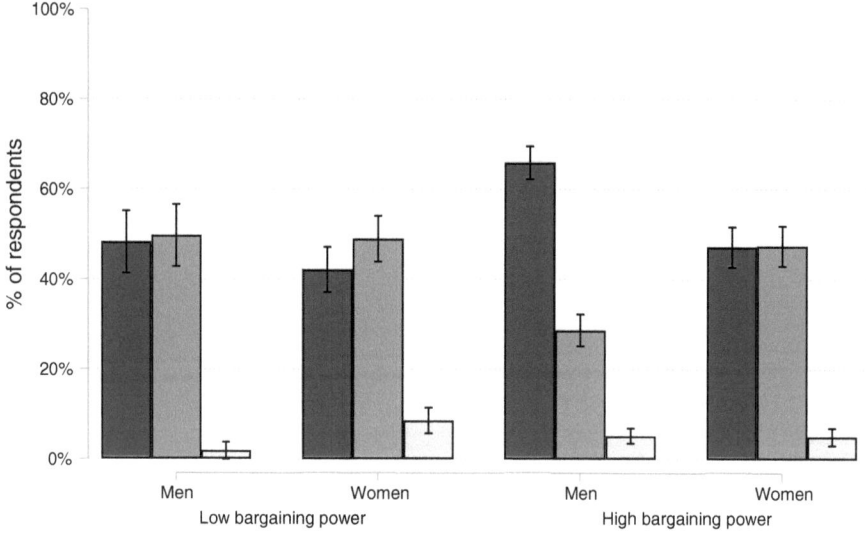

(c) By intra-spousal preference differences

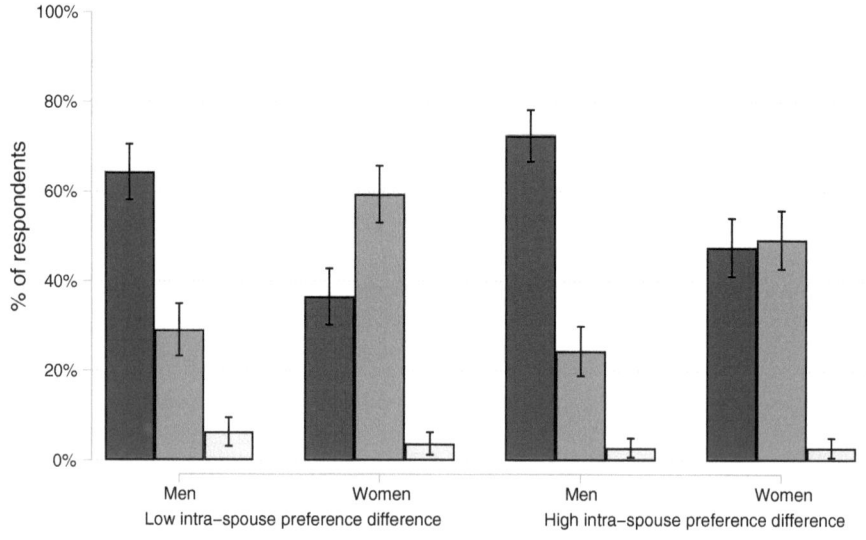

FIGURE 4.7 (*cont.*)

preference differences do not positively correlate with women's vote autonomy. Panel A reveals that political interest is negatively correlated with vote autonomy for women; women who are more interested in politics are significantly more likely to say that a male household member has the most say over their vote choice. Panel B shows that bargaining power, measured by whether women are employed, the highest household income earner, personally own land or livestock, is uncorrelated with women's vote autonomy. Panel C provides evidence of the same for intra-spousal preference differences. Additionally, bargaining power is positively correlated with men's reported vote autonomy, but political interest and intra-spousal preference differences are not. These correlations are systematically explored in the next chapter.

Women have internalized their roles as political subjects of the dominant men in their households, and men enforce these roles through fear. Not even strong exit options (employment, income, land, and assets) enable women's vote autonomy. Explicit coercion is difficult to observe as it is invisible until it is transgressed. To definitively prove the use of coercive tactics to an enforced equilibrium, we must observe responses to challenges to that equilibrium. While Chapter 8 will more explicitly demonstrate the strong and violent responses of men to women's demands for political agency, Vinod's expectation of retribution (mirrored in similar responses by many others) to a hypothetical act of norm deviance by a woman provides strong evidence of the use of coercion to uphold the patriarchal political order.

Strategic Household Mobilization and Family-Centered Clientelism

I have argued that strategic politicians are likely to benefit from household cooperation. If households vote as a unit, then a savvy politician would only need to mobilize one member of the household to capture its votes. Satisfying the common demands of an entire household is much less costly than fulfilling the unique demands of all household members, particularly given the variation in preferences shown in Figure 4.6. If politicians strategically mobilize key household members under the assumption that doing so is equivalent to mobilizing the entire household, then they reinforce the household as a political unit. As a result, such strategic mobilization of men would provide another mechanism through which household political cooperation may be sustained.

An observable implication of this argument is that only a limited number of household members should be mobilized to vote and that these should be mostly men. Figure 4.8 tests this expectation and visualizes intra-household vote mobilization. It shows the average number of people from the same household who reported being mobilized to vote by gender, conditional on at least one person being mobilized to vote. Figure 4.8 shows clear evidence of

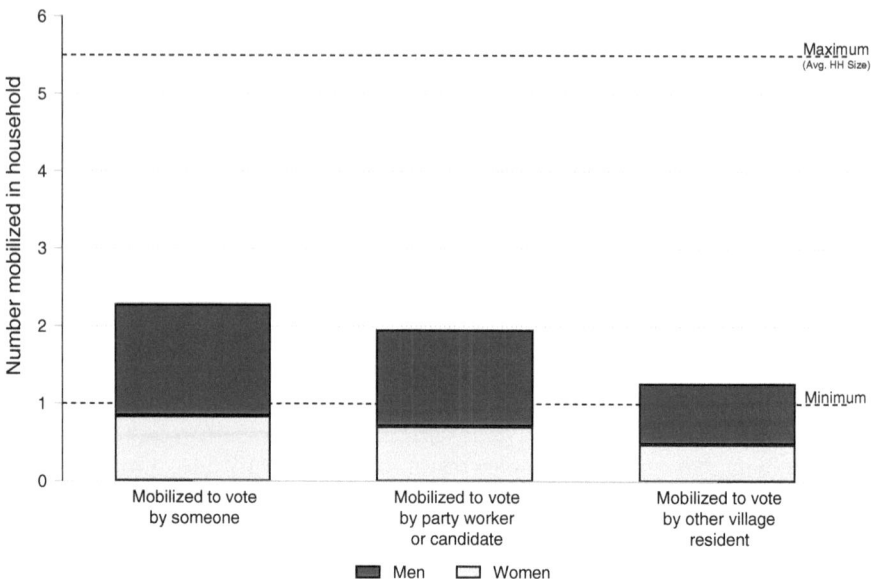

FIGURE 4.8 Only a few household members are mobilized to vote
Note: The figure plots the average number of household members, by gender, who were mobilized to vote by each type of actor conditional on at least one person from the household being mobilized to vote in each of the three ways. Data are from the census survey conducted in Villages A and B.

household-based political mobilization: while the average household has 5.5 adults, only 2.3 of them were mobilized by a political party on average. This is a fraction of those who eventually vote (see Figure 4.1). This is even more striking given the multiplicity of parties mobilizing votes, suggesting that parties must take similar approaches to whom they mobilize to vote. Additionally, while only 34 percent of all individuals were mobilized to vote, at least one person in more than 80 percent of households was mobilized. Electoral mobilization touches nearly every household but less than a majority of citizens, providing compelling evidence for a household-centric mobilization strategy.

Discussion of the household as the critical unit of electoral mobilization came up in a large majority of qualitative interviews, particularly with men. For example, an interview with a male ward member who described how he mobilized votes while campaigning revealed the explicit authority given to the male head of household and the expectation that women will defer to that authority:[35]

---

[35] Male elected ward leader, 30 years old, OBC.

INTERVIEWER: When you used to visit [constituents'] houses for their vote, whom did you talk to?

WARD MEMBER: To the head of the family.

INTERVIEWER: Mostly who is head of the family in these houses in your village?

WARD MEMBER: We mostly consider male member as head of the family. Mostly men talk to men. And women have to follow whatever men say. If [men] say that we would vote for Congress and not for BJP, then [women] will have to accept that.

INTERVIEWER: If a wife wants to vote for some other party, can she do that?

WARD MEMBER: No, she can't do that.

Similarly, a Brahman village elder named Mukund describes how candidates go door to door, but only the opinion of the head of household matters in the family members' vote:[36]

INTERVIEWER: And, during elections, how do they do campaigning?

MUKUND: They visit door to door and say "Ram Ram" and ask for votes.

INTERVIEWER: And what are your thoughts with regards to women voters?

MUKUND: The head of the family, he can vote for the sarpanch, and he would ask his family members to vote for the same. Women voters don't go beyond the head of the family. In our village, whatever the head of the family will say, the ladies will vote for that person only.

This household-based mobilization coincides with promises to deliver desired goods and services and, in a few instances, with explicit vote buying. Nearly all interviews describe how candidates promise to address problems in the village or provide access to a targeted government scheme. For example, Thakur succinctly describes prevalent patterns of mobilization and vote decision-making:[37]

INTERVIEWER: And when they come to your house, asking for votes, whom do they ask for?

THAKUR: First, they will ask the elder son.

INTERVIEWER: And what all promises they make?

THAKUR: They tell about many works. They will dig this well and even give rebate in electricity.

INTERVIEWER: And if we talk about your family, how do you decide that whom to vote for?

THAKUR: If I tell or the elder son tells that you have to vote for this particular candidate, then you have to vote for that person only.

Gender importantly shapes patterns of electoral mobilization: women are much less likely to be mobilized to vote than men. Figure 4.8 demonstrates that while both men and women are mobilized to vote, the scale of mobilization of men is much greater than that of women. On average, 43 percent of men were directly

---

[36] Mukund (pseudonym), male, 61 years old, GC.
[37] Thakur (pseudonym), male, 52 years old, ST.

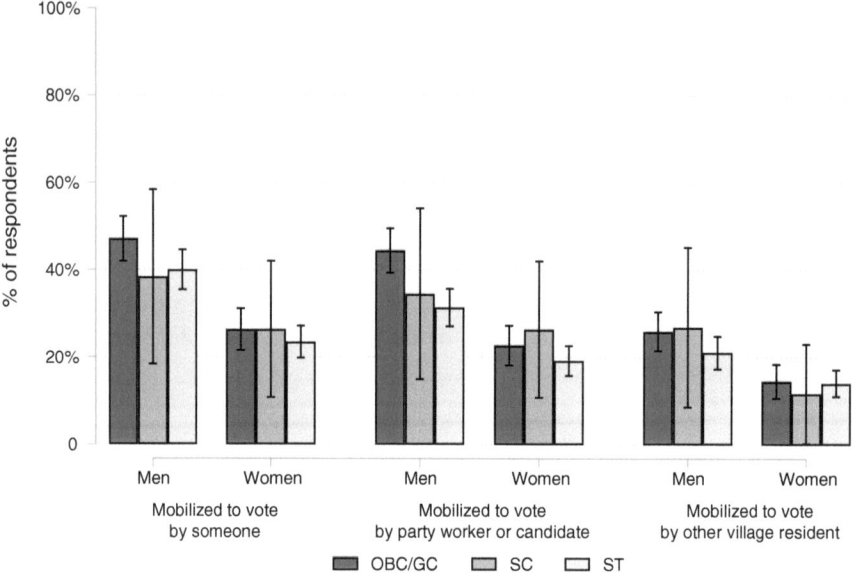

FIGURE 4.9 OBC men are the most likely to be mobilized to vote, but caste category does not condition women's electoral mobilization
Note: The figure plots the average percent of respondents, by caste category and gender, who were mobilized to vote by each type of actor. Data are from the census survey conducted in Villages A and B.

mobilized by a party worker or candidate, compared to only 25 percent of women. Figure 4.9 provides further evidence of gender inequality in electoral mobilization by comparing the share of men and women in Villages A and B that stated they were mobilized to vote in the most recent national election. Men across caste groups were mobilized to vote at much higher rates than women, particularly by political entrepreneurs. Furthermore, on average, men stated that 98 percent of those who approached them to encourage them to vote were male; women reported this to be 90 percent on average. Electoral mobilization is a man's game.[38] These dynamics introduce an additional mechanism for the inefficiency of household political cooperation: If politicians are only speaking to men, how can they be aware of women's distinct interests? Liaqat shows that they are not.[39] He demonstrates that politicians in Pakistan had significantly weaker prior knowledge of women's political preferences than men's, introducing welfare losses for women.

[38] Goyal (2021) demonstrates that the presence of women party workers improves the electoral mobilization of women.

[39] Liaqat (2019).

Caste category also conditions who is mobilized to vote, but only for men. Figure 4.9 shows that there is no significant difference between women from different caste groups with respect to their reported rates of electoral mobilization. OBC men, on the other hand, report significantly higher rates of electoral mobilization than ST men, particularly mobilization by party workers and candidates. OBC and ST men do not differ in their reporting of informal mobilization by others in their communities. Given OBC economic and political dominance in these communities, it is not surprising that OBC men would be targeted in political mobilization at higher rates. What is striking, however, is that these political caste dynamics do not translate into differences across women.

These results provide evidence that a broader system of political mobilization and representation supports the household's centrality in politics and in determining women's political behavior. The unitary household not only benefits those in the household with power but also benefits political entrepreneurs. The incentives of powerful men to ensure household cooperation facilitate the collective support of this institution and perpetuate its prominence.

DISCUSSION

This chapter evaluates the central tenet of my theory that the household acts as a coordinating unit of political behavior and that households act as a unit in political decision-making. Drawing on description of a large-scale survey with all adult residents of two villages and qualitative interviews with dozens of women and men, I document the existence of household political cooperation as an institution. Women (and men) regularly align both their vote choice and their political behavior more broadly with their household, but power hierarchies within the household and inequalities in coercive power elevate the status of men in this process. In fact, younger men's political agency approximates that of women.

Importantly, coordinated household behavior does not indicate maximized household welfare nor an efficient representation of women's interests. Men and women have different political preferences, both on average and within the same household. Assumptions of common household preferences are unwarranted given the evidence. We, therefore, cannot explain the perpetuation of household political cooperation with efficiency arguments of perfectly shared preferences.

Instead, the evidence suggests that household political cooperation is upheld both by within-household coercion and strategic electoral mobilization. Coercion is evidenced through both the deep internalization of the authority of elder men in all domains and the use of fear as a suggestion of repercussion for violation of the institution. Drawing on a hypothetical scenario posed in interviews, I demonstrate men's expectation of punishment for women who speak up in political spaces – punishment not extended to men in the same position. I also show that women's vote autonomy is uncorrelated with their political interest, bargaining power, and intra-spousal preference differences.

Elites seek out men when mobilizing political support, giving men further opportunities to voice their demands. Political party workers and candidates more heavily mobilized electoral support from men than women but did so by maximizing the number of households reached. This suggests that politicians benefit from an organized household vote bloc.

Ultimately, these findings show that women's exclusion from political spaces begins in the household. Their limited autonomy from the household (and limited agency within it) likely inhibit their ability to contest household control. As a result, we would expect women with greater autonomy and bargaining power in the household to be more independent political agents and engage in greater political action.

5

Political Behavior under Household Cooperation

How does household political cooperation shape women's and men's political behavior? I have hypothesized that, assuming households are coordinated, household members with the greatest bargaining and coercive power, the lowest costs to participation, and the greatest preference for participation are most likely to participate in forms of politics for which a household political division of labor is expected. All household members, however, are expected to participate when it is in the household's interests – that is, when there are increasing marginal returns to additional participation. Women's cooperation with the household is expected to imply their political exclusion between elections, their political participation on election days, and limited agency in all political decision-making. A second key hypothesis is that women's autonomy from the household – that is, breaking free of household cooperation – will positively correlate with their political participation.

I test both hypotheses – that power in the household and autonomy from the household correlate with women's political participation – by evaluating the correlates of within-household and within-village political participation. I provide considerable evidence in line with these two expectations. Within the household, the women (and men) with more bargaining power are more likely to participate in non-electoral politics but, as expected, are no more likely to vote. However, even accounting for bargaining power and resources, women's participation remains well below that of men, and women's reported political interest is uncorrelated with their political behavior, both suggesting the possibility of coercion. Even more, when comparing women at the village level, women's non-electoral political participation is negatively associated with gender-biased attitudes held by dominant members of their household. Instead, women with more autonomy from the household are significantly more likely to participate in non-electoral politics, and the determinants of their political behavior mirror those of men. Taken together, this provides strong evidence in support of both a coordinated household that elevates dominant members and a pathway to participation for women rooted in their autonomy from that household.

MODELING POLITICAL PARTICIPATION

To evaluate these hypotheses, I use regression analysis to correlate individual-level attributes with two measures of political participation, voting[1] and engaging in any of six nonvoting participatory acts in the past year (attending a village assembly meeting, contacting or making a claim on the local Panchayat or Block government, attending a party meeting, protesting, and campaigning on behalf of an electoral candidate), comparing only within households. By including household fixed effects and leveraging the fact that the census data measure the behavior of all adults in each household, the reported relationships indicate the importance of individual attributes in determining which household members participate in various political activities. I include household fixed effects to further control for unmeasured differences that vary only at the household level, such as the number of children in the household. However, this does not permit the inclusion of attributes that are constant across household members, such as caste category. It also does not allow for an understanding of how the characteristics of any individual household member affects others in the household.

Second, I evaluate which men and women in a village are most likely to participate in politics, allowing for cross-household comparisons by regressing the same set of attributes plus household-level attributes on political participation and including village fixed effects. Again, I benefit from having near-complete data on all village residents that enables a deeper understanding of within-village behavior. These models are reported for all adults and then separately for women and men in the two census villages. All models report robust standard errors, but results are robust to clustering standard errors at the household-level.

---

[1] Voting is measured as whether the respondent self-reports having voted in the most recent national election, which occurred only a few months prior to data collection. On average, voting in national elections has the largest electoral gender gap as women (and men) report higher turnout in local as opposed to state and national elections. However, the vast majority (89 percent) of women and men reported turning out to vote. This suggests that these measures may be subject to social desirability bias, despite the fact that they followed best practices and included language suggesting that non-voting is common and acceptable. Importantly, if this is indicative of socially desirable reporting, the scale of this bias does not extend to other forms of participation as substantially fewer people report non-electoral participation (73 percent of men and 24 percent of women). If high reported rates of voter turnout are in fact indications of social desirability bias, the divergent patterns of reporting on voting and non-electoral participation may, in fact, be evidence of the very patterns purported to underlie the differential gender gaps: women are/feel compelled to vote but are not expected/allowed to participate otherwise.

In both sets of models, I correlate political participation with four theoretically motivated sets of indicators: measures of autonomy from the household, costs and benefits to participation, power in the household, and demographic characteristics. The theoretical model described in Chapter 3 yields a set of hypotheses around the conditions under which autonomy, household power, and social perceptions will affect women's political behavior. The models presented here are intended to test these hypotheses.

Autonomy from the household is measured as the share of a respondent's reported political discussion ties with people from outside their household and, more generally, by the respondent's number of political discussion ties (out-degree of political network). Out-degree captures the number of people with whom the respondent reports discussing politics and does not include the set of people who themselves name the respondent as a political discussion partner. Use of out-degree is meant to capture the respondent's own perceptions of their network size and composition, though results are robust to including total political discussion network degree.

Costs to political participation are measured in three ways. I proxy for informational costs with a respondent's years of education and how many correct answers they provided to three questions on political knowledge (whether they know how to file an application for services, whether the village chairperson seat was reserved in the last election, and how many days of work are allowed in the large national workfare scheme). Informational costs are also a function of network size, measured as the out-degree of political network (as described above). I proxy for resource costs with a respondent's personal annual earnings. Finally, to measure perceived social costs, the models include the predicted proportion of adults in the village that the respondent believed would report anti-female attitudes regarding women's political participation; predicted village gender bias is the answer to the question: "Out of one hundred typical people over 18 years old who live in this village, how many say that 'women should attend the Gram Sabha instead of staying at home to take care of their kids'?" For those who provided an answer, the average predicted number of villagers who would agree with this statement was 25.5 (26.8 for female respondents and 24.3 for male respondents), signaling widespread belief that only a minority of people in their communities would support women's political participation. The 318 respondents who reported that they did not know were assigned the mean value of 25.5 to avoid losing these observations in the analysis.

Strength of preferences is estimated by a respondent's level of political interest, which is measured by an indicator of reporting some or a lot of interest in politics. This enables an examination of whether those most inclined toward politics within a household and village are also those most engaged in politics.

Bargaining power (exit options) is measured using an index for intra-household bargaining power, which is the sum of indicators of whether the respondent personally owns land or livestock (measures of control over commonly assumed joint assets),[2] whether they worked for pay in the past year, and whether the respondent was the highest earner in their household.[3]

Coercive power and coercion are difficult to measure, so I proxy for the likelihood of a respondent experiencing coercion – the within household limiting of their free political participation - using an indicator of whether the person in the respondent's household with the greatest bargaining power expressed normative attitudes against women's political participation. All respondents were asked two questions related to their beliefs about women's role in politics. To minimize social desirability bias, these questions were phrased as paired statements, and respondents were asked to choose which statement they most agreed with. The first set of paired statements asked whether the respondent believed that (a) women should attend the Gram Sabha or (b) women should stay home to take care of their kids. The second set of statements asked whether the respondent believed that (a) women should be encouraged to stand in elections or (b) women should stay home to take care of their kids. A respondent is identified as demonstrating gender-biased attitudes if they did not select (a) for both of these questions; 34 percent of all respondents and 42 percent of respondents who have the highest level of bargaining power in their household are coded as holding normative attitudes against women's political participation. This measure is not included in models using household fixed effects as it has no within-household variation.

Demographic characteristics include indicators for caste category,[4] age, and marital status. The models with all adults include an indicator for whether the respondent is female to evaluate whether women are less likely to participate in politics even after controlling for all of the aforementioned factors.

HOUSEHOLD POWER AND POLITICAL PARTICIPATION

I hypothesize that if households coordinate their political behavior, those in the household with the lowest costs to political participation and strongest preferences for participation will participate in non-electoral forums, but these factors should be uncorrelated with voting. Table 5.1 tests this hypothesis by modeling the within-household correlates of voting and non-electoral participation. Several insights emerge in support of this hypothesis.

First, factors expected to lower informational costs – education, political knowledge, and political network size – are all positively and significantly correlated with non-electoral political participation but not voting.

---

[2] Brulé (2020b).

[3] This is measured by taking data on annual earnings for each household member, winsorized to remove outliers, and then comparing within-household earnings.

[4] The models include indicators for being from an ST or SC group. The reported coefficients are relative to both members of OBCs and GCs. Given the very small number of GC adults in these two villages (20 adults or 1 percent of the population), they are clustered with OBC adults.

TABLE 5.1 *Bargaining power and network size are strong predictors of non-electoral participation and vote autonomy*

	Vote in National Election		Any Non-electoral Political Participation		Has Most Say Over Vote	
	(1)	(2)	(3)	(4)	(5)	(6)
Female	-0.055*** (0.015)	-0.006 (0.021)	-0.502*** (0.021)	-0.343*** (0.033)	-0.182*** (0.023)	-0.102*** (0.032)
Proportion of Political Network from Outside the Household		0.045 (0.032)		0.074 (0.046)		0.085* (0.050)
Size of Political Discussion Network (Out-degree)		0.002 (0.006)		0.043*** (0.008)		-0.011 (0.010)
Years of Education		-0.002 (0.002)		0.013*** (0.003)		-0.002 (0.004)
Political Knowledge Index		0.013 (0.011)		0.086*** (0.016)		0.024 (0.017)
Personal Income (10,000s Rs.)		0.007 (0.005)		-0.002 (0.007)		-0.002 (0.008)
Perceived Share of Population Politically Gender Biased		0.000 (0.000)		-0.001 (0.001)		0.001 (0.001)
Interested in Politics		0.065*** (0.017)		0.066** (0.026)		0.005 (0.028)
Bargaining Power Index		0.004 (0.010)		0.037** (0.014)		0.049*** (0.016)
Age		0.005*** (0.001)		0.003*** (0.001)		0.008*** (0.001)
Married		0.194*** (0.027)		0.061* (0.034)		0.061* (0.036)
N	1,721	1,721	1,725	1,725	1,721	1,721
Dependent Variable Mean	0.89	0.89	0.48	0.48	0.53	0.53
Fixed Effects	HH	HH	HH	HH	HH	HH

Note: ***, **, * indicates significance at the 1 percent, 5 percent, and 10 percent levels, respectively. Robust standard errors are reported. Data are from the census survey conducted in Villages A and B. All models include fixed effects as specified.

123

An additional network tie is associated with a similar increase in the likelihood of participation (around 4 percentage points) as roughly three additional years of education. These indicators of informational costs are uncorrelated with voting. Personal income, which is expected to reduce resource costs, and perceptions of community gender bias, which I argue proxies for perceived social costs, are uncorrelated with non-electoral political participation and voting. Political interest, a proxy for an individual's strength of preference for political participation, is positively correlated with both forms of political participation.[5] Taken together, these results support the argument that non-electoral participation within the household is more likely to be allocated to those with higher personal benefit and lower costs for non-electoral forms of participation.

Bargaining power is uncorrelated with voting but is positively and significantly correlated with non-electoral political participation. A one-unit increase in the bargaining power index, the equivalent of entering the labor force or becoming the highest earner, is associated with a 4 percentage point (or roughly 10 percent) increase in the likelihood of non-electoral participation and vote autonomy vis á vis those in your household. Other potential indicators of intra-household power, such as education, age, and being married, are also positively associated with non-electoral participation, providing evidence in support of the role of power in household political decision-making in determining non-electoral political participation within the household.

An evaluation of the correlates of vote autonomy further reveals the importance of household power in structuring within household political behavior. Vote autonomy is positively associated with men, age, bargaining power as defined by exit options, and, to a noisier extent, autonomy from the household and uncorrelated with all measures of the costs and benefits of political participation, including political interest. This suggests that while households may allocate political participation to those with the lowest costs and strongest preferences, voting decisions are more likely to be determined by bargaining power.

A fully saturated model, interacting gender with all covariates, reveals that these dynamics are largely similar for both men and women in the household (see Table A5.1). For non-electoral participation, only the relationship between political interest and non-electoral participation is marginally conditioned by gender (p = 0.085), with political interest having a larger correlation for men. In fact, the positive relationship between political interest and non-electoral participation is nullified for women: political interest is uncorrelated with women's non-electoral political participation and positively correlated with

---

[5] The relationship between political interest and participation is unaffected by the inclusion of the political knowledge index, suggesting a low correlation between these measures.

men's participation. The same is true to a larger and more statistically meaningful extent with vote autonomy: women who report an interest in politics are 11 percentage points less likely to have the most say over their vote than men who report an interest in politics. This provides strong evidence of the suppression of women's political inclinations within the household and inefficiencies in the determination of political participation. Unsurprisingly, gender also conditions the relationship between age and vote autonomy, with a stronger age gradient for men than women.

Even after controlling for inequalities in the costs and benefits to participation and intra-household power, women participate significantly and substantially less than the men in their households in non-electoral politics and have less autonomy over their vote choice but are no less likely to vote. This corroborates figures in Chapter 4 depicting a within-household gender gap in political agency, but further reveals that these gender gaps are not exclusively the result of intra-household bargaining and resource inequalities. Comparing the size of the coefficient on gender between the models in Table 5.1 that do and do not include these measures of resources and power demonstrates that a large portion of the gender gap in non-electoral participation and vote autonomy remains unexplained by these covariates. While it is possible that the remaining gender gap could be driven by other, unmeasured indicators of bargaining power and resources, it is unlikely that this would explain the remaining 34 percentage point difference in men's and women's political participation. Instead, the remaining differences in political behavior between women and men may be evidence of coercion and other difficult-to-measure forms or suppression.

Ultimately, Table 5.1 provides evidence in line with the existence of household political cooperation and in support of the hypothesis that, conditional on household political cooperation, those with the most power in the household have more say in political decisions and are more likely to participate in costlier, non-electoral forms of political participation. It also reveals, in multiple ways, how household political participation inefficiently allocates and potentially suppresses women's political action and agency.

AUTONOMY FROM THE HOUSEHOLD AND POLITICAL PARTICIPATION

I have additionally argued that women's political participation more broadly will correlate with their autonomy from the household. Table 5.2 tests this hypothesis by modeling the within-village correlates of voting and non-electoral participation and comparing the drivers of men's and women's political participation.

The puzzle of women's political participation is acutely clear in models 1 and 4 of Table 5.2: there is a large and significant gender gap in non-electoral

TABLE 5.2 *Household autonomy is a strong predictor of women's non-electoral political participation*

	Vote in National Election			Any Nonvoting Political Participation		
	All	Men	Women	All	Men	Women
	(1)	(2)	(3)	(4)	(5)	(6)
Female	-0.006			-0.326***		
	(0.019)			(0.030)		
Proportion of Political Network from Outside the Household	0.027	0.036	0.016	0.115***	0.034	0.108**
	(0.029)	(0.097)	(0.031)	(0.040)	(0.119)	(0.043)
Size of Political Discussion Network (Out-degree)	0.003	0.002	0.007	0.042***	0.042	0.039***
	(0.005)	(0.005)	(0.009)	(0.007)	(0.009)	(0.012)
Years of Education	0.001	0.005**	-0.002	0.007***	0.013***	0.001
	(0.002)	(0.002)	(0.003)	(0.003)	(0.004)	(0.004)
Political Knowledge Index	0.009	0.013	0.001	0.093***	0.088***	0.089***
	(0.009)	(0.012)	(0.015)	(0.014)	(0.019)	(0.020)
Personal Income (10,000s Rs.)	0.007**	0.000	0.0012**	-0.000	-0.010	0.014
	(0.004)	(0.005)	(0.005)	(0.006)	(0.007)	(0.009)
Perceived Share of Population Politically Gender Biased	-0.000	-0.000	-0.001	-0.001	-0.001	-0.000
	(0.000)	(0.001)	(0.001)	(0.001)	(0.001)	(0.001)
Interested in Politics	0.048***	0.028	0.069***	0.086***	0.118***	0.060**
	(0.015)	(0.019)	(0.022)	(0.022)	(0.034)	(0.030)
Bargaining Power Index	0.013	0.010	0.027*	0.032***	0.029*	0.038**
	(0.009)	(0.010)	(0.016)	(0.012)	(0.016)	(0.019)
HH Member with Most Bargaining Power Gender Biased	-0.011	-0.012	-0.008	-0.030	-0.002	-0.057
	(0.014)	(0.018)	(0.022)	(0.020)	(0.029)	(0.028)**
Age	0.006***	0.004***	0.007***	0.002***	0.002	0.002*
	(0.001)	(0.001)	(0.001)	(0.001)	(0.001)	(0.001)

Married	0.159***	0.226***	0.137***	0.027	0.085**	−0.014
	(0.026)	(0.038)	(0.036)	(0.029)	(0.043)	(0.040)
Scheduled Tribe	0.010	−0.011	0.019	−0.021	−0.032	−0.021
	(0.015)	(0.018)	(0.025)	(0.022)	(0.031)	(0.033)
Scheduled Caste	−0.003	−0.009	−0.005	0.058	−0.050	0.139*
	(0.042)	(0.049)	(0.063)	(0.055)	(0.079)	(0.072)
N	1,721	853	868	1,725	853	872
Dependent Variable Mean	0.89	0.92	0.86	0.48	0.73	0.24
Fixed Effects	Village	Village	Village	Village	Village	Village

Note: ***, **, * indicates significance at the 1 percent, 5 percent, and 10 percent levels, respectively. Robust standard errors are reported. Results are robust to clustering standard errors at the household-level (available on request). Data are from the census survey conducted in Villages A and B. All models include fixed effects as specified.

political participation (37 percentage points) and no gender gap in voter turnout. Importantly, this gender gap in non-electoral participation persists even after controlling for autonomy from the household, costs to participation, power in the household, and demographic characteristics. This suggests limited explanatory power of observable measures and cross-sectional variation for the gender gap in political participation. In Chapters 7 and 8, I consider interventions that shift the distribution of women's autonomy and take aim at this persistent gender gap.

Women's, though not men's, non-electoral participation is strongly associated with their autonomy from the household. Non-electoral political participation is expected to be higher for women in the village with larger political networks and a smaller share of their political network from their household (see models 3 and 6). Essentially, women are more likely to engage in non-electoral politics when they discuss politics outside of their households. Women whose entire political network is comprised of people outside of the household are 11 percentage points (or 45 percent) more likely to participate in non-electoral politics as compared to women whose entire political network is comprised of people inside of the household, holding the size of the network constant. The size and composition of women's political networks, however, do not correlate with voting. Furthermore, while the size of men's political networks is positively correlated with their non-electoral political participation, the household within those networks is statistically irrelevant for their behavior (see models 2 and 5). This is likely because men rarely report discussing politics within their households: 4 percent of men's political discussion ties are from their household as compared to 40 percent for women. Taken together, these results provide evidence for the importance of networks in non-electoral political behavior and the primacy of autonomy from the household for women's non-electoral political participation.

Women's political behavior, both voting and non-electoral political participation, is also correlated with their household bargaining power. The women in the village with greater bargaining power are significantly more likely to be politically active. This aligns with the expectation that bargaining power enables women's power in household decisions and potentially also limits their exposure to coercion if they can exit the household.

Further, while there is no distinguishable relationship between a woman's perceptions of gender bias in the community and her political participation, there is a negative relationship between the presence of a dominant household member who holds gender-biased attitudes and women's non-electoral political participation. Women in households where the most dominant household member (the one with the greatest bargaining power) reports beliefs that women should not participate in politics are 20 percent less likely to participate in non-electoral politics, though they show no difference in voting behavior.

The size of this relationship is the same as that of increasing a woman's bargaining power index by one point (i.e., gaining ownership over land or assets or joining the labor force) and as that of increasing the size of a woman's political network by one tie. Given the challenges of measuring coercion, this result provides suggestive evidence of the role of dominant household members in women's political decision-making.

Men's behavior also reflects patterns of patriarchal decision-making. Men's non-electoral political participation is significantly correlated with their bargaining power, marital status, and education. Not all men participate in politics; it is more commonly those with the greatest authority and power particularly in the household. In interviews, men also attributed their lack of political participation to being uneducated. When asked whether he attends the village assembly meeting, Kuldeep replied, "Yes, I sometimes do. But as I am illiterate, I don't understand much. If I were educated, I would have kept something in mind."[6] This is borne out in Table 5.2, as education is positively correlated with non-electoral political participation for men, though not for women.

Importantly, political interest is positively correlated with both men's and women's political participation, suggesting that political participation is, at least at a village level, more likely to be allocated among those who care about politics. Women who report an interest in politics are 6 percentage points (or 25 percent) more likely to participate in non-electoral politics.

It is also worth noting that caste category only marginally shapes political participation, and its effects are dwarfed by those of gender. Indicators of whether a respondent is a member of a Scheduled Caste (SC) or Scheduled Tribe (ST) are insignificant in all models, with the one exception that SC women are marginally more likely to participate in non-electoral politics than OBC/GC and ST women. There are no differences between ST and OBC/GC populations with respect to political participation, which is striking given these groups comprise 97 percent of the population of these villages. Table A5.2 reports the results of a fully saturated model, interacting indicators for SC and ST identity with all covariates. This table reveals that the correlates of political participation for both men and women are statistically identical when comparing ST and OBC/GC respondents. The one exception is that political knowledge has a larger relationship to voting for ST men and women. This provides strong evidence that, while a defining feature of society, caste category does not substantially differentiate the correlates of political participation in these communities.[7]

---

[6] Kuldeep (pseudonym), male, 36 years old, ST.

[7] Dynamics for SC respondents do differ from those of OBC/GC respondent; however, these results must be interpreted with caution, as the data include only twenty-six male and thirty-four female SC respondents.

To further evaluate the hypothesis that women's political participation is a function of their autonomy from the household, I compare the political behavior of women who have low versus high levels of autonomy from the household in Table 5.3. I categorize women as having high levels of autonomy if (1) the household comprises less than 42 percent of their political network (the average share for women reporting any political ties) and (2) they report discussing politics with at least one person. Table 5.3 estimates the correlates of women's electoral and non-electoral participation compared to other women in their village and reveals three main findings.

First, high-autonomy women are more likely to be politically active than low-autonomy women: the average rate of non-electoral participation is twice as high for high-autonomy women (34 percent versus 17 percent). As a further indication of the link between household autonomy and political participation for women, Figure A5.1 shows that women's participation in politics may increase after their husband dies: widows are more than five times more likely to attend village assembly meetings than similarly aged married women.[8]

Second, bargaining power and the gender attitudes of dominant men in the household significantly correlate with women's political behavior only for women who have low autonomy from the household. Low-autonomy women are more likely to participate in politics if (1) they have more bargaining power and (2) the person with the most bargaining power in their household does not express views against women's political participation. These results are in line with my theory of household cooperation, as bargaining power is expected to increase a woman's power in household decision-making and raise the costs to coercion, and gender-regressive attitudes held by the dominant household member are expected to proxy for possible coercion. As a result, these results indicate that women whose political lives are more centered on the household may politically participate when coercion is less likely. Political interest is also uncorrelated with participation for low-autonomy women.

Third, the two strongest predictors of non-electoral participation for high-autonomy women are the size of their political network and their interest in politics, implying that high-autonomy women are better able to translate their political interest into political participation. Even more, non-electoral participation is uncorrelated with power within the household for this group, suggesting that having autonomy from the household enables women's political participation even in more unequal household contexts. When you compare

---

[8] While substantively large, this difference is not statistically significant likely given the low number of widows in the data set (62). Married women in this figure are sampled to match this sample size and reflect a similar age distribution to widows.

TABLE 5.3 *Network size and political interest predict the political participation of women with high autonomy, while bargaining power predicts the political participation of women with low autonomy*

	Vote in National Election		Any Nonvoting Political Participation	
	Women	Women	Women	Women
	Low Autonomy	High Autonomy	Low Autonomy	High Autonomy
	(1)	(2)	(3)	(4)
Size of Political Discussion Network (Out-degree)	0.006 (0.014)	0.024 (0.015)	0.022 (0.015)	0.062 (0.024)**
Years of Education	−0.002 (0.004)	−0.005 (0.006)	−0.004 (0.005)	0.014 (0.008)*
Political Knowledge Index	0.007 (0.024)	−0.001 (0.022)	0.094 (0.026)***	0.070 (0.036)*
Personal Income (10,000s Rs.)	0.019 (0.009)**	0.003 (0.008)	0.024 (0.013)*	0.009 (0.017)
Perceived Share of Population Politically Gender Biased	−0.001 (0.001)	−0.002 (0.001)***	0.001 (0.001)	0.000 (0.001)
Interested in Politics	0.088 (0.033)***	0.026 (0.036)	0.024 (0.038)	0.112 (0.055)**
Bargaining Power Index	0.012 (0.023)	0.010 (0.023)	0.041 (0.022)*	−0.010 (0.040)
HH Member with Most Bargaining Power Gender Biased	0.016 (0.033)	−0.038 (0.033)	−0.096 (0.034)***	−0.021 (0.055)
Age	0.010 (0.001)***	0.004 (0.002)**	0.001 (0.001)	0.005 (0.003)**
Married	0.175 (0.048)***	0.063 (0.057)	−0.019 (0.044)	0.032 (0.094)
Scheduled Tribe	−0.016 (0.038)	0.048 (0.042)	−0.021 (0.042)	0.065 (0.062)
Scheduled Caste	−0.097 (0.105)	0.144 (0.048)***	0.119 (0.091)	0.274 (0.150)*
N	462	290	465	291
Dependent Variable Mean	0.82	0.91	0.17	0.34
FEs	Village	Village	Village	Village

Note: ***, **, * indicates significance at the 1 percent, 5 percent, and 10 percent levels, respectively. Robust standard errors are reported. Results are robust to clustering standard errors at the household-level (available on request). Data are from the census survey conducted in Villages A and B. All models include fixed effects as specified.

the determinants of non-electoral political participation for high-autonomy women (model 4 of Table 5.3) and the same for men (model 5 of Table 5.2), you see that they are nearly identical, i.e., the behavior of women with high levels of autonomy is similar in its determinants to that of men. The same cannot be said for women with low levels of autonomy.

DISCUSSION

In this chapter, I test the argument that, conditional on household cooperation, four variables predict women's degree of political participation – their bargaining power, male coercive power, their costs to and preferences for participation, and their autonomy from the household. Autonomy from the household emerges as a clear and significant predictor of women's non-electoral political participation. I show that women with limited autonomy from the household are less likely to participate in politics in between elections than men, and that their participation increases as their bargaining power rises and decreases as men's coercive authority escalates (having a gender-biased dominant male is associated with significantly lower political participation for women). Significantly, political interest is negatively correlated with women's political participation and positively correlated with men's political participation when comparing within households. Voting is largely uncorrelated with these characteristics. I further demonstrate that women with greater autonomy from the household are more likely to participate in politics in between elections than those with less autonomy, and that their participation is less defined by intra-household power dynamics. The political behavior of women with high levels of autonomy from the household is a function of the same characteristics as men's political behavior (network size, political interest, and education). More generally, non-electoral political participation is more likely for those in the household with attributes that lower the costs to political participation, as predicted.

The preponderance of evidence in this section is consistent with the existence of the institution of household political cooperation and supports my core argument that this institution constrains women's non-electoral political participation. Both intra-household resource inequalities, which manifest as inequalities in bargaining power and higher costs to participation, and coercion are evident as underlying this relationship. An important conclusion of these results is that both resources and norms matter for women's political participation but in a specific way: how they structure power within the household. Given the prevalence and resilience of patriarchal norms, these findings highlight that boosting women's inclusion should start by understanding the mechanisms to their autonomy from the household.

6

The Patriarchal Political Order

Networks and the Nature of Political Organization

What are the implications of household political cooperation for larger patterns of political organization? This chapter documents the political order built on household political cooperation and examines the broader implications of this order for women. To do so, I compare the structure and organization of men's and women's social and political ties using network data from the census survey of adults in two villages in rural Madhya Pradesh. Prior network studies have demonstrated how ethnicity is distributed across networks and examined its implications for political behavior,[1] but this work has largely overlooked gender differences in the nature of political connections. This chapter compares the size of men's and women's political networks, the gender homophily of political networks, the share of ties within the household, the centrality of men and women to the entire network, and the level of connectivity between individuals and political elites to reveal a politics marked by male power.

Village politics is structured around men with women existing largely on the periphery. Women have significantly fewer political ties than men, their ties are much more rooted in the household, and they are less central and less influential within the broader village network. Importantly, women's lack of political ties is not the result of their more general isolation, as they have more social connections than men. And men's political ties are almost exclusively with other (powerful) men. This pattern creates a broader political network with densely connected men as political insiders and sparsely connected women as political outsiders. Politics is, instead, organized around identities that are shared within households, but that stratify villages across households. Caste defines the structure of political connections in rural Madhya Pradesh.

---

[1] Larson and Lewis (2017).

The consequences of this gendered political organization are clear and acute. Women have less access to and lower levels of political information. Women are also perceived to be less influential in village politics and have less access to those with influence. Even the most well-connected women are but a fraction as central to the village network as the most well-connected men. And those well-connected women are better tied to men in their village than other women, supporting the idea that power comes from proximity to men. Influence and ties are more evenly distributed, however, across caste groups.

These findings highlight how women's relatively low rates of non-electoral political participation exist within, and are supported by, a broader order in which men capture political networks, political spaces, and – ultimately – political power. Investigating the contours of this political order is critical for understanding the pathways to women's political inclusion. Change on the margins is unlikely to yield widespread inclusion unless it addresses the broader political order that benefits from (and upholds) women's exclusion.

ANALYZING NETWORK DATA

Evaluating the role of networks and ties in shaping political behavior raises empirical challenges on two fronts. First, isolating the effect of having access to particular networks or additional ties requires parsing out the confounding effects that drive people to have those ties in the first place. Put another way, individuals select into networks for many reasons, and, for example, the types of women who have more political ties may be prone to political participation for reasons unrelated to their networks. Understanding how political ties encourage or discourage political participation therefore involves identifying variation in their ties that is uncorrelated with any other factor related to their selection into networks. Chapter 7 overcomes these methodological challenges by evaluating the effect of a program that arbitrarily expanded women's ties in some villages but not others. In this chapter, I instead describe and evaluate how men and women are distributed in village networks, and therefore do not examine what makes some men and women better connected than others. This chapter is therefore a descriptive exercise designed to understand the distribution of political relationships within rural villages.

The second empirical challenge associated with evaluating the importance of network ties for political behavior relates to measurement. The theory proposed in this book focuses on the role of an individual's political ties but also argues that the structure of a village network, particularly how gender is distributed in the network, affects the nature of gendered political participation. While an individual woman's ties are expected to affect her political participation (shown to be correlationally true in Chapter 5), so too does the broader structure of women's ties in the village network. A woman who has many ties in the community is expected to participate in politics more than one who is politically isolated, but the degree and kind of political participation are expected to be shaped by how many other women are connected – and with whom they are connected. This suggests that an empirical evaluation of the proposed theory must capture the attributes of both individual ties and the broader network.

Studies, like this one, that use surveys to measure interpersonal networks face a trade-off between the number of individuals surveyed and the number of networks surveyed.[2] Prior work has navigated this trade-off by (1) sampling a small number of individuals from a large number of networks,[3] (2) sampling a large number of individuals from a small number of networks,[4] or (3) sampling a large number of households, but only one individual from the household, from some intermediate number of networks.[5] When only some individuals from a network are surveyed, as in (1) and (3), the resulting data typically underrepresents women either due to difficulties in accessing them or a focus on heads of households (who are predominantly male). Measuring networks for only heads of households would distort network characteristics if these individuals are more connected or differ systematically from the general adult population. It also does not allow for an understanding of the role of the household in network relations – a factor I have argued is critical in an evaluation of women's political behavior. It is therefore difficult to accurately evaluate women's ties – particularly to understand how the potentially conflicting identities of being both a woman and a member of a household interact to shape their political behavior.

To capture the complexity of women's political relationships, and to explore how gender operates within political networks, this chapter draws on data from the census survey administered to all adults in two villages in Madhya Pradesh. These are the same data analyzed in Chapters 4 and 5, but instead of focusing on the distribution of power and participation within households, here I look at the distribution of power and participation across the entire village network.

I again leverage responses to a series of name-generator questions that asked respondents to list up to five people from their village with whom they socialize and with whom they discuss politics. Respondents were also asked to name up to five people from their village with whom they discuss economic matters, who influence their political beliefs, who they influence politically, who they believe voted similarly, and with whom they have jointly acted by either attending a public meeting together or approaching a government official together. Additionally, respondents were asked to identify the most influential people in the village and indicate whether they had been in contact with them in the past year.

---

[2] Studies of online networks, for example, do not necessarily face this trade-off or require surveys to map the network.

[3] See, for example, Alatas et al. (2016); Baldassarri (2015); Banerjee et al. (2013); Jackson, Rodriguez-Barraquer, and Tan (2012).

[4] See, for example, Larson and Lewis (2017).

[5] See, for example, Gulzar, Khan, and Sonnet (2020).

THE NATURE OF POLITICAL ORGANIZATION

Identities can structure network relations in many ways with different implications for the flow of information and potential for coordination within and across identities. For example, as Miguel and Gugerty suggest, when ties are denser within ethnic groups, we would expect to see greater coordination around those ethnicities.[6] Figure 6.1 uses simulated data to present three possible network structures in line with different ways in which identity can shape network ties. In these graphs, each circle, called a node, represents one person within the network. Nodes are shaded based on their identity group. The lines between nodes, known as edges, reflect ties between two individuals, and the arrows at the ends of each edge denote the direction of the tie (who reports being connected to whom). For example, if one person reports a tie with another person, the two nodes representing those two people will be connected by an edge with an arrow depicting it is the first person who reported the tie. The more edges radiating from a node, the larger the size of that node's network.

Panel A of Figure 6.1 depicts a network where two identity groups are enmeshed and connected to each other. Based on visual inspection, identity does not obviously structure this network, as nearly all members from identity group A are connected to members from identity group B in roughly the same proportion as they are connected to members from identity group A. Neither identity group is visually more central (having more edges or linking many other nodes together). On the other hand, Panel B represents a network where identity group B is visually more central than identity group A. Members of group A are connected to others in the network only through their ties to members of group B (closer to what is known as a star network). Members of group B have more connections in general than members of group A, and it would take fewer steps to reach any other node in the network (in common parlance, they have fewer degrees of separation from everyone else in the network). One implication of a network structured like this is that for information to reach a member of group A, it must flow through members of group B. Finally, Panel C shows a network where identity groups A and B are better connected with members of their own group than members of the other group and the two identity groups are only connected through a few key nodes (closer to what is known as a bowtie network). This network structure more closely resembles Miguel and Gugerty's description of Kenyan networks, where ethnic groups had dense ties with each other but few connections with members of other ethnic groups. Here, we would expect information to flow more easily within identity groups than across.

---

[6] Miguel and Gugerty (2005). See also Larson and Lewis (2017) for an empirical test of this hypothesis.

(a) Hypothetical network 1 (mesh)

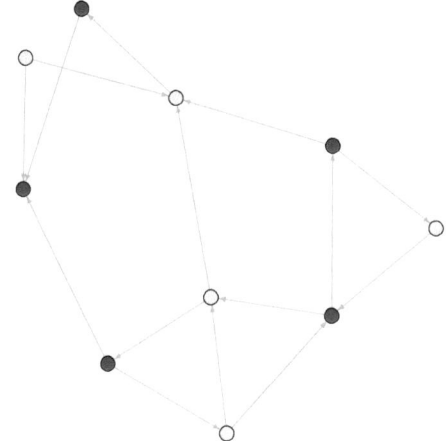

(b) Hypothetical network 2 (star)

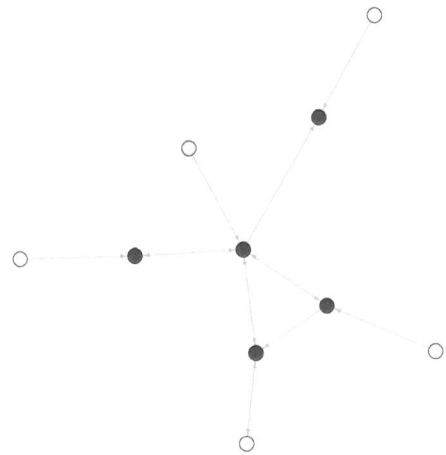

(c) Hypothetical network 3 (bowtie)

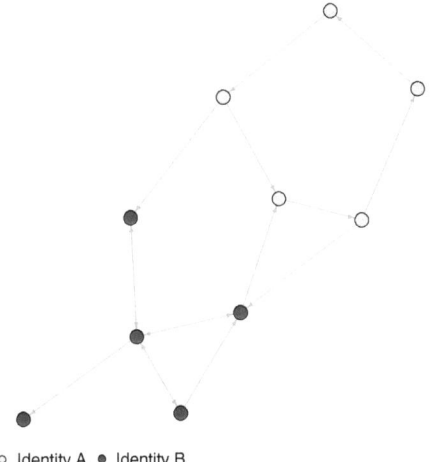

○ Identity A ● Identity B

FIGURE 6.1 Simulated hypothetical network structures

I have argued that household political cooperation leaves women's political ties concentrated in the household to a greater extent than men. As a result, we would expect village political networks where men are well connected to each other and central and women are connected largely through the men in their households. This would most closely resemble the simulated network in Panel B of Figure 6.1, where identity group B represents men and identity group A represents women. The implications of such a network are that information would flow through men, and men, given their centrality and the greater density of their within-group ties, would be better able to coordinate as a group.

To explore whether gender is distributed in village political networks in line with this expectation, Figure 6.2 visualizes the political discussion connections of Indian villagers in Village B.[7] In this graph, each node is a surveyed resident of the village, and each edge indicates when one node reports discussing politics with another. This network is directed, meaning that connections can be unreciprocated: an individual can report being connected to someone who does not in turn report being connected to them. The direction of the connection is denoted with an arrow.

I draw four conclusions from this network map. First, men are much more central to the broader village political network, as evidenced by their tight cluster in the center of the graph and the greater density of reciprocal nodes. Second, women are much more dispersed than men throughout the political network, and many women appear to have nonreciprocal ties. The density of ties between women appears to be lower than the density of ties between men. Third, there are, however, two important deviations from this pattern: a small cluster of women in the top left and one in the bottom right of the political network map that are largely disconnected from the central cluster of mostly male nodes and where a few women are densely connected to each other. This suggests that there are women who engage politically with other women, but also these few politically connected women remain "outsiders" to more central, male-dominated village networks. Fourth, there are many isolates – nodes not connected to any other nodes – in Village B's political network, indicating a nontrivial share of both men and women who report that they discuss politics with no one.

The first two suggest that the way gender is distributed in this village's political network most closely resembles the star network in Panel B of Figure 6.1. These patterns align with the implications of household political cooperation, which is expected to yield male authority and political centrality and tie women to politics largely through the men in their household. Importantly, the third conclusion – that a few clusters of politically connected

---

[7] Villages A and B were randomly sampled from the set of villages surveyed in 2016. I do not include a network map of Village A, as its population is too large to permit a clear map of connections, but the broad patterns hold, as shown later in the chapter. Village names are anonymized for respondent confidentiality.

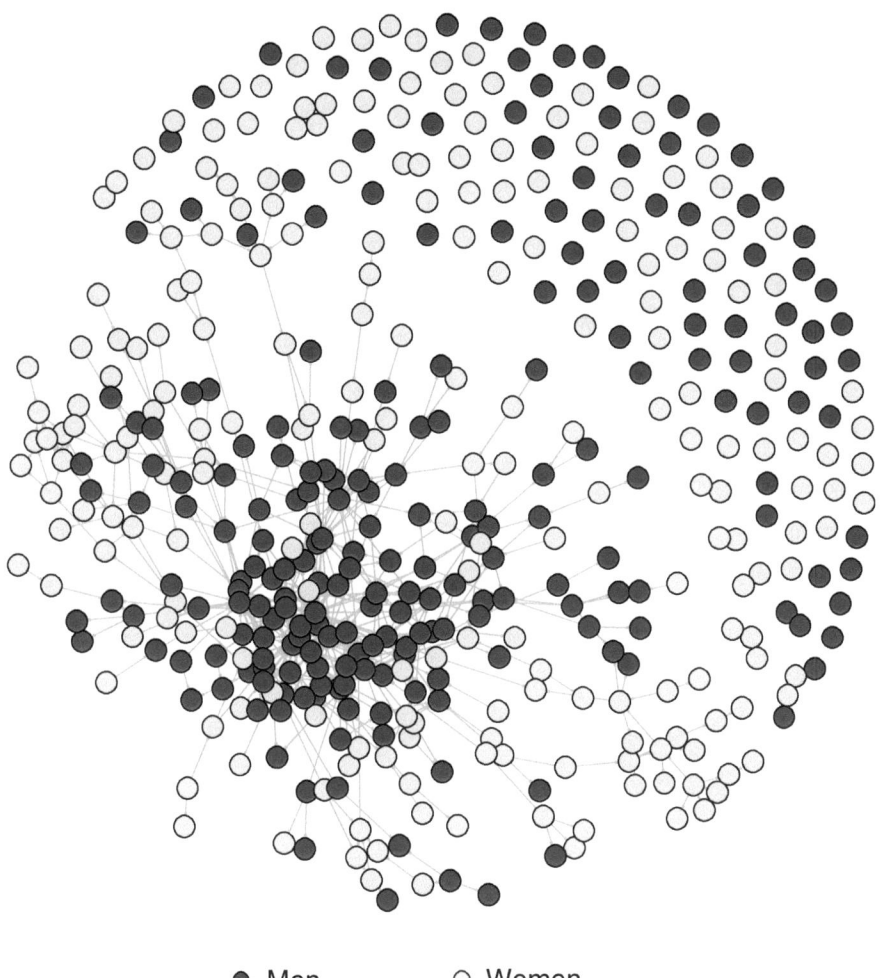

● Men   ○ Women

FIGURE 6.2 Village B's political discussion network is centered around men
Note: The figure plots the political discussion network in Village B, differentiating nodes by gender. Data are from the census survey conducted in Village B. The network map removes survey nonrespondents for ease of interpretation.

women exist – suggests that some women are able to operate outside of their households and that doing so is associated with dense ties among only women. The consequence of this is relegation to the periphery.

Is this simply a function of women's social isolation, or does gender impact women's political lives in distinct ways? To answer this, I compare the distribution of gender in Village B's political network (see Figure 6.2) with the same in its social network (see Figure 6.3). In contrast to the political network, in the social network, men and women both appear to be well connected, and neither

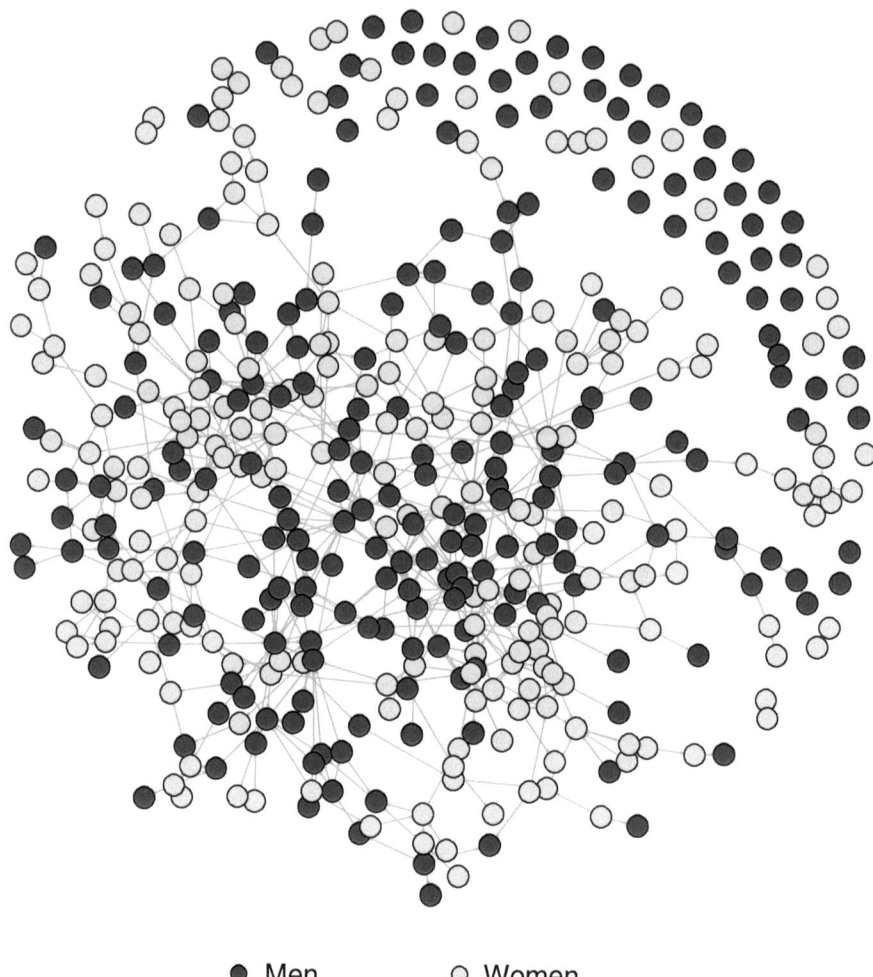

● Men   ○ Women

FIGURE 6.3 Women and men are dispersed in Village B's social network
Note: The figure plots the social network in Village B, differentiating nodes by gender. Data are from the census survey conducted in Village B. The network map removes survey nonrespondents for ease of interpretation.

gender emerges as being particularly central. Gender is more dispersed in this network and does not visually define the network structure. Village B's social network more closely resembles the network structure in Panel A of Figure 6.1. Women appear to have as many social ties as men, but these ties do not translate into political ties, suggesting that the way that gender structures the political network is not merely a function of women's more general isolation and attachment to the household.

Another implication of household political cooperation is that politics is expected to be structured around identities shared at the household level, such as caste in the Indian context. Figure 6.4 evaluates the distribution of caste category in the political network in Village B, a village that is largely comprised of people from Other Backward Classes (OBC) and Schedule Tribes (ST). OBC dominance is evident in the map of Village B's political network: they populate much of the center of the political network, though there are many central ST nodes as well. Unlike gender, though, caste category quite strikingly structures the political network in Village B. Political connections are densely concentrated among members of the same caste category. The distribution of caste category more closely resembles the bowtie network in Panel C of Figure 6.1 and aligns with findings from many other studies that show that members of ethnic groups are densely connected with each other and disconnected from members of other ethnic groups.[8] In fact, the two clusters of well-connected women shown in Figure 6.2 are exclusively caste category homogeneous, with that in the top left comprised of only OBC women and that in the bottom right comprised of only ST women. Figure 6.4 provides clear evidence that caste category organizes politics in this village and is in line with the expectation that, with household political cooperation, identities shared at a household level yield denser political ties than those shared within households.

Network and graph theory provides a set of tools to evaluate these visual inferences by providing measures of both node (individual) and network characteristics. Four measures, two describing the attributes of particular nodes and two describing the structural features of a network, are particularly useful when evaluating whether men's and women's positions differ within a network.[9]

At the node level, an individual node's degree is the number of connections (edges) a node has to other nodes in the network: out-degree is the number of nodes the individual reports being connected to, and in-degree is the number of nodes that report being connected to the individual. An individual's centrality to the network (how important they are to the network) is measured in two ways. Eigenvector centrality measures the influence of an individual node in a network by assigning greater weight to nodes that are connected to other central or important nodes and is measured as eigenvalues. Betweenness centrality measures an individual node's influence in a network based on the extent to which it connects or lies between other nodes. It is measured as the number of shortest paths between the other nodes in the network that pass through the individual node. Betweenness centrality suggests that other nodes may be dependent on more central nodes for access to information or resources.

---

[8] Fearon and Laitin (1996); Larson and Lewis (2017).
[9] Ward, Stovel, and Sacks (2011) summarize the basics of applied network analysis and its history in political science.

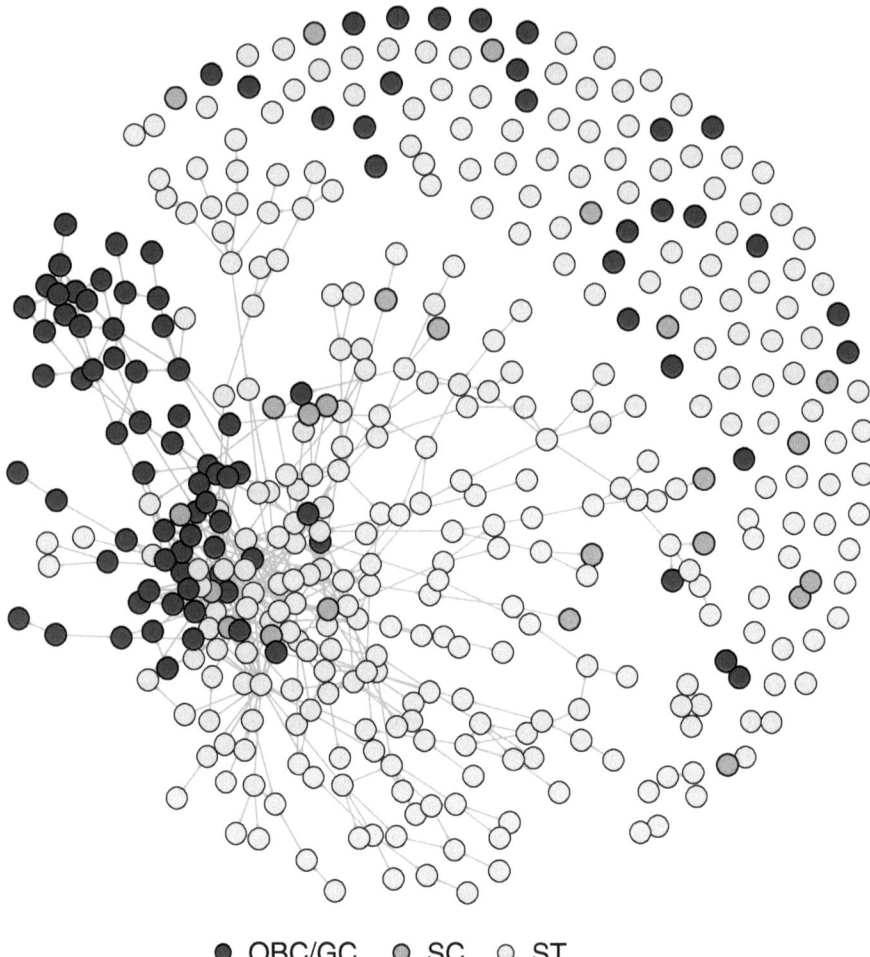

● OBC/GC   ● SC   ○ ST

FIGURE 6.4 Village B's political discussion network is divided by caste category
Note: The figure plots the political discussion network in Village B, differentiating nodes by caste category. Data are from the census survey conducted in Village B. The network map removes survey nonrespondents and those who do not report caste category for ease of interpretation.

At the network level, a network's density is the proportion of potential connections in the network that are actual connections. Denser networks are assumed to permit greater information transmission and sanctioning capacity.[10] A network's reciprocity evaluates the likelihood that nodes in a directed network both report being tied to each other.

---

[10] However, Larson and Lewis (2017) show that less dense and more heterogeneous networks facilitate greater information transmission.

Table 6.1 reports measures of these attributes for the political networks in Villages A and B for the entire adult population of each village (1,357 and 491, respectively). The differences in population size allow for a comparison of network structure and women's position within networks in both a relatively small village and a relatively large one. However, the majority of the analysis will compare across individuals within each network as opposed to comparing networks across villages.

Political networks in these villages are quite sparse (as shown in the low density scores in Table 6.1), meaning that very few of the potential connections are reported as actual connections. Additionally, there are low levels of reciprocity between ties: only 9 percent of ties in Village A and 6 percent of those in Village B are reciprocated, meaning both nodes report being connected to each other. Both of these characteristics imply that information flows are quite constrained in these communities.

Men's and women's political connections and position in the village political network differ significantly and in important ways. Women have significantly fewer political connections than men: in both villages, women have one to two fewer political ties than men on average.[11] Women also have less influence in both village's networks than men based on two measures of centrality. In fact, of the top twenty most central individuals in Village A's and Village B's political discussion networks, only three are women in each village with respect to betweenness centrality; only eight are women in Village A, and none are women in Village B when measured using eigenvector centrality.

Caste category, on the other hand, only marginally differentiates network ties. OBC and GC populations do have more political ties and greater centrality in the village political network on average, though these differences are not statistically significant. While centrality is not statistically different across caste groups on average, our qualitative fieldwork suggests that caste importantly shaped political influence. Before administering the survey in these villages, my research team conducted a series of qualitative case studies in each village to understand village dynamics. This involved compiling a list of the most influential and politically powerful members of the village through conversations with a diverse set of village residents. Political influence and power, as defined through these qualitative interviews, were disproportionately skewed in favor of male OBC residents. In Village A, roughly 70 percent of those named as most

---

[11] Women are also less likely to participate in civic groups. Figure A6.1 displays clear gender disparities in associational group participation, which represent community members' institutionalized connections. More than half of the adult men in both villages reported belonging to at least one civil society group, compared to less than one-fifth of women (a 32 percentage point difference). Figure A6.2 demonstrates the validity of these conclusions from the sample of seventy-six villages in Madhya Pradesh surveyed in 2016 and, by comparing spouses, shows that associational membership is distributed unequally among men and women even within the same household.

TABLE 6.1 *Women have fewer political ties and are less central to the village network*

	Village A		Village B	
Total Nodes	1,357		491	
Total Links	1,830		563	
Density	0.001		0.002	
Reciprocity	0.087		0.057	
	Men	Women	Men	Women
Average Degree	3.686	1.985	3.118	1.863
Average Eigenvector Centrality	0.012	0.005	0.021	0.000
Average Betweenness Centrality	1130	334	98	22
	OBC/GC	ST	OBC/GC	ST
Average Degree	3.078	2.687	3.170	2.437
Average Eigenvector Centrality	0.010	0.008	0.019	0.009
Average Betweenness Centrality	836	665	79	55

Note: The table reports attributes for the political discussion network by gender and caste category in two villages. Data are from the census survey conducted in Villages A and B. The network is defined at the village level, and respondents were asked to name up to five individuals from their village, including family members, with whom they discuss politics. Bolded numbers signal a statistically significant difference at the 5 percent level across groups with p-values calculated from a simple t-test for the difference in means across gender or caste groups. Density is the proportion of all potential connections that are actualized. Reciprocity is the proportion of all connections that are reciprocated. Degree is defined as the total number of connections for a given node. Eigenvector centrality measures the influence of a particular node, giving greater weight to nodes that are connected to other nodes. Betweenness centrality also measures the influence of a particular node but gives higher weight to nodes that connect many other nodes.

influential were OBC, and the remaining 30 percent were ST, even though OBC residents comprise only 42 percent of the village population and ST residents make up 51 percent. In Village B, 38 percent of those named as most influential were OBC, and 58 percent were ST; the village population is 21 percent and 69 percent, respectively. Few, however, were women.

In addition to comparing the average size and centrality of women's and men's networks, we can also compare the composition of their networks. Table 6.2 reports the average network size and composition of political discussion networks for women and men. Reported averages combine responses from both villages and focus only on the composition of nodes named by respondents.

On average, women report speaking with 1.34 others about politics, compared to 1.76 for men. Each man is, on average, named as a political discussion tie by 1.92 others, while each woman is on average named by only 0.81 others. These results reflect both gendered differences in access to political discussion partners as well as gendered differences in the conceptualization of what constitutes political discussion. Since men view politics as more pervasive and

TABLE 6.2 *Women's political networks are caste homogeneous but gender heterogeneous*

	Political Network	
	Men	Women
Degree: Number of Ties	3.674	2.139
Out-degree: Number of Ties	1.755`	1.333
In-degree: Number of Ties in	1.919	0.806
Age	41.543	38.392
Years of Education	7.084	4.356
% Women	0.025	0.638
% Coethnic	0.735	0.905
% General Category	0.007	0.013
% Other Backward Class	0.490	0.341
% Scheduled Caste	0.010	0.020
% Scheduled Tribe	0.474	0.615

Note: The table reports the average composition of men's and women's political ties. Data are from the census survey conducted in Villages A and B. All percentages are relative to the total number of nodes out reported (i.e., out-degree). Statistics in bold denote that the difference in means across men and women from a simple t-test is statistically significant at the 0.05 level.

less practical, the set of people with whom they could potentially discuss politics is much larger. Women, by contrast, see politics as pragmatic, and so may be only likely to discuss politics with those who would align with their practical needs.

Table 6.2 further shows that men almost never report discussing politics with women. Men's reported political discussion networks are comprised of only 2.5 percent of women on average. Women have much more gender-diverse networks. Women's reported political discussion networks are comprised of 64 percent women, showing that they politically engage with both women and men. Importantly, this suggests that men do not report reciprocity of ties with women, meaning that women state that they speak with men about politics, but men do not report speaking with women about politics. Women thus believe they are more connected to men than men believe they are connected to women.

Finally, politics is clearly organized around caste category. Both men's and women's political networks exhibit a high degree of homophily with respect to ethnicity: 91 percent of those with whom women discuss politics and 74 percent of those with whom men discuss politics are coethnics, meaning from the same caste category. The greater propensity for women to be connected to coethnics seems to derive from their lower likelihood of discussing politics with OBC community members and greater likelihood of doing so with ST community members. In part, this is because households are almost always coethnics; women's greater ties to the household imply a greater representation of coethnics within their networks.

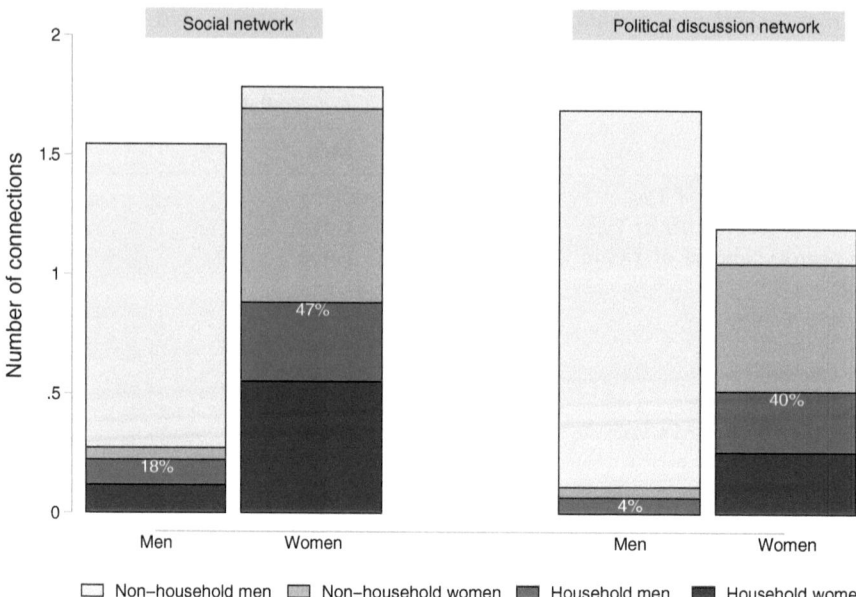

FIGURE 6.5 The household comprises a significantly larger share of women's networks than men's

Note: The figure plots the average network size for men and women across networks of people with whom they socialize and discuss politics. Shades differentiate the gender and household composition of these networks. Data are from the census survey conducted in Villages A and B.[12]

While the connection between ethnic ties and household ties may be implied, it has important consequences for women's access to influence. As I noted earlier, our qualitative work revealed the differential patterns of influence across caste communities, and specifically the disproportionate dominance of OBC populations in village politics. Since men are more likely to be connected to OBC residents, they are also more likely to be connected to influential nodes of the network. Additionally, the dominance of the household in women's networks, and its implications for the ethnic homogeneity of their networks, imply that caste-based interests are likely to receive greater discussion, salience, and representation.

The importance of the household in women's political discussion networks is made even clearer in Figure 6.5, which plots the household and gender composition of reported social and political ties for men and women. It differentiates between ties inside and outside the household by gender to highlight compositional differences in networks across men and women.

---

[12] Village names are anonymized to protect respondent confidentiality.

I include social ties as a useful comparison to understand whether the reported patterns are simply reflective of women's overall isolation or whether political ties are distinct.

A substantially greater share of women's than men's ties across both networks are from within the household: 47 percent of women's social ties are from the household, compared to only 18 percent of men's ties. This difference is starker for political networks: 40 percent of women's reported political ties, but only 4 percent of men's, are from the household. The household is a key political domain for women, but does not even register as a locus of political discussion for men. In describing whom he speaks to about the village, Ram Singh stated, "I chat with people with whom I have a brotherhood."[13]

Women report much more gender diversity in their networks than men, yet this derives almost exclusively from ties within the household: women report spending time with and discussing politics equally with the men and women in their household but generally only with other women outside of their household. Men report being tied to very few women inside or outside the household, particularly with respect to political discussion. Network size and composition are also largely similar across caste categories, and the household comprises a substantially larger share of women's networks across all caste groups (see Figure A6.1).

Finally, while women report larger social networks than men, they discuss politics with substantially fewer people on average. Men, by contrast, discuss politics with more people on average than they spend time socializing. These findings suggest a surprising puzzle: women have as many (if not more) social ties than men, but substantially fewer political ties. Why do women's social connections not foster political discussion and political connections? Two additional facts about the nature of men's and women's ties help elucidate this puzzle.

First, there is little overlap between individuals' social and political networks: only 20 percent of men's and 27 percent of women's political ties are also reported as social ties. This suggests that political and social networks are quite distinct; people do not report discussing politics with those they socialize with.

Second, women have fewer political ties than men partly because women are less likely to be seen as belonging to others' political networks. On average, women report discussing politics with fewer people than men (out-degree), and fewer people report discussing politics with women than with men (in-degree). However, the difference between the average in-degree for men and women is substantially larger than the difference in the average out-degree. In Village A, the average political in-degree is 0.827 for women and 1.998 for men, yielding a difference of 1.171. Yet the average political out-degree is 1.167 for women

---

[13] Ram singh (pseudonym), male, 45 years old, ST.

and 1.697 for men (a difference of 0.53). This means that while men discuss politics with 0.53 more people than women on average, others report discussing politics with 1.171 more men than women. Put simply, women believe they are more connected to men than vice versa, which suggests that women are less valued as political discussion partners than men.

These discrepancies may be partly attributed to the different ways in which men and women conceptualize politics and, therefore, political discussion. As described in Chapter 4, men described politics as factionalism, partisanship, and competition for power, while women described politics as service delivery and the catering to local needs. Women, in interviews, stated that political discussion is largely practical, targeted at clear goals and needs, while men considered it to be more conceptual, ranging from debating beliefs and interests to strategizing and coalition building to more regularized conversations about village happenings. Differences in the way that men and women conceptualize politics and its role in their daily lives likely shape who they see as part of their political network and when they deem regular interactions to be political interactions.

The broader structure of political ties in these villages provides strong evidence of a patriarchal political order – a political order structured around the household (and shared household identities) and that relegates women to the periphery. Women are less politically connected than men, report more connections to men and to the household, and, as a result, are less central to the village network than men. Men are densely connected with other men, generally other men from their caste group, and largely fail to register women as political actors. Given that network ties have been shown to shape access to information and the ability to coordinate with others,[14] the implications of this organization of politics are vast. Not only do men have more power in the household (as shown in Chapter 4), this evidence suggests that men have more power in their communities and are likely able to wield this power to entrench their political authority. The impacts of this organization of politics, and the mechanisms through which this organization of politics may perpetuate a patriarchal political order, are discussed next.

BROADER IMPACTS OF THE STRUCTURE OF POLITICAL ORGANIZATION

Access to Political Information

Within the social networks literature, a key benefit of larger networks is greater access to information.[15] Given that it is costly to acquire information about politics, network ties can help reduce the individual costs of obtaining such

---

[14] Sinclair (2012).   [15] Huckfeldt and Sprague (1987); Huckfeldt (2007).

information.[16] Individuals with more political ties are therefore expected to be more knowledgeable about the political process and the challenges associated with navigating it. In addition, the greater the heterogeneity within an individual's set of ties, the more likely they are to have access to new and diverse information.[17] Women's large share of ties within the household imply that their access to political information may be limited. If most of women's information about politics comes through members of their household, they are both less likely to have access to important information and even more likely to abide by the interests of others in the household, as they know little else. The control of information is, therefore, one potential mechanism through which men can perpetuate their political dominance in the patriarchal political order.

This yields the expectation that women will have less political information than men and that political information will be positively correlated with the size of a person's network and the share of that network outside of the household. To explore these hypotheses, census survey respondents were asked three questions related to their knowledge of the political system: (1) do they know how to submit an application to the local government, (2) was the local government chairperson seat reserved for a woman in the last local election, and (3) how many days of work are guaranteed by the Mahatma Gandhi Employment Guarantee Scheme (MGNREGS).[18] Responses to these questions were coded as being either correct or not; "don't know" responses were included as incorrect responses. The last row of Table 6.3 presents the mean averages of these measures: 47 percent of all respondents stated they knew how to file an application, 69 percent correctly provided the reservation status of the chairperson seat, and only 27 percent correctly stated that the MGNREGS program guarantees 100 days of paid work. In addition, these three measures were summed to determine the total number of questions correctly answered by a respondent (1.43 on average).

Table 6.3 evaluates the relationship between an individual's network characteristics and political information by correlating the size of men's and women's political networks, the share of the household within that network, and their network centrality with the four measures of political knowledge. All models include village fixed effects to compare respondents within a given village network, and robust standard errors are reported, though results are robust to clustering standard errors at the household-level.[19] Additional

[16] Krishna (2002a); McClurg (2003); Chandra (2007); Sinclair (2012).   [17] Alatas et al. (2016).
[18] MGNREGS is an Indian labor law that guarantees every citizen 100 days of work each year on government workfare programs. It is the largest social security program in the world, and is heavily utilized by equal numbers of male and female rural residents. Therefore, we would expect that, if information about the program was purely a function of participation, there would be little or no difference in responses across genders (Narayan and Das 2014).
[19] Results are available on request.

TABLE 6.3 *Women, those with less education, and those with smaller political networks have less knowledge of politics*

	Knowledge: N Correct			Know How to File Application			Know Reservation Status			Know MGNREGS Rules		
	(1)	(2)	(3)	(4)	(5)	(6)	(7)	(8)	(9)	(10)	(11)	(12)
Female	-0.643*** (0.040)	-0.501*** (0.040)	-0.451*** (0.048)	-0.299*** (0.022)	-0.203*** (0.022)	-0.191*** (0.028)	-0.140*** (0.022)	-0.125*** (0.023)	-0.094*** (0.028)	-0.204*** (0.021)	-0.173*** (0.022)	-0.167*** (0.026)
Years of Education		0.064*** (0.005)	0.061*** (0.005)		0.043*** (0.003)	0.042*** (0.003)		0.007** (0.003)	0.006 (0.003)		0.014*** (0.003)	0.013*** (0.003)
Degree of Political Discussion Network			0.023*** (0.005)			0.008 (0.002)***			0.004 (0.001)***			0.011 (0.002)***
% of Political Network from Household			-0.060 (0.080)			-0.006 (0.043)			-0.072 (0.046)			0.018 (0.037)
Rank of Political Discussion Centrality			-0.004 (0.018)			-0.002 (0.010)			0.008 (0.011)			-0.010 (0.010)
N	1,725	1,725	1,725	1,725	1,725	1,725	1,725	1,725	1,725	1,725	1,725	1,725
Dep. Variable Mean	1.43	1.43	1.43	0.47	0.47	0.47	0.69	0.69	0.69	0.27	0.27	0.27
Fixed Effects	Village	Village	Village	Village	Village	Village	Village	Village	Village	Village	Village	Village

Note: The table reports the correlation between gender, education, political network characteristics and political knowledge. Data are from the census survey conducted in Villages A and B. ***, **, * indicates significance at the 1 percent, 5 percent, and 10 percent levels, respectively. Village fixed effects are included, and robust standard errors are reported. All models include covariates for age, caste category, marital status, and employment status.

correlates of political knowledge, such as caste category, age, marital status, and employment status, are included but not shown.

Table 6.3 yields three key insights. First, there is a large and significant gender gap in political knowledge. We can compare the size of the coefficient on the indicator for being female across the three models with different controls to determine the extent to which this gender gap is driven by gendered inequalities in the included covariates (education and networks). Without accounting for any other attributes, women were 30 percentage points less likely to state that they knew how to file an application than men (model 4). This drops to 20 percentage points after accounting for differences in the underlying distribution of education (model 5), which suggests that gender inequalities in education partly underlie but do not fully explain gender inequalities in political knowledge. This gender gap in knowledge of filing an application drops to 19 percentage points once political network characteristics are accounted for. Similar patterns attain across all domains of political knowledge. There is a large gender gap in political knowledge that is related to underlying gendered differences in both education and political network characteristics (education is more important), but this gap persists and is large even after accounting for education and networks.

Second, the size of a respondent's political network is positively and significantly correlated with political knowledge. This size of this correlation is largest for knowledge of the MGNREGS program and self-reported knowledge of how to file applications with local governments. The bureaucratic processes associated with non-electoral political participation in rural India are complicated. The larger relationship between network size and knowledge of more bureaucratic systems suggests that political networks may facilitate the gathering of information needed to navigate these opaque structures. For knowledge of the rules of MGNREGS and the reservation status of the elected official in the last election, the size of the coefficient on political network size is almost as large as that for years of education; discussing politics with one additional person has a similar impact on political knowledge as an additional year of education.

Finally, the household share of a respondent's political network and their overall network centrality within the broader political discussion network are uncorrelated with political knowledge. Network size, rather than composition, is more predictive of political knowledge. This suggests that, conditional on network size, women (and men) are not punished with respect to political knowledge for having a greater concentration of the household as political discussion ties. Overall, these findings suggest a positive relationship between political network size and political knowledge, but gender inequalities in network characteristics and education explain only some of the prevalent and large gender inequalities in political information.

Access to Influence

By conferring access to influential nodes, networks can shape which individuals are able to make their voices heard and who is considered the most important to target when mobilizing electoral support.[20] This is particularly important in patronage democracies, where ties to political elites and entrepreneurs can manifest in direct material gains.[21] The gendered nature of political networks, and particularly women's status as political outsiders, may therefore preclude their access to influence (and thus key material resources) and reify men's political dominance.[22]

It is difficult to measure influence and access to it. I have discussed one measure of influence – network centrality – which captures the density of an individual's network ties. Centrality in these political networks is gendered, and men are significantly more likely to be central than women, meaning they have denser ties and fewer degrees of separation from others in the network. Men's greater centrality has implications for their ability to coordinate with others to achieve their desired wishes, make demands on key nodes, and gain valuable political information.

Here I explore two additional conceptions of influence. First, I look at subjective reporting by respondents of who has influence over their everyday beliefs and behaviors. Respondents were asked to separately name up to five members of their village, including household members, who (1) influence the respondent's political beliefs and (2) are politically influenced by the respondent. The only cue provided to respondents regarding how to conceptualize influence came from the following sentence read prior to requesting the list of names: "Sometimes when we talk to people about politics, they can change how we see issues and influence our beliefs." These measures, therefore, likely capture influence in everyday interactions and are more akin to evaluating the capacity for coordination (social pressure). They do not necessarily equate influence with power in village politics; those who influence an individual's day-to-day life may not be those with the most power to influence village outcomes.

Second, I more explicitly measure the influence that is likely related to political power by identifying those within the village network who shape overall village outcomes. Respondents were asked to name up to five people in the village who they believe are the most influential and were then asked to identify whether they had spoken with any of them in the last year. The Hindi

[20] Rosenstone and Hansen (1993).

[21] Brusco, Nazareno, and Stokes (2004); Stokes (2005); Chandra (2007); Nichter (2008); Kitschelt and Wilkinson (2007); Stokes et al. (2013); Auerbach (2016); Larreguy, Marshall, and Querubin (2016); Auerbach and Thachil (2017); Bussell (2019).

[22] Lizzeri and Persico (2004) and Rueda (2005) provide examples of how the inclusion or exclusion of political outsiders can shape the direction of policy either in favor of or against outsiders' preferences.

version of this question used two different words for influence (शक्तिशाली और प्रभाशाली) meaning powerful and influential to signal that this was asking about village authority. Since these are subjectively identified influential people, this should be a conservative measure of access to influence.

Respondents were then read a list of previously identified village leaders (including equal numbers of men and women) and asked whether they would feel comfortable approaching that person if they had a problem. Village leaders were identified through a series of qualitative interviews conducted by the research team in the weeks preceding the survey. Small focus groups were conducted in each hamlet of the village, and respondents were asked to name the most influential men and women in the village. From the set of unique names provided, seven names were randomly sampled in Village A, and eight names were randomly sampled in Village B, evenly stratifying on gender. Only seven names were sampled in Village A because only three female names were elicited (an indication in and of itself of women's limited political influence in a village with an adult population of 1,357). Ties to the same set of names was asked of every respondent in the village. As an objectively identified measure of access to influence, we would expect to see lower rates of reported ties.

Looking first at individual-level influence over day-to-day lives, Table 6.4 presents the number of people respondents reported that they influence as well

TABLE 6.4 *Women have less influence over others*

	Influences Me		I Influence	
	Men	Women	Men	Women
Degree: Number of Ties	2.321	1.197	**1.532**	**0.338**
Out-degree: Number of Ties	1.032	0.803	**0.787**	**0.194**
In-degree: Number of Ties	1.290	0.394	**0.746**	**0.144**
Age	45.055	41.320	39.331	37.847
Years of Education	7.010	5.505	**6.942**	**5.026**
% Women	0.019	0.481	**0.032**	**0.764**
% From Household	0.049	0.256	**0.089**	**0.244**
% Coethnic	0.767	0.825	0.751	0.842
% General Category	0.005	0.010	0.011	0.024
% Other Backward Class	0.479	0.453	0.433	0.572
% Scheduled Caste	0.005	0.017	0.026	0.019
% Scheduled Tribe	0.503	0.512	0.510	0.385

Note: The table reports the average composition of men's and women's influence networks. Data are from the census survey conducted in Villages A and B. All percentages are relative to the total number of nodes out reported (i.e., out-degree). Statistics in bold denote that the difference in means across men and women from a simple t-test is statistically significant at the 0.05 level.

as the number of people they believe influence them alongside the characteristics of these ties. Women report being influenced by substantially fewer people (0.8 vs. 1.03 for men) and having less influence over others than men (0.19 vs. 0.79 for men). Women have less influence over men than vice versa. Comparing the gender composition of influence networks reveals that men do not believe that women influence their political beliefs or that they influence women's political beliefs; 98 percent of those who men report being influenced by are men, and only 3 percent of those they believe they most influence are women. This provides further indication that men do not register women as political actors. Women, however, report that they influence other women's political beliefs but are themselves influenced more by men; 76 percent of the individuals women believe they influence are women, while only 48 percent of those who women report being influenced by are women.

Clearly, men hold more influence over women than women hold over men, even if men do not see it. Women, themselves, do not believe they have much influence over others. The implication of these broader networks is that women are exposed to influence and persuasion but are rarely the purveyors of influence. If those with influence have more agenda-setting power even in everyday relationships and are better able to coordinate (apply social pressure) to enact their wishes, this suggests the likely elevation of men's interests.

It is also worth highlighting the concentration of influence within ethnic groups. More than 75 percent of all people reported in day-to-day influence networks are coethnics (from the same caste group). This corroborates evidence that politics, including political influence, is organized around ethnicity. People see their own political beliefs as being most shaped by those from their caste and tribal community.

Turning to village-wide influence, Panel A of Figure 6.6 reports the number of influential people in the village, as defined by the respondent themselves, to whom the respondent reports being tied. There are clear and substantial gender disparities in access to subjectively identified influential villagers: nearly 74 percent of women reported no ties to the influential people they themselves identified, compared to only 28 percent of men. These gender disparities are not the result of gendered differences in the number of influential people identified. On average, men report 2.5 influential people and women report 2.3 influential people; however, on average, men report being tied to 1.3 of these influential people, while women report being tied to only 0.4 of them. While women can recognize influence in their villages, they also recognize their lack of access to it.

I also analyze the characteristics of those named by villagers as influential. Across both villages, 100 unique people were named as being influential. Of those, only seventeen were women, highlighting gender disparities in village influence. Only one of these seventeen women was named as influential by more than ten villagers, and she was only named thirteen times. By contrast, seventeen men were named by more than ten villagers, and seven men were each

a) Ties to subjectively-named influential nodes

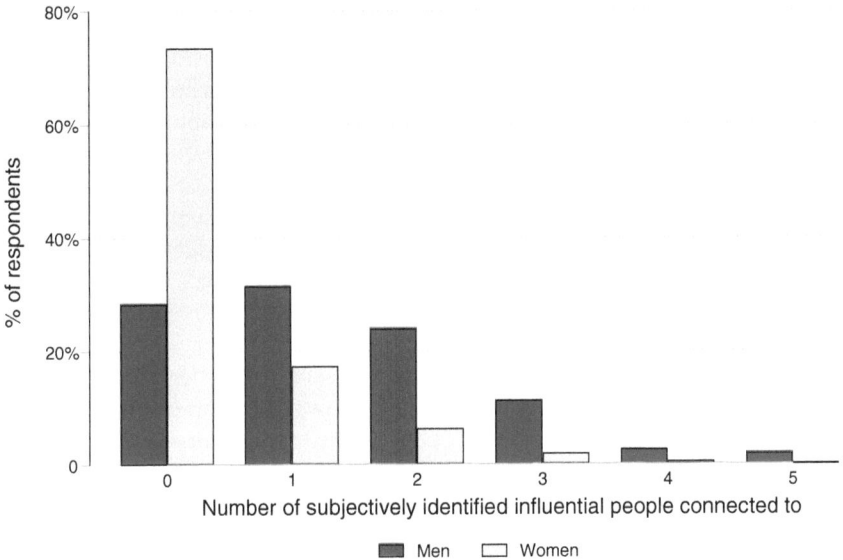

b) Ties to objectively-named influential nodes

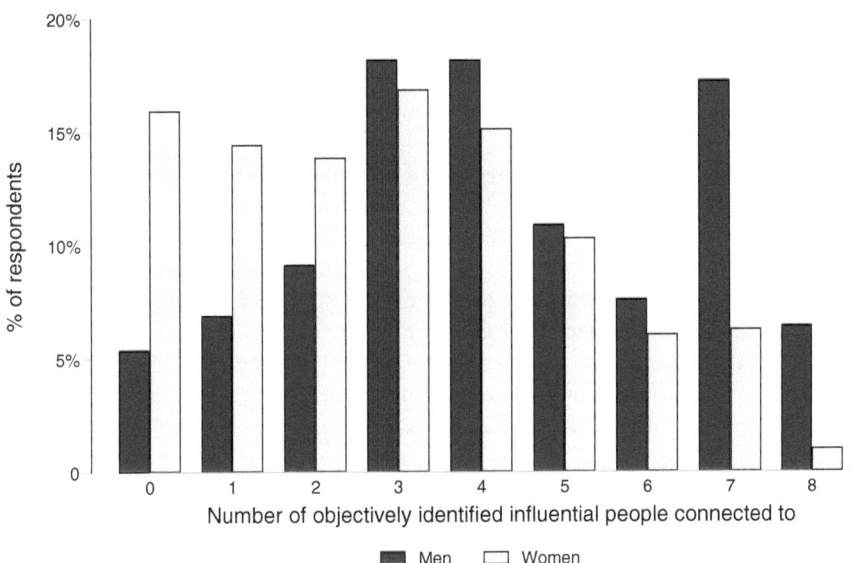

FIGURE 6.6 Women have fewer ties to subjectively and objectively named influential nodes

Note: The figure plots the average share of men and women who report different numbers of ties with influential nodes in their community. Data are from the census survey conducted in Villages A and B.

named by more than 100. The most influential man in Village A was named by 490 villagers, roughly half of the village population. To put this into perspective, if I define being influential as having at least 5 percent of the village name a person as such, then zero women and ten men would be considered influential.

Comparing across social categories, 51 percent of those who were named as influential are ST, and 37 percent are OBC. The relative population shares of these groups are 58 percent and 31 percent, respectively, suggesting that subjectively identified influence is generally representative of caste category, though OBCs are marginally overrepresented among those with influence. The most named influential person was OBC (named by 490 villagers), followed by an ST man (named by 295 villagers). Unlike gender, this reveals that influence is not held exclusively by members of one ethnicity but is, instead, distributed more proportionately across ethnicities.

Panel B of Figure 6.6 provides further evidence of gender inequalities in access to influential community members. It shows the number of objectively identified influential people in the village who the respondent says they would feel comfortable approaching. Roughly 16 percent of women reported that they would not be comfortable approaching any of the named influential community members, compared to only 5 percent of men. Similarly, only 6 percent of women reported being comfortable approaching all identified influential villagers, compared to 22 percent of men. In general, the distribution for women is visibly more left-skewed than the distribution for men. On average, men report being comfortable approaching 4.3 of the 7 named influential villagers in Village A and 4.0 of the 8 named in Village B, while women report being comfortable approaching only 3.3 influential villagers in Village A and 2.0 in Village B; a basic t-test indicates that the gender differences in both villages are statistically significant.

Importantly, 50 percent of the names of influential villagers that we provided to respondents were women, and yet women still reported substantially fewer ties to these pre-identified influential villagers. This suggests that women even lack access to important women in their communities. In fact, male respondents reported being more comfortable than female respondents in approaching our identified influential women in the community: men, on average, reported being comfortable speaking with 1.0 of these 3 named influential women in Village A and 1.7 of the 4 named in Village B, while women, on average, said they were comfortable speaking with 0.7 influential women in Village A and 1.0 in Village B. Strikingly, 50 percent of all men (compared to only 25 percent of women) in both villages stated that they would be comfortable approaching all four objectively identified men. Even more striking, only 8 percent of women in both villages stated that they would be comfortable approaching all objectively identified women.

This evidence makes clear that women have little ability to influence the lives of other citizens and little access to village power. Men's greater connections with influential people are likely to cement their voices and interests within politics. Women face much steeper hurdles to both raising their voices and ensuring that they are heard. The distribution of power and information within village politics and across men and women (favoring men) enables the perpetuation of household political cooperation and women's political exclusion.

DISCUSSION

In this chapter, I have shown that gender is distributed in political networks in rural Indian villages in such a way as to inhibit women's political authority and power. Men monopolize the center of the village network, while women are relegated to the periphery, connected largely to others in their household and to other women. Men see themselves as only politically connected to other men and do not reciprocate ties with the women in their households. Caste, as opposed to gender, divides and organizes village politics.

These patterns of political connection contrast starkly with patterns of social connection, where women report as many (if not more) ties than men. Women discuss politics with only a small fraction of those with whom they spend their free time. Women's political isolation is, therefore, not a function of a more general social isolation. Fundamentally, this suggests that to understand why women's political participation is low, we must explore why their social ties are apolitical.

Political spaces led – and dominated – by men are more easily availed of by men. Women who attempt to enter these spaces are viewed as trespassing where they do not belong. In such a system, the constraints on women's political participation are twofold. First, women lack the political connections that facilitate the accumulation of information and influence they sorely need. I show that women have less information about how to navigate political action than men and that their limited political ties contribute to this inequality. Women are also not deemed politically influential and not tied to those with political influence. I have shown clearly that political power is almost exclusively concentrated within men. The structure of political connections, in part through the way that it structures access to information and influence, contributes to the perpetuation of the patriarchal political order.

Second, the evidence in this chapter suggests that for women to gain access to such a system to which they are so clearly political outsiders amounts to their contesting the political power cemented within networks of men. Men clearly benefit from the nature of political organization and women's deference to household authority. Demanding political inclusion is likely to be met by resistance from those with the greatest stake in the current system, namely those highly central and influential men. The structure of political networks documented in this chapter, and the ability of men to coordinate given the density of ties with each other, likely facilitate this resistance to political authority challenges.

Ultimately, the patriarchal political order is marked by two key characteristics: the primacy of male-led households and the dominance of men in larger political networks. Chapter 4 provided ample evidence of the primacy of households in political decision-making and electoral mobilization and the authority of elder men in these domains. Chapter 5 demonstrated the role of the household in constraining women's non-electoral political participation and documented the positive relationship between autonomy from the household and greater political engagement for women (and not for men). In this chapter, I have provided evidence for the second condition: the dominance of men in the village political network. Taken together, this evidence supports the existence of a patriarchal political order and demonstrates the many ways in which this order elevates the status of men and subordinates the political action of women. In the next section, I will evaluate whether expanding women's political ties outside of the household opens space to contest this political order.

PART III

THE UNRAVELING

7

The Power of Autonomy from the Household and Women's Collective Action

Access to politics brings power. But I have demonstrated that women in India have little access to politics – largely because the powerful men in their household perpetuate their dominance by suppressing their political actions. Since the household is the principal institution constraining women's agency, to obtain agency women must either break free from household cooperation or achieve greater equality and power within the household. Contesting intra-household power structures to demand agency within the household, however, is enormously costly, particularly when broader community power structures reinforce and support household power structures. Doing so is likely to spark substantial resistance from those with power inside and outside the household. Without structural transformations that upend these age-old hierarchies and power structures, intra-household power is unlikely to be meaningfully redistributed.

While the path for women may seem bleak, in this chapter I show that it is possible for women to become politically active and make traction on their empowerment even without changing the structures of inequality and coercion that constrain them in the first place. In a context of strict patriarchy and gender inequalities in access to social and economic institutions, I suggest that increasing women's political autonomy from the household is a promising route to their empowerment.[1] I document how a financial inclusion program created and institutionalized spaces for women to convene outside of their households and fostered solidaristic ties among women that were then deployed via collective action to demand political representation. Such gender-based collective action made these women's political emancipation possible.

---

[1] This builds on work in Chhibber (2002) that also argues that autonomy from the household is a key driver of women's political participation in India. See also Prillaman (2021).

Specifically, I study women's participation in self-help groups (SHGs),[2] which are small, women-only microcredit groups that have become India's largest female empowerment program over the past decade.[3] If the model of women's political behavior I have proposed is correct, then participation in SHGs should increase their political participation, even (and especially) if social norms and household dynamics continue to reinforce women's exclusion from politics. I leverage a natural experiment and data from more than 2,000 women from 152 villages across rural Madhya Pradesh to document how the implementation of SHGs in five districts of rural Madhya Pradesh had large and meaningful consequences for women's political behavior. I draw on interviews with fifty women in these villages to examine the underlying processes of change.

I demonstrate that participating in these apolitical women's groups allowed women to form deep political connections outside of their households. Regular interactions in these groups supported the development of trust and solidarity among women,[4] which created space for them to share grievances and recognize commonalities in their collective experiences.[5] The groups' lending practices facilitated the goal of mutual benefit and reliance, which fostered trust and solidarity.

These women's groups acted as laboratories for democratic deliberation, providing a supportive institutional space for them to experiment with using their voice and with civic engagement. In many groups, the discussions extended beyond finances into social, familial, and political issues. Such emerging political dialogue allowed women to explore their interests, recognize commonalities across each other's experiences, develop confidence and authority, and accumulate civic skills. These new forms of association gave women a distinct vantage point from which to evaluate their social position and question the social and political orders in which they existed.[6] Women often recognized a common desire for inclusion, status elevation, and increased power within the household, creating a group consciousness and furthering the sense of solidarity among them. Women's very identity was thus renegotiated in these group spaces.

By fostering strong ties and a shared identity between women as well as greater political consciousness and interest, these groups challenged internalized beliefs about women's unsuitability for politics and provided them with tools to demand agency and autonomy. Regular political discussions outside the household changed women's information set and activated gendered

---

[2] These SHGs were mobilized by the nongovernmental organization (NGO) Professional Assistance for Development Action (PRADAN), who has worked in rural India for over twenty-five years to mobilize women into SHGs.

[3] Sanyal (2014); Brody et al. (2015).

[4] Feigenberg, Field, and Pande (2010), Sanyal (2014), and Kumar et al. (2019) also show that SHG and microcredit group participation increases women's social capital.

[5] Karpowitz and Mendelberg (2014); Putnam (2000); Baldassarri (2015).   [6] Kabeer (2012).

interests that other household interests had subjugated. Strong ties with other women also encouraged them to become political agents and to protect fellow group members when they demanded agency. Women often recounted how they, as a group, would speak with angry male family members to demonstrate it was not just one woman demanding agency alone. Group solidarity in some cases was so strong that members intervened to protect each other from physical abuse.

In addition to serving as spaces that fostered political interest and agency, the women's groups I studied also provided the tools for political action and the ability to overcome the transaction costs of collective action. These groups, built on a foundation of solidarity and norms of reciprocity, gave women the organizational capacity to act collectively to combat the social forces of coercion.[7] Group participation provided women with the common drivers of collective action: a shared identity, a recognition of a common injustice, and the belief that group mobilization could address those injustices.[8] When group discussions led women to recognize their shared interests and to develop a group consciousness of gender inequalities, the groups often mobilized to contest these inequalities and improve the representation of their interests through collective action.[9] Within these institutional spaces, women identified strategies to contest social norms, constraints on mobility, and threats of backlash. The SHGs created opportunities for gender-based collective action, as networks facilitated information acquisition and group bargaining and provided the institutional structures to enforce group-wide action. Women's groups therefore play two key roles: (1) they give women political autonomy from the household through expanded political networks, and (2) they provide an institutional structure to facilitate the collective action needed for women to exercise agency in political spaces.

Yet, SHG members did not equally experience the positive impacts of participation. The positive effects were strongest for women who held more dominant positions in community caste hierarchies. While SHG participation increased political participation for all women, the effect is twice as large for Other Backward Class (OBC) women compared to Scheduled Tribe (ST) women. This may reflect higher-caste women's greater ability to traverse political boundaries or the fact that OBC women had the lowest rates of political participation a priori, as the SHG intervention simply equalized women's participation.

Furthermore, only women who were members of SHGs reaped the benefits of group creation: I observe no spillover effects on the political participation of women not in SHGs but in villages with SHGs. This suggests that the mechanisms of empowerment for SHGs are tied to group participation itself.

---

[7] Morgan-Collins (2021).   [8] Van Zomeren, Postmes, and Spears (2008).
[9] Sanyal (2009), too, demonstrates the potential for SHGs to generate collective action, most commonly against shared injustices.

SHGs were most likely to increase political participation if groups had developed high levels of trust and solidarity. Many groups were purely trans-actional, and regular meetings failed to foster discussion of difficult issues such as gender discrimination and household coercion. Other groups were even contentious, as they replicated social inequalities from the broader community. I show that group solidarity – measured as (1) whether groups discussed social issues during meetings and (2) whether group members spent time together outside of meetings – positively correlates with which SHG members partici-pated in politics. Group diversity, however, is generally uncorrelated (and may even be positively correlated) with which SHG members ultimately became more politically active. While group diversity may have inhibited social trust and coordination in some instances, in others it may have enabled a stronger attachment to the commonalities of experiences as women.

The results described in this chapter clearly demonstrate that expanding women's networks and giving them greater autonomy from the household can ignite their political empowerment. The evidence provides substantial scope for optimism. Even without changes in their economic position or a priori patriarchal norms, women mobilized collectively to demand access to political institutions and the representation of their voices in political dialogue. What precipitated this change was an apolitical external intervention that brought women together, away from their households, and provided a formal space for connection. These conditions allowed women to demand power – agency over their own political lives. While the power of the patriarchal household may be deeply entrenched, these findings illustrate that external interventions that create the conditions for women's autonomy can spark change that has the potential to challenge the patriarchal political order.

SELF-HELP GROUPS

In India, SHGs have become the most popular associational group among women and the most wide-reaching public policy aimed at women's empower-ment: more than ninety million women had joined a government-run SHG as of 2023. More broadly, mobilizing women into women-only groups, including various types of microcredit groups, has become a global tool to increase development and financial inclusion.[10]

A Brief History of SHGs

Across India, SHGs have become a cornerstone of policies designed to empower women. They developed out of the microcredit movement that began in the early 1980s. In 1983, Muhammad Yunus first introduced the concept of

---

[10] Banerjee (2013).

microcredit through his organization, the Grameen Bank, in Bangladesh. Microcredit targeted the poor and those who would typically struggle to access credit due to limited collateral or would pay high interest rates to moneylenders. To insure against default, collateral was provided through the innovation of group lending, where members of a microcredit group bore joint liability for each member's loans. Rotating savings and credit associations predated, but are distinct from, microcredit in that they are largely informal; savings and credit are derived from personal contributions as opposed to outside bank linkages. Group lending was premised on group trust and social pressure. Women were the primary beneficiaries of microcredit, arguably because of their relative deprivation, greater investment potential, and higher responsiveness to social pressure.

Throughout the 1980s and 1990s, the microcredit model grew exponentially across the globe, particularly in lower-income countries. It became a key strategy of the World Bank based on the belief that inadequate access to capital trapped people in poverty, known as the "financial self-sustainability paradigm."[11] In its early stages, microcredit was largely implemented by nonprofits and NGOs that believed the financial self-sustainability paradigm was key to poverty relief and development. As the high demand for microcredit became clear, private and for-profit businesses entered the market, which has led to criticisms that microcredit has been used to exploit the poor.[12]

In the late 1980s, development NGOs operating in India adapted the typical microcredit group into what became known as SHGs. SHGs are microcredit groups that expect to operate indefinitely and support the collective action by the group for mutual benefit. These informal savings and credit institutions are typically comprised of 10–20 women from the same village who meet regularly. Unlike more typical microcredit groups, SHGs sometimes help groups achieve their goals through trainings such as programs to improve farming and agricultural practices. SHGs are typically federated institutions: 15–20 SHGs form a cluster association, and all SHGs within a block (the administrative unit just above village) constitute a federation.

The rise in microcredit corresponded with an increasing focus on women's empowerment – particularly, enhancing women's agency to improve their own social position. SHGs sought to achieve the dual goals of empowering women and addressing credit constraints. The government-led Women's Development Programme, for example, mobilized women into informal groups in rural Rajasthan with the aim of fostering mutual gains.[13] NGOs, including PRADAN and Self-Employed Women's Association, studied the microcredit and empowerment models and initiated some of India's first SHGs.

---

[11] Robinson (2001).   [12] Sanyal (2014).   [13] Das (1992).

Throughout the 1990s and early 2000s, SHGs expanded across India largely at the hands of NGOs. Funding for these NGOs came from government and donor agencies. Recognizing that SHGs had the potential to empower women and reduce poverty, the Government of India initiated a national SHG program in 2011 with the creation of the Ministry of Rural Development's National Rural Livelihoods Program (NRLM). The NRLM aims to scale SHGs across India and has mobilized more than ninety million women into SHGs since its inception. It is one of the largest poverty alleviation programs in the world, and SHGs remain the backbone of the government's approach to women's empowerment.

Yet, SHGs and microcredit more generally have been shown to only modestly improved individuals' financial situations. While some studies have found that they improve households' financial positions,[14] others have concluded that microcredit poorly translates into long-term financial stability,[15] and nearly all such studies have shown that women retain almost no control over the money borrowed, instead transferring the loans directly to men.[16] SHGs have also exhibited potentially adverse effects, such as perpetuating women's vulnerability and even heightening the risk of violence against women in response to negative financial returns.[17]

More recent scholarship has argued that microcredit, and specifically SHGs, should be evaluated only on the basis of their financial merits. While the principal goal of microcredit programs is to address individual credit constraints and lift households out of poverty (what Sanyal[18] calls the "financial mechanism"), their design and the way in which they are delivered through groups suggests they also have the potential to improve women's lives by creating social capital (what Sanyal calls the "associational mechanism").[19] While SHGs and microcredit have been shown to have tenuous benefits for long-term financial well-being and women's economic empowerment, a growing body of evidence suggests they have substantially increased women's social capital.[20]

PRADAN

One of the first NGOs to mobilize SHGs in 1987 was PRADAN, which is a large rural livelihoods development organization that has mobilized more than 850,000 women into SHGs across seven states in India. In Madhya Pradesh, PRADAN began mobilizing women into SHGs more than twenty years ago. In the villages I study, the average SHG age is six years. PRADAN works with

---

[14] Brody et al. (2015).   [15] Banerjee (2013).   [16] Sanyal (2014).
[17] Rahman (2019); Goetz and Sengupta (1996).   [18] Sanyal (2014).
[19] Feigenberg, Field, and Pande (2010; 2014); Sharma (2008).
[20] Feigenberg, Field, and Pande (2010; 2014); Sharma (2008).

the poorest and most socially disadvantaged households; more than 65 percent of its beneficiaries are from Scheduled Castes (SCs) and STs.[21]

PRADAN recruits women to join SHGs and institutionalizes procedures of informal savings and credit sharing. It also provides livelihood promotion within SHGs to facilitate better and more efficient farming practices. To organize an SHG, PRADAN team members enter a village and share information about the groups with women in the community and their families. Once 10–15 women display an interest, PRADAN organizes them into an SHG. Several SHGs will be formed in each village with the average PRADAN program village in Madhya Pradesh having 6.6 SHGs. These women often come from the same hamlet and are usually from similar caste groups. Yet 39 percent of PRADAN's SHGs in Madhya Pradesh are heterogeneous on caste category: the average heterogeneous group include 59 percent ST members, 9 percent SC members, and 31 percent OBC members.[22] PRADAN's external mobilization of these groups likely increases their diversity, since selection into groups has been shown to create homogeneous networks.[23] Overall, PRADAN's SHGs in Madhya Pradesh as of 2021 were comprised of 78 percent ST women, 4 percent SC women, and 15 percent OBC women and these women come from forty-four distinct castes (*jatis*) and tribes.

When women are recruited to join an SHG, they are informed about the financial benefits of microfinance, particularly relative to extortionary money lending, and of improved farming. The economic nature of these groups – particularly, the access to capital – motivates male household heads to give permission for women to participate. Qualitative conversations with PRADAN staff and SHG members suggest that, if such groups were identified initially as political spaces seeking to generate broader social change, men would likely prevent women's participation as they do with other political spaces.

RESEARCH DESIGN AND DATA

To examine how SHGs affect women's political participation, I study their rollout by PRADAN in rural Madhya Pradesh. I leverage an arbitrary geographic boundary used to determine which villages were eligible for SHGs to identify the effect of women's groups on political participation across 152 villages in the state. Control villages were selected via pair matching on observables to further ensure villages across this boundary are similar. I discuss the details of this methodology below.

---

[21] Based on data from PRADAN's internal management information system data on SHG beneficiaries in study regions.
[22] Based on data from PRADAN's internal management information system data on SHG beneficiaries.
[23] Alesina and La Ferrara (2000).

Sampling Villages

There are two principal challenges associated with estimating the impact of SHG participation on women's political outcomes. First, if NGOs want to capitalize on existing women's mobilization, they may create SHGs in villages where women are the most politically active. It may be easier or more successful to recruit women who are already actively engaged in community institutions and are more participatory in nature. Comparing villages with and without SHGs therefore risks conflating their effect with that of more fundamental underlying differences in the extent to which women participate in public life. Second, since not all women in a village join SHGs, it is possible that the types of women who join are fundamentally different from those who do not. If, for example, the types of women who join SHGs are more likely to want to engage in community institutions generally, then comparing women in SHGs with those not in SHGs may capture these underlying differences in participatory propensity as opposed to the effect of the SHG.

To address the first concern related to the selection of villages for SHGs, I exploit plausibly exogenous variation in access to SHGs resulting from an arbitrary boundary used to determine which villages were eligible for PRADAN's SHG intervention.[24] Villages were generally eligible for the SHG intervention based on their location relative to the nearest PRADAN field office: only those within a set kilometer radius were eligible for the intervention due to daily travel constraints for the field staff. The specific distance varied by PRADAN field office and was a function of the terrain and road quality.[25] The average distance for the travel radius was 30 km. While the location of PRADAN's field offices was not arbitrary (though it was remote), the boundary of implementation is unlikely to be correlated with indicators of women's empowerment. This arbitrary boundary allows us to assume that villages just outside the boundary should be identical to those just inside it on both observable and unobservable characteristics. In other words, women's political participation should have been the same in villages on either side of the boundary before PRADAN implemented SHGs. Thus, comparing just those villages close to the boundary should remove concerns that fundamental differences across these villages, as opposed to SHGs, are driving any observed effects.

Roughly, 60 percent of the villages in the implementation areas received the SHG intervention. Given that the primary purpose of SHGs was to improve access to credit and women's livelihoods, PRADAN selected the villages within the boundary that were more economically deprived, targeting villages with large ST populations who have historically had limited land ownership,

---

[24] Dell (2010).
[25] This boundary was not a hard-and-fast rule codified in PRADAN's operating protocols but was an informal rule used to select villages to work in. I learned of this informal practice through conversations with PRADAN staff and subsequently verified it in each implementation team.

challenges with regular cultivation, and high poverty rates. To ensure that the villages outside the boundary were the most like those inside the boundary, I selected comparison villages through a pair-matching process. Combining this forced similarity on observable characteristics with the presumption of similarity on unobservable characteristics due to geographic proximity allows me to estimate the causal effect of SHG program access.[26] I identified the villages most similar to those that received the SHG intervention on characteristics, such as the share of the population from STs. to ensure balance across the treated and control villages on observable, village-level covariates. The villages were selected as follows:

- For each district, all villages that had received the intervention were geo-located.
- A circular boundary was drawn around these villages, with the radius equal to the distance to the furthest village. This circle is what I call the implementation boundary.
- All villages in the same district but outside this boundary were identified, leaving a 1 km gap from the boundary given the fuzzy nature of the boundary.
- All treated villages within the boundary were matched to control villages outside the boundary using coarsened exact matching on district, population size, female population proportion, and tribal population proportion. Pairs were then selected by minimizing geographic distance.

The final sample includes 152 villages (76 treated and 76 control), which represent the best matches, i.e. those that minimize geographic distance within possible matched pairs. Since SHGs were created in treated villages at different times, this yields different treatment durations, as all villages remained treated until data collection. Figure 7.1 depicts the sampled villages by the year when SHGs were first instituted.

The key identifying assumption for my research design is continuity: treated (those that have SHGs) and control (those that do not have SHGs) villages across the border should be identical on observable and unobservable characteristics. To prove that they are identical on observable characteristics, Table A7.1.1 compares the balance in village-level pretreatment measures using data from the 2001 census of India. Village-level covariates are statistically identical across the treated and control villages, with the exception that control villages had higher pretreatment literacy rates. Since education is positively correlated with political participation, this suggests that any treatment effect would be attenuated. There is no statistical difference between treated and control villages with respect to the terrain or distance to towns, which confirms that the boundary does not coincide with major geographic barriers.

---

[26] Keele and Titiunik (2015).

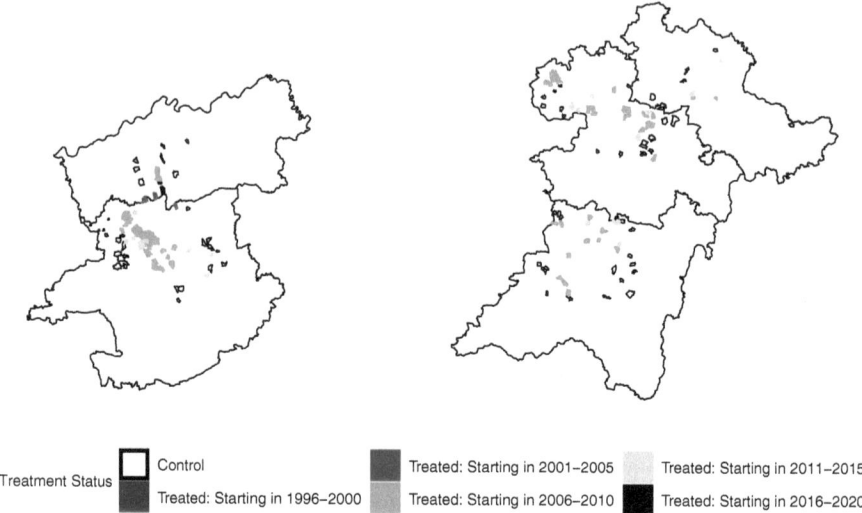

FIGURE 7.1 Treated and control study villages by district and year of first SHG
Note: The map shows Balaghat, Betul, Dindori, Hoshangabad, and Mandla districts in Madhya Pradesh – the districts in which PRADAN works.

Table A7.1.2 compares the balance in person-level measures that are unlikely to have changed as a result of the treatment. Most individual-level covariates are statistically equivalent across the treated and control villages. However, women in the control villages are on average older than those in the treated villages and may also be more likely to be from a Scheduled Tribe. I also show in Table A7.1.3 that the villages that received the intervention within the boundary were not substantively different from those that did not receive the intervention within the boundary.

Sampling Respondents

The second challenge of understanding how SHGs affect political participation is differentiating between the characteristics of those who join SHGs and the effect of the SHG. This is made even more difficult by the fact that data on women's political participation are severely limited. There were no data on women's political participation, particularly non-electoral participation, for the study villages prior to our data collection. Gender-disaggregated turnout data are ad hoc, and several attempts to work with the state election commission suggested that they either do not exist or would be impossible to get. While many local officials collect attendance rosters from public assembly meetings, there is no systematic process of collecting or recording this information. Many officials did not have or could not share their rosters. Others were willing to share but only retained these records for meetings in the past year (well after

SHGs had been started in many villages). Many villages did not hold village meetings as often as constitutionally mandated and were even less likely to have systematic data. These rosters were unreliable and likely biased, and many women reported being forced to go to the meeting to sign the register (as there is a mandate of a quorum of women) and then were told to leave. Where possible, I verified that self-reported data were reflected in meeting rosters.

I, therefore, needed to collect data from individuals about their political behavior. To understand the effect of SHG participation, as opposed to SHG access, I needed a large enough sample of respondents who were SHG members. But sampling only SHG members makes it difficult to understand whether SHG participation or underlying differences between those who do and do not join SHGs is driving any observed effects. I address these competing concerns in two ways.

First, to ensure sufficient representation of SHG members, I conducted an in-person survey with 15 women from each of the 152 sampled villages in 2016, creating a total sample of 2,152 women. All respondents were surveyed by female surveyors, and all surveys were conducted in complete privacy. In treated villages, respondents were randomly sampled from lists of SHG members provided by PRADAN. In control villages, they were randomly sampled from person-level census data collected by the state of Madhya Pradesh in 2011, restricting to adult, ever-married women to match the eligibility criteria for SHGs.

The different sampling procedures raise concerns of selection bias, as only treated women in treated villages were surveyed. If those who selected into SHG participation (treatment) are different from those sampled in control areas, then the observed effects could be the result of these underlying differences rather than the intervention. To address this concern using this sample, I first show that selection into SHGs is almost entirely driven by financial need as opposed to political participation. Selection into SHGs is largely a function of economic need: women want access to cheaper credit. My survey data reveals that 96 percent of treated women stated that they joined the SHG to obtain improved financial access or agricultural training. Fewer than 1 percent said that they joined because they wanted to meet other women. This economically based selection into SHGs is unsurprising given that most women were only allowed to join these groups because they were seen as bringing financial benefit to the household. As I will describe, household members attempt to prevent women's participation in SHGs once they realize they pose a challenge to their authority.

Qualitative conversations with SHG members reveal that, while economic need is the principal reason for joining, women typically join only after they are invited to do so by a friend or neighbor. When I asked SHG members why they did not include other low-income women in their village, they said they simply had not thought to do it. This does suggest that many women already have a foundational relationship with other SHG members and so these groups cannot be seen as a random pairing of women. At the same point, it was apparent from my observation of dozens of these groups that many of these women were not accustomed to conversing with each other on more serious concerns or political matters.

To ensure that the women I study in control villages are most likely those who would select into SHG participation if they had the option, I match women across the treated and control villages on pretreatment indicators of economic need. I did this using genetic matching on land ownership, age, education level, marital status, and ST/SC status. While this does not guarantee that women in control and treated villages are identical on average except for their participation in SHGs, it does make it more likely. As evidence in support of this, Figure A7.2.1 shows that the husbands of sampled female respondents in treated and control villages are identical with respect to their political participation. The matched sample allows me to estimate how SHG participation, not just SHG access, shapes women's political outcomes – that is, the average treatment effect on the treated.

Second, to further mitigate concerns of fundamental differences between SHG members and nonmembers, I conducted a supplemental survey in all study villages in two of the five districts (Betul and Hoshangabad), which make up 40 percent of all villages in the study (62 villages). In this supplemental survey, women in treated villages were sampled using the same strategy as in the control villages; they were randomly sampled from census lists of adult, ever-married women. As a result, in these treated villages, I have data on both women who joined SHGs (treated women) and those who did not (untreated women in treated villages). Comparing all sampled women across treated and control villages in this supplemental survey therefore eliminates concerns of bias due to selection into SHGs. However, by comparing averages across all women, not just those who joined SHGs, the effect of the SHG intervention will be muted if it only benefited those who joined SHGs. Figure A7.2.2 shows that the political behavior of untreated women in treated villages is statistically identical to that of women in control villages, suggesting that any effects of treatment do not spill over to non-group members. The results from this subsample of villages are presented alongside the full village sample. Data from this supplemental survey are pooled with data from the original survey to ensure sufficient representation of treated women in the sample.

Estimating the Effect of SHG Participation

I estimate the effects of SHG participation on political outcomes in two ways. First, using the entire sample of villages and only SHG members from treated villages, I estimate the difference between pairs of matched villages by including matched-pair fixed effects.[27] Essentially, this specification estimates the average difference in women's political outcomes across all pairs of villages that are identical on observable characteristics. The results from this analysis reflect the estimated average effect of treatment on women who joined SHGs by using the matched sample of individuals and assuming that selection into treatment is uncorrelated with outcomes. This is referred to as the average treatment effect on the treated (ATT). To improve efficiency, I also control for individual-level covariates known to correlate with political participation, including years of education, acres of land owned by the household, whether the respondent is Hindu or from a Scheduled Tribe, age, marital status, and the number of children at home. I cluster standard errors at the village level, since that is the level of the treatment assignment.[28]

Second, using the subsample of the sixty-two villages in which a random sample of all women was surveyed, I estimate the same matched-pair fixed effects model of the effect of SHG membership on political outcomes as above. I deviate from the first estimation approach by instrumenting for individual-level SHG membership (i.e., treatment take-up) with village-level assignment to treatment. While SHG membership is nonrandom, village treatment assignment arguably is. I therefore leverage the random variation in village-level treatment assignment to induce random variation in SHG membership. Essentially, when only some people in treated villages comply with the treatment (join an SHG), the instrumental variables approach allows for an estimate of what share of those in treated villages are so-called noncompliers (imagining there should be the same share of noncompliers in control villages had they had the chance). It uses this estimate to weight the overall estimated treatment effect (the effect comparing all women in treated villages with all women in control villages). This generates an unbiased estimate of SHG participation on political outcomes, assuming that those who do not participate in SHGs are unaffected by the treatment. I provide support for this assumption in Figure A7.2.2, which shows that untreated women in treated villages show the same level of political participation as women in control villages. Again, the results in this model reflect the estimated average effect of treatment on women who joined SHGs but do so with less potential for bias (as well as a smaller sample size and so greater uncertainty around the estimates). I will refer to this as the complier average treatment effect (CATE) because it estimates the effect of treatment on compliers: those who joined SHGs when they were available.[29]

---

[27] The results are robust to alternative geographic regression discontinuity specifications, such as the cubic functional form proposed in Dell (2010), and to subsetting to various bandwidths, as shown in Appendix A3.

[28] The pair-matching estimating equation is: $Y_{k,i} = \gamma D_{k,i} + \beta X_i + \alpha_p + \varepsilon_k$, where D is the treatment status of individual i in village k, X is a matrix of individual-level covariates, and α_p are matched-pair fixed effects. γ is the estimate of the impact of the treatment, D, on Y.

[29] Estimates from this sample that do not instrument for treatment take-up and simply compare all women in treated and control villages (i.e., the intent-to-treat effect) can be found in the Appendix to this chapter.

Descriptive Evidence on the Impact of SHGs

In addition to estimating the causal relationship between SHG participation and political outcomes, I draw on several additional data sources to understand how and why SHGs shape women's behavior. First, I utilize data from the census survey conducted in a subset of six villages from the full sample of villages considered in the main analysis. Two of these villages (A and B, as described in Chapters 4 and 6)[30] were not eligible for the SHG intervention because they were outside the implementation boundary. Villages C and D (the treated villages) were eligible for the SHG intervention because they were inside the implementation boundary. Within these treated villages, 27.9 percent of adult women selected into SHG membership. According to administrative data from PRADAN, Village C had four SHGs; the oldest was just over 10 years old at the time of data collection and the youngest was just over 2 years old at the time of outcome data collection. Village D had six SHGs ranging in age from less than 1 year old to nearly 10 years old at the time of outcome data collection. The census survey data from these four villages will be used to understand differences in networks across control and treated villages and across women who did and did not join SHGs in treated villages.

Second, I leverage a variety of questions asked only of SHG members in the full sample survey in Madhya Pradesh to understand group dynamics and how group characteristics correlate with political participation. Surveyed SHG members were asked about the nature of the discussion in SHG meetings, their relationship with other SHG members, activities undertaken by the SHG, as well as their perceptions of the group composition. I pair this individual-level survey data with administrative data from PRADAN, which captures SHG group characteristics, including group age and various measures of group diversity. These two data sets were combined through a fuzzy matching process on SHG member name, SHG member spouse name, and village. I use these data to understand how various group characteristics correlate with SHG group dynamics, such as the degree of trust and solidarity in the group, and to understand *which* SHG members ultimately engage in politics.

SHGS AND POLITICAL BEHAVIOR

I have suggested that SHGs have the potential to shape women's political agency and political participation, thus leading to greater political empowerment overall. If households represent the primary constraint on women's political agency, then their agency can be developed either by increasing women's voice *within* the household or increasing their autonomy *from* the household. I explore the effect of SHGs on both manifestations of women's

---

[30] Villages are referenced by anonymous letters because respondent anonymity could be questioned if village names were revealed, since all adults in the village were surveyed.

agency. I then evaluate whether this increased agency yielded greater political action by examining the impact of SHG participation on various measures of political participation.

Impact on Political Agency within the Household

Participating in SHGs may increase women's political agency within the household either by increasing their bargaining power or reducing men's coercive power over them. Women's bargaining power may rise if the credit access generated by SHG participation affords them more authority in household decision-making or gives them greater financial protection. Alternatively, SHG participation may reduce men's coercive power if women can mobilize their collective strength to challenge men's authority.

Figure 7.2 displays the impact of SHG participation on various indicators of women's financial and political decision-making and economically based bargaining power. Each point reflects the estimated impact of SHG participation on each dependent variable shown on the y-axis, and each line represents the 95 percent confidence interval around this estimate. The black points report the average treatment effect on the treated – that is, the effect of SHG participation using the full sample of villages and the matched sample of women across treated and control villages. The gray points report the complier average treatment effect – that is, the effect of SHG participation using the subsample of villages and instrumenting for SHG membership with village-level SHG implementation.

The top two lines provide evidence that SHG membership increased women's involvement in their own political decision-making. Women in SHGs were more likely to say that they participate at all in the decision over whether they vote or attend village assembly meetings, though this positive effect is only significant when looking at the subsample of respondents in two districts (the CATE). Additionally, women's participation in SHGs is shown to increase their consumption-related decision-making participation in both specifications, but again only significantly affects women's participation in decisions over land purchasing when looking at the subsample of villages.[31] These effects, however, should be interpreted with some caution, as more than 70 percent of women reported that they were included in household decisions even in control villages, as the survey question only asked about involvement in

---

[31] Differences between the CATE and ATT estimates may be due to differences in the underlying sample of districts. SHGs in the two districts studied in the subsample used for the CATE are, on average, older than SHGs in the other three districts; they also surround the statewide PRADAN headquarters. It is possible that SHGs in these two districts had more intensive treatment than SHGs in the remaining three districts. When the ATT analysis is subset to only those two districts, the Gram Sabha decision-making coefficient becomes significant at the 5 percent level. Alternatively, it could be that the CATE specification itself reduces bias, more accurately parses selection into SHGs, and therefore leads to different coefficients.

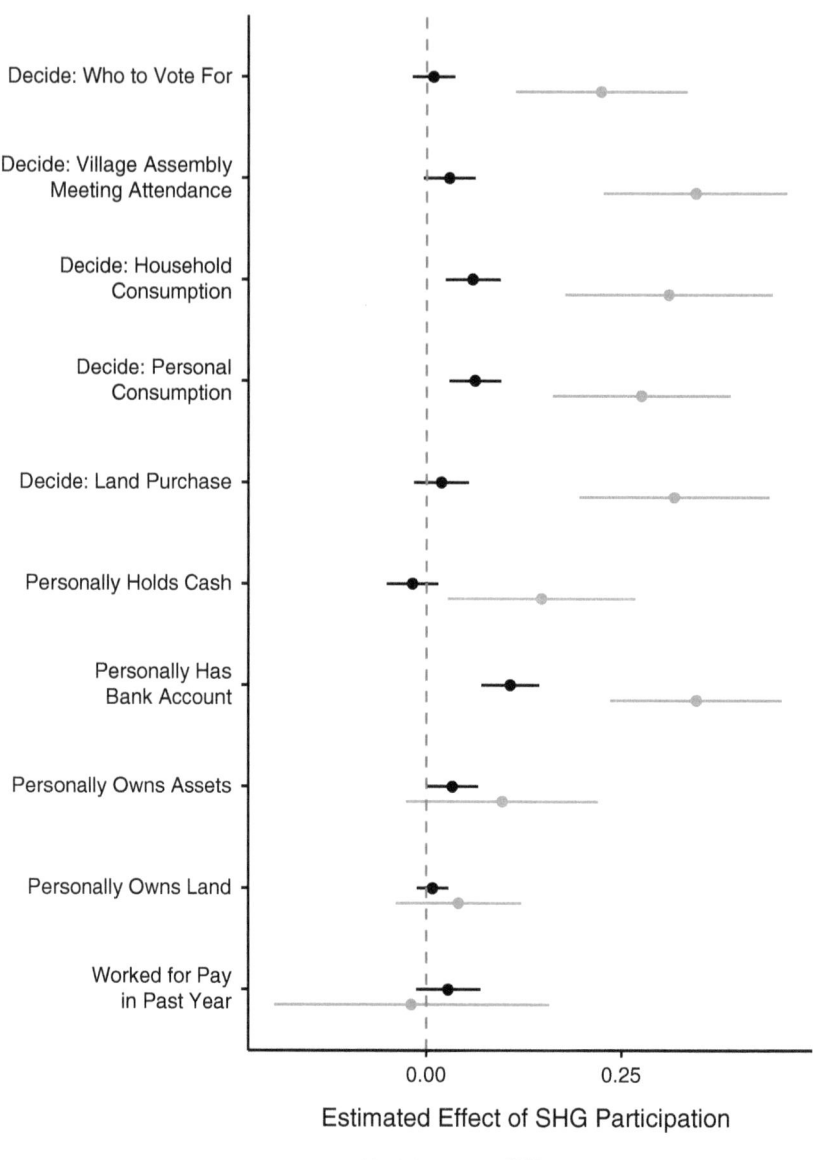

Estimated Effect of SHG Participation

Model: ● ATT   ● CATE Subsample

FIGURE 7.2 SHG participation increased women's role in household decision-making but did not shift their bargaining power

Note: The figure shows the estimated effect of the SHG intervention on a series of indicators of decision-making and bargaining power. Estimated effects from two models are shown along with corresponding 95 percent confidence intervals. Each variable on the y-axis is a distinct dependent variable, and point estimates are the effect of the SHG treatment on each outcome. Underlying models include village pair-matched fixed effects, and individual covariates and standard errors are clustered at the village level. Data are from the 2016 sample survey in 152 villages in five districts of Madhya Pradesh.

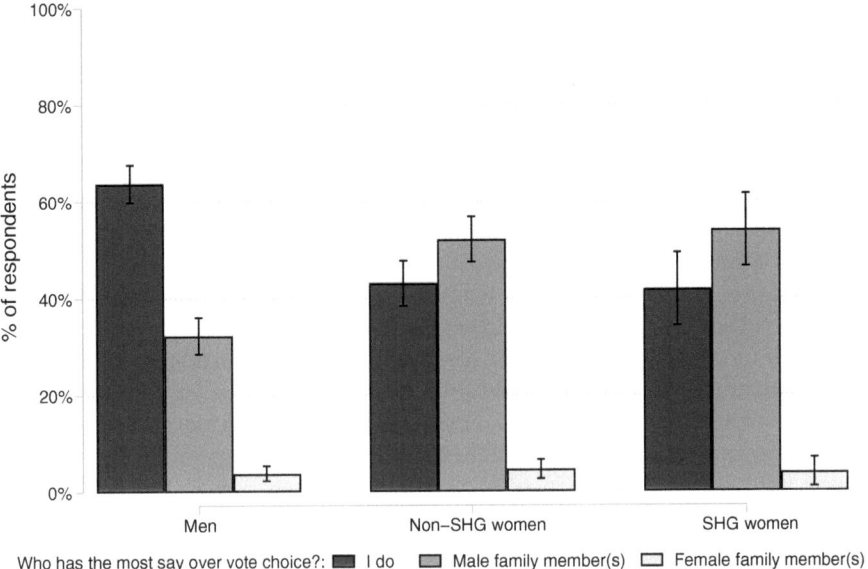

FIGURE 7.3 SHG women and young men report the same vote autonomy as non-SHG women

Note: The figure plots the share of women, by SHG membership status, who report having the most say over their voting decision, who report a male family member having the most say, and who report a female family member having the most say. Data are from the census survey conducted in Villages C and D. Error bars denote 95 percent confidence intervals around the reported means.

each decision as opposed to final authority. These results thus suggest that participating in SHGs increased women's role in household decision-making on the margin but cannot be considered definitive proof of agency within the household.

Drawing on more explicit measures of political agency in the household from the census survey conducted in Villages C and D, Figure 7.3 describes the average share of women in these villages that report that they have the most say over their own vote choice, differentiating women in these villages who had joined an SHG and women who had not. There is no significant difference in these two villages between women who had and had not joined an SHG with respect to vote autonomy. This suggests that the impact of SHG participation on within household empowerment may be limited; however, these results should not be interpreted causally, as they reflect a comparison within two villages between women who (nonrandomly) selected into SHG membership and those who did not.[32] Qualitative interviews with fifty SHG members and

---

[32] Results from Figure 7.3 are robust to comparing women within the same households based on SHG membership status.

twenty-one non-SHG members across ten villages provide somewhat more support for the hypothesis that SHGs can increase women's agency in the household: women who were members of SHGs were 14 percentage points more likely to state that they had agency over their vote choice (69 percent vs. 55 percent for non-SHG members), even though many still suggested that male relatives were consulted in their vote decision-making. SHG members were also 14 percentage points less likely to indicate that their households aligned their vote choices, though still 61 percent stated that their households acted as a unit when voting. Taken together, this evidence suggests that SHG participation may increase some women's agency over their political decision-making within the household but that these impacts may be limited.

The bottom half of Figure 7.2 illustrates that SHG participation does not systematically or substantially improve women's financial bargaining power. It reports the effect of the SHG intervention on five common indicators of bargaining power, including whether the respondent personally holds cash, has a bank account, owns assets, owns land in their name, and worked for pay in the past year. Unlike decision-making, these measures of bargaining power capture the respondent's financial independence, which may lead to more exit options and be a mechanism underlying household agency. While there is a positive and significant effect on having a bank account, there are no significant differences in women's asset ownership or labor force participation.

Overall, Figures 7.2 and 7.3 show that women in SHGs report having a larger but still limited role in decision-making, including political decision-making, but are no more likely to own assets, hold cash, or be employed. This suggests that participation in SHGs may give women some autonomy from the household but does not fundamentally alter the underlying structures that keep them tied to the home. Economically based bargaining power derived from improved access to credit through SHGs is therefore unlikely to be driving the demonstrated improvements in decision-making.

Impact on Political Autonomy from the Household

Participating in SHGs may also increase women's autonomy from the household, allowing them freedom from the household as opposed to power within it. Autonomy from the household is most likely if SHGs provide women with stronger political connections outside the household so that they have more channels of information and potential support when choosing to act in a way that deviates from the household. SHGs increase women's contact with each other and therefore foster the growth and strengthening of women's networks.[33] In some cases, SHG members may already be connected through a social network, and participation in SHGs simply formalizes and transforms

---

[33] Feigenberg, Field, and Pande (2010).

that existing relationship. In other cases, SHGs may bring women who were not already socially connected into contact with each other. As shown in Chapter 6, women's networks exhibited high degrees of homophily with respect to social categories. The external mobilization of SHGs may bring women into contact with others from their village with whom they did not previously have strong ties.

Figure 7.4 estimates the impact of participating in SHGs on the size of women's networks, the nature of women's political discussions, and an index of women's mobility, including whether they left the village in the last month and whether they are allowed to visit health centers, homes of relatives or friends, local markets, or a local public meeting alone, or travel a short distance by train or bus. SHG members in treated villages reported having significantly more (female) friends and that they turn to their friends when in need more often than similar women in control villages, suggesting that SHG participation deepened connections. The SHG intervention also has a robust and positive impact on women's mobility, which suggests that women move about their community more as a result of being a part of an SHG.

Utilizing data from the census survey, Table 7.1 reports the average size and composition of women's political networks in two control villages (A and B) and non-SHG and SHG women in two treated villages (C and D). Since the number of villages included is small, comparing women across control and treated villages could simply reflect differences in these villages that are unrelated to SHG implementation. And since SHG members are nonrandom, comparing SHG members and nonmembers in treated villages could simply reflect underlying differences in the types of women who join SHGs.[34] However, both sets of comparisons help illuminate differences in the network size and composition of SHG members.

Table 7.1 reveals that SHG women's political networks are significantly different from non-SHG women's political networks in both degree and kind. SHG women discuss politics with, on average, 0.8 more people than non-SHG women in the same village – that is, with 38 percent more people. Importantly, this is not just driven by social desirability in SHG women's reporting that they speak to more people; other people in the network are also more likely to name SHG members as political discussion partners (in-degree). Additionally, there is no significant difference between SHG members and non-SHG members' social network size, suggesting SHGs may help to specifically catalyze political discussion. This aligns with the reported effects of SHG participation on political

---

[34] SHG members reported only modest differences from non-SHG members with respect to their social networks, providing some suggestive evidence that these comparisons are justifiable, as the types of women who join SHGs in treated villages are not substantially different in terms of their sociability than those who do not join SHGs. Furthermore, a comparison of women in control villages with non-SHG members in treated villages shows they closely resemble each other with respect to social network size and composition.

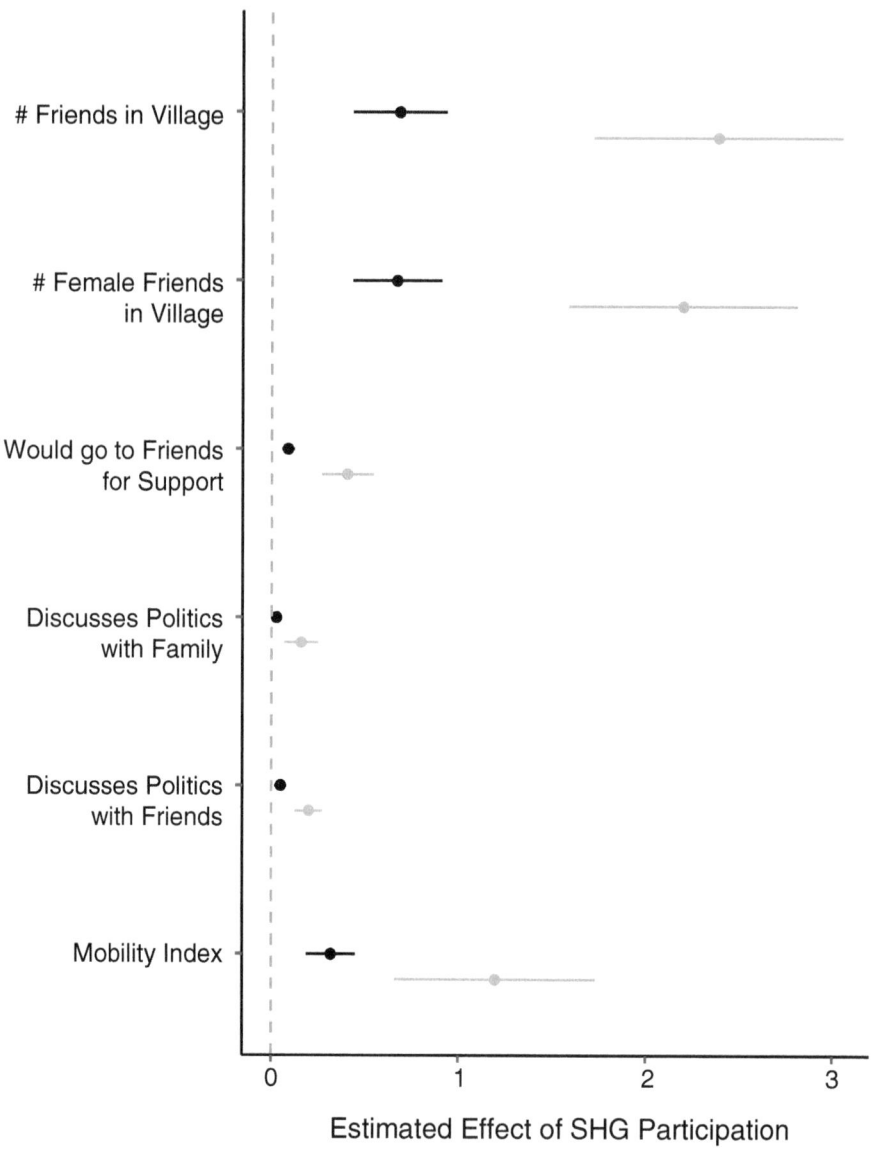

FIGURE 7.4 SHG participation increased women's connections and mobility
Note: The figure shows the estimated effect of the SHG intervention on a series of indicators of connections, political discussion, and mobility. Estimated effects from two models are shown along with corresponding 95 percent confidence intervals. Each variable on the y-axis is a distinct dependent variable, and point estimates are the effect of the SHG treatment on each outcome. Underlying models include village pair-matched fixed effects, and individual covariates and standard errors are clustered at the village level. Data are from the 2016 sample survey in 152 villages in five districts of Madhya Pradesh.

TABLE 7.1 *SHG members' political networks are larger and include a greater share of women than non-SHG members' political networks*

	Political Network		
	Control	Treated	
	All Women	Non-SHG Women	SHG Women
Degree: Number of Ties	2.139*	1.957	2.721*
Out-degree: Number of Ties	1.333*	1.283	1.535*
In-degree: Number of Ties In	0.806	0.674	1.186
Age	38.392	40.739	37.673
Years of Education	4.356	3.800	2.780
% Women	0.638	0.601	0.688
% From Household	0.402	0.365	0.284
% Coethnic	0.905*	0.773	0.702*
% General Caste	0.013	0.028	0.012
% Other Backward Class	0.341*	0.329	0.110*
% Scheduled Caste	0.020*	0.075	0.062*
% Scheduled Tribe	0.615	0.535	0.769

Note: The table reports the average composition of women's political networks by village SHG treatment status and SHG membership status. Data are from the census survey conducted in four villages, two without PRADAN SHGs (Villages A and B) and two with PRADAN SHGs (Villages C and D). All percentages are relative to the total number of nodes out-reported (i.e., out-degree). * denotes that the difference in means across women in control villages and SHG women in treated villages from a simple regression with village-clustered standard errors is statistically significant at the 0.05 level. Bold indicates that the difference in means across non-SHG women in treated villages and SHG women in treated villages from a simple regression is statistically significant at the 0.05 level.

discussion in Figure 7.4. Here, women in treated villages discussed politics more and were more likely to do so with friends than women in control villages. While not shown in Table 7.1, even in treated villages, women comprise only 4 percent of men's political networks. This suggests that while women are becoming more politically connected to each other, they are not becoming more visible or relevant as political actors to men.

Not only do SHG women discuss politics with more people, a larger share of those with whom they discuss politics are women. Women who were members of SHGs had a larger share of their political network comprised of women than both non-SHG women in their own village and women in control villages. The average non-SHG woman in control villages stated that she discusses politics with 1.29 people (out-degree), of which 60 percent are women. The average SHG woman stated that she discusses politics with 1.54 people, of which 69 percent are women.

The greater share of women in SHG members' political networks is mirrored by a reduced share of household members in such networks. Women who were members of SHGs, on average, reported that 28 percent of those with whom they discuss politics are from their household, compared to 37 percent of non-SHG women from the same village and 40 percent of women in control villages. The relatively smaller role of the household in SHG members' political networks suggests the SHG's potential to reduce women's attachment to their household as the locus of political discussion.

Finally, there are additional important compositional differences when comparing non-SHG and SHG women's political networks. SHG women, on average, discuss politics with people who are less educated, younger, less likely to be OBC, and more likely to be ST than non-SHG women. These differences could reflect the characteristics of those who select into SHGs or could suggest that participating in SHGs appears to have enabled women to connect more with women of different backgrounds than they may have otherwise.

These shifts in the nature of women's ties have important consequences for the broader political networks in their villages. Figure 7.5 maps the political discussion network in Village D, one of the two treated villages included in Table 7.1. Village D's political network is strikingly different from that of Village B, shown in Figure 6.2 in Chapter 6. In Village B, women were disconnected from each other and attached largely to a few men, who were well connected and at the center of the network. Village D, instead, features a large and dense cluster of women on the left side of the figure. Furthermore, a majority of SHG members are present in and at the center of this cluster of women. Men remain well connected to each other, but have visibly fewer links to women. The way that gender is distributed in the political network in this village bears similarity to the way that caste category was distributed in the political network in Chapter 6, suggesting that gender may be becoming a cleavage in Village D.

In combination, the evidence in Figures 7.4 and 7.5 and Table 7.1 suggest that SHGs expanded and reshaped women's political networks and gave them greater autonomy from the household and more connections to other women, particularly other group members. It also suggests that this has consequences for the nature of political organization in a village, with gender emerging as a clearer political identity and more salient political cleavage.

Impact on Political Participation

Does SHG membership lead to greater political action? Figure 7.6 reports the estimated impact of the SHG intervention on measures of electoral and non-electoral political participation, including whether the respondent stated that they had voted in the previous local and state elections and whether in the past year they had attended a village assembly meeting, contacted or filed an application with the local Panchayat government, contacted or filed an application with the Block government, campaigned in an election (e.g., mobilizing

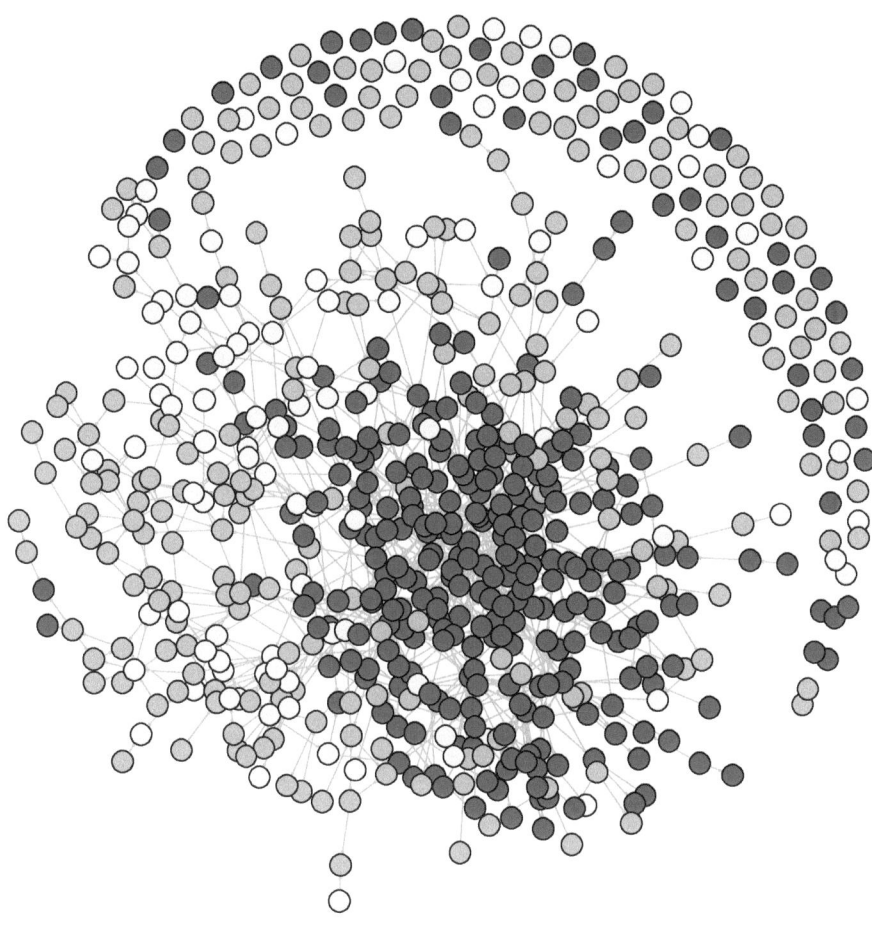

● Men   ○ Non–SHG Women   ○ SHG Women

FIGURE 7.5 Women, particularly SHG members, are densely connected in Village D's
political discussion network
Note: The figure plots the political discussion network in village D, differentiating nodes by gender
and SHG membership. Data are from the census survey conducted in Village D. The network map
removes survey nonrespondents for ease of interpretation.

electoral support or attending a campaign rally), or attended a party meeting.
I also estimate the effect of the SHG intervention on an indicator for whether
the respondent had participated in any non-electoral political activity.

Figure 7.6 illustrates that the SHG intervention had a robust, positive impact
on nearly all measures of non-electoral political participation. SHG members
were 17 percentage points more likely to attend a village assembly meeting,
10 percentage points more likely to make a claim on the Panchayat, and

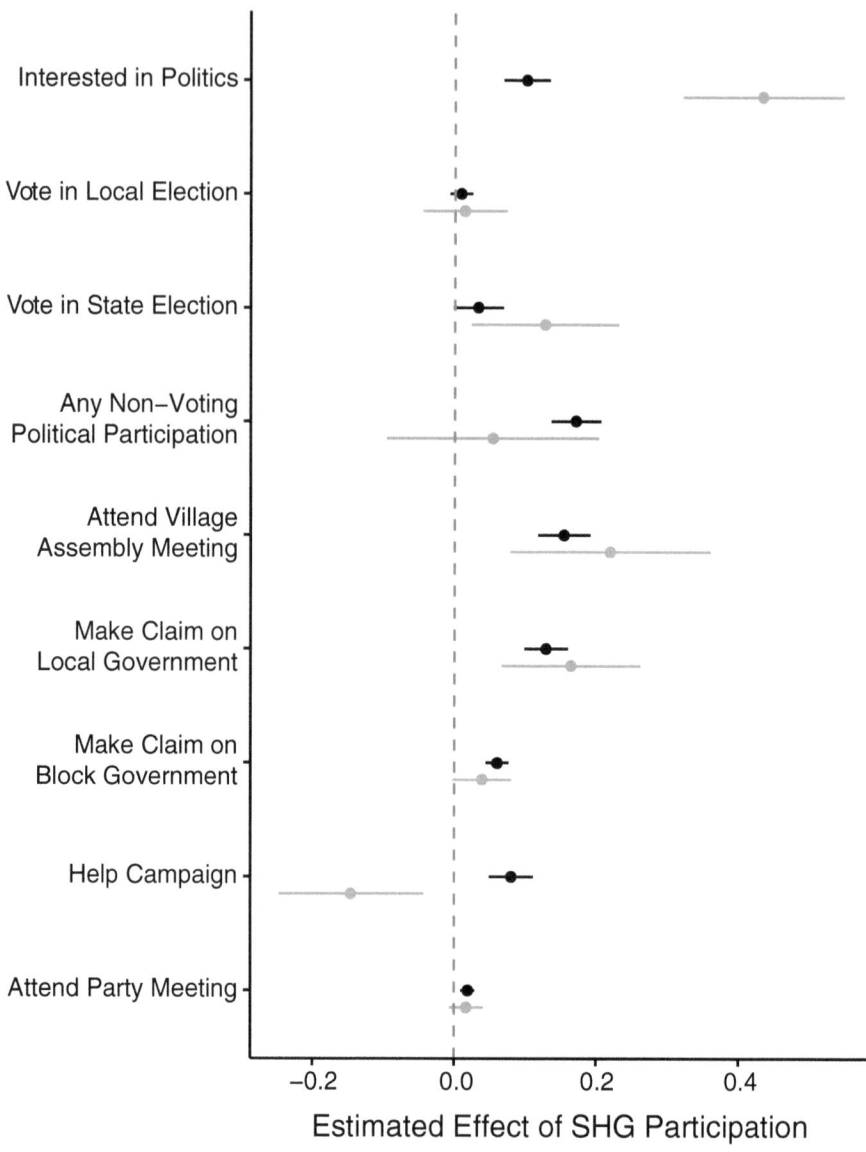

FIGURE 7.6 SHG membership robustly increases women's non-electoral political participation

Note: The figure shows the estimated effect of the SHG intervention on a series of indicators of political participation. Estimated effects from two models are shown along with corresponding 95 percent confidence intervals. Each variable on the y-axis is a distinct dependent variable, and point estimates are the effect of the SHG treatment on each outcome. The underlying models include village pair-matched fixed effects, and individual covariates and standard errors are clustered at the village level. Data are from the 2016 sample survey in 152 villages in five districts of Madhya Pradesh.

4 percentage points more likely to make a claim on the Block. The size and significance of these effects hold when using the data from the subsample, although the effect on any non-electoral participation is attenuated by the negative effect on campaigning in this sample.[35] These effects are substantively meaningful, as they suggest a nearly 100 percent increase in political activity for women in treated versus control villages above the baseline of 22 percent of women in the control villages having attended a village assembly meeting in the past year. Figure 7.6 also reveals that SHG members were significantly more likely to report an interest in politics. This finding suggests that SHGs help women recognize that politics is a legitimate interest for women and elevates the importance of politics in their lives.

The robust positive relationship between SHG membership and non-electoral political participation holds throughout the country. Table A7.4.1 uses data from the nationally representative Indian Human Development Survey to correlate rural women's SHG membership, alongside other confounding variables, with their attendance at village assembly meetings. This survey included only one question on political participation, which was only asked in the supplemental women's survey and therefore does not permit comparisons between men and women. While the results in Table A7.4.1 cannot be interpreted causally, they do indicate that there is a large and significant positive correlation between SHG membership and women's political participation across India (and across implementing organizations), even after controlling for resources and indicators of bargaining power.

The effect of SHG participation on voting is less robust; there is no discernible effect on voting in local elections and a positive effect on voting in state elections only in the CATE specifications (see Figure 7.6). This is likely because even non-SHG women vote at high rates, as my theory would predict. It could also be, however, that voting does not have the social costs that accompany public forms of political participation, and is therefore less likely to benefit from women's groups.

SHG membership, also, does not affect political participation equally for women of all caste categories (see Figure 7.7, which plots the heterogeneous effects of SHG participation by caste category for the full sample of villages). While women from all caste groups experienced a large and positive shift in their political behavior as a result of the SHG intervention, the effects are largest for OBC women, particularly with respect to attending village assembly meetings. OBC women's meeting attendance increased significantly more than that of ST women (evident in the lack of overlap between their confidence interval bars). This could be because SHGs are more likely to empower women from groups that are more likely to hold political power in the village.

---

[35] It is plausible that SHG members in this community were less likely to campaign as a result of their SHG membership, given that campaigning generally involves working with political insiders outside of the SHG.

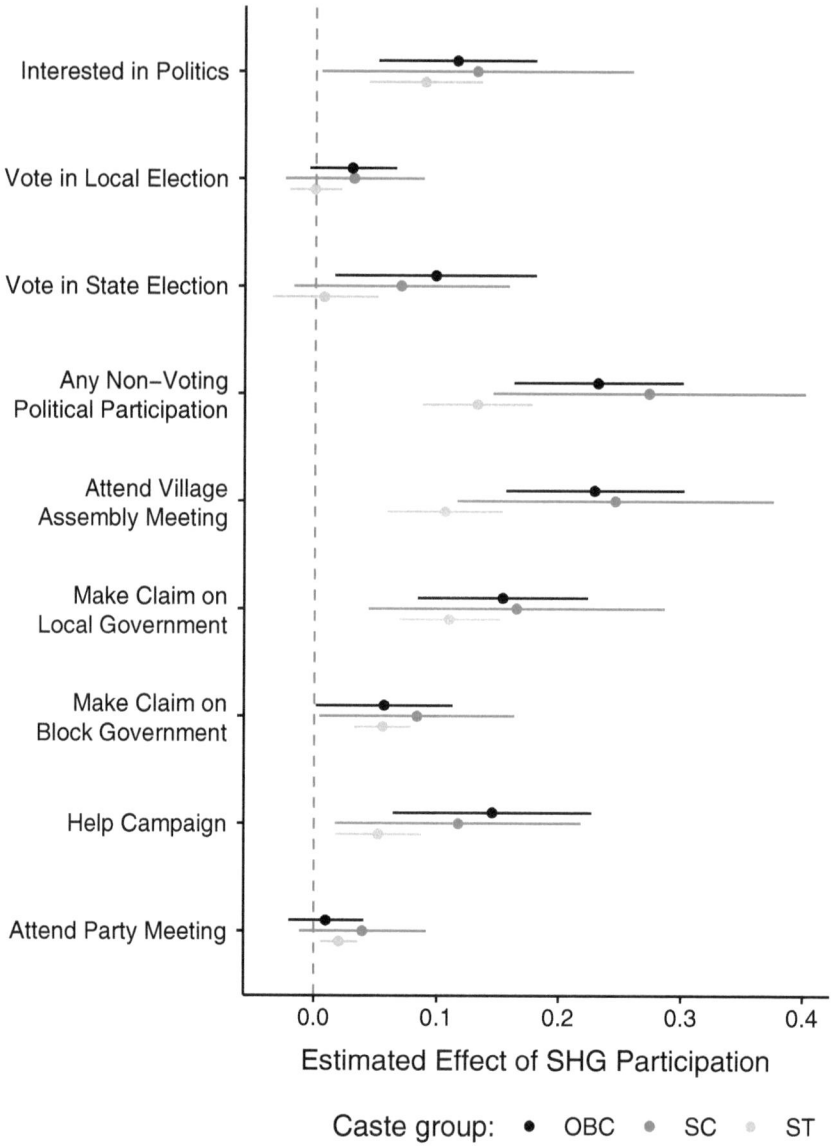

FIGURE 7.7 SHG membership increased OBC women's political participation
marginally more than ST women's political participation
Note: The figure plots the marginal effect of the SHG intervention from a model that interacts
treatment status with caste group along with corresponding 95 percent confidence intervals. The
reported effects are only for the model that uses the full sample of villages and denotes the average
effects for those in SHGs. Each variable on the y-axis is a distinct dependent variable, and point
estimates are the marginal effect of the SHG treatment on each outcome. Underlying models include
village pair-matched fixed effects, and individual covariates and standard errors are clustered at the
village level. Data are from the 2016 sample survey in 152 villages in five districts of
Madhya Pradesh.

However, OBC women also had the lowest rates of political participation in control villages, suggesting that caste power does not necessarily translate into greater empowerment for women. Given OBC women's relatively worse baseline position, it could be that SHG membership affected all women equally, helping OBC women to catch up to others and resulting in identical rates of participation for all women. In control villages, 15 percent of OBC women had attended a village assembly meeting, compared to 25 percent of ST women. In treated villages, the figures were higher and much more similar: 37 percent and 35 percent, respectively. This suggests that SHG membership helped close the caste-based gap in women's political participation. Finally, given that caste-based differences in the effect of SHG participation are only significant for village meeting attendance, it could be that OBC women face greater social resistance to their political participation in such public spaces and therefore benefit more from the collective action introduced by SHGs. Appendix A5 further demonstrates that the effect of SHG participation on political participation does not vary based on age (Figure A7.5.1) or the amount of land owned (Figure A7.5.2).

SHGS AND WOMEN'S COLLECTIVE ACTION

SHGs clearly increase women's political participation. But why? I have argued that, principally, SHGs enable women's social solidarity and, in turn, support women's collective action. According to the proposed model, women's political participation is constrained by both a lack of autonomy from the household and the likelihood of experiencing a backlash for deviating from norms. Overcoming such obstacles inside and outside the household from a position of social inferiority requires more than just desire, skills, or resources. In the absence of institutions that protect women's right to political inclusion, collective action among women, I have argued, allows for the credibe contestation of this coercive power. If SHGs build women's social solidarity, then women will be in a better position to jointly mobilize and demand representation in political spaces.

Social psychological theories of collective action have highlighted the importance of group-based social identity. Van Zomeren, Postme, and Spears summarize this literature and argue that collective action is possible through shared feelings of injustice, a shared and politicized group identity, and the belief that action is likely to successfully challenge these injustices.[36] Social capital theorists suggest that collective action is rooted in trust and solidarity, which facilitates social capital and the expectation that others will also act for the collective good even if there are no immediate benefits to them.[37] Both sets

[36] Van Zomeren, Postme, and Spears (2008). See also McAdam (1995).
[37] Putnam, Leonardi, and Nanetti (1994); Brehm and Rahn (1997); Putnam (2000); Krishna (2002a).

of theories suggest that collective action, particularly action aimed at social change, requires strong ties among groups that share collective goals.

SHGs are expected to shape women's political behavior by transforming their networks, creating a formal space for women to develop solidaristic bonds and social capital, raising the salience of gender and women's interests (and thus inculcating a shared identity among women and an awareness of gender-based discrimination), and providing an organizational structure to foster and support collective action. The high transaction costs to collective action are, therefore, overcome through group information-sharing, discussion-based preference negotiation, and joint accountability. Groups that fail to develop solidaristic social capital are less likely to overcome these transaction costs and generate political change.

Trust, Solidarity, and Group Politicization

While SHGs formally focus on financial access, the regular group meetings create an institutionalized space for women to convene. Regular participation in credit groups has been shown to increase women's social capital.[38] The concept of group lending was founded on the premise that localized group trust facilitates financial cost sharing.[39] Trust and solidarity within these networks are considered critical to their economic success and viability; weekly interactions are encouraged to build and strengthen these relationships. Unlike other microfinance models, such as general savings groups and village savings and loan associations, SHGs have no set time horizon or payout period, which is likely to foster deeper social capital within the group. These institutions, therefore, serve as an ideal case to evaluate the role of social networks and social solidarity in women's political behavior, as they are not explicitly political spaces, yet they seek to form strong social ties.

Additionally, because SHGs are formal spaces, they are likely to build networks in meaningfully different ways than passing social exchanges.[40] The institutionalized group space provides a structure for women to meet, get to know each other, and share their life experiences. Regular meetings are likely to foster group discussions of personal and community concerns. Even conversations about daily activities can have a political tinge, as the economic division of labor that determines how most women spend their time also shapes their interactions with public services. For example interviews regularly highlighted the difficulties women face in collecting water. One woman explained that during the dry season, when their village faced water shortages, she would walk for two hours to collect clean drinking water for her family. While sharing

---

[38] Feigenberg, Field, and Pande (2010).   [39] Besley and Coate (1995); Ghatak (1999).
[40] Auerbach (2017).

such incidents may not be interpreted as political discussion, these experiences are inherently political and gendered.

I spent several months visiting and observing SHGs in Madhya Pradesh. While my presence in these spaces likely led to atypical meetings, I was struck by the variation in the discussion I observed. A typical meeting would usually begin with everyone sitting in a circle and the SHGs bookkeeper updating on group finances (e.g., collecting new savings, discussing loan disbursement, etc.). Women would discuss the status of their farms and current economic troubles. Since most women used loans to improve their farming techniques, women were always very eager to share their innovations, such as new crops, trellis farming, and new irrigation structures. These conversations, however, often quickly turned into exchanges about the challenges women faced in meeting the livelihoods needs of their households. Sometimes these conversations focused on women sharing their unique economic struggles or farming plights (e.g., a bad crop season, unexpected expenses, etc.). More often, however, these conversations turned toward the failures of their local government to provide the services they needed to improve their farm's productivity or ease their daily survival. The most common of these conversations centered on water, be it drinking water, water for irrigation, or water for livestock.

At this point, the meeting would usually have concluded all formal requirements, and so women would just chat informally. Some women would leave as their responsibilities beckoned. Those who stayed would generally chat in a circle, usually with one or two very vocal women leading the conversation. These conversations almost never covered village gossip (most gossip happened as women waited for the meeting to start) but were usually spaces of grievance sharing. Women would describe a challenge in their life, and others would chime in with support and advice. The nature of these grievances varied substantially across meetings. Sometimes they remained wholly focused on economic challenges. Sometimes they became more generally targeted at ineffective local leaders. Women would regularly describe their frustration with leaders they did not think had provided the services needed or promised. Sometimes these discussions turned toward more personal concerns, such as domestic struggles. One of the most memorable days I spent in the field involved shadowing SHG meetings in two villages. In the first, women openly discussed the challenges of intimate partner violence in their group. One woman even pointed to another and shared that, in the previous year, she (her friend in the group) had been abused and that the group had spent many meetings discussing and strategizing over how to improve her situation. In the second meeting, after already more than an hour of conversation, women shared some of their frustration with having to navigate permission from men to move outside of the home. One woman started to share about the abuse she was experiencing at home, and she was immediately (and subtly) silenced by others in the group. While I do not know what women whispered to her, the change in her behavior suggested that they enforced a norm that such

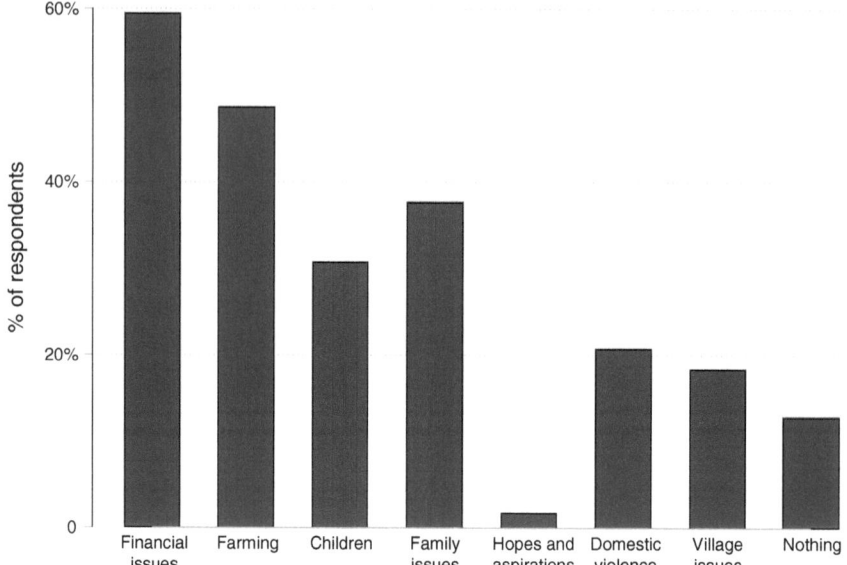

FIGURE 7.8 Women discuss economic, governance, and personal issues in their SHG meetings

Note: The figure plots the share of SHG members who reported discussing various topics in SHG meetings. Data are from the full sample survey in seventy-six treated villages and reflect responses from 721 SHG members. The results are identical when analyzing survey data from the 2,200 SHG members in villages not included in the matched sample. Respondents were asked what topics were discussed in SHG meetings apart from group finances. Multiple responses could be recorded for each respondent.

discussion was not acceptable in the group or in my presence. These two meetings were striking in their difference. In one, women not only discussed some of the most intimate and vulnerable details of their lives but also took pride in the role the group played in improving their lives. In the other, the conversation was bound by internal norms defining acceptable topics.

Figure 7.8 shows the distribution of reported discussion topics in SHG meetings from the sample of treated villages. Unsurprisingly, the most common topics of conversation pertained to financial issues and farming challenges. However, 30 percent of SHG members said they discuss their children with the group, and nearly 40 percent stated that they discuss family issues. Additionally, roughly 20 percent of the women reported discussing domestic violence with their SHG. More than half (57 percent) of SHG members report discussing children, family issues, hopes and aspirations, or domestic violence. To address concerns that women might underreport the frequency of conversations about domestic violence since this is a sensitive and private topic, my survey included a list experiment designed to solicit accurate rates of domestic violence discussion. A random half of SHG members were asked how many of three topics they had discussed in group meetings, including farming techniques, movie stars, and concerns about children. The other half were asked how many of four topics they had discussed, adding domestic violence to the list. The difference in means between the average number of topics discussed by women who saw only three topics and those who randomly saw four should reflect a more accurate rate of domestic violence discussion. Evidence from this list experiment suggests that 43 percent of SHG members likely discussed domestic violence with their group.

An additional indicator of group solidarity is whether group members meet with each other outside of SHG meetings. Exactly 50 percent of SHG members stated that they spent time with their fellow group members outside of group meetings. The qualitative interviews highlighted the depth of solidarity felt by group members and the SHG's role in creating these ties. Women were asked how close they felt to their fellow SHG members. Coded data from interviews with SHG members shows that 57 percent of women reported strong ties with fellow SHG members, 8 percent reported mixed ties, 16 percent reported neutral ties, and only 11 percent described ties as weak. While this suggests that a majority of women felt they had developed strong solidaristic bonds with their fellow SHG members, a nontrivial share of women reported no strong connections (or even weak attachments) to group members. It is important to highlight that the SHGs studied in this chapter had been convening for an average of six years and a range of one to twenty-five years; these measures may thus reflect the maturity of SHG solidarity after many years of repeated interaction.

Some women described their relationship with other SHG members as being like sisters: "We are ten women. We are like friends to each other. We are like friends or sisters to each other. If anyone of us has any problems and she alone cannot solve it, then all of us try to solve it. When all of us come together, then it becomes easy."[41] Others highlighted the trust they have in their fellow group members: "I have trust that they will come running. They will tell something that do this or do that. They will take time. They will help. I have this much trust. I don't know if they will help or not. But I have trust in them."[42] Several interviewees mentioned that regular discussions fostered close bonds. When asked how close she is to other members of her SHG, Shanti bai responded, "We are quite close. When the group was not formed, then it was weird in the beginning, because we were not aware of each other's nature. There were many women I didn't know. But because we meet often and discuss frequently, now we feel that she is my person, and those who are not, we don't feel the same with them because we don't meet like this."[43] In line with this last statement, Figure A7.2.2 shows that the benefits from SHG participation for political

---

[41] Shivati bai (pseudonym), female, 42 years old, ST.
[42] Kastori (pseudonym), female, 26 years old, ST.
[43] Shanti bai (pseudonym), female, 31 years old, ST.

participation do not extend beyond the SHG itself: non-SHG members in villages with SHGs participated in politics at the same rate as women in villages without SHGs.

When do SHGs become explicitly political? Figure 7.8 suggests that just under 20 percent of SHG members stated that they discuss village issues in their group (though many other listed topics of conversation could be considered political). SHG members were also asked how often the group met to jointly petition government officials or political leaders for either village development or personal matters. Exactly 50 percent of SHG members reported having jointly petitioned the government with their SHG in the past year (average of 3.2 petitions). Again, this suggests that nearly half of SHGs evolve from transactional financial institutions into spaces for political dialogue and coordination.

To understand why some groups are more likely to develop solidaristic bonds, Table 7.2 correlates group- and individual-level characteristics with the two aforementioned indicators of solidarity and two indicators of group politicization. These models evaluate whether group heterogeneity and group age correlate with group dynamics.[44] Group diversity is measured using PRADAN's administrative data to create (1) a measure of whether a group includes both OBC and ST women, since these are the two largest caste groups in these villages and (2) a measure of the number of castes (jatis) represented in each group. Group measures are then fuzzy matched to survey respondents based on SHG member name and spouse name, yielding an 85 percent success rate. I also measure group diversity as reported subjectively by the SHG members, based on responses to the question "Are the members of your SHG mostly from the same jati?" and similarly for political party. Group age is measured using administrative and survey data. Administrative data reflect the number of years since SHG formation, and survey-based measures reflect how long each respondent has been a member of the SHG. I additionally control for the SHG members' loan portfolio as reported by survey respondents along with district fixed effects.

The first four columns of Table 7.2 evaluate the correlates of group solidarity. Contrary to expectations, group heterogeneity is either uncorrelated or positively with whether SHG members report discussing social topics or spending time together outside of group meetings. In fact, the objective and self-reported measures of jati diversity both suggest that more homogenous groups with respect to jati are less likely to discuss social topics. Similarly, political homogeneity is negatively correlated with social group discussion. Additionally, group age and individual member time in SHGs are uncorrelated with both indicators of group solidarity.

Likewise, group heterogeneity and age are largely nonpredictive of group politicization. Group heterogeneity is weakly correlated with the frequency of

---

[44] Kochar et al. (2020); Sheth et al. (2021); Sanyal (2014).

TABLE 7.2 *Group heterogeneity and age are largely uncorrelated with group solidarity and politicization*

	Spend time with SHG members outside meetings		Discuss social things in SHG		Discuss political things in SHG		Petition local government with SHG	
Individual-level covariates:								
SHG is mostly from same jati	0.037 (0.044)		-0.118 (0.044)***		-0.057 (0.032)*		-0.036 (0.046)	
SHG is mostly from same political party	0.033 (0.041)		-0.081 (0.042)*		0.087 (0.037)**		0.002 (0.036)	
Years spent in SHG	0.005 (0.006)		-0.006 (0.006)	-0.002 (0.006)	-0.008 (0.006)	-0.006 (0.005)	0.005 (0.005)	0.012 (0.005)**
Total loans received from SHG	0.005 (0.005)		0.010 (0.004)**	0.006 (0.004)*	0.008 (0.004)*	0.007 (0.004)*	0.007 (0.004)*	0.006 (0.004)
Group-level covariates:								
Mixed OBC/ST group		0.006 (0.053)		0.009 (0.055)		-0.072 (0.038)*		0.067 (0.063)
Number of jatis/tribes in SHG		-0.034 (0.025)		0.081 (0.034)**		0.026 (0.019)		0.031 (0.026)
Age of SHG	-0.006 (0.009)	-0.009 (0.008)	0.008 (0.007)	0.002 (0.008)	0.005 (0.007)	0.005 (0.007)	-0.001 (0.010)	0.006 (0.008)
N	614	590	614	590	590	614	590	614
Dependent Variable Mean	0.49	0.50	0.57	0.57	0.19	0.19	0.44	0.45
Fixed Effects	District	District	District	District	District	District	District	District

Note: The table plots the estimated relationship between group heterogeneity and age, and group solidarity and politicization. ***, **, * indicate significant at the 1 percent, 5 percent, and 10 percent levels, respectively. District fixed effects are included, to allow for comparison across villages. Village-clustered standard errors are reported. Data come from both the full sample and the resample in seventy-six villages. Only SHG members are included. SHG loan amount is measured in thousands of rupees and has been winsorized to remove outliers.

political discussion: groups with both OBC and ST women are marginally less likely to discuss politics, but again there is a positive correlation between self-reported jati heterogeneity and political discussion. Political homogeneity is positively and significantly correlated with more political discussion, meaning that women who believe they share partisan affiliation with the majority of group members are more likely to report greater political discussion within the group. But this does not translate into differences in the probability of group petitioning. While these results do not precisely explain why (or when) some groups develop stronger social ties and become politicized, they do suggest that within-group caste heterogeneity does not hinder the formation of social capital, and may even support it. This is potentially important when thinking about how and when SHGs become spaces for developing a shared gender identity.

Spaces for Identity Creation

In the process of developing solidaristic bonds, participation in women's groups is also likely to facilitate the development of a shared gender identity. Common experiences and challenges are likely to emerge in group discussions, particularly with respect to women's subordination. Reserving these spaces for women allows group members to recognize their similarities, the most salient of which are shared experiences of inequality.[45] By identifying shared experiences and struggles, women may come to see that their personal experiences of discrimination are part of broader systemic patterns of discrimination.[46] Group membership can thus raise women's awareness of sexism and shared grievances, even without explicitly aiming to do so, and reveal that these gendered interests are underrepresented in political spaces.[47]

For example, a focus group that I conducted with an SHG in Madhya Pradesh in 2017 had been discussing their challenges with domestic violence in the community and how they were working to stem such violence. One woman shared that prior to joining the group, she was unaware that other women had experienced such violence; she had assumed that it was her fault that her husband regularly abused her. She said she had been ashamed to talk about these experiences but now realized that if she had done so, she would have found many other women in similar situations. One of the coercive tools of the patriarchal order is the ability to make women feel ashamed of the oppression they experience and therefore to stay silent. Women's groups can help break this silence.

Figure 7.9 reports the estimated effect of SHG membership on self-reported attitudes toward gender discrimination and gender norms. While the results are noisy, SHG participation appears to be somewhat correlated with more progressive gender attitudes. Group membership significantly reduced women's

---

[45] Kabeer (2012).   [46] Sapiro (1983).   [47] Kelly and Breinlinger (1996).

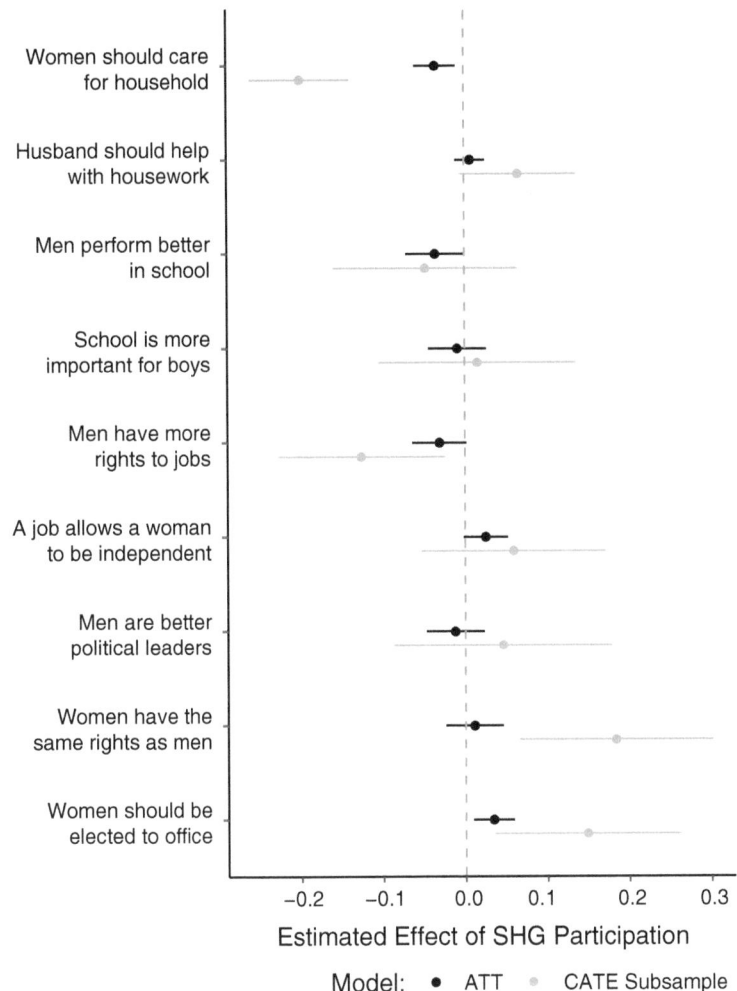

FIGURE 7.9 SHG membership marginally shifted women's attitudes toward gender equality

Note: The figure plots the marginal effect of SHG participation on women's attitudes toward gender equality. Estimated effects from two models are shown along with corresponding 95 percent confidence intervals. Each variable on the y-axis is a distinct dependent variable, and point estimates represent the effect of the SHG treatment on each outcome. Underlying models include village pair-matched fixed effects, and individual covariates and standard errors are clustered at the village level. Data are from the 2016 sample survey in 152 villages in five districts of Madhya Pradesh.

belief that caring for the household is primarily the responsibility of women and increased women's belief that women have the same rights as men and that women should be elected to office. Yet SHG participation did not meaningfully change many attitudes related to gendered norms and acceptable behaviors,

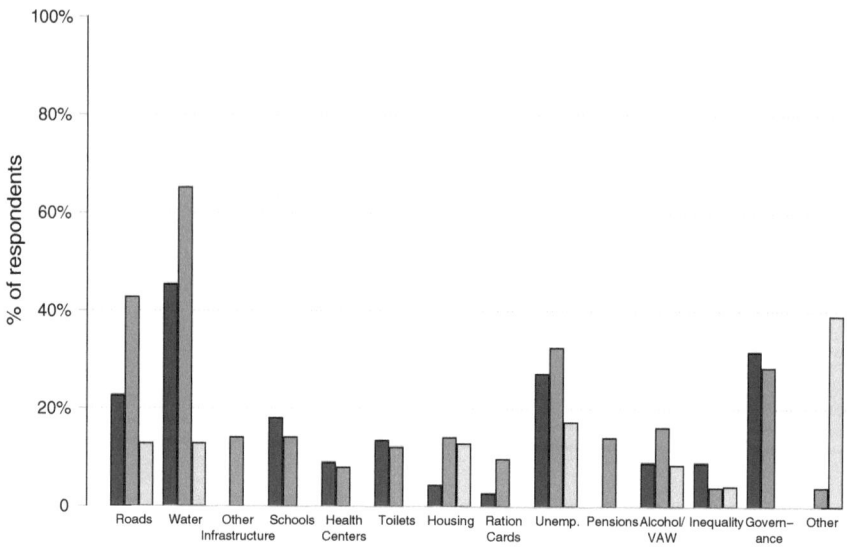

FIGURE 7.10 SHG members report different political preferences than non-SHG members

Note: The figure plots political preferences for non-SHG and SHG women alongside domains of SHG political mobilization. Data are from qualitative interviews with seventy-one women (50 SHG members and 21 non-SHG members) across ten villages in Betul district of Madhya Pradesh. Reported categories are not mutually exclusive, so the shares presented indicate the share of women that reported each domain as either a big problem in their village or a domain of political mobilization.

particularly those pertaining to education and labor market institutions. The results displayed in Figure 7.9 suggest some reconsideration of dominant gender paradigms, though more would be needed to reduce internalized beliefs about women's place in society.

Another indication that SHGs help women develop a shared identity is the activation and mobilization of gender-based interests. Drawing on data from interviews with fifty SHG members and twenty-one non-SHG women, Figure 7.10 documents which issues women believe to be the biggest problem in their village alongside which issues SHGs mobilized in support of. Women who were members of an SHG were more likely than women who weren't to say that roads, water, housing, violence against women, ration cards, unemployment, and pensions were big problems in their villages. Previous research has shown that water and roads disproportionately affect women,[48] suggesting that greater recognition of these problems may be the result of a

---

[48] Chattopadhyay and Duflo (2004).

greater awareness of gender-based interests. Non-SHG women were marginally more likely to report that schools, health centers, and toilets are serious problems in their village. These differences are in part because SHG members named more problems on average than non-SHG women (2.8 problems vs. 2.0 problems on average, respectively). However, Figure A7.6.1 demonstrates that SHG women and non-SHG women have marginally distinct political preferences when looking at only the most important problem named in the census survey. Like with attitudes toward gender equality, the marginal differences in women's preferences suggests that SHG participation may shift women's political priorities but does not fundamentally alter the nature of women's political preferences. However, the sizable difference in the number of reported problems in the village suggests that women may be more inclined to openly articulate these preferences.

While SHG participation did not substantially alter the distribution of preferences among women, SHGs mobilized around a distinct subset of women's interests. Figure 7.10 also reports the share of SHG members that reported collectively mobilizing around each issue area, conditional on having mobilized at all. The most common issue that SHGs mobilized to address was water provision: 32 percent of SHG members reported in interviews that their SHG had mobilized for this purpose. Across the developing world, water has become a key policy area for women, given their disproportionate role in collecting it.[49] It is, therefore, unsurprising that, when women mobilize as a group, they are most likely to do so in support of improved water provision. Other common areas in which SHG members mobilized included the provision of roads, housing support, unemployment, and alcohol prevention/violence against women.

The results related to women's mobilization around alcohol prevention and violence against women reveal the role that SHGs play in defining women's interests and actions. When asked about the biggest problems in their village (prior to any mention of the SHG), few women autonomously named alcoholism or gender-based violence, although SHG members were substantially more likely to do so than non-SHG women (14 percent vs. 9 percent). However, when discussing the domains around which their SHG had mobilized, 20 percent of SHG members highlighted mobilizing around these issues. This aligns with the prevalence of discussing domestic violence within SHGs reported earlier (23 percent of SHG members explicitly reported such discussion and a list experiment estimates 43 percent engaged in such discussion).

Alcohol consumption and violence against women are commonly identified as "women's issues" in India; many states, including Madhya Pradesh, have proposed policies that would prohibit the sale of alcohol and these policies have been articulated as a response to women's concerns. For example, in the state of

---

[49] Chattopadhyay and Duflo (2004).

Bihar, where such a policy has been implemented, an op-ed written by the Chief Minister of Bihar, Nitish Kumar, stated that "women self-help groups, Jeevika, were rewarded for their efforts to make villages alcohol-free," directly attributing prohibition to SHG mobilization.[50] SHG women's mobilization around alcoholism and gender-based violence highlights how gendered group spaces can elevate the salience of interests more specific to women's experiences and provide spaces to coordinate around those shared interests. The finding that at least a quarter of SHGs discussed domestic violence speaks to the solidarity and trust shared among women in these groups and indicates that a broader feminist consciousness-raising is occurring in some of these women-only spaces.

Knowledge and Efficacy

Participation in women's groups can also help women develop civic skills that are likely to improve perceptions of both individual and group-based efficacy. The belief that political action has the potential to be effective is particularly critical for those who have been subordinated by existing institutions and therefore do not trust them. In interviews, the most commonly cited benefit to membership in SHGs was increased confidence. Many women described themselves as afraid and incapable of speaking with strangers prior to joining the group. Through regular and institutionalized interaction with women in the SHG, they described the process of developing their voice. SHGs acted as laboratories for political participation, providing an opportunity to experiment with deliberation. In these meetings, women explored alternative preferences, practiced deliberation, developed confidence and authority, and, as a result, strengthened their civic skills.[51] Batesha, a thirty-four-year-old SC woman, described the process of practicing voice and learning about deliberation by saying:

Earlier, we did not go to Gram Sabha. Since I joined the SHG, I go. I feel that I got the experience of what it is like to speak in the Gram Sabha from my time in the SHG. Before this, I didn't know how the Gram Sabha was conducted, what they said, and what is being done. . . . However much information we get in SHG, men in the village don't have that much information. Men don't have as much information as women have now. Men didn't think about the development of the village until now as compared to women. Today, women are ahead of men in knowing what kind of development there should be in the village; how much improvement there should be.[52]

Figure 7.11 reports the effect of the SHG intervention on an index of subjective and objective political information, an index of perceptions of

[50] Kumar (2018).
[51] Burns et al. (2001) documented the importance of civic skills for non-electoral participation in the United States and attributed the development of these skills to participation in social institutions.
[52] Batesha (pseudonym), female, 34 years old, SC.

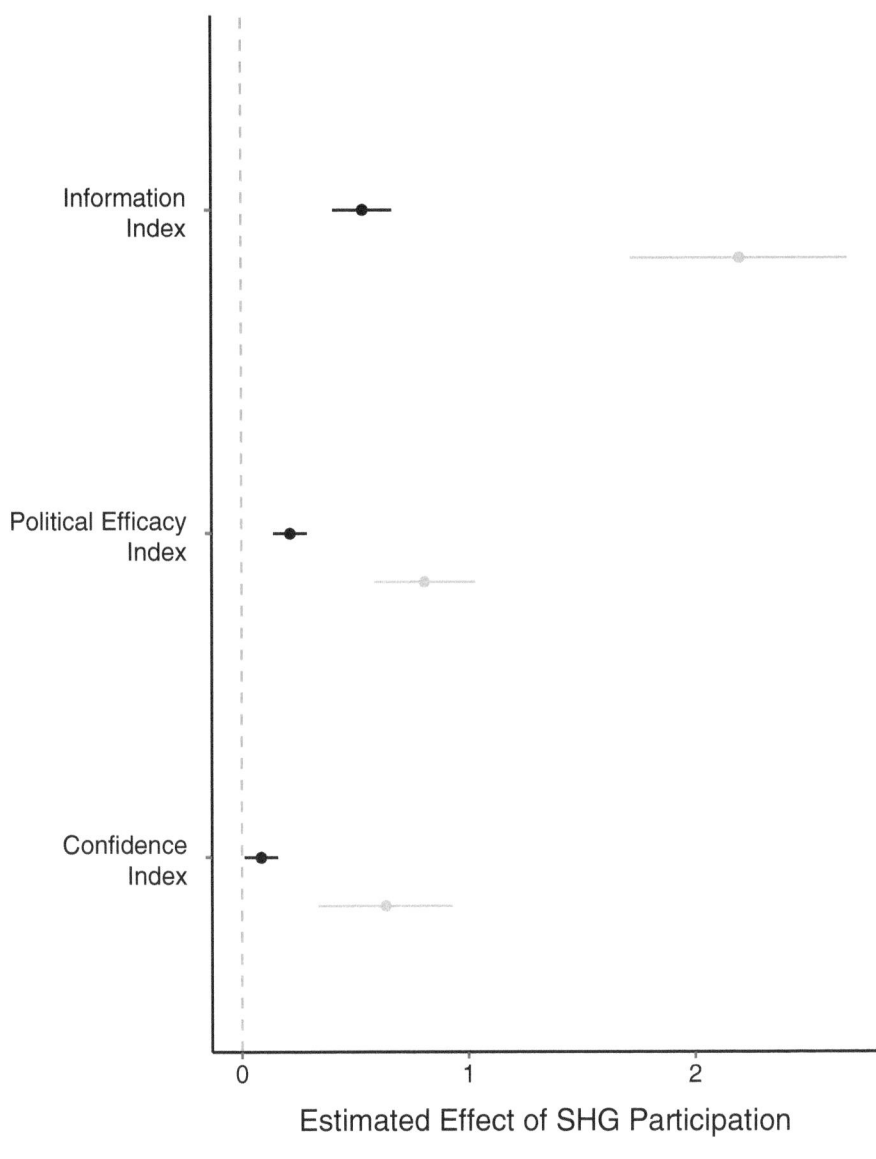

FIGURE 7.11 SHG participation increases civic skills

Note: The figure plots the estimated effect of the SHG intervention on women's information, political efficacy, and confidence. Estimated effects from two models are shown along with corresponding 95 percent confidence intervals. Each variable on the y-axis is a distinct dependent variable, and point estimates are the effect of the SHG treatment on each outcome. Underlying models include village pair-matched fixed effects, and individual covariates and standard errors are clustered at the village level. Data are from the 2016 sample survey in 152 villages in five districts of Madhya Pradesh.

political efficacy (i.e., whether the respondent would feel comfortable speaking up, considers themselves qualified to participate in politics, and feels they could do a good job as village chairperson), and an index of civic skills (i.e., whether the respondent is confident, can confidently speak to strangers, and can confidently speak in front of a group). It shows that SHG participation has a positive and significant effect on political information across nearly all indicators. Women in treated villages were more likely to state that they know the names of political leaders and that they know how to make a claim and were more likely to correctly identify the program specifics for Mahatma Gandhi National Rural Employment Guarantee scheme. The treatment also demonstrably increased women's confidence, sense of political efficacy, and civic skills. Women in treated villages were 10 percentage points more likely to report that they would speak up at the village assembly meeting and were significantly more likely to state that they felt confident.

Igniting Collective Action

Given the social costs associated with violating norms against women's political participation, women's political participation is expected to increase most when group structures are used to mobilize collective action and demand the right to public participation, even in the face of social sanctioning. Collective action among a critical mass of women is expected to enable them to demand representation in public political spaces and provide protection from household contestation, as women can lean on each other to sanction household heads when they lash out.[53] Yet, collective action bears high transaction costs, as groups must identify and negotiate which interests to mobilize around and enforce group participation. As a result, collective action is most likely when groups have formed solidaristic bonds, developed a sense of shared identity, and believe such action is likely to be effective.[54] With sufficient solidarity, group members can also utilize group spaces to plan and coordinate collective action – a process that parallels the cooperation of political behavior that occurs within households – and apply social pressure to each other to ensure participation.

Qualitative interviews highlighted how women gained access to politics as a group. The interviews were coded to reflect whether women reported that their SHG attended the village assembly meeting together or collectively mobilized in some other way to achieve a shared goal. Strikingly, more than 80 percent of the interviewees said their SHG had explicitly coordinated to attend the village assembly meeting as a group, and 60 percent reported that their group had collectively mobilized in some other way to achieve a shared goal. Women stated that SHGs would discuss upcoming village meetings and plan to attend them together. They would go door to door before a village meeting to collect

---

[53] Kanter (1977); Dahlerup (1988).   [54] Van Zomeren, Postme, and Spears (2008).

all SHG members so they could enter as a group. This was partly a response to direct experiences of backlash; women in one village shared with me that men tried to forcibly remove them from the village meeting by beating them with sticks. In subsequent meetings, these women were able to withstand these threats because they had shown up in sufficient numbers.

Group collective action can also be deployed to ensure women's continued presence in SHGs. In my conversations with SHG members, many described how their husbands had become concerned with their continued participation in the group, particularly after women appeared more confident and empowered, and that the SHG strategized on how to enable their continued participation in the group. In one SHG meeting I visited, women described how the husband of one group member tried to restrict her attendance at public meetings. The SHG members shared that they discussed the matter and jointly showed up at her home, demanding her right to attend. A focus group participant described this coordination:

We have done many things in the village. We have solved issues for children in the village. We have also fought for the prohibition of alcohol. A new team from our SHG has been formed on the issue of intoxication. If women are being beaten or harassed by men, then we help them. We go to the Panchayat together. Wherever is any issue, all we sisters go there collectively.[55]

Santosh, the husband of an SHG member, described how women contested backlash through collective action:[56]

INTERVIEWER: And if we talk of women of your village, do women in your village go to the Gram Sabha?

SANTOSH: Yes, SHG women surely attend Gram Sabha, and nowadays women are going more.

INTERVIEWER: And do men in the village think something about women who attend the Gram Sabha?

SANTOSH: They used to, but not anymore.

INTERVIEWER: What did they think before?

SANTOSH: They thought that they are women and what can they do by attending Gram Sabha.

INTERVIEWER: Even now, does this happen in your village?

SANTOSH: No, but in few houses, it might, but nowadays men listen more to women.

INTERVIEWER: When you have attended Gram Sabha, what points are raised by women?

SANTOSH: If she is having a problem with her husband, then she will complain about it; if her husband is beating her, then she tells that only, and the Panchayat officials would say that they cannot get involved in personal life. Once a lady had raised that point, and the Panchayat officials told her that she needed to resolve it within your

---

[55] SHG focus group led by the author, July 8, 2016.
[56] Santosh (pseudonym), male, 32 years old, ST.

family. All the women in the SHG come together if they have some problem in the village. Here there is a problem of liquor, and SHG women came together and they said that they could approach the police to get it stopped, and the women held a rally, where women got together, and they had support from higher-level officials who call us and ask if they can help us out.

INTERVIEWER: Ok, after formation of the SHG, was there any progress in this village?

SANTOSH: It is all good but nothing as per progress of the village; changes are there, as now ladies are not having problem in their houses.

Santosh's description of the process of change within his village reaffirms several of the dynamics expected in my argument: men initially questioned and challenged women's participation in public spaces, women gained access to these spaces by collectively organizing, and this collective action was leveraged to address women's needs and particularly to demand autonomy from the house and protection from violence. It also highlighted the many hurdles that women face in becoming seen as political agents: households that abuse and restrict them, community members that shame and sanction them, and politicians that devalue their issues.

Group collective action is often critical to securing agency to leave the house, to ensuring women's voices and demands were heard in spaces where they were typically absent or silenced, and to protecting them from community-level backlash. Women shared that they were only allowed out of their homes if they traveled as a group. They also reported both a fear of speaking alone and the expectation that their demands would not be heard unless they entered meetings with a critical mass. It is well documented that women's voices are less likely to be heard and addressed in public spaces, particularly when men dominate positions of political authority.[57] Collective participation ensured that they would be considered politically relevant. And in many cases, women's strength in numbers also provided physical protection.

I estimate the correlates of political participation for SHG women in treated villages in Table 7.3 to empirically test whether SHG members who reported group-based collective action were more likely to participate in politics than those who did not. This model controls for group solidarity, group diversity, group age, and traditional correlates of political participation, including education, income and consumption, free time, and demographics, to attempt to rule out potential factors that might affect both women's political participation and the likelihood that SHGs collectively act.

I find that group-based collective action – whether a respondent reports that their SHG had collectively petitioned the Panchayat – is strongly and positively correlated with attendance at village assembly meetings. This correlation holds in both significance and size even after controlling for resources and group characteristics. Substantively, this documents that the SHG members who stated that they collectively acted with their SHG were more likely to participate in

[57] Karpowitz and Mendelberg (2014); Parthasarathy, Rao, Palaniswamy (2017).

TABLE 7.3 *SHG collective action is associated with SHG members'*
political participation

	Attend village assembly meeting	
Individual-level covariates:		
Petition local government with SHG	0.197	0.188
	(0.043)***	(0.041)***
Discuss political things in SHG	0.092	0.060
	(0.044)**	(0.054)
Spend time with SHG members outside meetings		0.076
		(0.038)**
Discuss social things in SHG		0.070
		(0.052)
SHG is mostly from same jati		0.020
		(0.049)
SHG is mostly from same political party		−0.005
		(0.039)
Time spent in SHG		0.001
		(0.007)
Total loans received from SHG		0.003
		(0.004)
Group-level covariates:		
Mixed OBC/ST group		−0.102
		(0.056)*
Number of jatis/tribes in SHG		0.071
		(0.026)***
Age of SHG		−0.004
		(0.008)
N	789	565
Dependent Variable Mean	0.42	0.43
Fixed Effects	District	District

Note: The table estimates the SHG-based correlates of political participation for SHG members. ***, **, * indicate significance at the 1 percent, 5 percent, and 10 percent levels, respectively. District fixed effects are included, to allow for comparison across villages since collective action is likely to be shared at the village-level, however, results are robust to the inclusion of village fixed effects. Village-clustered standard errors are reported. Data come from both the full sample and resample in seventy-six villages. Only SHG members are included. SHG loan amount is measured in thousands of rupees and has been winsorized to remove outliers. Models control for general covariates of women's political participation, including education, household monthly expenditures, acres of land owned, housing material, labor force participation, social category, number of children at home, amount of time spent working or on domestic work, religion, age, and marital status.

politics than SHG members who did not report collective action. The reported occurrence of political discussion in an SHG is also positively associated with attendance at village assembly meetings though not statistically different from zero with the inclusion of control variables. Additionally, both measures of group solidarity – whether SHG members discuss social issues at group meetings and whether group members spend time together outside of meetings – are positively and significantly correlated with women's political participation. Contrary to expectations, group diversity (i.e., having multiple jatis represented in a group) is positively correlated with women's political participation, suggesting the potential for women to traverse traditional social boundaries in pursuit of a common goal.[58] These results suggest that group dynamics and particularly group political coordination likely facilitate individual political action.[59]

ALTERNATIVE EXPLANATION: ECONOMIC RESOURCES

SHGs are fundamentally spaces of economic exchange. Thus, an alternative mechanism linking SHG participation to political participation could be through higher incomes or greater financial security. The link between SHG participation and political participation may be purely a function of new economic resources:[60] access to credit may provide households with greater financial security and, therefore, the ability to devote more free time to pursuits such as political participation.

Figure 7.12 estimates whether the SHG intervention affected economic resources and suggests that any impact of the SHG intervention on political behavior is unlikely to be due to increased financial resources. There is no robust relationship between SHG participation and assets, consumption, food security, or access to quick credit, even though the main purpose of SHGs is to provide access to finance. While there is a positive effect of SHG participation on monthly household expenditure, it is not accompanied by changes in consumption or assets. This supports the evidence in Figure 7.2 that SHG participation did not affect financial indicators of bargaining power. These findings are in line with those of past studies on how microcredit affects economic empowerment, which find tenuous effects at best.[61] While access to microcredit has been shown to generally encourage business creation, it has not improved

---

[58] Varshney (2001).

[59] It is difficult to distinguish whether collective action is driven by group members' own initiation or whether PRADAN (the organization mobilizing the SHG) encouraged this behavior. The organization's role was intended to largely facilitate SHG coordination, and not to promote particular ideologies or behaviors. Interviews with PRADAN staff suggested that they viewed their job as providing information on finances and livelihoods and facilitating additional conversation only if initiated by the women, though they did discuss suggesting village assembly attendance when women articulated shared frustrations. Interviews with SHG members never mentioned that a PRADAN implementer alone determined their behavior. Even if the organization did encourage this behavior, it is still through collective action that women gained entry into political spaces. This would not undermine the observed effects but highlights the need to better understand when and how groups capitalize on their collective action potential.

[60] Schlozman, Burns, and Verba (1994); Burns, Schlozman, and Verba (2001).

[61] Banerjee et al. (2013); Brody et al. (2015).

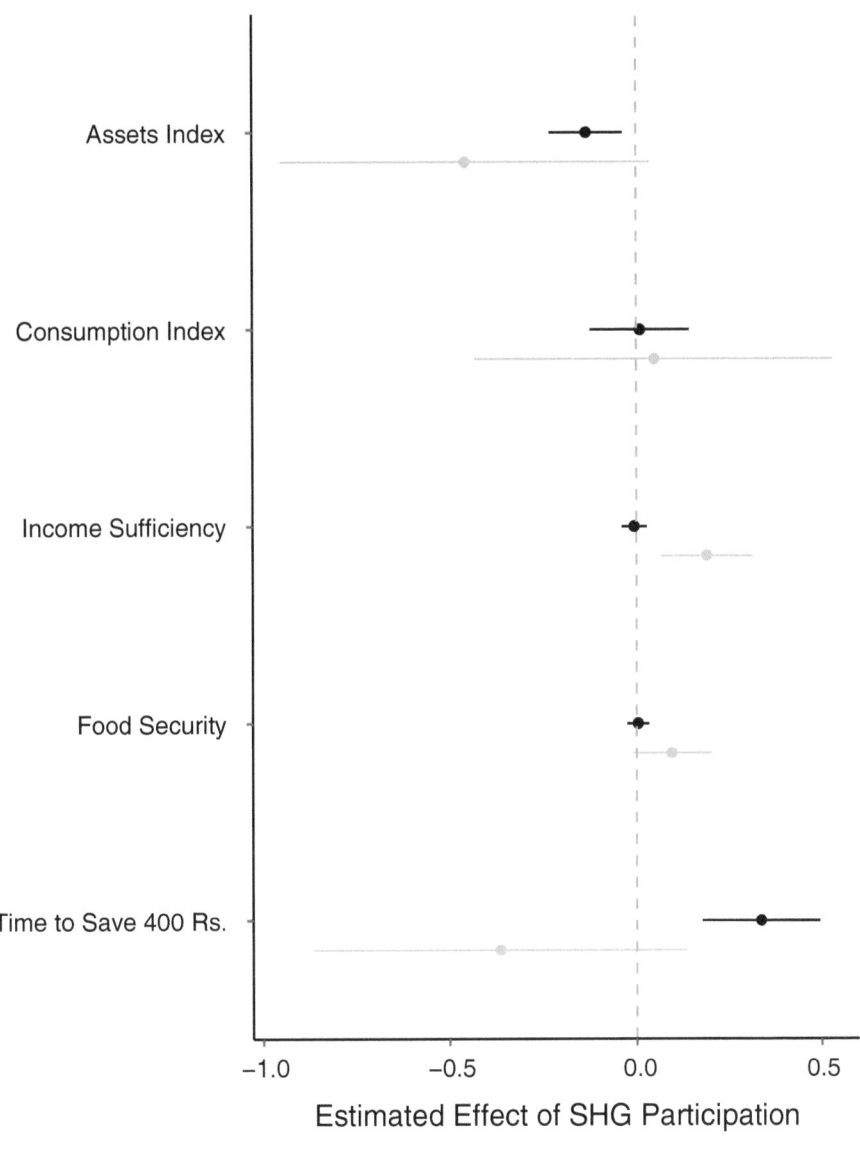

FIGURE 7.12 SHG participation does not robustly increase women's economic resources
Note: This figure plots the effect of the SHG intervention on women's economic resources. Estimated effects from two models are shown along with corresponding 95 percent confidence intervals. Each variable on the y-axis is a distinct dependent variable, and point estimates denote the effect of the SHG treatment on each outcome. Underlying models include village pair-matched fixed effects, and individual covariates and standard errors are clustered at the village level. Data are from the 2016 sample survey in 152 villages in five districts of Madhya Pradesh.

consumption or incomes, likely due to the challenges associated with turning credit into long-term profit generation.[62]

DISCUSSION

In this chapter, I have shown that an apolitical external intervention – the creation of microcredit groups – can dramatically increase women's political participation, even when structures of inequality inside and outside the household remain unchanged. The principal mechanism driving this effect appears to be how participating in these groups expanded and restructured women's political networks, expanded their political autonomy from the household, and facilitated women's collective action to gain entry into previously exclusionary political spaces. For a majority of the SHGs studied, group meetings became spaces for social and political discussion and planning, transcending their intended function as spaces for financial management. In these groups, women collectively organized to gain access to political spaces and make demands on local governments, often on issues of water provision and protection from alcoholism and domestic abuse. SHG members' political participation was much lower if their group did not collectively organize and, more generally, these positive outcomes on political participation only benefit women who were members of the SHG and do not spill over into the behavior of non-SHG members.

I also show that participation in these groups increased women's reported decision-making power within the household, particularly with respect to political decision-making, but did not robustly improve their agency in voting, bargaining power, or economic position. This suggests that it is possible to radically increase women's political participation through solidaristic networks and autonomy from the household, even without fundamentally altering the underlying structures that keep women dependent on the household.

The age-old adage is true: there is strength in numbers. The effect of women's groups on political action far eclipsed that of other interventions shown to increase women's political participation.[63] These microcredit groups, which have become the largest female empowerment policy in India, have proven to be spaces in which women can gain access to political spaces. Yet, the evidence in this chapter also reveals the limits to women's political empowerment: women's political participation, though not always their completely political agency, is enabled through collective action, but such collective action bears high costs. Only some groups were able to surmount the hurdles to collective action through sufficient solidarity to ignite political change. In the next chapter, I will consider how group solidarity can be spurred through external intervention and critical consciousness-raising.

---

[62] Banerjee et al. (2013); Brody et al. (2015).
[63] Chattopadhyay and Duflo (2004); Robinson and Gottlieb (2019).

8

Consciousness-Raising as the Ignition for Collective Action

Women constitute a diverse group with many varied interests that span multiple crosscutting identities. This diversity can make it difficult to generate solidarity among women and hamper efforts to mobilize against shared injustices.[1] The finding that the institutionalization of women's groups in and of itself led to a dramatic change in women's political behavior is therefore remarkable. I expect that the more that women are able to connect with a gender-based group consciousness and develop a shared identity, the more likely they are to engage in gender-based collective action. This chapter evaluates the importance of solidarity for women's political behavior and shows that autonomy from the household alone is limited in its scope for empowerment.

In her description of consciousness-raising, Batliwala writes:

The process of women's empowerment must begin in the mind, by changing women's consciousness. This means changing a woman's beliefs about herself and her rights, capacities, and potential; creating awareness of how gender, as well as other socio-economic and political forces, are acting on her; helping her break free of the sense of inferiority that has been imprinted since earliest childhood; enabling her to acknowledge and rejoice in her strengths, knowledge, intelligence, and skills. Above all, supporting her to recognize her innate right to self-determination, dignity and justice, and to realise that it is she, along with her sisters, who must assert that right, for no one who holds power will give it away willingly.[2]

Consciousness-raising has long been considered a critical first step toward group mobilization.[3] If a marginalized group does not have a shared identity and an awareness of how that identity intersects with inequality and

---

[1] Teele (2018); Morgan-Collins and Natusch (2021); Crenshaw (1990).   [2] Batliwala (1994: 8).
[3] Sapiro (1983).

discrimination, it is unlikely to undertake joint action.[4] Gender consciousness-raising has thus been seen as particularly critical given how deeply women in patriarchal societies internalize gender roles and norms.[5] Consciousness-raising programs, more broadly known as gender mainstreaming programs, seek to facilitate a shared bond and sense of identity among women by making them aware of the gendered struggles they experience.

Traditional approaches to empowerment have coupled external intervention with consciousness-raising based on the premise that empowerment is impossible without consciousness.[6] This also formed the basis of the movement around consciousness-raising groups by US feminists in the late 1960s and 1970s.[7] This chapter tests this premise. While I have shown that simply participating in an apolitical women's group can increase women's political participation, groups that transformed into spaces of solidarity, political discussion, and deliberation were more successful at mobilizing collective action. Under what conditions will women's groups undergo such a transformation, and what role does group consciousness play in this process?

In this chapter, I evaluate the impact of a gender consciousness-raising intervention delivered to a set of Self-Help Groups (SHGs) on women's attitudes, group dynamics, and ultimately political behavior. The gender program was developed and delivered by PRADAN and a feminist nongovernmental organization (NGO), Jagori, to a set of SHGs in rural Madhya Pradesh through a pilot program sponsored by UN Women from 2011 to 2015. The program was designed to raise women's awareness of gender inequalities, encourage discussion of social and political issues pertinent to women, and ignite collective action among them by fostering a shared group identity. The program implemented a series of gender trainings in some of PRADAN's SHGs. I examine whether participation in these training sessions activated stronger attachments to gender as an identity, stimulated political discussion within SHGs, and ultimately led to women's collective action in political spaces. Since the pilot program was not randomized, I pair match villages that did and did not receive the gender trainings to estimate their effect on women's political behavior.[8] Knowledge of the assignment mechanism is used to justify this identification approach.

---

[4] Klein (1986).   [5] Kabeer (2012).

[6] Batliwala (1993, 1994). Cornwall (2016) demonstrates that projects that include consciousness-raising have a much more transformative impact.

[7] Sarachild (1978).

[8] The villages studied in this chapter that did not receive the gender mainstreaming program overlap with those studied in Chapter 6. The villages studied that *did* receive the gender program are new to this book and are not evaluated in any other chapter. None of the villages studied in Chapters 1–7 received the gender program. Chapter 1 describes the overlap of the study villages across chapters.

I find that this gender program is associated with significantly higher levels of political participation among SHG members. Women who took part in the program also had more information about the political process and a greater sense of political efficacy. These differences are among SHG women, and so reflect an additional improvement in political outcomes above those from simply participating in SHGs (as shown in Chapter 7). I also establish that this program is associated with a greater likelihood that SHGs were collectively oriented toward politics and concentrated this orientation on issues of particular concern to women, namely water provision and the prevention of gender-based violence. Yet women showed no difference in their attitudes about the role of women in society after the training; in some instances, they vocalized even less support for gender equality.

Why would a gender consciousness program empower women to engage in political action but entrench gender-biased beliefs? I argue that women experienced a backlash in response to their participation in the gender program. SHG members in villages with the gender program reported more than 200 percent more harassment and public shaming than SHG members in villages that were not offered the gender program. This backlash provides evidence of the coercive nature of the patriarchal political order – when challenged, those with power responded with backlash. Faced with such resistance, women may have responded by signaling their compliance with dominant norms. Many women characterized their political action as bringing generally valuable development to their communities, thus recasting their political empowerment as complying with norms of women's broader caretaking. Others, however, responded by demanding institutional protections from gender-based violence, thus demonstrating how women's demands for empowerment are both a cause and a consequence of broader structures of coercion and oppression.

Ultimately, women's experiences of backlash and resistance in response to their empowerment are evidence of the critical need for collective action. While women's groups may or may not endogenously transform into spaces for collective action for a variety of reasons, understanding the efficacy of external attempts to raise group consciousness can highlight the importance of group discussion and social solidarity in engendering collective action and political participation. These findings, therefore, deepen our understanding of why, how, and when group participation generates shifts in women's political behavior. And how those whose power is threatened respond to challenges to their patriarchal authority.

A GENDER CONSCIOUSNESS-RAISING PROGRAM

Trainings as a Tool for Women's Empowerment

Training has become a key policy and development tool to improve public service delivery, combat sexism and sexual harassment, and stimulate women's empowerment.[9] Many of these development-oriented trainings have been designed to boost the participation of underrepresented groups in political decision-making.[10] The World Bank alone has spent more than $85 billion in the last ten years on local participatory development projects.[11] Participatory programs targeting women have been deployed with the hope of reducing the disparities in participation that result from underlying inequalities in education. The motivating idea is that providing women with information about the political process and opportunities to act on this information will motivate them to become more actively engaged. Despite great promise, there is little evidence that participatory programs have increased civic participation overall or among underrepresented groups. Most of the available evidence suggests that such programs have had limited effects on both participation and improved public goods provision;[12] in several cases, conservative gender norms have worsened women's representation in public spaces and discussion.[13]

An alternative approach has focused on explicit gender mainstreaming trainings. Officially endorsed by the United Nations in 1997, gender mainstreaming is "the process of assessing the implications for women and men of any planned action...It is a strategy for making women's as well as men's concerns and experiences an integral dimension of the design, implementation, monitoring, and evaluation of policies and programs in all political, economic, and societal spheres so that women and men benefit equally and inequality is not perpetuated."[14]

Several NGOs in India have introduced gender mainstreaming to reduce gender inequalities. When deployed in classrooms, these programs have been shown to substantially increase young boys' and girls' support for gender equality.[15] Gender mainstreaming has also been initiated to turn existing SHG institutions into spaces for gender consciousness-raising.[16] And, more recently, the Government of India has started to roll out gender mainstreaming trainings to government-organized SHGs. Such trainings seek to raise awareness of the particular challenges that women face in their daily lives as the result of systematic inequalities between men and women, which is expected to encourage women to challenge prevailing norms.

The Gender Equality Project

PRADAN and Jagori jointly piloted the Gender Equality Project (GEP) through a partnership with UN Women between 2011 and 2015 in eight districts in four

---

[9] Daly (2005); Walby (2005); Mansuri and Rao (2012); Dobbin and Kalev (2019).
[10] Olken (2010).   [11] Mansuri and Rao (2012).
[12] Mansuri and Rao (2012); Ananthpur, Malik, and Rao (2014).
[13] Gottlieb (2016b); Beath, Christia, and Enikolopov (2013).   [14] United Nations (1997).
[15] Dhar, Jain, and Jayachandran (2018).
[16] Mehra and Gupta (2006); Devika (2016); Holden et al. (2016).

states in India, including Madhya Pradesh. The GEP aimed to deliver a gender mainstreaming program in SHGs by providing SHG members with information and educational materials about gender inequality in the community and in the political process, including through a series of gender trainings. As PRADAN described, "besides working in the area of economic empowerment, the focus was now also on impacting the well-being of these women and achieving that by following a rights-based approach, by which women can make claims to their rights and entitlements."[17] The program's goals included "enhanced autonomy of women, enhanced respect and influence of women within the family and neighborhood and informal/formal local governance bodies, assured access of women to various basic services/programmes run by the government."

Jagori prepared educational materials on gender and women's empowerment that drew on its decades of experience with feminist organizing and working with the Mahila Samakhya program, a women's education program. The GEP training materials were implemented through a cascading model. Jagori identified and hired a resource person placed in each implementing PRADAN team, who were experts in the field of gender. PRADAN similarly identified one staff member in each team to lead on the gender work, who received a series of trainings by Jagori on gender and patriarchy. The resource person, working with support from the PRADAN team gender lead, then led a series of intensive trainings to identified Community Resource Persons (CRP), who were SHG members that showed strong leadership skills and a proclivity for work in the domain of gender. One CRP was selected for every two to three villages. After their extensive training, CRPs were then deployed to share the gender training materials with the SHGs in the two to three villages where they live and work. SHG members were not required to participate in the program, but trainings and information dissemination by CRPs were typically implemented during existing SHG meetings. In total, the GEP program included 8–10 training sessions over a three-year period.[18]

The gender trainings focused on four key themes: (1) the roots and manifestations of gender norms in the household and society, (2) enhancing women's agricultural livelihoods opportunities and power in agricultural decision-making, (3) the political process and how to engage with it, and (4) gender-based violence.[19] Each domain had a series of activities intended to highlight

---

[17] Singh (2014: 5).
[18] My analysis considers the possibility that observed effects could also be due to behavioral cues from this normative program. Contradictory findings with respect to gender attitudes suggest effects due to behavioral cues may be minimal.
[19] For a deeper discussion of the goals of each area, see PRADAN and Jagori (2016).

core dimensions of the theme and open dialogue on the issue. For example, in one of the sessions on gender norms, women were shown a scale and a pile of rocks. They were first asked to think about what they do on a typical day and mention each activity that benefits the household. They were then asked to place a rock representing the difficulty of that activity on one side of the scale. Women were then asked to repeat the process on the other side of the scale, but for the men in their household. At the conclusion of the activity, the trainer moderated a discussion on the value of women's work for the household and how this often does not translate into decision-making and bargaining power. In another activity, outlined in detail in Appendix A8.1, participants were encouraged to think about the differences between biological sex and gender and to recognize how gender roles are defined and enforced throughout the life cycle. They compared two infants born into the same family at the same time, Kamal and Kamali (one boy and one girl). Standing up, they took a step backward to symbolize each type of discrimination discussed and a step forward to indicate a privilege. At the end of the activity, the group discussed the physical distance between Kamal and Kamali and the various forms of discrimination that led to this distance.

After conducting several trainings on what gender is and how gender inequalities manifest in daily life, the sessions concentrated on inequality within economic and political institutions. A key focus of this program was to inform women of their rights and entitlements in the political system. The gender trainings formally made SHGs a space for political discussion. For example, the institution of reserved seats was explained to women through a series of activities. While most women had heard of reservations, their understanding of the institution was often incorrect, with many women believing that open seats were reserved for men, and that women could only run for reserved seats. Similarly, SHGs were encouraged to think about the public services with which women engage most often and their level of satisfaction with such services. Participants were also taken as a group on a set of exposure visits to institutions such as local government offices. During these visits, all participants were introduced to the institution and to political leaders and were given assistance in engaging with the institution. For example, in a visit to the Panchayat office, women were shown how to complete an application for government services, such as improved roads or water. During elections, women were taken to meet party representatives.

Finally, the gender trainings included a series of modules on women's role in economic institutions and the provision of livelihoods. These trainings focused on women's role in farming, since this is the primary source of income for most households in these villages. Through a series of activities, the trainings encouraged women to consider why men are in charge of agricultural decision-making, such as which crops to plant, even though women share in much of the labor of planting and harvesting. These modules also discussed the allocation of land titles and their links to the dowry system.

RESEARCH DESIGN

The gender program was allocated at the village level; thus, all SHGs in the selected villages participated in the program. I compare data on SHG members from villages that received this program and SHG members from villages that did not to estimate its effect on SHG members.

Since the villages that received the gender mainstreaming program were not randomly chosen, this makes it difficult to attribute any observed differences between participant and nonparticipant villages to the program. The principal concern is that recipient villages may have been different on the outcomes we care about *even before they received the program.* The observed differences after the program could, therefore, be the result of either the program or those preexisting differences across villages that did and did not receive the program.

Understanding how villages were chosen for the gender program – that is, the assignment mechanism – can help address these concerns. Assignment to the program occurred in two stages. First, PRADAN's central office selected three districts in Madhya Pradesh to be a part of the pilot program – Balaghat, Betul, and Dindori – based on their relatively "poor economic, social and gender indicators."[20] PRADAN operates one team in each district, so this amounted to selecting three field teams in the state to implement the gender program. District selection is likely to downward bias any results, as women in these districts were selected for their relatively greater disempowerment and were, therefore, likely to have worse political and social outcomes prior to the intervention.

Second, since the program required PRADAN team members to undergo intensive training so they could deliver the training to CRPs and SHGs, field-level staff in each pilot district were asked whether they wanted to opt into the program or not. Conversations with team members suggested that the decision was largely based on available time and general interests as opposed to characteristics of the population that each team member worked with. For example, one team member shared that they had done their schooling in agricultural methods and were therefore more invested in other training programs around livelihoods. Another team member said they opted into the program because they had time and had observed the need in their communities for gender trainings, suggesting some link between community characteristics and program receipt but in such a way as to downward bias results.

In general, team member assignment to villages is arbitrary and largely based on the needs of the team. Differences in villages across team members are therefore most likely the result of differences across the capacities of the team members, not an underlying difference in the village populations. It is unlikely that team members who opted into the gender trainings were already working in villages that had more active or gender-progressive SHGs a priori. In fact, the majority of team members I spoke with who opted into the program stated that

[20] Singh (2014: 6).

they had done so because they had observed the opposite; women were less engaged in gender equality issues. If this is true, then again, any comparison would likely lead to downward bias estimates of the program's effect, since it was implemented in areas with the most challenging circumstances. It is possible, however, that team members who opted into the gender program were a priori more likely to introduce gender concepts into their SHGs. However, only 35 percent of the PRADAN staff in these districts were women, which was part of the motivation for the gender programming in the first place.

It is, therefore, important to find an appropriate counterfactual for each treated village – that is, a village that is identical to the treated village on all observable and unobservable characteristics except that it did not receive the gender mainstreaming program. This is made challenging by the fact that I do not have data on SHG members' gender attitudes or political participation prior to their participation in the program. Given these challenges to causal inference, I triangulate three approaches to estimate the effect of the gender program.

In the first approach, I leverage the fact that the gender pilot program was only implemented in three districts in Madhya Pradesh. Previously, I argued that the PRADAN central office selected these districts due to their relatively worse outcomes prior to the program. I, therefore, compare villages in these three districts with those in two neighboring districts to estimate the effect of the pilot program. Since this approach does not differentiate between villages in the three program districts that did and did not receive the trainings, this eliminates concerns of village-based selection into program participation. As a result, these estimates can be seen as the intent-to-treat (ITT) effect or the effect of having *access to* the program as opposed to *participating* in the program. The key assumption is that the districts that had access to the program are similar to those that did not. To satisfy this assumption to the best of my ability, I first compare gender program districts with neighboring non-gender program districts, assuming that geographic proximity implies commonality on many unobservable attributes such as culture and norms.[21] I also pair match villages in gender program districts with those in non-gender program districts on observable characteristics from the national census conducted just prior to program implementation in 2011. I match the villages using Mahalanobis distance matching with replacement[22] on literacy rates, female literacy rates, and population proportions as indicators of gender norms, education rates,

---

[21] These districts are all geographically proximate, but two program districts (Balaghat and Dindori) abut one nonprogram district (Mandla), and the other program district (Betul) abuts the other nonprogram district (Hoshangabad).

[22] Matching with replacement has been shown to reduce bias in estimates (Abadie and Imbens 2006). I additionally match with replacement to allow for exact matching on the abutting district. Matching without replacement would remove roughly 75 percent of Betul's villages, as Hoshangabad is a smaller district.

population size and composition, land arability as a proxy for industry, and road and electricity access as measures of development. This results in 202 unique villages in program districts, of which 62 received the gender program,[23] and 60 unique villages in nonprogram districts. Appendix A8.4 demonstrates the robustness of the results to alternative matching strategies.

The second approach builds on the first but more explicitly evaluates village-level *participation* in the gender program as opposed to program access. The ITT results from the first approach are likely to underestimate the program's impact if it only benefited those who directly participated in it. Using the same matched village sample as the first approach, I estimate the effect of village-level participation in the gender program by instrumenting for gender program participation with gender program access. This estimation strategy leverages arguably arbitrary variation in the district-level assignment to treatment to induce arbitrary variation in the village-level treatment. Essentially, it models which villages in treated districts "comply" with the treatment (i.e., get the gender program) and then weights the estimated effect of the program by the share of villages that complied. This approach reduces concerns of village-level selection due to team member selection into the program and permits an unbiased estimate of participation in the gender program, assuming that villages that did not participate in the program are unaffected by the treatment (which is possible, since attributes of treatment were assigned at the district-level) and that district selection into treatment is unconfounded. The former assumption is somewhat validated based on the results from the third approach I describe later, which shows that treated villages in treated districts experience substantially higher outcomes than control villages in treated districts. These estimates can be interpreted as the complier average treatment effect (CATE) or the effect of the gender program on those villages who complied with (participated in) the program.[24]

These two approaches only allow for unbiased estimates of the treatment effect if the districts that received the gender program were identical to those that did not prior to the program's implementation. To address the concern that this assumption can not be validated, I take a third approach that compares villages that did and did not receive the gender program *in the same district*. This method removes concerns of bias at the district level but raises concerns of bias at the village level. On the one hand, this holds constant the presence of gender programming at the PRADAN team-level, presenting a hard case to observe effects. On the other hand, if the villages that received the

---

[23] Gender program participation was recorded by the PRADAN implementing teams and shared in 2016.

[24] It is important to note that this still averages over impacts at an individual-level as only some SHG members in a village received the gender training program. I do not have data on which SHG members received the trainings (nor on the degree of receipt) and since the gender program was allocated at the village-level, I do not attempt to parse person-level variation in program participation.

program looked different than those that did not before the program was implemented, then we cannot unbiasedly estimate its impact. In this within-district approach, I address this concern by matching treated villages with control villages within each district based on their observable characteristics[25] using census data from 2011, which was collected just before the gender trainings began. Ideally, we would match villages on all variables that are correlated with both treatment assignment and the outcomes of interest. I match villages within a district on their overall literacy rate as well as the literacy rate for women as aggregate measures of education level. I also match on the percent of the total population employed as well as the percent of women employed as aggregate measures of employment status. Given that PRADAN team members could opt into providing the program, assignment to treatment was a function of their population targets and the ease of implementing the program. To account for village-level confounders, I further match on total population size, the proportion of the population that were women, the proportion of the population that were from a Scheduled Tribe (ST) or Scheduled Caste (SC), total land area, forest land area, and non-cultivable land area, as well as whether there was access to the village via a paved road and whether the village has domestic electricity.

Again, the villages are matched using Mahalanobis distance matching with replacement on the same variables used in the first approach, which results in sixty-two unique villages that received the program and forty-seven unique villages that did not. Villages are pair matched without replacement to maximize efficiency, and the remaining control villages are dropped.[26] I additionally assume that team member selection into treatment is either uncorrelated with unobservable village characteristics, which is potentially reasonable since all of the villages that each team member worked in (not just those with better outcomes) would receive the program, or that any unobservable differences are likely to downward bias estimates, because team members stated that they selected into program participation because they wanted to redress inequalities they observed. That said, these results on their own should be interpreted with caution. These estimates can be seen as the average treatment effect on the treated (ATT) or the village-level effect of the gender program in program districts.

I rely on the robustness of the results to the three empirical approaches as evidence of likely causation. It is also worth noting that the majority of the results presented in this chapter, including those on backlash, are in line with the qualitative endline conducted by PRADAN and Jagori.[27] All said, future work should endeavor to more systematically assess the impact of this and similar programs.

---

[25] Ho et al. (2007).   [26] Imbens and Wooldridge (2009).   [27] PRADAN and Jagori (2016).

Data and Estimation

Again, a key challenge associated with estimating the effect of the gender program is the availability of data on women's political behavior. I use data from the 2016 sample survey, which included fifteen SHG members from each village randomly sampled from lists of all SHG members in the village. Women from this survey who were considered treated in Chapter 7 are considered as nonprogram participants in this chapter (except in the ITT estimates that average across program and nonprogram participants in participant districts). Data from women who participated in this program has not been analyzed elsewhere in this book.

To estimate the effect of the gender program, I use three specifications that correspond to the three approaches outlined. The first approach assigns treatment to all villages in the three program districts. The second approach assigns treatment at the village level based on program participation, instrumenting for this village-level treatment with district-level treatment. The third approach subsets to only the three participant districts and assigns treatment at the village level based on program participation. All specifications include individual- and village-level covariates and matched-pair fixed effects to compare within observably similar treatment-control pairs.

Despite matching on observed village-level covariates to ensure balance at the village level, it is important to include relevant covariates at the individual level to reduce concerns of confounding and to, more precisely, estimate effect sizes. In all specifications, I include individual-level measures of education level, the amount of agricultural land owned by the household, whether the respondent is ST or SC, Hindu, or married, the respondent's age, and how many children are living at home. I also include village-level covariates for the village's total population, the proportion of the population that is female, the proportion of the population belonging to a Scheduled Tribe or Caste, the overall literacy rate, the female literacy rate, the total employment rate, the female employment rate, total land area, forest land area, non-cultivable land area, whether the village is accessible via a paved road, and whether the village has electricity in domestic households. Standard errors in all specifications are clustered at the village level since this was the unit of treatment assignment.

Village-level matching removes concerns of selection bias if assignment to treatment is exclusively based on these observable characteristics. However, this is a strong assumption and requires that no unobserved factors correlate with both treatment and the outcomes of interest. Ideally, to evaluate this assumption, we would be able to observe political participation and other outcomes in all villages both before and after treatment. However, this is not possible given the paucity of data on women's political behavior. Instead, I validate the assumption that treated and control villages are similarly on observable and unobservable characteristics by (1) demonstrating balance at both the village and individual levels in observable variables shown to correlate with women's political participation and (2) evaluating the impact of the gender trainings on men's political behavior (see Appendices A8.2 and A8.3 to this chapter).

To provide a deeper understanding of the process of change and to validate the conclusions from the statistical evaluation, I include evidence from qualitative interviews conducted in ten villages that received the gender program and ten villages that did not; five SHG members were randomly sampled for interviews from each village. The interviews were conducted in 2018 and were not done in any of the pilot GEP villages. Instead, following the sample survey data collection in 2016, the GEP program was randomized to a set of villages that had not been a part of the pilot. This study is ongoing, but the interviews evaluated here were conducted after roughly one-third of the gender program had been delivered to villages. While this marks only a partial treatment, I utilize observations from these interviews to understand the underlying mechanisms of change. Importantly, the women interviewed who had received the gender program had been randomly sampled *and* randomized into program participation. I rely as much as possible on the women's own words as they detail their experiences in the SHG and in negotiating access to political spaces. Where relevant, I quantify these experiences and compare them across SHG women who participated in the gender trainings versus those who did not to demonstrate the broader applicability of their experiences.

THE GENDER PROGRAM AND WOMEN'S POLITICAL PARTICIPATION

Did participation in gender trainings increase women's political participation? Figure 8.1 reports the estimated impact of the gender program on voting in state and local elections alongside six measures of non-electoral participation and a measure of political interest. Across all empirical specifications, there is a positive and significant relationship between access to and participation in the gender program on most indicators of women's non-electoral political participation. The effects are strongest for the most public form of political participation – attendance at village assembly meetings. Participation in the gender program is estimated to increase the likelihood of a woman attending a village assembly meeting by 23 percentage points according to the CATE estimate (a 69 percent increase above the nonprogram group mean). Additionally, SHG members in villages with the gender program were more likely to make claims on local government offices, especially block offices that require travel and are therefore quite public. SHG members were 15 percentage points, or 214 percent, more likely to have made a claim on the block government in the past year compared to SHG members who had not participated in the gender program. As expected, the effect size estimated in the CATE model is larger

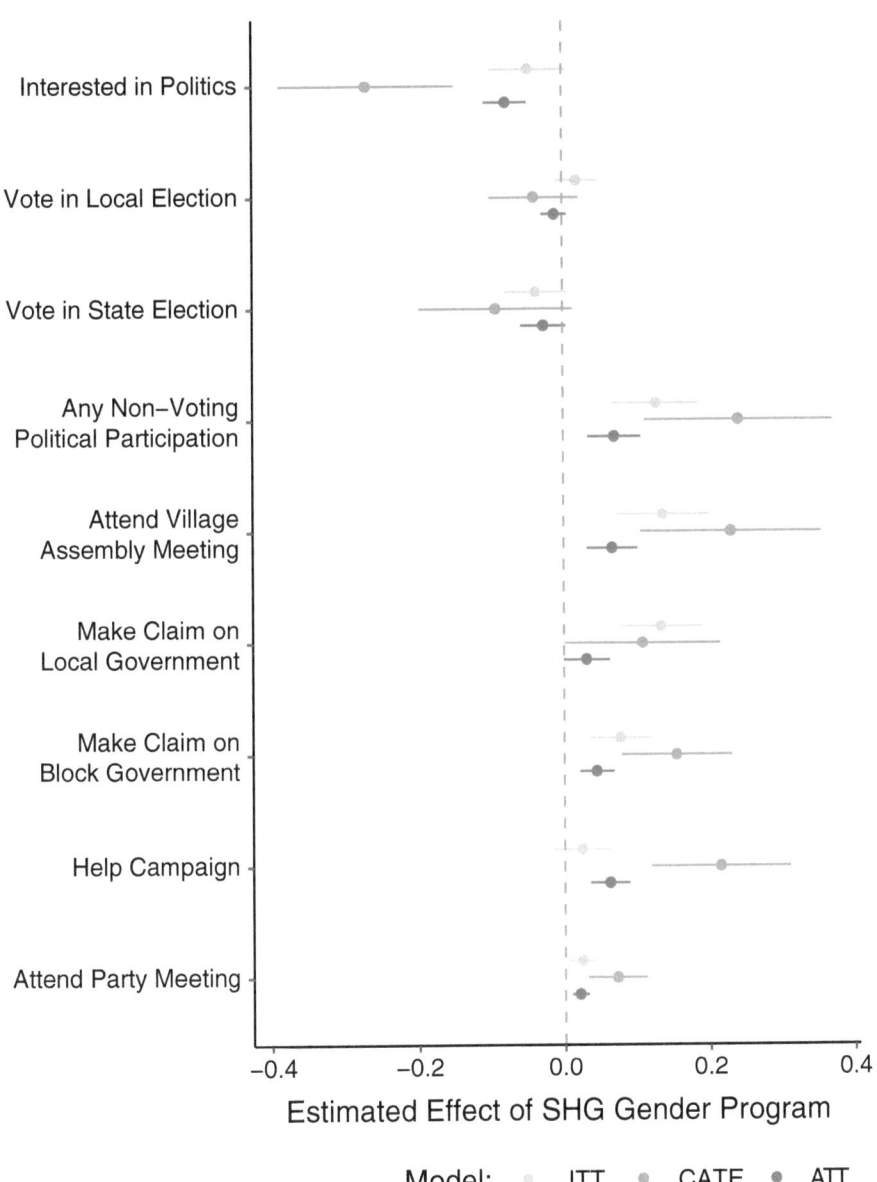

FIGURE 8.1 Participation in the gender training program significantly increases women's non-electoral political participation

Note: The figure plots the effect of the SHG gender training program on women's political participation. Estimated effects are shown along with corresponding 95 percent confidence intervals. Each variable on the y-axis is a distinct dependent variable, and point estimates are the effect of the gender training treatment on each (as estimated by the corresponding model). The underlying models include village pair-matched fixed effects (as per the noted specification), and individual covariates and standard errors are clustered at the village level. Data are from the 2016 sample survey in five districts of Madhya Pradesh.

than those in the ITT models, which suggests that it is program *participation*, rather than access, that more strongly shapes political participation.

Importantly, the observed positive effects on women's political behavior hold for both types of political participation that were directly discussed in the gender trainings (local public meetings, contacting local leaders) and for those that were not directly discussed in the trainings (campaigning, party participation, contacting block leaders). While this does not rule out the possibility that women were normatively influenced by the trainers, it does suggest that their greater engagement was not simply them just "doing as they were told"; it, instead, indicates a shift in their broader political engagement. It is also important to note that these results pertain to behavior more than a year after the completion of the gender pilot program.

However, the treatment has no discernible effect on voting behavior in either local or state elections. This could be a result of the already high rates of voter turnout (93 percent in local elections and 78 percent in state elections in control villages) or the way that gender trainings shape women's behavior. My proposed argument suggests that women's turnout at the polls is not constrained by limits on women's autonomy; if anything, it is enhanced. Voting is therefore not expected to benefit from the social solidarity and collective action that come from group-based discussion and mobilization.

These findings contrast with evaluations of other development-oriented and civics training programs, which detect a negative effect on women's political participation.[28] These studies have all highlighted that attempts to empower women in conservative societies have often backfired by worsening women's position in society. The link between the gender program and reported political interest may reflect similar dynamics at play. Depending on the specification, there is either no relationship or a negative relationship between the gender program and women's reported political interest. This is surprising in light of the positive relationship between the program and political participation. And, as will be shown in the next section, this aligns with results of the gender program on other attitudinal measures, which I suggest may be indicative of strategies that women deploy in the face of backlash to appear more norm-abiding.

A key difference between these past programs and this program is the composition of the group receiving the program. Typical group-based trainings are delivered to mixed-gender groups, which often include a quota for women. Critical to my theoretical argument is the development of solidarity and social capital among women specifically. Mixed-gender groups are unlikely to foster such solidarity and have, instead, often been shown to reproduce gender inequalities within group dynamics.[29] Much past research has found that

---

[28] Gottlieb (2016b); Van der Windt, Humphreys, and Sanchez de la Sierra (2018); Clayton (2015); Beath, Christia, and Enikolopov (2013).

[29] Karpowitz, Mendelberg, and Shaker (2012); Fearon and Humphreys (2018).

women's inclusion in mixed-group empowerment programs can depress their political participation, as women face backlash and compensate for contra-norm behavior (attending the trainings) by reducing their civic participation.[30] While the results for political interest suggest some limitations to empowerment in line with the results from mixed-gender groups, it is possible that the positive relationship with political participation is evidence of the value of social solidarity in gender homogeneous groups for collective action.

PATHWAYS TO PARTICIPATION

Women in the village of Khimsar[31] have historically been beholden to traditional patriarchal norms. Leelavati, a thirty-four-year-old ST mother, describes how it has undergone a transformation in the last few years:

Earlier, women didn't have the courage to go out of their house and tell somebody about their sorrow. They used to get beaten at home, and they used to sit at home. If a woman tried to do anything, then she was given divorce. It used to happen this way. Now, women never take a divorce. They live their own life the way they want to live.[32]

Leelavati appeared frustrated when describing her childhood and the ways in which her life had been dictated by a set of rules that no one seemed to be able to justify. She first questioned these unjustified but well-monitored rules when she started menstruating while at school. After coming home with stains on her clothes, all her mother told her was that she could not cook and must sit outside. Leelavati shared, "But I said that if you want to sit, you can, but I won't sit outside. But my mummy said that you would not cook and you will have to stay outside now, and you would sleep there too. I said that I would not sit, and I straightaway went inside." After defying these rules for a day, Leelavati was forced into submission. She said that over time, she grew into the "habit" of this practice, and she observed other girls doing the same. Yet she refuses to banish her own daughter from the house when she is menstruating.

Women in Khimsar have renegotiated these norms via explicitly coordinated action among women – a change Leelavati attributes to the introduction of SHGs five years ago. Through her participation in the SHG, Leelavati began to understand that the unexplained rules that had governed her life were up for contestation:

The role of men in our society is the same as it was before. Men are always ahead, and so nobody says anything to them. They always comment on women only in terms of their failures. Nobody says anything to men in the family, or in the society or the village. Men don't need to [contest their position in society] as they are always ahead in everything. Nobody makes them go back. They do so only with women. However, men do wrong also. If a man is going in the wrong direction, nobody will say anything to him. But if a

---

[30] E.g., Gottlieb (2016b).   [31] Village name has been changed to ensure respondent privacy.
[32] Leelavati (pseudonym), female, 34 years old, ST.

woman does something wrong, then people will comment on her. But none of them has the courage to say anything to men. However, if women were more like men, then no man would have the courage to say anything to her. Men are ahead, and people don't find any mistake in them.

Leelavati's participation in the gender program in her SHG provided her with a language for the discrimination she had experienced. This program involved conversations with her fellow group members about discrimination and motivated them to actively work in their village to renegotiate women's position in their society:

Suppose in our society somebody says that a boy can study outside, but we won't send our girls out. Then we try to counsel them that there is no difference between a boy and a girl. Girls can also study outside, and nothing will happen. We counsel the people in society. Then they also understand it and realize that it's true; there is no difference between boys and girls. They also realize that, and now they are educating their girls as much as they are educating their boys. So we try to put this matter in the community, and they understand that there is no inherent discrimination. So they also don't do any kind of discrimination.

Leelavati directly attributes the changes in her life to her participation in an SHG. She describes her relationships with the other SHG members as involving love. She knew the group had a special bond when all of the women showed up to build the house of one of their members who was in dire economic straits. The bond that they have formed has led them to share experiences that historically would have been kept private. Her SHG has become a place where women discuss their challenges related to poverty, domestic violence, and alcoholism.

But beyond discussion, Leelavati relays countless stories of the SHG mobilizing to act in support of their group's goals. After a group member experienced repeated violence within her household, the entire group showed up to speak with her husband: "We counseled that man that she is our group member, and if he beats her, we will file a case. One day we surrounded him at nine o'clock in the night. All members did that. Then we abused him a lot. Now he does not abuse anyone." Leelavati describes another incident where women mobilized a rally in support of alcohol de-addiction and coordinated with the SHGs in the two neighboring villages. Following this rally, the SHG women went into the homes of the alcohol dealers and forcibly destroyed the alcohol.

In these instances, women took justice into their own hands, as the police and elected officials were not responding to their concerns. Leelavati's SHG, however, also worked within existing formal political institutions to seek change:

It's about going to the Panchayat (local government). If anybody is not getting a ration card or their pension, then we file an application for that. We gave for a hand pump, and work has been done on that. We gave for a bridge, and work has been done on that also. We gave for a toilet, and work has been done on that also. Earlier, women didn't go to the Panchayat. But since women have associated with the SHG, they have started going to the Panchayat. If a Gram Sabha [village assembly meeting] is held, then women go there for sure. They go, and they sit in front of men. Earlier, women were scared to do this. But today they are not scared. They talk with men face-to-face, and they even go and sit in front of them.

Leelavati believes that women have become more successful than men at resolving their issues. According to her, men often only ask for help to build their houses or address their household's personal needs. Women, by contrast, desire improvements for their entire village. But this has been an uphill battle. A fellow SHG member ran for the village chairperson seat in the last election against a man in the village and lost. As Leelavati described, all of the men voted together to ensure the male candidate was elected, and even though the entire SHG voted for their fellow member, it was not enough to counteract the coalition of men in the village. "The men would say that it is good if we elect a man as sarpanch (village chairperson). He is even educated, and he will do better work. That's why he was selected as sarpanch."

Leelavati's experience of the gender program was different from that of Santari, an SHG leader from a nearby village. Santari[33] was elected by her SHG to serve as their representative to facilitate the gender trainings. She worked with the PRADAN training implementer to learn about the gender trainings and to help ensure that her SHG participated and understood the materials. Santari traveled to the closest town, Betul, to learn about the trainings and to work with the PRADAN team members and other SHG representatives for three to four days. With the help of the PRADAN team implementer, she then shared the trainings with her fellow SHG members. Santari described her personal experience:

Earlier, I faced many restrictions. Then I gradually became fearless. Some women say that a woman is bad because she hasn't had a child or she doesn't have a husband, but such things should not be told to anyone because we are also women. Right? So I tell women not to say such things. She is also a woman like us. They all are living their lives, and let them live their life, but don't restrict anyone for anything. I now tell such things to other women.

Participating in these gender trainings led Santari to question many of the gendered practices and inequalities that she had been socialized to believe. They highlighted women's commonalities and shared identity for her.

All of the women in Santari's SHG became more attuned to gender inequality after the training and recognized experiences of discrimination as systemic and shared with other women. She spoke of the conversations they had during the gender trainings. A fellow group member shared that her husband forced her to have sex against her will when she was pregnant. Another shared that her

---

[33] Santari (pseudonym), female, 30 years old, ST.

husband abused her after the birth of their daughter. Santari explained, "If there is discrimination with anybody, then women tell the problem ... Women have a lot of problems. Many men are of this type. In the gender training, women tell all this. Then women get together and discuss it." Women's common experiences of discrimination and subjugation led to a deeper attachment to their identity as women and a desire to rectify these inequalities, as Santari described earlier.

Enlivened and motivated by these trainings, Santari said that she and her SHG wanted to act to improve their village because they had the right to have their voices heard. "I became fearless even though I didn't used to come out of my house before." When asked why women needed to go to Panchayat meetings, Santari said, "[Men and women] cannot have the same issues. Only women can understand their problems. Although a few men may understand women's wants, the general perception among men is that women should not do things and why would they do this, etc. Because men think like that, that is why women should speak up." She shared that their SHG had fought to have an Anganwadi (child healthcare) center built so their children could have good meals and petitioned the Panchayat to bring more work for women in the village.

However, Santari and her group faced substantial backlash from the men in their community. To discourage the women from attending the Gram Sabha, the men in a nearby village explicitly withheld information about when the meeting would occur:

It used to be that we learned about when the Gram Sabha was happening from the men in the village where the Panchayat office is. But they stopped telling us. And I said to them, "Why do you take women for campaigning during sarpanch election? But when we are going for a meeting, you say things like 'Is it that all men of the village are dead? Is that why women are going?'" I would say, "Is it only the men that have elected the sarpanch? The Panchayat is made for everyone. So everyone can come and sit here. It's not like women or girls can't sit. They can sit." When I speak, all men and women look at me, wondering how it is that I am raising my voice. My fellow SHG women asked, "Aren't you afraid?" I said, "Why get afraid? They are also human beings, and I am also a human being. He is higher in post, so what? We should not hesitate while speaking." [Other SHG members] are afraid that they will be defamed.

Santari's household also disliked her new behavior. Her in-laws, in particular, were unhappy that she was traveling alone to attend the gender trainings in Betul. She explained:

When I went to attend the meeting, in the beginning, they said, "Why are you going to meetings so late in the night? What type of meeting is it?" They were scolding us [Santari and her husband]. My in-laws would tell my husband that their daughter-in-law hasn't come home yet, and you have allowed her to go. "She would walk away one day and leave you. She has bad habits; she is roaming, and you are not saying anything to her." So he called me one night, asking where I was. He was getting the noise of the vehicle on his phone. So he believed that I was telling a lie. He said that "You are going somewhere, and you are making me look a fool. Does any meeting happen till so late in the night? Which meeting is conducted at night?" He started asking questions.

Then the other SHG members visited her husband and told him of the import-ance of the gender trainings and convinced him that there was nothing illicit about her travels. Santari shared that after those conversations, her husband was more encouraging of her participation and even stood up to his parents. But other husbands in the village were not so understanding; they would question their wives and use Santari as an example. As Santari shared, women in her SHG were afraid they would be defamed in the same way she had been:

From that day, some women thought that I am involved in politics and that I am a very dangerous woman. I said, "Yes, I am a dangerous woman. I am doing politics." I don't mind saying such things because I know that we should discuss these things in our group, and we shouldn't feel bad about it. If people question it, it doesn't matter. But some men tell such things to our husbands. Then they don't tolerate it and tell us to stop going to the SHG meetings. These are the problems for some of our members. Some of them no longer trust me as a result.

Santari said that three to four women left the SHG because of these incidents. As a result, they had to consolidate two SHGs into one. When asked what the biggest problem facing her village was, Santari responded that it is the distrust sown by men among the women of the SHG. So while the gender trainings led to deeper conversations about inequality and discrimination within Santari's SHG, they also generated substantial backlash that sought to undercut the group's trust and solidarity.

Responses to Women's Political Mobilization

Several women interviewed for this study described experiencing resistance to their group's efforts to mobilize to gain entrance into political spaces. Past research has demonstrated the frequency of backlash to women's political ascension,[34] including the widespread deployment of violence.[35] This resistance is often framed in the language of patriarchal norms: men question why women want to participate in politics when it is not their place. In the small number of cases in which women did not describe substantial resistance, they had negoti-ated their access to political spaces by highlighting that their participation was bringing development to the village, something they said they were uniquely positioned to do. As Leelavati shared:

Women should go to Gram Sabha for the development of their village. Women are aware of what kind of problems are there in the village and how we can improve the

---

[34] Gottlieb (2016b); Clayton (2018); Brulé (2020a, 2020b); Blackman and Jackson (2021).
[35] Krook (2020); Krook and Sanín (2020).

village. All the problems are discussed in Gram Sabha, and only if we raise them will there be an improvement in the village.

In these accepting communities, women's political participation was framed as being for the good of everyone in the village. Meera, an elected official, explained, "Women are more mature [since the formation of SHGs]. They understand their responsibilities to the village."[36] In this way, women can define their participation as being in accordance with norms of women's care for the community, which can help prevent these behaviors from being sanctioned. As Leelavati shared, "[silencing of women] doesn't happen anymore because now everybody knows that women in the SHG are getting a lot of work done." Politically active women in villages without the gender program shared similar stories of acceptance of their political behavior: since SHGs were seen as spaces for economic improvement, women's political action was assumed to align with the community's broader economic goals.

Rachpa articulated the strategic value of women's mobilization when asked for his thoughts about the village's SHG by sharing that "the SHG became [secretary] of the school and they cook food and distribute food to the children, which is their responsibility. They serve different foods; they give green peas vegetable and other green leafy vegetables. They are good because of that, as it is their responsibility to cook and serve food and serve them."[37] Similarly, Nanhu shared that "many improvements have come to the village [since SHGs]. We have hand pumps now. Roads are cemented now. We have school here. Community hall has been constructed."[38] Even elected officials see the strategic value of supporting women when they organize around development. Ishawar, a village chairperson, described the impact of SHGs in his village: "Yes, changes have come. Earlier there was no unity among women. Now they are united. When any program is organized, all women come together. They have raised their demand for development. I have provided them whatever they required. I have helped them and they also help me."[39]

In other villages, the gender program redefined community perceptions of SHGs, which came to be seen as spaces that were antagonistic to broader community norms and a threat to the preservation of men's dominant position in society. In villages where women faced resistance, men (and often older women within the household) sanctioned these norm-violating behaviors by attempting to shame women and their households, withholding information and political access, and even using intimidation and threats of force.

While few men would openly share negative opinions about SHGs in interviews, Dumari described his dislike for SHGs, which he associated with their

---

[36] Meera (pseudonym), elected ward member, female, 25 years old, OBC.
[37] Rachpa (pseudonym), male, 50 years old, ST.
[38] Nanhu (pseudonym), male, 28 years old, SC.
[39] Ishawar (pseudonym), elected village chairperson, male, 35 years old, ST.

uselessness for himself: "The SHG is a useless thing. Good things have not happened because of them; rather, bad things are spreading. The SHG is formed with 10 people. They all deposit 10 Rs each. But anyone takes 1000 Rs and doesn't repay, then 10 Rs of everyone is lost. They neither feed their children nor take their own meal, but they lose their money."[40]

Figure 8.2 illustrates how the gender program affected SHG members' reported experiences of domestic violence, verbal abuse by their husbands at home and in public, the practice of witch-hunting, and the practice of throwing stones at women in public spaces. While the program had no effect on the reported incidence of domestic violence, women in villages with the gender program experienced significantly more humiliation and threats by their husbands in front of others: SHG women in villages that had received the gender program were 18 percentage points, or 200 percent, more likely to be humiliated by their husbands and experienced similarly large effects on the likelihood of being threatened according to the CATE models. Women in gender program villages were also significantly more likely to report that women were shamed in public by the throwing of stones.

These effects only appear when evaluating women across pilot and non-pilot districts – not when comparing across treated and untreated villages within pilot districts. However, when comparing the experiences of physical and verbal abuse only for non-SHG members, I do not detect any statistically significant underlying differences between pilot and non-pilot districts. Nor are there statistically significant differences in the rate of abuse across SHG members who had not received the gender program across pilot and non-pilot districts. Along with the fact that the gender program had no discernible effect on physical violence, this suggests that the underlying differences in the rates of abuse across pilot and non-pilot districts are unlikely to be driving these results.

Mobilization in the Face of Resistance

Why would women continue to mobilize and engage in political participation if it engendered such extreme backlash? Resistance to women's mobilization constrains their ability to participate in political spaces and contest gender inequalities. Participation in the gender program led to a significant increase in the shaming and humiliating of women. Yet, this backlash was the result of women's fight to renegotiate norms and practices. Their mobilization sought to shift norms regarding acceptable behavior for men and women and to directly combat the mechanisms of resistance they were experiencing. The gender program ultimately united women behind a shared desire to improve their position in society and reduce men's ability to control and coerce their behavior. While not all SHGs were as successful as Leelavati's in mobilizing and

---

[40] Dumari (pseudonym), male, OBC, 45 years old.

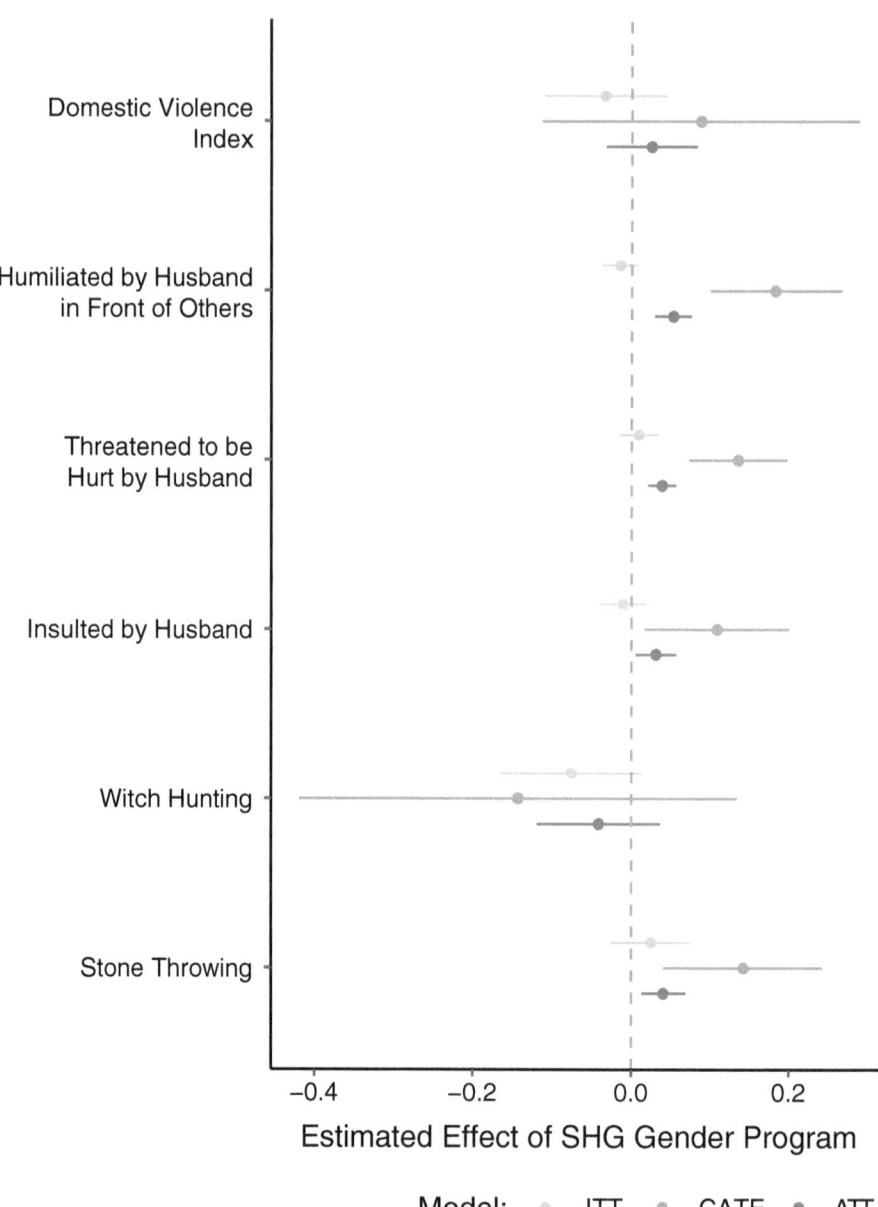

FIGURE 8.2 Women who participated in the gender training program experienced higher levels of public shaming and violence

Note: This figure plots the effect of the SHG gender training program on women's experiences of domestic violence, shaming, and verbal abuse. Estimated effects are shown along with corresponding 95 percent confidence intervals. Each variable on the y-axis is a distinct dependent variable, and point estimates are the effect of the gender training treatment on each outcome.

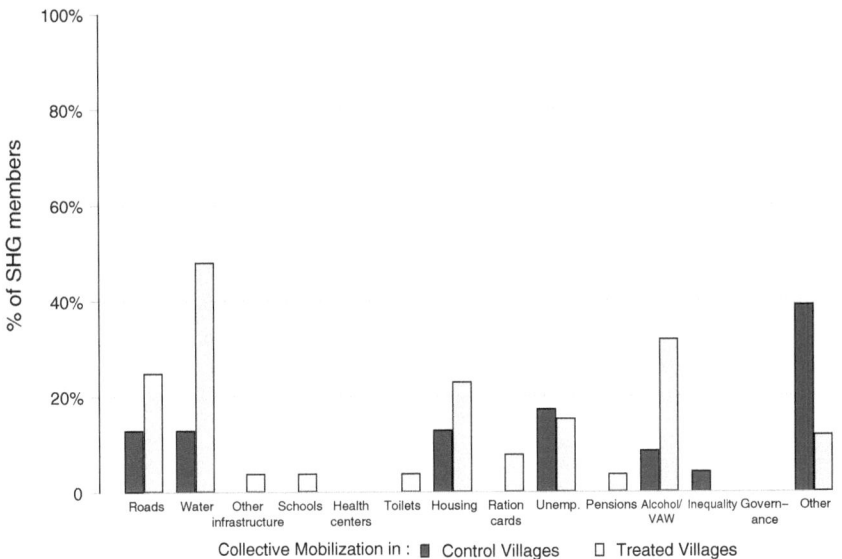

FIGURE 8.3 SHG members who participated in the gender training program collectively mobilized around different issues than SHG members who did not
Note: This figure plots political preferences and domains of political mobilization for control and treated SHG women. Data are from qualitative interviews with 100 SHG members, of which 50 are in ten treated villages, and 50 are in ten control villages in Betul district of Madhya Pradesh. Reported categories are not mutually exclusive, so the shares presented are the share of women who reported each domain as either a big problem in their village or a domain of political mobilization.

generating social change, the benefits of engaging in the political system were clear to women: political representation meant change and voice.

Figure 8.3 analyzes interview data with fifty women who participated in the gender program and fifty women who did not and compares the activities reported for which SHGs had collectively mobilized (which are not mutually exclusive). It makes clear that SHG members who received the gender trainings were more likely to report collective mobilization, and they mobilized around different issues than SHG members who had not received the trainings. They tended to mobilize around two issues: (1) the provision of public services disproportionately used by women and (2) the prevention of gender-based violence. Leelavati and the women in her village gained access to political spaces by mobilizing around underprovided public services that arguably improved the development of the village as a whole. Under the economic division of labor established in much of rural India, women are responsible for collecting water. When it is scarce or if water sources are not available, women must often walk several kilometers, sometimes for hours, to fetch water for their household. Mobilization around the provision of water indicates that women have recognized a shared interest in improving the provision of public goods related to their ascribed domestic responsibilities. While women have a disproportionate stake in the provision of these services, and therefore a very clear motivation to act politically to improve their provision, mobilization in favor of these public services does not challenge the patriarchal social order and was less likely to encounter resistance.

Leelavati and Santari also discussed how they actively mobilized to reduce the incidence of gender-based violence. As Figure 8.3 indicates, nearly 30 percent of all SHG members interviewed who had participated in the gender program reported collectively mobilizing against gender-based violence – and by extension, the consumption of alcohol, which is often assumed to trigger it. While many women experienced harassment and resistance from men in their communities in response to their mobilization, it is the potential for that harassment itself that ignited women into action. Resistance is the likely response to demands for power and a renegotiation of norms; it prevents women from independently demanding political change. As shown in Leelavati's example of the abusive husband or Santari's example of the restrictive in-laws, collective action by women can credibly challenge the backlash to women's demands for empowerment.[41]

Women's continued mobilization, therefore, gives them greater power to enact social change. As Santari describes, their continued persistence and group mobilization have gradually led some men and village elites to accept them:

Men always consider women as wrong. They say, "Why would women go there? What is their need? When men are already there, why would women go to Gram Sabha?" Many men think like that. People from our villages think like that. But now, some people are starting to understand it a bit. We don't listen to anyone, and we do whatever we want to do. So now men know that SHG women will listen to whatever you say; it does not make a difference to them. A few men now understand that women should come and sit in the Gram Sabha. They even ask us that why we don't come when we can't make it. Even the sarpanch would also ask that why you did not come. He asks us now.

One husband, supportive of his wife's participation in the SHG, articulated this exact pathway of inclusion when asked what changes he has observed in women since the formation of SHGs: "What has changed is [women] have gotten united, and they are capable to fight for injustice. They cannot fight it alone, but if ten women are there and having some problem with a man, then they all can fight."[42]

Mobilization in these domains required women to have shared some of their most intimate struggles with explicit violence and to have chosen to act as a group to ameliorate these struggles. Discussion of, recognition of, and mobilization around gendered issues such as water provision and gender-based violence require high levels of trust and solidarity within a group. The gender

---

[41] Weldon (2002); Htun and Weldon (2018, 2012).
[42] Heera (pseudonym), male, 27 years old, ST.

consciousness-raising program triggered these conversations. As Visaniya shared, after revealing that her husband is an "oaf" (a *baangad(r)*), "I speak to [my SHG] about these things; they know everything about me. The group is like family."[43] Or, in Bhagwati's words, "We are all like sisters."[44] Many women stated that the gender trainings had led to explicit changes in the way they spoke. Ramkali shared:[45]

INTERVIEWER: Did you see any change in your way of thinking?
RAMKALI: I see the change slowly.
INTERVIEWER: What kind of change?
RAMKALI: It so happens that we consider girls as weak and boys as strong. Even in education, boys will study well and be well. But both girls and boys are equal. And yet, a boy is considered more. But both are equal. Boy is also same, and girl is also same.

Explicit discussion of gender inequality, such as with respect to education, as Ramkali mentioned, created space within SHGs to explore discrimination and injustice. Women, as a result of the gender trainings, developed a group consciousness around what it means to be a woman and the gender roles they had been assigned since birth. By opening space to discuss their shared identity, the gender program also facilitated deliberation of these norms and how best to respond to shared grievances. As shown in Figure 8.3, in many cases this led to direct mobilization around women's common struggles.

The qualitative interviews with women provide further evidence that the gender trainings boosted women's political mobilization. Figure 8.4 plots the share of SHG members in villages with and without the gender program who, in qualitative interviews, stated their SHG discussed politics, attended the village assembly meeting together, or collectively mobilized in some other way. It is important to note that SHG members in all villages reported high levels of collective action; even in villages that did not receive the gender program, almost 80 percent of SHG members stated that they had attended a Gram Sabha meeting with their SHG at some point. However, women in villages who received the gender program reported even higher rates of collective action.

Not all SHGs exhibited such high levels of solidarity and social capital. Some women admitted to being scared that the other women in their SHG would steal their money or that they would not benefit from participation. Yet, such social capital is key to transforming these groups into spaces of collective action. Figure 8.5 compares the impact of the gender program on SHG members' political participation separately for women who were members of SHGs that were homogeneous with respect to caste category and women who were members of SHGs that were heterogeneous with respect to caste category.

---

[43] Visaniya (pseudonym), female, 37 years old, ST.
[44] Bhagwati (pseudonym), female, 36 years old, ST.
[45] Ramkali (pseudonym), female, 40 years old, ST.

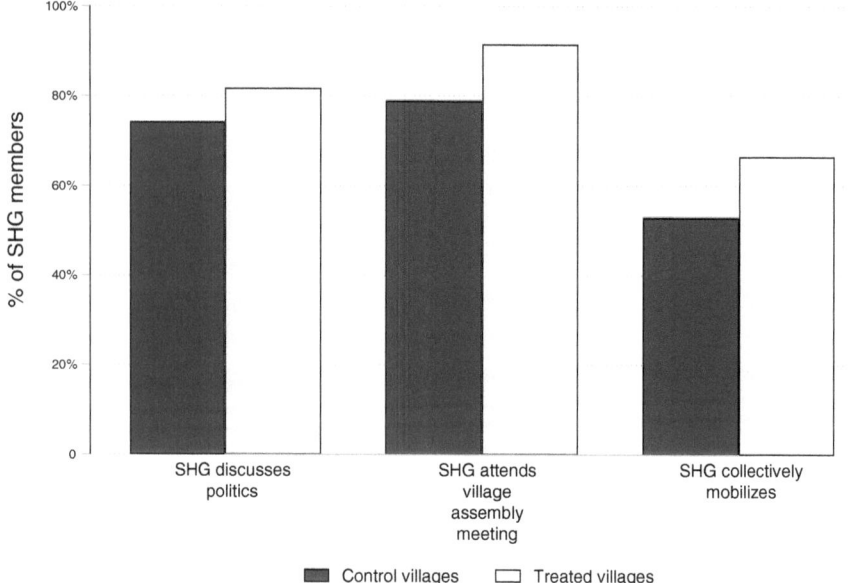

FIGURE 8.4 SHG members who participated in the gender training program collectively acted more than those who did not
Note: This figure plots the share of SHG members that reported political discussion and collective action by treatment status. Data are from qualitative interviews with 100 SHG members, of which 50 are in ten treated villages, and 50 are in ten control villages in Betul district of Madhya Pradesh.

Group composition is measured using administrative data on all group members provided by PRADAN. Data are then fuzzy merged with survey responses by SHG member name, SHG member spouse name, and village, with an 85 percent successful match rate. Estimated effects are generated by interacting this indicator for group heterogeneity with treatment.

The results in Figure 8.5 demonstrate that women's political participation was significantly higher in villages with the gender program for women in homogenous groups than for those in heterogeneous groups (as determined by nonoverlapping confidence intervals for the two groups). The difference between gender program and nonprogram villages is particularly striking for women's attendance at village assembly meetings. There are similar differences with respect to voting in local elections. Several interviews suggested that some SHGs attempted to get one of their members elected to local office, which could explain why the voting effect only holds only for local elections.

I also compare measures of group solidarity and politicization in response to the gender program. The program sought to create space for SHGs to become political, fostering political coordination and eventually political participation. Did participation in this program change women's social and political attachment to their SHGs? Figure 8.6 estimates the differences in measures of SHG solidarity and politicization for villages that did and did not receive the gender

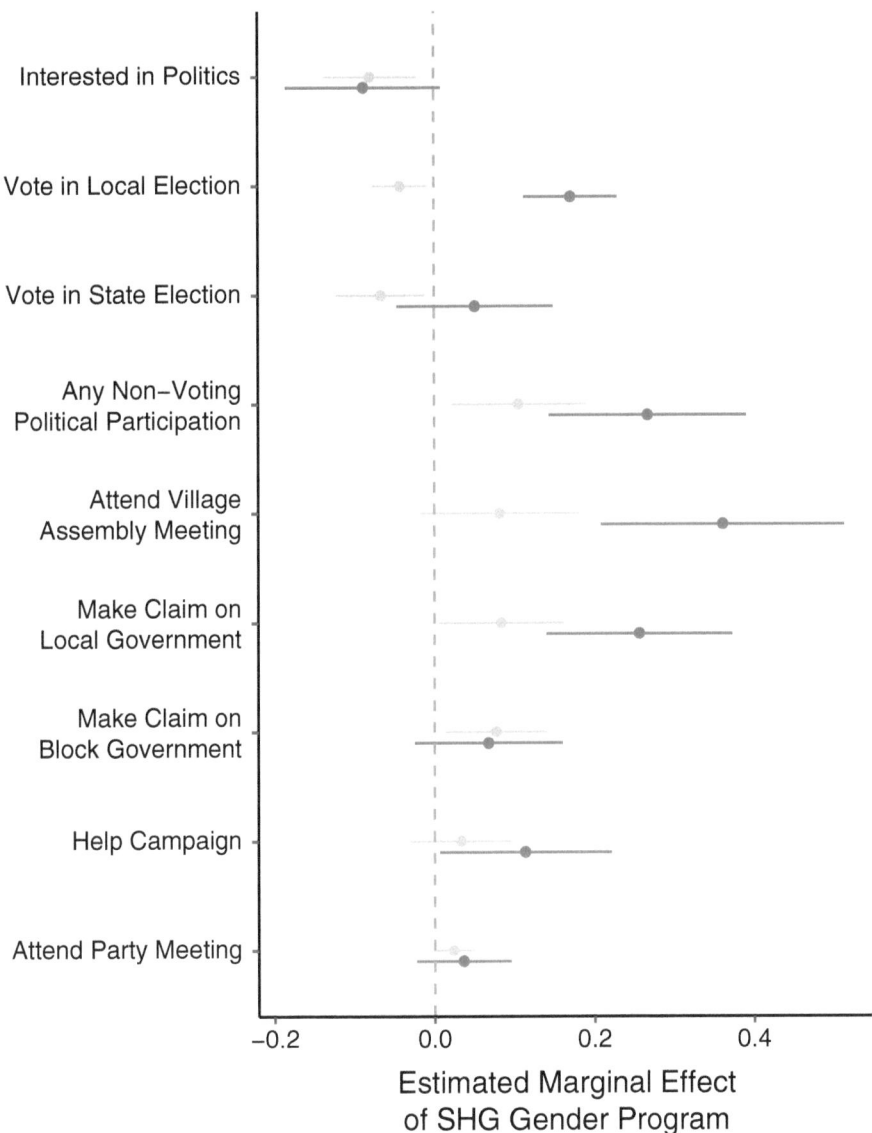

FIGURE 8.5 SHG gender trainings had a larger impact on the political behavior of women in caste homogeneous groups

Note: The figure plots the marginal effect of the SHG gender training program on women's political participation by group caste composition. The results are estimated by interacting an indicator for group heterogeneity with village-level treatment. The results presented indicate the marginal effect of the gender program for each type of group composition. Estimated effects are shown along with corresponding 95 percent confidence intervals. Each variable on the y-axis is a distinct dependent variable, and point estimates are the effect of the gender training treatment on each outcome. Estimates are reported from the ATT model, as group selection is constant within the implementing team but is likely confounded by many characteristics across implementing teams.

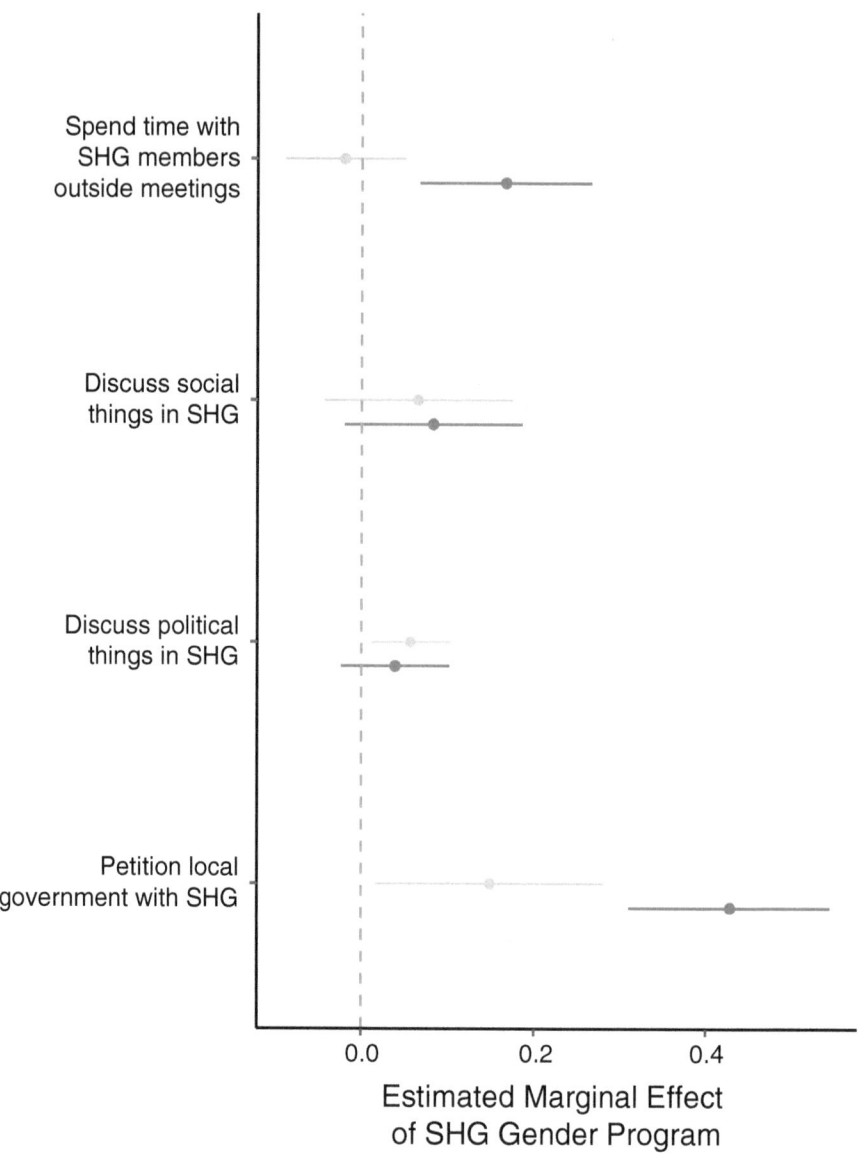

FIGURE 8.6 Caste homogeneous groups that received the gender program were more likely to act collectively than heterogeneous groups

Note: The figure plots the marginal effect of the SHG gender training program on SHG solidarity and politicization by group caste composition. The results are estimated by interacting an indicator for group heterogeneity with village-level treatment. The results presented show the marginal effect of the gender program for each type of group composition. Estimated effects are shown along with corresponding 95 percent confidence intervals. Each variable on the y-axis is a distinct dependent variable, and point estimates indicate the effect of the gender training treatment on each outcome. Estimates are reported from the ATT model as group selection is constant within implementing team but likely confounded by many characteristics when looking across implementing teams.

program separately for women in caste homogeneous and caste heterogeneous groups. Women in caste homogeneous groups who participated in the gender program were significantly more likely to report spending time with SHG members outside of group meetings and petitioning the local government collectively with their SHG than women in caste homogeneous groups who did not participate in the program (the error bars do not transect zero). These women were also significantly more likely to report spending time with SHG members outside of group meetings and petitioning the local government collectively with their SHG than women in caste heterogeneous groups who also participated in the gender program (the two bars do not overlap). This suggests that caste homogeneity may have augmented the program's impact on group solidarity and the likelihood of group collective action. Importantly, women in all villages that received the gender program had greater political coordination as a group than women in nonprogram groups.

Taken together, these stories and results demonstrate that the gender program helped to stimulate collective action and political participation and did so largely by fostering social solidarity within SHGs around gendered interests. However, they also show that not all groups responded to the gender program in the same ways. Some groups responded by organizing around more norm-abiding yet still gendered issues, such as public goods provision. Other groups respondent by acting in norm-deviant ways against gender violence and subjugation. And caste homogeneous groups were more likely to develop solidaristic ties, engage in collective action, and participate in politics.

THE GENDER PROGRAM AND ATTITUDES

A principal goal of the gender training was to foster a group consciousness around gender inequalities. A group cannot be expected to mobilize in its interests until these shared interests and struggles are identified.[46] The trainings therefore sought to open space for women to recognize how gender discrimination shapes the lives of women, for example, by highlighting the differences between sex and gender and drawing attention to ascribed gender roles. Through such consciousness-raising, women are expected to recognize their shared interests and strengthen their social capital.

Participation in the gender program is, therefore, expected to lead to more gender-equal beliefs. Figure 8.7 evaluates this hypothesis and displays the differences in various attitudes toward gender equality between program and nonprogram villages. Surprisingly, SHG members who participated in the program exhibited either no difference in their attitudes toward gender equality or less support for gender equality than SHG members who did not participate in the program: they were significantly less likely to say that women have the same rights as men, that women should be elected to office, and that husbands should help

---

[46] Sapiro (1983); Klein (1986).

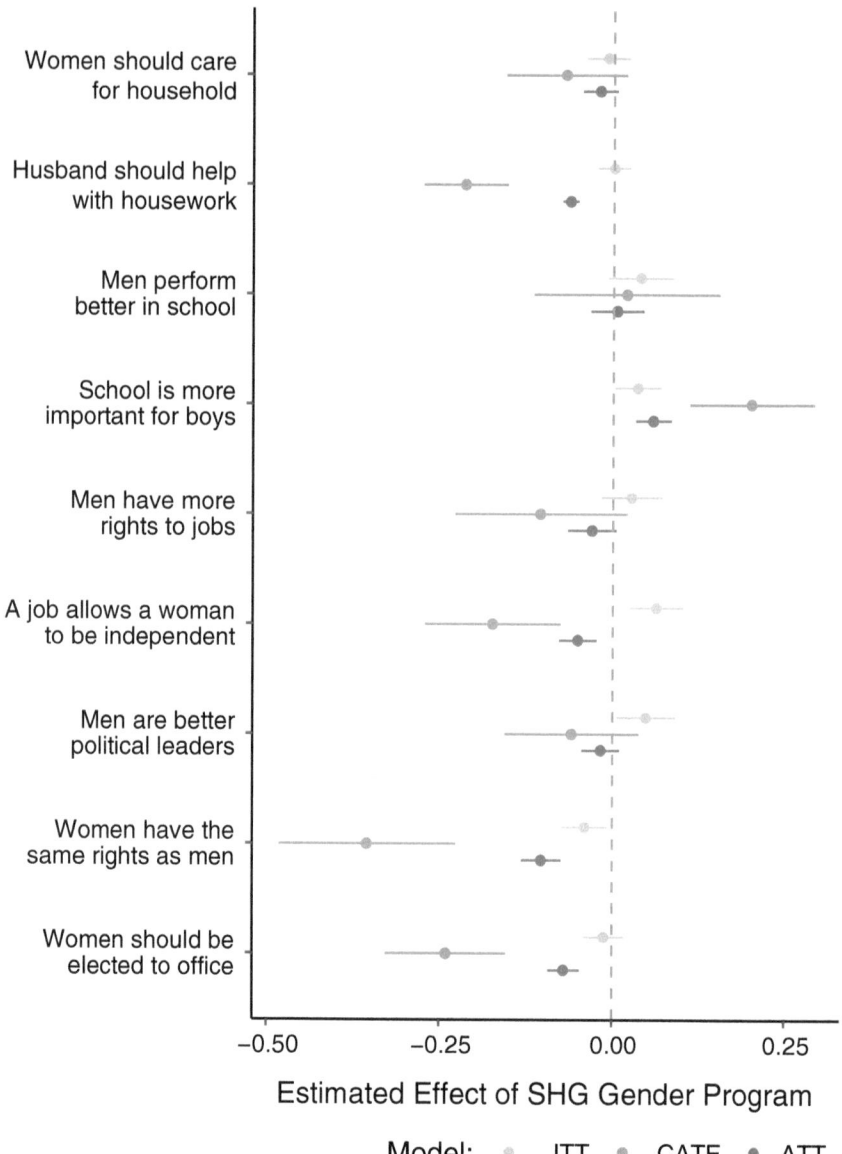

FIGURE 8.7 The gender program has no robust impact on women's attitudes toward gender equality

Note: The figure plots the effect of the SHG gender training program on women's attitudes toward gender equality. Estimated effects are shown along with corresponding 95 percent confidence intervals. Each variable on the y-axis is a distinct dependent variable, and point estimates indicate the effect of the gender training treatment on each outcome.

with housework, and significantly more likely to say that school is more important for boys. These effects do not differ based on SHG member caste category or age, or by the group's caste composition. Across all women who participated in the gender program, 51 percent stated that men perform better in school, 61 percent responded that school is more important for boys, 65 percent that men have more right to jobs, and 60 percent that men make better political leaders.

Why would participating in a program designed to increase awareness of gender-based discrimination and overall gender consciousness *deepen* attitudes against gender equality? It is difficult to directly explain why program participation had such an unintended impact. Prior research has shown that experiences of backlash, such as those experienced by the SHG participants in this study, can cause women to align more closely with dominant normative ideals, particularly in conservative societies. For example, quotas for women in government office and development councils have been shown to have no effect on women's attitudes toward gender equality[47] and a negative effect on women's political participation when male attitudes toward gender equality have worsened.[48] Other studies have shown that women who are most at odds with male preferences are most likely to censor their own behavior,[49] building on a large literature on the internalization of unequal gender norms as a response to conditions of oppression.[50] Appendix Figure A8.3.1 illustrates that men are significantly less likely to espouse gender-equal attitudes in communities that received the gender program. This suggests the possibility of attitudinal and normative backlash in response to programs that seek to generate normative change.

However, despite the backlash that women experienced as a result of the gender program, women's political participation was still higher in communities that received the program. Figure 8.8 documents the program's impact on SHG members' political participation by both reported attitudes toward women's gender equality[51] and reported experiences of domestic abuse. The figure indicates that attitudes on gender equality did not condition the effect of the gender program on women's political behavior (despite nearly 50% of women being categorized as having gender unequal views). Nor did experiences of domestic abuse. Women who stated that women are inferior to men had significantly higher levels of political participation in communities that received the gender trainings than

---

[47] Clayton (2018); Van der Windt, Humphreys, and Sanchez de la Sierra (2018).
[48] Gottlieb (2016b); Clayton (2015).   [49] Khan (2021).
[50] Allport, Clark, and Pettigrew (1954); Sen (1987); Jost and Banaji (1994); Szymanski, Kashubeck-West, and Meyer (2008).
[51] Women are coded as holding gender unequal views if they responded somewhat or strongly agree with at least four of the following five statements: (1) education and skills are more important for a boy than a girl, (2) women should take care of most of the household duties, (3) when jobs are scarce, men should have more right to jobs than women, (4) on the whole, men make better political leaders than women, and (5) on the whole, men perform better in school than women. Results are robust to different codings of gender attitudes, including using responses to each question individually.

(a) By attitudes toward gender equality

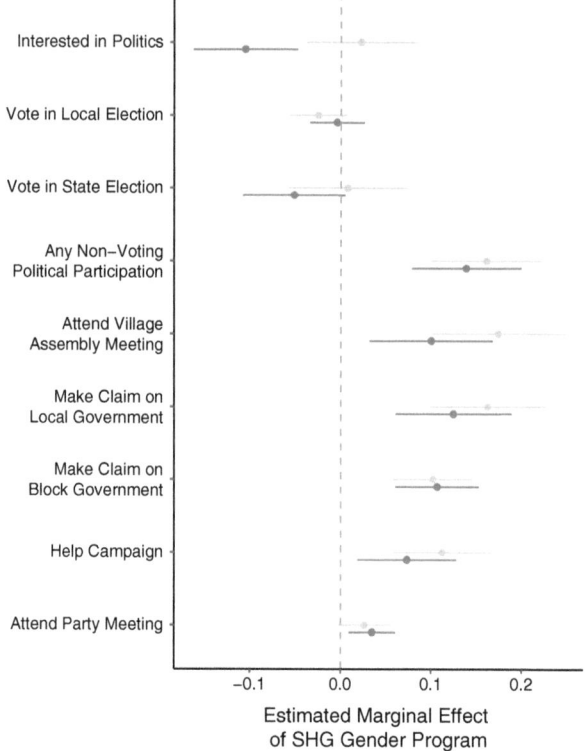

FIGURE 8.8 The impact of the gender program on women's political participation is not conditioned by women's attitudes toward gender equality and experiences of domestic abuse

Note: The figure plots the marginal effect of the SHG gender training program on women's political participation by gender attitudes and experiences of domestic abuse. Women are coded as holding gender unequal views if they responded somewhat or strongly agree with at least four of the following five statements: (1) education and skills are more important for a boy than a girl, (2) women should take care of most of the household duties, (3) when jobs are scarce, men should have more right to jobs than women, (4) on the whole, men make better political leaders than women, and (5) on the whole, men perform better in school than women. Women are coded as having experienced domestic abuse if they reported having experienced any form of physical or verbal abuse. The results are estimated by interacting an indicator for gender unequal attitudes and experience of abuse with village-level treatment. The results presented show the marginal effect of the gender program for women of each type. Estimated effects are shown along with corresponding 95 percent confidence intervals. Each variable on the y-axis is a distinct dependent variable, and point estimates indicate the effect of the gender training treatment on each outcome. Estimates are reported from the reduced form of the CATE model but are robust to all specifications.

(b) By experiences of domestic abuse

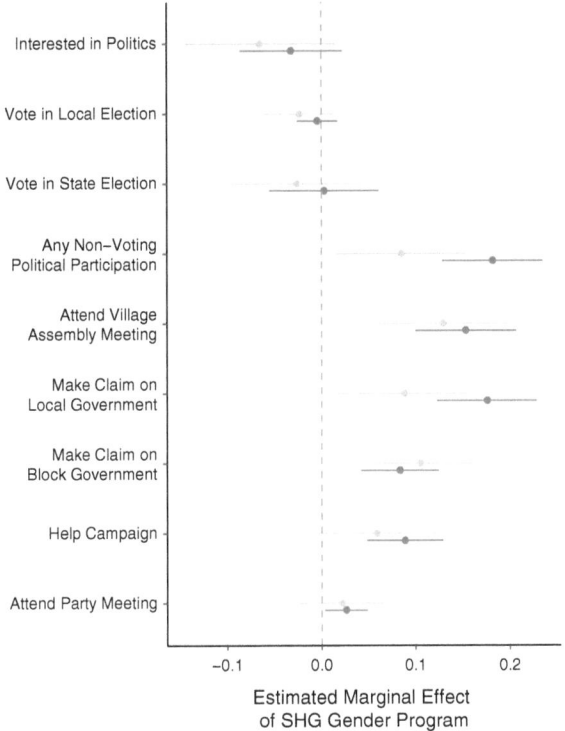

FIGURE 8.8 (*cont.*)

similar women in communities that did not receive the gender trainings. The same is true for women who reported more gender equal views. This suggests that women's responses to the gender program were largely unaffected by individual characteristics, even those most likely to diminish the efficacy of a gender consciousness-raising program, and supports the argument that the program's impact on women's political behavior is likely driven by coordinated, group-based collective action, enforced by within-SHG social sanctioning.

A secondary goal of the gender program was to enhance women's understanding of their political rights and entitlements and how to demand them. Gender trainings may have an individual-level effect on political participation through political information, political resources, and civic skills.[52] Figure 8.9 evaluates whether this program had the intended effect of increasing women's

---

[52] Finkel and Ernst (2005); Verba, Schlozman, and Brady (1995); Soss (2002).

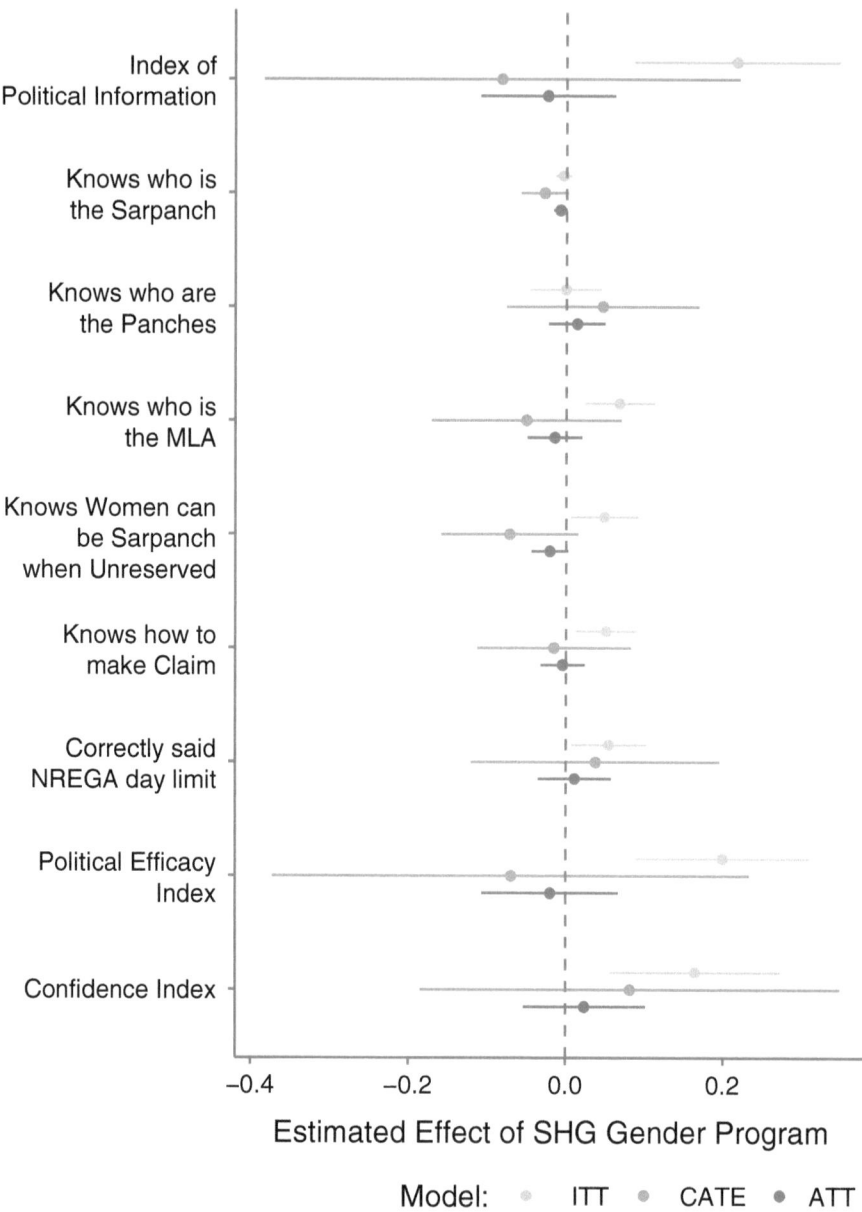

FIGURE 8.9 The gender program had only a marginal impact on women's knowledge of
politics, beliefs of political efficacy, and confidence
Note: The figure plots the effect of the SHG gender training program on women's information,
political efficacy, and confidence. Estimated effects are shown along with corresponding 95 percent
confidence intervals. Each variable on the y-axis is a distinct dependent variable, and point estimates
are the effect of the gender training treatment on each outcome.

understanding of the political process by looking at the treatment effect on various measures of political knowledge. The information index captures measures of subjective and objective political knowledge, including whether the respondent reported knowing who the *sarpanch* (village chairperson) or any of the *panches* (village ward members) were in their village, whether they knew who the MLA was for their region, whether they stated that they knew how to make a claim for services to the Panchayat, whether they knew that women could become the *sarpanch* even if the seat was not reserved, and whether they could accurately state the maximum number of days of work provided by MGNREGS (a government workfare scheme). The index of beliefs of political efficacy is derived from the answers to four questions: "Do you feel that sometimes politics and government seem so complicated that a person like you can't really understand what is going on?" "Do you consider yourself well qualified to participate in politics?" "Do you feel that you could do as good a job as sarpanch as most other people?" "If you were to attend a Gram Sabha or community meeting, would you feel comfortable speaking up?" The confidence index is composed of three dichotomous survey questions of confidence in different settings: whether a respondent sees themself as confident generally, when speaking to a stranger, and when speaking in front of a group.

The gender program had a positive effect on an overall index of six measures of political knowledge when comparing women who did and did not participate in the program within the same district (ATT), but had no discernible effect when comparing women across pilot and non-pilot districts (CATE). When looking at the components of the index, it is clear that the observed positive effect in the ATT model is driven by greater awareness of less generally known aspects of the political system. For example, women in villages that received the gender program had a more accurate and nuanced understanding of the reservation process relative to those in the same district who did not receive the program. Women in villages with the gender program were also more likely than those in villages in the same district that did not have the gender program to state that they knew the name of their state legislative assembly member (MLA), that they knew how to file a claim with the local government for services, and to correctly state that the welfare program allows for 100 days of work.

Beyond the substantive information acquired from the trainings, simply participating in the sessions and group discussions may have strengthened women's beliefs of their own efficacy within the political system or their confidence to engage with others. Such psychological shifts are most likely to stem from experience and practice communicating political ideas and organizing political activities, which were core components of the gender program. Figure 8.9 demonstrates that women who participated in the gender program reported higher levels of perceptions of political efficacy and an index of reported confidence when compared to women who did not participate in the program within the same district (ATT), but again with no discernible difference when compared to women in nonprogram districts (CATE). These results suggest that the gender program can positively shift women's knowledge, efficacy, and confidence but that these effects are limited and may not be causally determined.

Overall, women appear to have become more regressive in their attitudes toward gender equality after participating in the gender program but also show some indications of having greater knowledge of the political system, higher perceptions of efficacy within the political system, and more overall confidence. I have suggested that these contradictory findings make sense through the lens of the process of norm renegotiation. By exposing women to new ideas, increasing their knowledge, and shifting their conceptions of their own capabilities, the gender program enabled women to act collectively and become more active political citizens. However, in doing so, women challenged long-held normative values that have suppressed their power. Women's demand for power – for agency over their political decisions and voice in political institutions – was met with substantial resistance from those whose power was most threatened. While experiences of backlash, including heightened shaming and humiliation, give women greater incentives to collectively organize against their oppression and demand protection from gender-based violence, they can also ignite a fear response that leads to the development of personal protection mechanisms such as the vocalization of more gender-regressive attitudes. The evidence I have shown makes sense when interpreted as a snapshot of women in the midst of the process of norm renegotiation.

ALTERNATIVE EXPLANATION: ECONOMIC RESOURCES AND BARGAINING POWER

It is also possible that the gender program could have shifted women's political behavior by changing household bargaining dynamics if the program provided women with more resources with which to negotiate a greater bargaining position. If greater political information, political resources, and civic skills increase bargaining power within the household, then they may be more likely to participate in politics even independently from the behavior of the group.[53] These mechanisms suggest an individual-level pathway for participation that is not tied to the network-based nature of training delivery. Given the persistent gender inequalities in political resources and civic skills, these individual-level effects are likely to be most pronounced for women. However, as noted earlier, such individual-level interventions have not been shown to increase women's political participation when delivered to mixed-gender groups in areas with gender-biased social norms.[54]

Figure 8.10 refutes these individual-centric explanations. It displays no positive correlation between the gender program and most indicators of

[53] Agarwal (1997).   [54] Mabsout and Staveren (2010); Gottlieb (2016b).

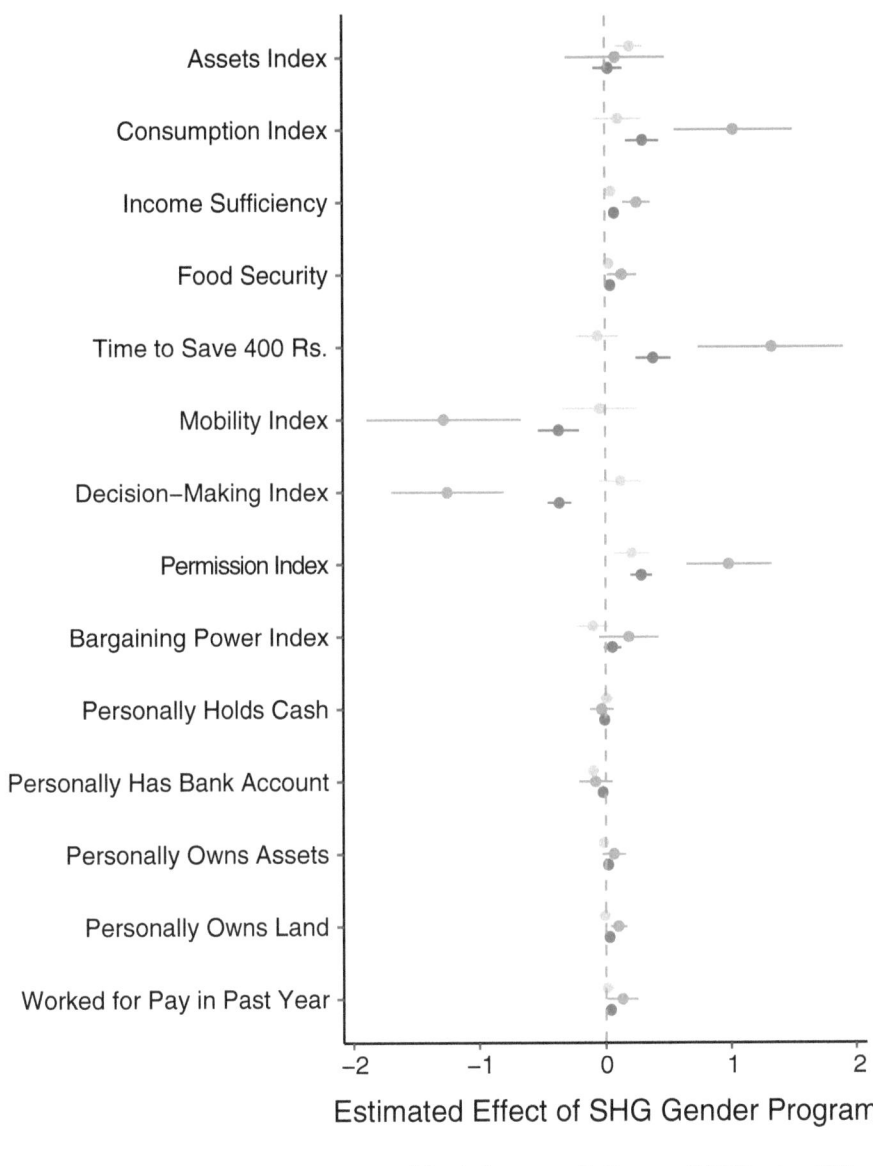

Estimated Effect of SHG Gender Program

Model: ◦ ITT • CATE • ATT

FIGURE 8.10 The gender program had no robust impact on indicators of bargaining power and economic resources

Note: The figure plots the effect of the SHG gender training program on women's economic resources and bargaining power. Estimated effects are shown along with corresponding 95 percent confidence intervals. Each variable on the y-axis is a distinct dependent variable, and point estimates are the effect of the gender training treatment on each outcome.

bargaining power. Women in villages that received the gender program reported that they have to ask for permission significantly less often than those in villages without the gender program, but also report less mobility overall and less decision-making power. These negative impacts on women's role in the household may be further evidence of a backlash. The gender program also has a minimal effect on women's economic resources: although women in villages that received the program do report greater consumption, they also report that it takes longer to save money. Overall, this suggests that the gender program did not fundamentally transform household relations; if anything, it may have worsened women's agency and authority within the household.

DISCUSSION

Two facts motivate the research discussed in this chapter. First, participatory programs targeting women have largely been unsuccessful at mobilizing their inclusion in political spaces. Second, as I have shown, women's connections with each other increase their political engagement. This chapter combines these facts to investigate whether externally delivering explicit gender consciousness-raising interventions to women's groups can activate those ostensibly apolitical groups toward collective action and political participation. In doing so, it parses out the impact of household autonomy from that of social solidarity among women and demonstrates that solidarity (conditional on autonomy) can strengthen women's political action.

In this chapter, I document the capacity for public policies and external actors to strengthen women's groups and build women's social capital. I show that a gender program delivered to SHGs coincided with higher levels of women's political participation more than the SHG intervention alone. Importantly, this relationship accompanied stronger solidarity among group members and greater group action directed toward distinctly gendered interests. Women who had participated in the gender trainings were significantly more likely to collectively act alongside their SHG, had somewhat more knowledge of the political system and how to engage in it, and had greater confidence in their ability to engage in public spaces. And when SHGs collectively mobilized in the public sphere, they did so in pursuit of improvements to the services that women use the most and reductions in gender-based violence.

The positive gains in women's political participation, however, were met with substantial resistance and backlash. Women reported higher rates of public shaming and threats of coercion. Their experiences highlight the serious challenges women face in the fight for their political inclusion and, ultimately, norm renegotiation. Women navigated this resistance in three main ways. In some instances, they reframed their political participation as norm abiding – that is, bettering the village as a whole rather than advancing their personal aims and goals. In other cases, SHGs with insufficient social solidarity withdrew in the face of resistance and even faced internal contestation. Finally, some SHGs countered resistance by engaging in strong and persistent collective action, particularly directed at reducing men's ability to use violence and harassment to oppress women.

These results constitute a snapshot of the lives of women in the thick of attempting to renegotiate gender-biased norms and generate social change. This process is anything but linear. While women responded to the gender program with increased political action, they were also more likely to vocalize attitudes antithetical to gender equality. These findings highlight the complex, and sometimes seemingly contradictory, ways in which women must respond to coercion designed to suppress their attempts at empowerment. However, this coercion and backlash create the conditions that can unite women in solidarity against their continued oppression.

Overall, these findings suggest that programs that seek to increase women's gender consciousness and civic engagement may only be successful if women have access to networks or groups that they can deploy to demand representation in the face of resistance. Findings from prior work suggest that backlash against women following campaigns for their political empowerment may inhibit program success.[55] Without strong social solidarity built on repeated engagement in an institutionalized setting, women's political participation may not have been possible in the current study's setting. Overall, these findings suggest that small tweaks to the design of participatory programs, namely in how they are delivered, can yield even larger gains to women's political inclusion and open up the necessarily conflictual process of norm renegotiation.

[55] Gottlieb (2016b); Clayton (2018).

PART IV

CONSEQUENCES OF INCLUSION

9

Women's Mobilization across India and Its Portents

In 1972, policemen raped a poor young tribal girl named Mathura who came to the station to file a claim. After seven years and multiple appeals, the Bombay High Court eventually found the policemen guilty of custodial rape. The Supreme Court overturned the ruling on the grounds that Mathura was "habituated to sexual intercourse" based on the two-finger test. Days later, the country erupted into protest. For the first time, Indian women turned out en masse to protest widespread violence against women.[1] These mass protests ignited the modern women's movement in India and led to the first major legal reform regarding violence against women.

In 2012, six men gang-raped Jyoti Pandey, a young medical student, in Delhi, on her way home from the movies; she died from her injuries several days later. Again, the country erupted in what proved to be a second watershed moment for the Indian women's movement. A new generation of women turned out to protest, demanding justice for Jyoti as well as broader policy change. These protests were the largest demonstration against gender-based violence ever seen in India.[2] Women from a wide range of backgrounds and ages coalesced around shared demands for safety, protection, and, most importantly, social change.

What I have shown throughout this book in a small number of villages in Madhya Pradesh mirrors the broader women's movement in India. Women have struggled to organize and act against their subordination, but when they have, they find commonality in the experience of subordination and coercion. In this chapter, I demonstrate how the patterns of political renegotiation in rural Madhya Pradesh resemble those observed across the nation, in both their demands and in their responses. Like self-help groups (SHGs) contesting

---

[1] Basu (2013); Weldon (2002).   [2] Pal (2018).

women's place in village hierarchies, women across India have found a voice through collective action, accomplishing reform and policy change that elevates the status of women through coordinated mobilization. Yet when the gender consciousness-raising program exposed women to feminist agendas, men in their village responded violently. Similarly, women's mobilization around their distinct issues and their success at achieving legal protection from violence have been met by both backlash and subversion.

In this way, the micro-dynamics of women's demands for political representation and the cyclical patterns of norm renegotiation observed in Madhya Pradesh exhibit similar patterns at the national level. Women often come together to contest the widespread coercion they experience. Men resist such mobilization: they leverage their resources to politically mobilize against women and deploy the very violence and intimidation that women are contesting to directly suppress their voices. While such resistance raises the costs of women's collective action, it also highlights the need for collective action to credibly contest women's shared experiences of oppression, coercion, and violence. And it is through this costly collective action that women can generate the legal and political change that will protect them from the resistance they face. The macro-dynamics of women's mobilization thus affirm and substantiate the power of collective action in their broader path to political empowerment.

The first goal of this chapter is to demonstrate the generalizability of this pattern of norm renegotiation around women's right to make political demands and demonstrate that women's political inclusion, particularly when it leads to attempts to change the social and political order, is marked by coercion and resistance. Yet a mechanism that enables women to contest this coercion – collective action – also supports their success in achieving their demands. The second goal of this chapter is to document the ways in which women's collective action can bring about political and social change and therefore to demonstrate the substantive consequences of women's political participation.

A BRIEF HISTORY OF THE INDIAN WOMEN'S MOVEMENT

Women in India have long been organized and actively involved in larger social movements, including during the movement for independence. Women were a critical constituency in the anti-colonialist nationalist movement in India in the first half of the twentieth century. This early mobilization focused nearly entirely on the nationalist agenda; little attention was paid to issues of gender violence or discrimination, which had been permitted under colonial family law.[3] Women were expected to protest within the framework of patriarchy to achieve the cross-gender goal of independence rather than advocate for their

---

[3] Patherya (2017).

specific demands or challenge patriarchal norms.[4] Independence leaders asked women to participate in mass movements in order to legitimize their demands, but to subjugate their interests to those of the male-dominated collective. Gandhi's first writing on women urged them to stop their demands for a "vote for women" and to, instead, take their proper place beside men, "helping their men against the common foe."[5] Women's political participation in India during the country's first decades as a nation state was defined by deference to male guardians and the regular suppression of gendered interests.

The women's movement in India did not become more generally established until the 1970s. A report titled "Towards Equality," commissioned by the Indian government at the urging of the United Nations, revealed that women's outcomes had worsened on most measures of empowerment and well-being relative to 1911. This coincided with a period of economic crisis that led many in the country, including women, to be disenchanted with the government's promises of greater equality.[6] Toward the end of the 1970s, autonomous women's groups began organizing in pursuit of legal protections for women. Spurred in part by the Mathura rape case, mass protests by women demanded reforms to laws regarding rape, widow burning, dowry violence, and other forms of violence against women.

In response to the rise in women's mobilization, legal reforms in the 1980s aimed to overturn discriminatory colonial laws and introduce new legislation that institutionalized equality and the protection of women. The new autonomous women's groups worked closely with the courts and the bureaucracy to facilitate legal reform,[7] and, in 1983, the Indian Penal Code was amended to increase the punishments for cruelty toward wives and dowry deaths. As a result of the accomplishments of the women's movement in generating policy reform related to gender-based violence, this decade has been coined the "golden age of feminist politics."

Many nongovernmental organizations (NGOs) entered the space of feminist activism in the 1990s – a period of "NGO-ized" and institutionalized feminism.[8] This led to a decline in autonomous women's groups and the diffusion and decentralization of the women's movement. To some, this was considered beneficial to the women's movement, as it enabled it to expand its reach, increase its institutionalization and ties with the state, and tackle a more diffuse set of women's interests. Various groups have fought for such diverse interests as the rights of lower-caste women, divorce reform, inheritance rights, prohibition, protection from gender-based violence, reductions in child marriage, environmental protection, unionization of domestic workers, and equal wages and employment opportunities.[9] However, critics expressed concern that the institutionalization of the women's movement and the introduction of

---

[4] Sen (2000).   [5] Gandhi (1920).   [6] Calman (1992).   [7] Pal (2018).   [8] Pal (2018).
[9] Ray (2000).

international and government donors would lead to its co-optation, inhibiting progress on larger issues of gender justice.[10] As evidence of greater deference to the state, this era was characterized by a greater focus on legal change.

The broader movement has also expanded to include communities historically excluded from feminist organizing, in part due to the diffusion of technology, and protesting has become a key site of women's activism. Beginning in 2012 with the gang rape and murder of Jyoti Pandey, the women's movement expanded and incorporated many student and youth activists who were not members of traditional feminist groups. Many of the largest protests in the past decade have not been organized directly by women's organizations but by student groups and online activists, shifting the organizational nature of the women's movement. Technology further enabled the elevation of women's voices that had historically been marginalized in the Indian women's movement, such as those of lower-caste and poorer women. The present-day women's movement is decentralized: women collectively organize around a wide range of interests and demands. Most notable, however, has been the rise in mass mobilization around violence against women over the past decade.[11] Protests related to violence have received international media attention and, to some extent, refocused attention in India on issues of gender-based violence.[12]

The lack of systematic historical data on women's protests makes it difficult to analyze trends in women's demonstrating. However, recent data compiled in the Armed Conflict Location and Event Database (ACLED) uses news reports to document all protest events reported in South Asia from 2016 to 2021. This includes both large-scale national protests as well as small-scale demonstrations, as long as a domestic media outlet reported on the demonstration. The ACLED data parses and codes the actors associated with each protest event, differentiating between primary and secondary actors and including women as one of the coded actors. I compiled and coded these data to create a dataset with all women-led protests in India for these five years. According to these data, women led 2,924 from 2016 to 2021, comprising roughly 5 percent of all protest events in the country each year.

WHAT WOMEN DEMAND

The women's movement in India has been internationally known for its mobilization around issues of gender-based violence, including child marriage, dowry, *sati* (widow burning), rape, sexual harassment in the workplace, domestic violence, witch-hunting, acid attacks, female feticide and infanticide, and communal and police violence. Molyneux conceptualizes such agendas as regarding feminist or strategic interests, namely those seeking to enhance the position of women in society at large.[13] However, the tenor of the women's

[10] Ray (2000).   [11] Pal (2018).   [12] Roychowdhury (2013).   [13] Molyneux (1998: 232).

movement in India has varied across space and time; some organizations demand the protection of gender interests, and others advocate for improved welfare and development more broadly.[14] These more practical or pragmatic interests, as Molyneux differentiates, generally arise out of women's position in society and the economic division of labor.[15]

Social movement theorists have sought to understand why (and under what conditions) women's movements diverge in this way. Amrita Basu compares social movements in Maharashtra and West Bengal and argues that the former was more militant and had greater participation by women[16] due to socio-economic and political differences across the regions, specifically differences in the distribution of caste and class and women's role in both hierarchies. Raka Ray more directly evaluates the nature of women's mobilization by comparing two social movement organizations led by women in similar socioeconomic contexts across Bombay and Calcutta, which differ mostly in the nature of their demands.[17] According to Ray, mobilization by women in Calcutta centered on pragmatism, which she explains is the result of a hegemonic political field with concentrated power and limited room for subordinate groups to independently mobilize around their unique interests. Bombay's women's movement, by contrast, was organized around feminist and strategic interests as a result of more fragmented power and heterogeneous organizations, which made it easier for women's groups to enter the movement market.

Basu's and Ray's accounts highlight how politics and culture shape the nature of women's mobilization. Women's collective action must navigate existing power structures to be successful. In some instances, women have the capacity to compete within the political field and collectively demand a share of overall power relations. In other instances, women face substantial hurdles to credibly challenging those with power. Where this is the case, it may be in women's practical interests to fold their demands into broader movement politics to make their interests more palatable to those with power. Thus, the patterns in broader movement politics echo those in the micro-movement politics observed in villages in Madhya Pradesh: women's collective action is often critical for the representation of their interests, but their capacity to demand power and representation varies based on their ability to traverse the political field, which Ray defines as a combination of a region's distribution of political power and overarching political culture.[18] As I have argued, this implies that the potential for backlash and co-optation (i.e., the distribution of coercive power) and the organization of politics (and the vested interests in women's subordination) shape the nature of women's demand-making and women's pathway to participation.

---

[14] Basu (1992); Ray (2000).   [15] See also Molyneux (1985).   [16] Basu (1992).
[17] Ray (2000).   [18] Ray (2000).

I use the ACLED data to evaluate the nature of women's collective demand-making across India from 2016 to 2021 to demonstrate the diffuse interests represented by women. Figure 9.1 plots the distribution of all women-led protests in India across a range of topic areas. The protest topic denotes the key demands made at each protest event, which was coded using the news headline and brief summary information provided by ACLED for each event. With the help of a research assistant, I iteratively developed a coding scheme to categorize protest events across aggregate topic areas, shown in Panel B of Figure 9.1. These topics were then further aggregated into broader topic areas, including gender-based concerns, identity-based concerns, economic concerns, service provision, government performance, and non-gender-based violence, as shown in Panel A of Figure 9.1. My research team then coded each of the 2,924 protest descriptions according to this coding scheme, with each protest event receiving one or more codes.

Figure 9.1 shows that, from 2016 to 2021, 40 percent of women-led protests targeted gender-based concerns (feminist or strategic concerns, according to Molyneux), the largest of which was gender-based violence. More than one in five women-led protests centered on issues of gender-based violence (as shown in Panel B). Women also frequently protested in favor of the prohibition of alcohol, which is commonly presumed to reduce gender-based violence, and against broader gender discrimination. Table 9.1 documents a random sample of the descriptions of these protests. From this snapshot, we see that women-led protesting around gender-based concerns included demands for statewide alcohol prohibition, justice in specific rape cases, more general protection from violence, protection from eve-teasing (street harassment), and the general upliftment of women. These protests spanned the country. They were organized by NGOs, women's organizations, student groups, and individual women themselves. And they ranged from the small-scale mobilization of a few women to demonstrations involving thousands of women. As highlighted in the history of the Indian women's movement and through broader, cross-national scholarship, policies designed to protect women from gender-based violence have largely resulted from women's mass mobilization.[19]

Yet, Figure 9.1 shows that women also regularly mobilized as a group around issues not targeting gender justice. More than half of the women-led protests focused on more pragmatic interests such as improved labor conditions and equal wages, better service provision, and frustrations with government performance and accountability. For example, roughly 5 percent of all women-led protests focused on improvements to education, just over 5 percent on water provision, and more than a quarter on government performance. As Table 9.1 shows, this included varied issues such as the use of alcohol to influence elections, punishment of corrupt politicians, and political

---

[19] Weldon (2002); Htun and Weldon (2012, 2018).

accountability for service delivery failures. Many of the protests around non-gender identity-based concerns concentrated on the 2019 Citizenship Amendment Act and its treatment of Muslims. Economically oriented protests focused on such varied topics as agricultural pricing and farm laws, bus fares, and demonetization (the 2016 outlawing of most cash in circulation in India).

Figure 9.1 suggests that national dynamics mirror those observed across villages in Madhya Pradesh: in some instances, women mobilize around violence and more explicitly feminist agendas, while in others, they mobilize around development and more general economic improvements (see Figures 7.10 and 8.3 in Chapters 7 and 8 for comparison). Women most often come together motivated by a shared desire to minimize their experiences of discrimination and violence. But they also find commonality in their daily experiences, traversing markets, politics, and social dynamics. The works of Molyneux, Basu, and Ray suggest, however, that we should see variation in women's mobilization that centers on feminist versus pragmatic interests.[20] Figure 9.2 documents the variation in protest frequency and type across Indian states. The left side documents the total number of women-led protest events in each state. The right side reports the share of protests that focused on a gender-based concern.

Figure 9.2 reveals that there is substantial variation across states with respect to the frequency of women-led protests, which is not well explained by state population size. For example, Kerala and Telangana are two states with similar populations, but Telangana had nearly three times as many women-led protests (96 as compared to 33 in Kerala). Manipur, one of the smallest states in India located in the northeast of the country, had nearly twice as many women-led protest events as any other state. This is largely attributed to the Meira Paibi, a historical women's movement focused on the protection of human rights rooted in broader statewide self-determination movements. In fact, the three states with the highest frequency of women-led protests since 2016 have all recently faced challenges to territorial control. Most states averaged roughly 100 women-led protests in the past 5.5 years.

However, Panel B of Figure 9.2 documents the substantial variation across states in the degree to which this mobilization by women centered on feminist issues, and this variation is not correlated with the frequency of women-led protests. In some states, such as Jammu and Kashmir, Bihar, and Maharashtra, only about 20 percent of women-led protests directly targeted gender-based concerns. In other states, such as Telangana, Uttarakhand, and Jharkhand, more than half of all women-led protests focused on gender-based concerns.

---

[20] Molyneux (1985), Basu (1992), and Ray (2000).

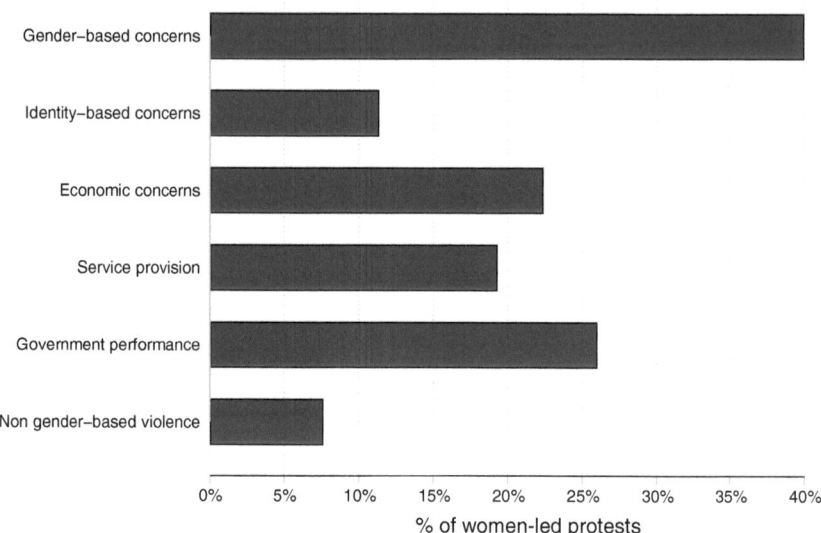

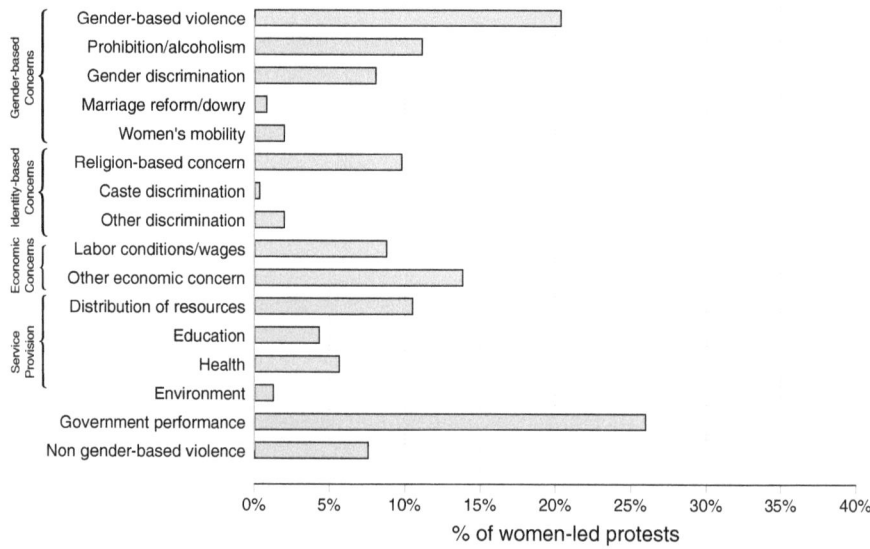

FIGURE 9.1 Women protest in support of both gender-based and development-oriented interests

Note: The figure plots the nature of women's protests across India, 2016–2021. Data are from the Armed Conflict Location and Event Data (ACLED) South Asia political violence and protest dataset and cover all reported political violence and protest events from 2016 to 2021 (Raleigh et al. 2010). These data were subset to protest and riot events for which the primary actors were women, yielding a total of 2,924 events. Event descriptions were then hand coded into the categories shown above.

TABLE 9.1 *Examples of women-led protest activities by coded protest topic in the ACLED database*

Protest Topic	Year	State	Protest Description
Gender-based Concerns	2016	Assam	On July 13, thousands of women came to the streets, protesting against child marriage. The women assembled at Tangla town, under ROSS, and other organizations.
	2016	Jammu and Kashmir	Hundreds of women held a demonstration over the rape and murder of a kidnapped girl in Domail area of Bhaderwah in Indian-occupied Kashmir.
	2016	Jharkhand	On April 10, 2016, over a dozen women, clad in pink saris (Gulabi Gang), protested outside the Governor's House in Ranchi (Jharkhand), seeking a total ban on alcohol in the state.
	2016	Karnataka	Members of the Karnataka Widow-Destitute Women Association staged a protest in Bhadravati city, demanding an increase in the pension amount paid to them by the government.
	2016	NCT of Delhi	On the occasion of International Women's Day, female students associated with ABVP in JNU tied black bands on their mouths and protested against the attacks on them.
	2016	NCT of Delhi	On May 4, women's organizations and citizens joined a protest outside Kerala House in New Delhi to protest against the rape and murder of Dalit law student Jisha on April 28 in Ernakulam.
	2016	Uttar Pradesh	All India Democratic Women's Association (AIDWA) members held a protest march against the rise of crime against women in the state.
	2016	Uttar Pradesh	Hundreds of schoolgirls protested in front of their village Vaidpura, close to Saifai city, Etawah district, to express their rage about eve-teasing incidents they were facing during their way to schools, demanding police action against the accused.
	2016	Uttarakhand	Women in large numbers from various areas of Uttarkashi district staged a protest in Mussoorie demanding the removal of a liquor vendor in their village and that they be supplied potable water supply instead.
	2016	Uttarakhand	Activists of the Akhil Bharatiya Janwadi Mahila Samiti held a rally in Dehradun demanding beneficiary schemes for the upliftment of women in the state.

(*continued*)

TABLE 9.1 (*continued*)

Protest Topic	Year	State	Protest Description
	2016	West Bengal	The BJP Mahila Morcha on Wednesday kicked off a ten-day march from Kamduni in North-24 Parganas district to Kakdwip in South-24 Parganas to protest against alleged rising atrocities against women across the state under the TMC regime.
	2017	Haryana	Girl students staged a protest at the Government High School in Kadarpur village in Gurgaon assumed on May 19, demanding an upgradation of their village school so that girls can complete Class 12 in their village school and not fall victim to sexual harassment while commuting to cities or other villages.
	2017	Manipur	District Women Committee, Bishnupur, under the aegis of United NGO Mission Manipur, carried out a strong protest against the April 14 gang-rape incident of Phaknung at Keinou today.
	2017	Uttarakhand	A number of women SHGs held protests at Thal village in Berinag in Pithoragarh on Friday, raising slogans against the government and demanding that liquor shops be closed down throughout the district.
	2018	Madhya Pradesh	Assumed on July 2, in Bhopal city (Bhopal, Madhya Pradesh), Bhopal Gas Peedit Mahila Udyog Sangathan (BGPMUS) activists demonstrated over an incident of the gang rape of a seven-year-old girl.
	2018	NCT of Delhi	On April 12, a group of students and women organizations held a protest at Parliament Street in New Delhi against the rape and murder of an eight-year-old girl in Kathua as well as the rape of another girl in Unnao.
	2019	Karnataka	On January 20, in Chitradurga city (Chitradurga, Karnataka), the Grameena Kooli Karmikara Sanghatane rural laborers' organization, including about 3,000 women, staged a *padayatra* (march) from Karnataka to Bengaluru to demand complete prohibition of alcohol.
	2020	Punjab	On May 6, 2020, women staged a protest in different villages of Nabha, Patiala (Punjab), against the state's decision to open liquor vends, fearing domestic violence during coronavirus.

Identity-based Concerns	2016	Maharashtra	Over 350 women activists belonging to Bhumata Brigade attempted to enter the Shani Shingnapur temple to break a 400-year-old tradition banning women from entering. Police stopped the women.
	2018	Uttar Pradesh	On March 18, Muslim women took out a protest march against triple talaq in Varanasi city (Uttar Pradesh).
	2019	Jharkhand	On November 13, tribals, including women, pulled down an under-construction boundary wall for a housing project at Kamargoda panchayat (Saraikela Kharsawan, Jharkhand), which was being erected by an alleged "outsider," demanding protection of their ancestral land.
	2019	Manipur	On February 10, women vendors clashed with the police in Khwairamband market in Imphal city (Imphal West, Manipur), during a demonstration against the Citizenship Amendment Bill. The police used tear gas shells and mock bombs, and the women retaliated by throwing objects and water bottles. Six women were injured.
	2019	Uttar Pradesh	On October 25, at least fifteen women from the Valmiki community protested when they were denied entry to a temple in the Bulandshahr district (Uttar Pradesh) because they were Dalits.
	2021	Jammu and Kashmir	On March 27, 2021, hundreds of JKAP members, along with its women's wing, held a protest at Jammu city (Jammu and Kashmir) to demand revision of the current geology and mining policy in order to safeguard the rights of natives on their natural resources.
	2021	Punjab	On February 18, 2021, various unions, including Kirti Kisan Union and the Istri Jagriti Manch, staged a protest in Nawanshahr (Punjab) against the arrest of Dalit activist Nodeep Kaur from the ongoing farmers' agitation.
Economic Concerns	2016	Jammu and Kashmir	The Pardesh Mahila Congress staged a demonstration against the center and state governments in response to their failures to control the price of pulses and vegetables.
	2017	Uttarakhand	Members of the Mahila Congress, along with members of district Congress unit, organized the statewide "Thali Bajao" protest program against demonetization at district headquarters of Uttarakhand state on Monday.

(continued)

TABLE 9.1 (continued)

Protest Topic	Year	State	Protest Description
	2018	Tamil Nadu	On January 23, in Thanjavur, agitations by the National Federation of Indian Women against the recent hike in bus fare continued with protests and slogans.
	2020	Punjab	On October 25, 2020, farmers from the BKU – along with women, children, youths, the elderly, laborers, artists and writers – burned effigies in Jalandhar district (Punjab) in a massive protest against recently passed farm laws.
	2021	Odisha	On January 23, 2021, police forcibly dispersed protesting Auxiliary Nurse Midwifes in Bhubaneswar (Odisha) during an ongoing protest demanding job regularization.
Service Provision	2016	Uttar Pradesh	A group of women from Sector A, Sitapur Road (Lucknow), gathered at the zonal office of Jal Kal (a welfare association) and blocked traffic in protest of dirty water.
	2016	Himachal Pradesh	Women of Nagri staged a demonstration in front of the office of the IPH Department in Palampur against the water crisis and demanded restoration of water supply to their villages.
	2016	Odisha	Women led by Mahila Congress leaders on Monday staged demonstrations at different districts of the state, protesting acute shortage of drinking water and state government's alleged failure to supply potable water to its people.
	2018	Tamil Nadu	On December 26, in Madurai city (Madurai, Tamil Nadu), hundreds of women staged a protest against the Corporation for not removing garbage dumped into the channel along the main road.
	2019	Telangana	On August 21, pregnant women and lactating mothers, along with villagers, staged a protest in front of local Anganwadi center in Rustapur village (Nalgonda, Telangana) against the contractor for supplying spoiled milk packets.
	2020	Assam	On January 24, protesters – including students, women, unemployed youths, flood victims, the landless, and the homeless – staged a rally at Sadiya (Tinsukia district, Assam) against the Citizenship (Amendment) Act, 2019 (CAA), including flood, erosion, loss of land, education, unemployment, roads, and electricity, among others.

Year	State	Description
2020	Bihar	On June 1, 2020, a large number of women associated with local female organization Bihar Mahila Samaj took out a protest march in Kishanganj city (Kishanganj, Bihar) against the alleged apathy of both the central and state government over the deaths of many migrant laborers due to thirst, hunger, and accidents in various parts of the country during the coronavirus pandemic. The agitation took place in all district headquarters of the state.
2020	Himachal Pradesh	On May 1, 2020, tribal women staged a protest in Keylong in Lahaul Spiti (Himachal Pradesh) demanding restrictions on entry of outsiders during coronavirus.
Government Performance		
2016	Manipur	Women vendors staged a sit-in-protest in front of the New Market complex today, claiming that absence of quality control in the construction of New Market complex and Tampha Keithel at Yairipok Bazar, Thoubal district, led to cave-in of its pillars in the massive earthquake that shocked the state early morning on January 3.
2016	NCT of Delhi	Workers of All India Mahila Congress took to the streets in the capital to protest against the latest Union Budget.
2017	Kerala	On December 1, in Poonthura of Thiruvananthapuram, hundreds of people, mainly women, from the fishing community blocked roads protesting the inefficiency and apathy shown by official agencies in bringing home over 200 fishermen trapped in the turbulent sea under Cyclone Ockhi.
2017	Manipur	Hundreds of women from various communities of Kangpokpi under the aegis of Kangpokpi Women Welfare Organization sit in protest against alleged demands and extortion in Kangpokpi town.
2018	Punjab	On December 20, around 300 women staged a protest at Mehatpur police station in Nakodar (Jalandhar, Punjab) against the failure of the police to take dowry and harassment cases seriously. The women claim officers at the station have ignored serious allegations of physical and mental torture.
2019	Manipur	On March 8, women staged a protest and blocked the road in Tekcham village (Thoubal, Manipur) by digging holes on the stretch, in protest against the prolonged inactivity of the state government to commence repair works on the said road.

(continued)

TABLE 9.1 (*continued*)

Protest Topic	Year	State	Protest Description
	2019	Uttarakhand	On September 26, women of Banskhera village protested in Kashipur (Udham Singh Naga district, Uttarakhand) against the practice of distribution of liquor to influence elections.
	2020	Kerala	On September 15, members of the BJP women's wing held a protest in Malappuram city (Malappuram, Kerala) demanding the resignation of a minister involved in a gold smuggling case.
	2020	Odisha	On November 8, over a hundred women under the banner of the Dalit and Adivasi Mahila Manch staged a protest, in Bhubaneswar (Odisha), demanding the arrest of BJP national vice president, in connection with the alleged Sarua land scam.
Non-gender-based Violence	2016	Manipur	Local women staged a demonstration in the area on Friday in protest against an incident, where suspected rebels exploded a hand grenade inside the residence of Ch Manglem Singh, a retired professor of Regional Institute of Medical Sciences (RIMS), here at 11.30 p.m. on Thursday.
	2016	Uttar Pradesh	Women are sitting on a dharna demanding the arrest of Jan Muhammad of Akhlakh, who is accused of cow slaughter in Bishada village.
	2018	Jammu and Kashmir	On June 18, the AIMC led a silent protest march in Jammu city (Jammu and Kashmir) against government forces' failure to protect people's lives and property in Jammu and Kashmir.
	2019	Uttar Pradesh	On June 10, members of the AIDWA and other women activists demonstrated in Lucknow city (Uttar Pradesh) to oppose the increase in crimes against minors.
	2019	West Bengal	On May 15, members of the BJP women cell workers held a silent protest near Mahatma Gandhi's statue in Kolkata city (Kolkata, West Bengal) in protest against vandalization and clashes between TMC and BJP supporters at the BJP President's roadshow in the city, on May 14.

Data are from the Armed Conflict Location and Event Data (ACLED) South Asia political violence and protest dataset and cover all reported political violence and protest events from 2016 to 2021 (Raleigh et al. 2010). These data were subset to protest and riot events, for which the primary actors were women, yielding a total of 2,924 events. Event descriptions were then hand coded into the categories shown above.

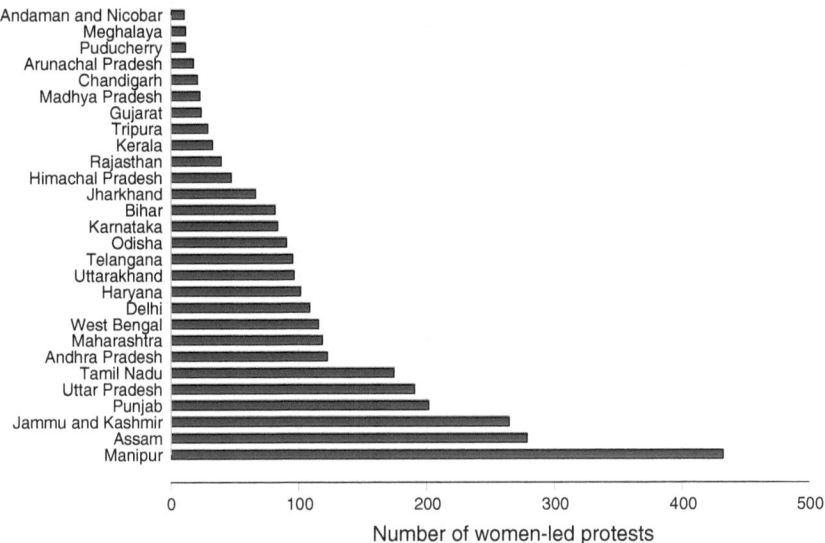

Number of women-led protests

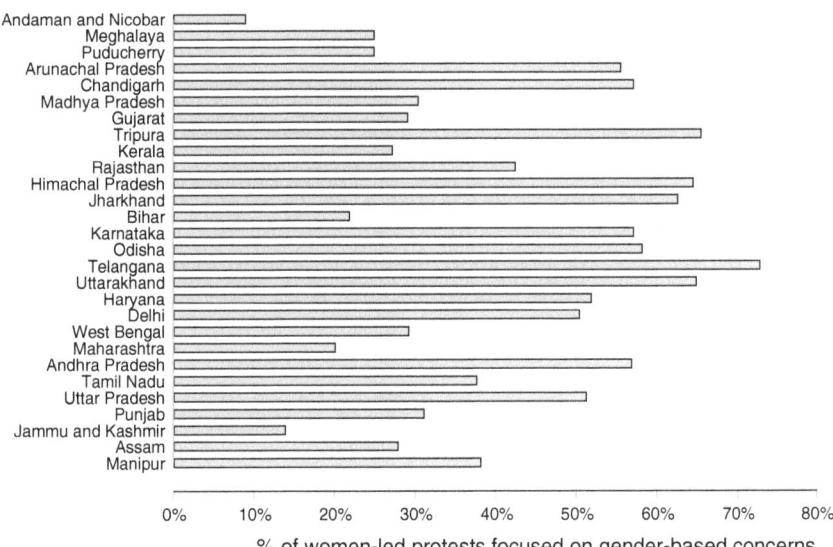

% of women-led protests focused on gender-based concerns

FIGURE 9.2 The frequency and nature of women-led protests varied substantially by state

Note: Panel A plots the total number of women-led protests in each state (subsetting to states with at least 10 protest events). Panel B plots the share of women-led protests in each state that were focused on gender-based issues. Data are from the Armed Conflict Location and Event Data (ACLED) South Asia political violence and protest dataset and cover all reported political violence and protest events from 2016 to 2021 (Raleigh et al. 2010). These data were subset to protest and riot events where the primary actors were women, yielding a total of 2,925 events.

While I do not aim to explain this variation, the intuition from past scholarship that the nature of women's demand-making is constrained by the environment in which the movement operates appears evident in the substantial variation seen across states. This implies that the diversity of interests among women can lead to diversity in their demand-making. It also suggests that the ways in which women traverse political climates may shape the nature of women's mobilization.

The women in Madhya Pradesh similarly navigated decisions about whether to elevate explicitly gendered issues or more normatively acceptable issues of community development. The two most common agendas of women's collective action in the villages I study were gender-based violence and the provision of water. Similarly, across India, the three most common agendas of women's collective action were gender-based violence, government performance, and service provision. While of a very different kind, structure, and scale, the micro-movements observed in a small number of villages in Madhya Pradesh resemble the broader women's movement in India.

The variation in the nature of women's collective action across India makes one point clear: women politically organize around distinct demands. This suggests that women's political inclusion has substantive implications; women's political action challenges the state to address distinct issues, implying the inefficiency of the patriarchal political order.

BACKLASH TO WOMEN'S ACTIVISM

In Madhya Pradesh, many of the women experienced social sanctioning and intimidation intended to suppress their political action after seeking entry into political spaces. This resembles more general patterns of resistance and backlash to women's activism. A notable example is the large-scale Aurat March (Women's March), which has taken place in Pakistan on International Women's Day for the past several years. In recent years, women have experienced physical intimidation and harassment while protesting; one year, they were pelted with stones as they marched.[21] Organizers have faced digital harassment and even legal allegations of blasphemy. Such experiences of resistance and backlash to collective organizing by women are not unique to Pakistan. Women across South Asia have experienced backlash to their political mobilization,[22] both directly and indirectly through the rise of men's rights groups and anti-feminist countermovements in response to the perceived

---

[21] Khan (2021); Javaid (2021).   [22] Brulé (2020a, 2020b).

threat of women's mobilization. The observation of backlash against women reveals the more general use of coercion to suppress women's political behavior.

Direct Resistance to Women's Political Action

Measuring backlash and resistance is challenging, as the methods of resistance are plentiful, their deployment often discreet, and their success marked by the inaction of women. As a result, explicit instances of backlash to women's mobilization are rarely documented. However, the ACLED database captures a sample of news headlines documenting direct and explicit instances of backlash. ACLED codes these events as either riots or experiences of direct violence against citizens. Many instances of explicit backlash will be missed by ACLED's inclusion requirements (reported by news media and identified as either political violence or protest). However, the sample of instances captured in these data provides a glimpse of the experiences of women activists and helps understand the threats and fears that many women contend with when deciding whether to raise their voices in protest. To identify such instances, my research team extracted all events in the ACLED database where women were identified as secondary actors and, reading through all event descriptions, coded events as backlash when the event action was a direct and negative response to women's behavior and choices.[23] Table 9.2 reports the thirteen such events that have been recorded in India since 2016.

Women experienced backlash for activities such as entering previously male-only temples; protesting religious marriage customs, eve-teasing (street harassment), and animal rights; seeking information regarding potentially corrupt behavior by politicians; and reporting as journalists. In most of these cases, women were violently attacked by groups of men. In two cases, women were killed. This backlash happened across India, including in both urban and rural communities, and targeted women of all backgrounds. The use of violence and intimidation against women engaging in legal, political action unified these experiences.

While incomplete, these data highlight the nontriviality of women's concerns over backlash to their political action. These patterns of resistance mirror those described in Chapter 8 in a few villages in Madhya Pradesh, where women also reported intimidation and physical violence in response to their collective organization. When the potential cost of political mobilization is violence or death, women's political action is undoubtedly highly constrained. This threat

---

[23] The vast majority of events where women were secondary actors were legal cases filed by women against either men or the police, largely due to experiences of violence. While this is also a potential indication of backlash, these events could not be linked to explicit behavior by women and so are not coded as backlash.

TABLE 9.2 *Coded instances of backlash to women in the ACLED database*

Year	State	Protest Description
2016	Maharashtra	Unknown assailants attacked Trupti Desai, a women's rights activist who, along with her followers, has been entering Hindu temples to pray following a Supreme Court decision. She was seriously injured.
2016	West Bengal	On Tuesday, a wife of slain TMC activist was burnt alive in Jamaitola village of Malda district, allegedly by INC activists. She was killed because she refused to withdraw a 2013 murder case against INC.
2017	Karnataka	On September 5, Gauri Lankesh, a prominent female Indian journalist, was shot dead at close range by unidentified gunmen at her residence in Bengaluru city (Karnataka).
2017	Karnataka	On October 14, in Bengaluru, a mob of unidentified actors attacked two women animal rights activists along with two police constables accompanying them when they tried to rescue cattle from an illegal slaughterhouse at Avalahalli near Thalaghattapura.
2017	Uttar Pradesh	Social women activists, expressing their views on triple "talaq" and "halala," were attacked by a group of about sixty persons in Lucknow on Sunday evening, who manhandled and abused them and called them anti-Islam.
2018	Kerala	Within the month of June 2018, in Cheruplassery (Palakkad, Kerala), a woman and SFI activist was allegedly raped by a CPI-M member inside the Cheruplassery area committee office. The CPI-M denied the allegations.
2018	Uttar Pradesh	On December 15, a woman was molested, and she and her family were attacked by ten local men armed with sharp weapons, in Machhrauli village of Jhinjhana area (Shamali, Uttar Pradesh), after she protested against eve-teasing by a group of local men.
2019	Assam	On September 28, a man physically assaulted a female journalist during news coverage in Guwahati city (Kamrup Metropolitan district, Assam). Later, the man was arrested by Paltanbazar police.
2019	Delhi	On November 30, a woman who was staging a solo protest in front of the parliament in New Delhi against the rape of a doctor in Hyderabad was allegedly detained and beaten up by the Delhi police.
2019	Jammu and Kashmir	On September 8, police damaged a female journalist's car with batons at a checkpoint near Jehangir Chowk in Srinagar city (Jammu and Kashmir), amid restrictions following the government's decision to repeal Article 370 and bifurcate the state into two union territories.
2019	Manipur	On July 4, unidentified gunmen fired at the daughter of a human rights activist in Imphal city (Imphal West district, Manipur). The girl managed to escape the attack with no injuries.

Year	State	Protest Description
2019	Meghalaya	On April 20, a woman was assaulted by the family of a council secretary, in Tohsildarpara (Bagicha) village under Mahendraganj area (Southwest Garo Hills, Meghalaya), after she filed a petition asking for details regarding alleged use of government funds by the secretary to construct a boundary wall around his house. [size=no report]
2019	Telangana	On January 23, in Hyderabad town (Hyderabad, Telangana), several Hindu organizations, including VHP, attacked a female journalist and her crew while they reported on their demonstration against the Sabarimala Ayyappa Seva Samajam issue.

Data are from the Armed Conflict Location and Event Data (ACLED) South Asia political violence and protest dataset and cover all reported political violence and protest events from 2016 to 2021 (Raleigh et al. 2010). These data were subset to protest and riot events for which the secondary actor were women, and then further to instances clearly indicatiing a backlash against women.

of coercion, however, highlights the value of women's collective action to safeguard against the credible resistance of those in power.

The Indian Men's Rights Movement

Out of the women's movement of the 1970s came the Dowry (Prohibition) Act (i.e., Section 498A of the Indian Penal Code in 1983). This act criminalized "cruelty" against women and protected women from harassment and abuse due to insufficient provision of dowry. The women's movement had protested and lobbied for these reforms after the continued murder of women related to dowry, as in the case of Tarvinder Kaur, who was burned to death by her mother-in-law and sister-in-law for failing to provide enough dowry.

Roughly two decades later, the men's rights movement saw small groups of Indian men come together in response to the Dowry (Prohibition) Act, which they claimed enabled unfair treatment of men by allowing the automatic arrest of men accused of dowry-related crimes. Men's rights activists argue that women exploit this provision by falsely claiming dowry abuse to punish their husbands. In a victory for the emerging men's rights movement, the Supreme Court repealed the law's automatic arrest clause, citing the potential for the abuse of men.[24] This clause was partially reinstated in 2019.[25]

---

[24] Bhattacharya (2017).   [25] Rautry (2018).

What started as small groups of disgruntled men has, over the past two decades, become a larger political movement.[26] It is largely coordinated by the Save Indian Family Foundation (SIFF), an NGO, and sees its core agenda as protecting men from gender-biased laws, feminist media, and a broader feminist agenda that threatens the traditional family. Politically, the movement operates largely through legislative advocacy but has also organized protests to demand legal reform.

SIFF defines itself as a response to the movement for women's empowerment in India. Its website describes its mission: "to expose and create awareness about large scale violations of Civil Liberties and Human Rights in the name of women's empowerment in India." Chowdhury highlights how "the demand for men's rights in India is to be explained by the reconstitution of patriarchy – expressed particularly in altered gender roles within the family – that has been necessitated by the dual pressures of economic change and feminist legal intervention in the previous two decades."[27]

From its origin to its current organizational structure, men's rights activists define their agenda as directly oppositional to that of women's rights activists. These groups have fought to overturn legal changes driven by the women's movement and have, in the case of the Dowry (Prohibition) Act, been successful. Notably, the men's rights movement does not actively contest the mobilization of women, but the mobilization of women aimed at feminist agendas. The rise of the men's rights countermovement is one example of backlash to women's demands for empowerment, and, as evidenced in SIFF's mission statement, has the direct goal of reestablishing patriarchy. The case of SIFF and the broader men's rights movement in India highlights men's capacity to leverage their social capital and economic resources to protect the dominant social order. This, along with the evidence in Table 9.1, suggests the generalizability of male-led contestation to women's empowerment across India.

DISCUSSION

The recent history of women's mobilization in India has largely focused on contesting violence against women and seeking greater legal protections for women. Yet, women have also mobilized around many other issue areas, including state performance and service provision. The diversity of women's demands can be attributed to both the diversity of their interests[28] and the social and political contexts in which they must negotiate for political voice.[29] Women's organizations, as others have argued, are more likely to focus on pragmatic issues as opposed to feminist issues when facing external constraints, which limits their efficacy in pushing feminist agendas. This highlights the first

---

[26] Basu (2015, 2016).   [27] Chowdhury (2014).   [28] Molyneux (1985, 1998).
[29] Basu (1992); Ray (2000).

way in which the threat of resistance can constrain women's political mobilization – by shaping which interests are elevated.

When women do advocate for gender justice, they are often met with direct and indirect resistance and backlash. Women's mobilization around gender-based violence and other gendered interests in India has led to a countermovement seeking to protect men's rights and traditional institutions. The men's rights movement, led by SIFF, challenges legal reforms designed to protect women's rights and has succeeded in at least one instance. Resistance to women's collective mobilization goes beyond the countermobilization by men and directly threatens women's safety. I document a small sample of instances of direct and violent backlash to women's mobilization. Such overt backlash to women's demands for political representation highlights the second set of constraints on women's political mobilization and political success.

The Indian women's movement and the nascent men's rights countermovement demonstrate the circuitous process of women's political empowerment, which I also document in the micro-dynamics of women's mobilization in Madhya Pradesh. Diversity among women creates challenges to organizing collective action. As a result, women's mobilization most commonly centers on their shared experiences of subordination and violence. Women's political action inherently challenges the social order, as women seek both political power for themselves and the curtailment of men's capacity to protect their own power. Unsurprisingly, this often leads to resistance from those with the greatest stake in the prevailing order. Such resistance is deployed through the very capacities from which women seek protection – violence and intimidation. This process of negotiating and renegotiating norms and power demonstrates the value of women's solidaristic collective action, without which men's resistance is likelier to succeed.

Yet the nature of women's political organization reveals the inefficiency of the patriarchal political order. Women across India collectively mobilize around their distinct interests; 5 percent of the country's protests were women-led and women-focused and more than 20 percent of their demands focused on gendered concerns. This is even more striking given the gendered inequalities in political participation across India. Such protests would be unnecessary if the existing political order efficiently represented women's interests. Women's political inclusion matters on both descriptive and substantive grounds, as it is likely to impact policymaking and politics.

Conclusion

Political Inclusion as a Path to Social Change

> *It took me quite a long time to develop a voice, and now that I have it, I am not going to be silent.*
>
> —Madeleine Albright

On January 1, 2019, 3.5–5 million women stood side by side in the Indian state of Kerala to protest gender inequality. They formed a 385-mile long "women's wall" (വനിതാ മതിൽ), unbroken and united, in what became one of the largest women-led protests in history.[1] Women joined the wall to demand entry to a space previously reserved for men, but, more generally, they came together to collectively demand progress on gender equality.

An Indian Supreme Court ruling on September 28, 2018, granted women legal permission to enter the Sabarimala temple in Kerala after three decades of prohibition, citing women's right to free worship. Since 1991, women had been banned from the temple on the grounds that their entry would defy prevailing customs and could lead to impurity in the temple. The 2018 ruling held that this law violated women's equal constitutional rights, including the free practice of religion.

Days later, as women were set to enter the temple, thousands of mostly male protesters descended on the temple to block their entry.[2] Many women trying to enter were physically and verbally harassed. Both leading national parties, the Bharatiya Janata Party (BJP) and the Indian National Congress (INC), usually adversaries, endorsed these protests, claiming the need to uphold traditions such as the purity of temples.[3]

---

[1] *The Times of India* (2019); Thiagarajan (2019).
[2] Ameerudheen (2018); Schwartz (2019); Reuters (2019).   [3] Unnithan (2018).

By January 1, no woman had entered the temple. In response to their continued and forced prohibition despite a legal ruling in their favor, women came together in what has become known as the women's wall protest. The next day, two women entered the temple unharmed with police protection. While protests against women's entry continued to rage, the state responded to women's mass mobilization by providing them the protection they were legally due.

The women's wall protest is an example of the dynamics shown throughout this book. The path to women's political empowerment, and ultimately the representation of their distinct interests, is anything but linear. Gaining political voice and demanding gender equality, as this case reveals, is at odds with tradition, customs, and norms. Progress engenders resistance. And resistance by those with power challenges women's ability to demand representation. In the case of the Sabarimala temple, the country's two largest political parties illegally opposed women's inclusion, and thousands of men stood against women's rights. The BJP even acknowledged that it opposed women's inclusion as part of its agenda, with a chief party official promising that the party would provide protection to the male protestors: "I assured [the chief priest] that we are with him and that contempt of court charge would not stand."[4]

In the rural villages of Madhya Pradesh that I have described and studied, women's households constituted a strong constraint on their political agency and behavior. In line with an informal institution – household political cooperation – designed to uphold patriarchal political authority, I find that women often align with their households in political decision-making. As both parties did in the Sabarimala case, men and political elites in the study villages benefited from women's political cooperation with the household. Coercing and constraining women's political behavior elevated men's political authority and ensured their political spoils. The result of the dominance of the institution of household political cooperation is women's limited political engagement except where their participation would benefit powerful men.

Economic resources, patriarchal norms, or political institutions alone cannot sufficiently explain patterns of women's political participation. The intersection of all three creates a patriarchal political order that elevates men's authority, suppresses women's agency, enables resistance to women's challenges, and ultimately bifurcates political power across genders.

How, then, can women achieve political representation? As with the women's wall, I suggest and show that women are able to contest resistance and demand political representation through joint collective action. Women can credibly challenge entrenched political power hierarchies and the political system that benefits from their subordination by coming together and standing in solidarity. They will often find support from others who have been excluded

---

[4] Express News Service (2018).

from the prevailing political order. A less publicized aspect of the women's wall protest was the parallel wall, formed opposite, where men and other allies stood in solidarity.[5] And, when successful, women's collective organization can yield political and policy change.

The renegotiation of power and voice is thus likely to be a circular process, in which forward motion is met by friction. This book has demonstrated the twists and turns of this process. In the beginning, we saw how the prevailing political system suppresses women's political voices to its benefit. In the middle, we explored how women have begun to challenge this system, more actively engage in politics, and raise distinct demands. By the end, we observed how women's more explicit mobilization around gender equality is met with backlash and resistance in attempts to curtail the demanded process of change.

Drawing on evidence from nearly 10,000 women and men in Madhya Pradesh, this book makes and defends three central claims: (1) households make political decisions jointly, (2) this elevates the voices of dominant men, suppresses (often coercively) the voices and political behavior of women, and inculcates vested interests in a larger patriarchal political order, and (3) autonomy from the household and collective action by women, in combination, empower women and challenge the patriarchal order.

In this book, I have evaluated a shock to a long-stable political order. It remains to be seen how India's political system (and politics in the study villages in Madhya Pradesh) will respond to this shock. Will there be a shift to a new order in which women are active members of political institutions and their voices are given equal weight in political processes? Or, will resistance prevail and bolster the exclusionary system that has dominated the country's politics for decades? Women's experiences elsewhere suggest possible paths this story may take.

This chapter outlines the possibilities that flow from the argument I have presented and defended. It demonstrates how my focus on women's lives reveals much larger processes of politics and development. It is becoming increasingly apparent that economic development does not necessarily increase women's agency. Although India's GDP has increased, female labor force participation has declined, particularly in the wealthiest households. My findings echo those in prior studies, which have concluded that economic transfers to women do not necessarily change household dynamics or give women greater agency.[6] Restrictive social norms tend to prevail. Despite decades of quotas, women remain substantially underrepresented in the Indian Parliament.

---

[5] The law prohibiting women from entering the temple was based on the Brahmanical Hindu religious doctrine of purity, according to which menstruating women and Dalits (historically known as members of the untouchable castes) are considered impure. These exclusionary rules are thus rooted in caste as well as gender hierarchies.

[6] Kabeer (2005); Duflo (2012); Khan (2021).

Yet, women are engaging in more collective action at both the micro and macro levels. Women lead hundreds of protests each year. India's most recent national election had the highest turnout of women in history: in many parts of the country, more women turned out to vote than men. From the women's wall to the numerous protests against gender-based violence, women continue to collectively demand progress on gender equality.

The COVID-19 pandemic exacerbated gendered inequalities and increased the deployment of coercion against women,[7] but is also a potent example of the power of women's collective action. When the initial lockdowns sent men home, women had less autonomy and more responsibility and care work than ever; violence against them rose exponentially.[8] The economic crises that occurred due to shifts in production disproportionately hurt women-dominated sectors, further reducing their resources and agency.[9] Yet, women known as "COVID-19 warriors" came together to manufacture personal protective equipment, disseminate health information, and operate community kitchens in a largely self-help group (SHG)–led movement[10] – a testament to the ability of women's joint action to benefit the broader good.[11]

These dynamics suggest that once we understand that the answer to the puzzle of women's political participation lies in the vested interests in women's subordination, the key question is: how do we meaningfully improve women's agency? I suggest the answer lies in fostering sustained and solidaristic collective action among women. If women's collective action is often deployed to enhance both gender equality and the broader good, then it bears even greater impact. The long-held assumption that economic development will beget gender equality has proven incomplete. These patterns instead suggest that in some instances, the reverse may be true: women's political empowerment, as a result of their historical position as political outsiders, may facilitate development. I explore this potential in this chapter and then consider the implications of this unanticipated accountability – namely, what does it mean to put development on the backs of women?

THE GROWING SHG MOVEMENT

SHGs at Scale

Since I conducted the majority of fieldwork for this book, India has experienced a dramatic rise in the prevalence of SHGs, which reflects how these groups have become a priority of the current government. In 2011, the Indian government's Ministry of Rural Development launched the National Rural Livelihoods

---

[7] Krishnakumar and Verma (2021). [8] UN Women (2020). [9] Agarwal (2021).
[10] Madan (2020); World Bank (2020). [11] Jain (2020).

Mission (NRLM) as one of its flagship programs.[12] The NRLM is a poverty relief program that creates and fosters SHGs. Its core tenet is that providing credit, livelihoods support, and self-employment opportunities to women's institutions will cascade into sustainable income generation and more widespread poverty relief. According to the NRLM, its core guiding principles include that "social mobilization and building strong institutions [SHGs and their larger federated structures] of the poor is critical for unleashing the innate capabilities of the poor" and "an external dedicated and sensitive support structure is required to induce the social mobilization, institution building and empowerment process."[13] Women and women's groups are thus assumed to be the bearers of development, which, in turn, makes women's empowerment possible. As of 2023, the NRLM had mobilized more than 90 million women into SHGs. The ultimate goal is to benefit 350 million women, or roughly 85 percent of the rural poor.

I have shown that participation in SHGs can lead to women's greater political participation by evaluating the implementation of the SHG program by one of the leading nongovernmental organizations (NGOs) in this space. Will this proliferation of SHGs by the government lead to the widespread political empowerment of women across India? Can SHGs accomplish these inclusionary successes at scale?

The national SHG program's impact on women's political empowerment will depend on its ability to foster the deep and solidaristic ties among women that are needed to motivate and transact collective action. I have shown that SHGs generate successful political action when group members come together to collectively demand access to political spaces, but such collective action is more likely when women have high levels of trust and recognize a common set of gendered interests.

Government incentives to create such social solidarity may be limited. The costs of deep engagement and institution building may be precipitously high when conducted at scale. Key to the development of women's social solidarity is the persistence of SHGs over time, since regularized interactions are needed to foster a shared group identity and strong bonds.[14] The SHGs that I studied had been meeting continuously for six years on average and, in some cases, more than two decades. It is therefore the *sustainment*, rather than the *creation*, of SHGs that likely led to women's political empowerment. A recent evaluation of the NRLM suggests that it has been difficult to build these lasting institutions at scale.[15] More than 10 percent of SHGs had disbanded. In my proposed framework for collective action, this suggests that national SHGs may address only

---

[12] The NRLM built on the previous Swarnjayanti Gram Swarozgar Yojana program, which mobilized women into SHGs as early as 1999. This program garnered mixed results and so was revamped and scaled in 2011 through the NRLM.

[13] Deendayal Antyodaya Yojanaj (2021).   [14] Feigenberg, Field, and Pande (2010).

[15] Kochar et al. (2020).

the informational costs of collective action but may face challenges in overcoming the bargaining costs (identification of common interests) and enforcement costs (building sufficient trust to ensure collective action) to collective action. Such challenges have likely inhibited other government programs that create connections between women, such as the Mahatma Gandhi National Rural Employment Guarantee scheme that provides public work opportunities and often brings women into contact via this work, from generating the collective action and political participation shown in this book. Inclusionary change is likely only if these goals are also built into the design and implementation of these programs.

Parallel Institutions of Governance

The proliferation of SHGs has also created a set of local institutions parallel to local government bodies. Given the cohesion and efficacy of SHG institutions in collective action, and the orientation of such action toward broader development and public goods provision, SHGs in much of India have taken on and been tasked with public service delivery. Once the government has built these institutions, they are easy to tap into to reach remote populations. Based on the assumption that SHGs may be more reliable and effective institutions for service delivery than local governments, many government and nongovernment schemes are now run through SHGs.[16] SHGs are presumed to provide economies of scope and scale and have been given responsibility for running local Public Distribution System (PDS) (ration) shops, delivering maternal and child health information, advocating for better nutrition, and recruiting youth into vocational training programs. In some instances, these outcomes reflect collective action on the part of SHGs that have observed local government failures to perform their responsibilities and act to fill the void. In other instances, these outcomes reflect state directives in recognition that well-organized SHGs may provide a deeper and more reliable reach into the periphery than the state apparatus. SHGs have therefore become a mechanism to increase state capacity.

While visiting a village in Bihar, which the government considers an exemplar of the SHG program, I saw firsthand how the PDS shop – which distributes subsidized food grains to households below the poverty line – was run by SHGs after their own recognition that the local government could not and did not do so effectively and their seeking authority from higher-level officials to overtake distribution. These groups were lauded for their efficacy in development-oriented action. This support and praise from higher-level government officials, and from the community benefiting from the action, helped these groups stand against backlash and legitimize their political presence.

---

[16] Gugerty, Biscaye, and Anderson (2019); Nichols (2021).

The contrast between the lack of transparency and efficiency in state officials' implementation of many government programs and the efficacy of SHGs
has led to direct investments in these informal institutions. The premise of the
NRLM – that mobilizing women into institutions is a mechanism for poverty
reduction – highlights the instrumentality of women's groups. Making such
groups a bureaucratic arm of the state may result in wider and more sustainable
development and may support women's political inclusion and contestation of
backlash, but also has the potential to co-opt women's groups to serve state
interests rather than women's autonomous interests.

Co-optation of women's groups would provide a distinct pathway to
women's participation through direct state mobilization as opposed to the
autonomous collective action described in this book. By engaging women's
groups within the broader state apparatus, women's political participation
becomes a given. The broader community will come to expect women's
involvement in public affairs, as the state-sanctioned deployment of SHGs for
service delivery increases the groups' legitimacy. But women's political participation is more likely to be oriented around community development and other
issues in line with the needs of the state. State sanctioning of women's political
participation is less likely to be perceived as a threat to the social order – and is
therefore less likely to be opposed. Kabeer et al. document how the NRLM
program, unlike its NGO forbears, anticipates continual investment in SHG
institutions to ensure they can deliver much-needed services, securing the
sustainability of women's political participation.[17] Women's political inclusion
under these conditions would be instrumentally valuable for the state and the
wider community.

When asked what villagers think about SHGs in the village, Somila[18]
replied, "Villagers say that they themselves have not attempted nor accomplished the amount of work that the SHG has done. Men in the village
especially say that whatever work men have not been able to do, women have
gotten it done and shown how." Kabeer et al. compares the reception of state-
organized and NGO-organized SHGs:

> [NRLM] SHGs were seen, and with justification, as a conduit for accessing various
> government schemes. As a result, women in Narharpur were actively encouraged by
> their families to join. By contrast, women in Bhanupratappur faced strong resistance
> from their families who considered that PRADAN [an NGO] was merely taking women
> away from their normal responsibilities without offering compensatory access to
> new resources.[19]

And, there is some debate as to whether the proliferation of these groups has a
political aim. Journalists have noted that "the push for rural livelihoods,
meanwhile, has been as political as policy-driven. Not only does it help the

---

[17] Kabeer et al. (2019).   [18] Somila (pseudonym), female, 35 years old, ST.
[19] Kabeer et al. (2021).

BJP portray itself as a pro-rural poor party, it also enables it to tap into the extensive SHG network to spread its message,"[20] and Prime Minister Modi has been noted as visiting these women's groups directly.[21]

State mobilization can thus help create broader constituencies in support of women's political participation, but does this represent inclusion and empowerment? If such state-mobilized participation is not built on solidaristic ties within SHGs, then women's participation may pose little threat to patriarchal norms and political systems in practice. If women engage politically before they develop a consciousness and group identity around gender inequalities, their participation is unlikely to be channeled to reduce injustice. At the extreme, women may gain autonomy from the household but find themselves under the control of the state. The trade-off in this scenario is growth in women's political participation and broader economic development at the continued expense of women's complete agency and the representation of their gendered interests. How these policies are designed, specifically how much solidarity among and autonomy for women they foster, is likely to determine whether such programs yield true empowerment.

PROSPECTS FOR INDIA

The anti-arrack movement is known in the Indian state of Andhra Pradesh as one of the biggest political successes of grassroots women's movements in India. In 1990, the National Literacy Mission launched a campaign in the Nellore district of the state to increase women's literacy and raise their awareness of the societal inequalities that perpetuate their deprivation and poor education, including discussing issues such as labor exploitation, dowry, caste, and gender-based violence. Groups of women regularly met to see performances by cultural troupes, or *kalajatra*, on these topics. This program was similar in many ways to the gender consciousness-raising program studied in Chapter 8.

In discussions that followed these meetings, the women of Dubagunta village shared their common experiences of domestic violence and pervasive economic destitution, which they attributed to men's widespread consumption of liquor (locally referred to as "arrack"); the average rural household in Andhra Pradesh spends an estimated 50 percent of its annual income on liquor.[22] In response, the women of Dubagunta mobilized a campaign to expel liquor vendors from their village on both feminist and economic grounds.[23] The women later recounted in a literacy primer, "We then told the *sarpanch* (head of the village council) to close the *arrack* shop. But we could not succeed. So the next day, hundreds of us marched out of the village and stopped a cart of

---

[20] Tewari (2018).   [21] *The Times of India* (2021).   [22] Pande (2000).
[23] Balagopal (1992); Frese (2012).

toddy. We told the owner to throw away the liquor. We said all of us would contribute one rupee to compensate his loss. He was terrified. From that day no toddy has entered our village."[24] When politics failed, women turned to collective action.

News of their success spread: women in other villages mobilized similar campaigns, which developed into a statewide movement. With support from the Progressive Organization of Women, women organized a large-scale protest in August 1992 to demand the statewide prohibition of liquor. This protest increased awareness of the movement, and over the following year, women continued to organize across the state. But this success was met with substantial resistance, largely at the hands of the police. In one of the largest instances of this backlash, the police physically assaulted attendees at a gathering of more than 500 women in October 1992 in Mahboobnagar district.[25] However, in October 1993, the state government of Andhra Pradesh officially banned the sale of liquor.

How did women's collective action, starting in just one village, ultimately lead to a statewide ban on alcohol? While the demands for prohibition arose out of a grassroots movement led by women, it successfully built into a statewide movement and shifted public policy. A key factor in its success was the overarching politics in Andhra Pradesh. At the time, the sale of liquor was an important source of revenue for the political parties in power, the INC and the Telugu Desam Party. Revenue from excise taxes had sextupled over the previous twenty years, driven almost exclusively by the growth in liquor sales.[26] Excise taxes on liquor comprised an important component of the budget but also facilitated rent extraction by those in power.[27] State officials thus had few incentives to support prohibition. The political opposition, namely the BJP and Communist Party of India (Marxist-Leninist) (CPI (ML)) parties, had substantial motivation to support prohibition not to protect women but to cripple their political opponents. Starting with the 1992 protest, both opposition parties helped organize the movement. Their support not only provided an organizational structure; it also helped women contest the considerable resistance to their campaign. By 1993, to avoid electoral losses, the chief minister, a member of the Telugu Desam Party, joined the opposition to support the prohibition of alcohol ahead of the 1994 elections.[28]

This book has highlighted how and when women organize collective action to redress persistent inequalities in the representation of women and women's interests. When will their inclusion become certain and their demands met? The politics of the anti-arrack movement highlight several important considerations when examining how and when grassroots women's movements will lead to changes in policy and, ultimately, practice. Principally, it suggests that to

---

[24] Quoted in Pande (2000: 134).
[25] Frese (2012). See also Reddy and Patnaik (1993) for a description of police coercion.
[26] Reddy and Patnaik (1993)   [27] Frese (2012).   [28] Balagopal (1992); Frese (2012).

understand the success of women's mobilization, we must evaluate the response of strategic political actors. The women in Andhra Pradesh accomplished their political goals by making their organizing a political threat, due to both the scale of their mobilization and their alliances with opposition political parties.

The creation of a gender-equal political order may rest in women's ability to identify other actors (with historical political power) who benefit from their inclusion and to build larger coalitions that allow them to contest entrenched political interests. There is evidence of this in Madhya Pradesh. While collective action was led by women, many men joined in support when they saw women's actions as improving their welfare. Understanding when and how women successfully navigate coalition building – and what, if anything, is lost in this process – will start to map the contours and scope of a gender-equal political order.

Prospects for Women in India

If women's political participation is constrained by a deeply rooted patriarchal political order, what are the prospects for Indian women? I have suggested that women's widespread political participation will likely result from their collective solidarity and autonomy from the household. As shown in the discussion of the NRLM, fostering connections among women has recently become a priority of the state, and the number of women collectively organized has grown exponentially in the past eight years. Other recent trends suggest that women in India are becoming more politically empowered: they have ignited change by standing for election, turning out to vote at unprecedented rates, and building grassroots movements demanding representation and improved governance.

Women's turnout has risen and now exceeds that of men in some states. This rise in turnout is driven by the countryside; women's voting in state and national elections in rural villages has risen, while voting in urban cities remains stagnant. While I have argued that turnout is often a poor indicator of women's political agency, this rapid shift in behavior likely reflects women's agentic decision-making; this increase in turnout has occurred without corresponding changes in men's behavior, suggesting that the tides of household vote coordination may be turning. Some have explicitly argued that women's higher turnout reflects their greater exercise of agency. Recent headlines have read "The rise of the female voting bloc,"[29] "How women are shaping political fortunes in India,"[30] and "How women voters are altering India's electoral politics."[31]

Key to this change is that women are now treated as a voting bloc: parties are responding to them as a group. Parties have promised financial assistance to women-led households, subsidized transport for women, updated maternity benefits, and introduced reservations for women in government jobs and on

---

[29] *The Indian Express* (2021).   [30] Mehta (2021).   [31] Verma and Barthwal (2021).

electoral ballots in the hopes of winning the support of this new voting bloc. Women's political participation has become strategically valuable for those with political power.

Gaps remain in our understanding of the drivers of this rise in women's turnout and whether women's turnout preceded its strategic electoral useful-ness or vice versa. Some have argued that this rise in voting reflects rising education levels among women, particularly young women.[32] Others reference the growing connectedness of women in villages, largely driven by the expan-sion of SHGs.[33] Why turnout rose remains unclear but, given the new strategic value seen in women's turnout, these shifts suggest that the tide for women's political representation throughout India, as in the villages studied in Madhya Pradesh, may be turning.

Whether the recent gains in women's political participation in India, and Madhya Pradesh more specifically, will be sustained depends on women's ability to navigate both resistance and co-optation. If women's collective mobilization enables them to not only gain access to political spaces but also to entrench and institutionalize their political presence, their long-term political incorporation will be more likely. Prior research has highlighted that once women obtain political office, they set in motion an acceleration effect that increases their political representation. Bhavnani shows that in Mumbai, women who are elected under reservations often stay in political office even after the reservation has been removed.[34] Bhalotra, Clots-Figueras, and Iyer demonstrate the same effects at the state level.[35] Goyal and Karekurve-Ramachandra suggest that there is even the potential for women to contest for higher office.[36] Several studies report that the election of a female leader increases women's political participation.[37] Furthermore, Beaman et al. dem-onstrate that exposure to female elected officials can improve perceptions of women's capacity as political leaders, suggesting the potential for normative change.[38]

This book is ultimately about more than just enabling women's nominal participation in political spaces. It is about ensuring that political institutions hear their voices and demands. Women's collective action has immense poten-tial to strengthen institutions and policies aimed at gender equality and gender justice, including policies targeting gender-based violence, women's inheritance and asset ownership, marriage and divorce, and protection from discrimin-ation. Across the globe, scholars have noted that policy changes that protect women's equal rights and institutionalize gender justice come largely in

---

[32] Mehta (2021).   [33] Vaishnav (2018).   [34] Bhavnani (2009).

[35] Bhalotra, Clots-Figueras, and Iyer (2018).

[36] Goyal (2020); Karekurve-Ramachandra (2021).

[37] Tripp and Kang (2008); Barnes and Burchard (2013); Chattopadhyay and Duflo (2004); Brulé (2020b).

[38] Beaman et al. (2009). See also O'Brien and Rickne (2016).

response to mass, autonomous women's movements.[39] Morgan-Collins shows that the greatest achievements of female suffrage expansion for the representation of women's specific interests occurred where women were well organized and coordinated in their political demands.[40]

The women's wall protest, the anti-arrack movement, the recent upswing in women's turnout, and the broader research on women's movements from around the world highlight that the substantive representation of women's interests occurs when they are seen as a unified and politically salient group. Only when their collective voice cannot be denied do we see policies and politics aligned with women's demands.[41] This highlights the importance of a constituency of women to hold those in power accountable to their interests. Absent such a strong accountability mechanism, women's political participation may be co-opted to serve the interests of those with power.[42]

While more research is needed to understand precisely how women entrench their political power, one condition seems critical: women must be able to resist co-optation by existing power holders. Once resistance fails to stop women's mobilization, those with power are likely to pursue a co-optative strategy to maintain their status. The success of women's movements has been attributed to their autonomous (nonparty-based) mobilization. While the anti-arrack movement motivated parties to concede to women's demands when it was electorally strategic to do so, few increased the representation of women on their candidate lists. In 2022, the INC promised to increase women's representation in state elections in Uttar Pradesh in response to women's rising turnout, but stopped at 40 percent of candidate nominations and only implemented this quota in a state where they yielded less than 3 percent of the vote. Strategic commitments to women's preferred policies may satisfy women in the short term, but unless parties incorporate women in all stages of the political pipeline and women continue to collectively hold politicians accountable to their interests, their demands are unlikely to be represented over the long term.

Women-Led Development

Evidence from the mobilization of SHGs in Madhya Pradesh and more broadly from women-led protests across India suggest that women's collective action is often oriented toward one of two core goals: (1) reducing the incidence of violence against women or (2) demanding the more effective and programmatic delivery of core public services such as water, sanitation, and food security.[43] Women's political inclusion, therefore, has the potential to transform both the

---

[39] Weldon (2002); Htun and Weldon (2012, 2018). See also Morgan-Collins (2021).
[40] Morgan-Collins (2021). [41] Weldon (2002); Htun and Weldon (2012, 2018).
[42] Bertocchi and Spagat (2001); Corntassel (2007); Nayak and Berkes (2008).
[43] See also Sanyal (2009) for confirmation of this. This aligns with Molyneux's (1985) categorization of women's interests.

lives of women and bring development to their communities. How and when this will happen depends again on how women's movements sustain and navigate various responses to their demands.

Past waves of politically incorporating outsider groups elsewhere have produced major shifts in the allocation of resources. For example, the expansion of the franchise in Western Europe led to the creation of the welfare state and universal education.[44] In the United Kingdom, it also led to a decline in personalistic and patronage politics and the rise in politics oriented around public goods.[45] In the United States, the expansion of the franchise led to an increase in health spending and a shift in policy toward women's priorities.[46]

Women's electoral representation has also been shown to improve the provision of public goods, particularly those that disproportionately benefit women and children and that have historically been underprovided, such as toilets, water, fuel, and healthcare. Studies have shown that women elected leaders are more likely to invest in public goods both as a reflection of their preferences and in response to their socialized role as caretakers. For instance, female village leaders in India improved the provision of water and roads in line with the preferences of the women in their communities.[47] Likewise, female leaders elected both with and without quotas in India invested more in public health and education.[48] Studies on the impact of women's political participation, which largely focus on extending the franchise, also highlight the impacts of women's inclusion on public health, education, and the size of the government.[49] However, survey data from Tunisia reveals that women are punished electorally (as measured in hypothetical voting experiments) for investing in gender-based issues and are rewarded substantially more for investing in public services more broadly.[50]

While women have been shown to favor the improved provision of public goods, there is also societal pressure for women to deliver public goods. There is strategic value in leveraging women's political participation for broader aims, potentially at the cost of their complete agency and true substantive representation. Women's position in the economic division of labor often make public goods more important for women than men. Wantchekon argues that "younger voters or rural women might be systematically excluded from the most common forms of clientelist redistribution, and those groups might therefore be more responsive to a platform of public goods. This would imply that initiatives to promote women's participation in the political process at all levels of government are likely to help improve the provision of public goods."[51] As political outsiders, women have less access to ineffective government institutions and officials. In Argentina, Daby shows that women are less able to

[44] Acemoglu and Robinson (2000).   [45] Lizzeri and Persico (2004).
[46] Lott and Kenny (1999); Aidt and Dallal (2008); Miller (2008); Morgan-Collins (2021).
[47] Chattopadhyay and Duflo (2004).
[48] Clots-Figueras (2011); Clayton and Zetterberg (2018).
[49] Ibid.; Carruthers and Wannamaker (2014).   [50] Blackman and Jackson (2021).
[51] Wantchekon (2003: 401). See also Vicente and Wantchekon (2009).

successfully mobilize votes through clientelist offers because of smaller networks.[52] They may also be less likely to extract rents from the political process due to their limited networks and inexperience in the political system. Local female politicians in Mumbai were found to be significantly less likely than their male counterparts to perform pure constituency service and to discuss issues of symbolism, identity, and individual exchange.[53] State officials, therefore, have incentives to capitalize on women's interests in public goods provision to achieve their broader development goals.

If, however, women are co-opted into the same relationships of dependency, patronage, and identity that have long characterized male politics, their inclusion may lead to few changes in governance patterns; it may even reinforce traditional power dynamics and governance systems, as these networks will be resilient to political challenge. Yet, if women create new networks beyond the purview of traditional clientelist ties, the quality of local governance could improve, and accountability gaps in local schools and clinics, leakages in social programs, and capture by local (predominantly male) elites could be rapidly reversed.[54] Women's political participation has the potential to help achieve broader development. But whether this reflects women's autonomous interests will depend on how women navigate politics and co-optation.

The path to inclusion matters as much as inclusion itself. Research on the impacts of female representation often fails to link women citizens' path to participation with that of women representatives' path to office and subsequent policy priorities. Unpacking this process will reveal a broader story about identity, inclusion, governance – and, ultimately, political and economic development. As women continue to gain access to political institutions, we can begin to answer three open questions: How does the political order change with women's political inclusion? What do these changes mean for policies aimed at gender justice and the provision of public goods? And through these processes, what does women's active participation in politics mean for long-run patterns of development and democracy?

STUDYING GENDER

My original goal with this study was to understand how social welfare policies indirectly affect political behavior in rural India. Yet, it soon became apparent that women were the focal point of this story. Women have become the nucleus of many such policies. The value of these policies has often relied on women's ability to raise incomes and consumption, but their targeting of women has consequences for broader political structures and norms. We, therefore, cannot understand the link between policy and behavior without appreciating the role of women in the broader political equilibrium.

---

[52] Daby (2021).   [53] Karekurve-Ramachandra and Lee (2021).
[54] Lizzeri and Persico (2004); Clayton et al. (2019).

This book tells more than a tale of women's political inclusion. When women enter politics en masse, the structure of political organization changes. Linkages between representatives and citizens change. Policies change. And eventually, a different path to political and economic development is created. But women's inclusion began here with a social welfare policy. A feedback loop between inclusion and development thus emerges.

Democracy often elevates some voices above others. Women's voices have long been (and continue to be) systematically suppressed. Understanding the underrepresentation of women in politics requires a deeper understanding of the broader social and political system. Social and structural forces have united to generate a political order in which women's limited political participation is only one outcome. My investigation of women's political participation therefore includes a variety of actors and institutions in order to better grasp not only why women do not participate, but also how others – particularly, within the household – benefit from a system that subjugates them. These dynamics span beyond India; men across the globe benefit from women's (lack of) political participation. Focusing on the incentives of those with power as a defining factor in women's political behavior, rather than assuming gender inequalities result from more passive forces, reveals a more complex process of political inclusion.

In trying to identify the common experiences of women, I have unavoidably left out many of the nuances of how identity shapes women's political lives. I have attempted to highlight how gender and caste intersect to shape women's lives, but much more needs to be explored in this domain. I have largely ignored the role of religion as an identity shaping women's political lives largely because the regions of India that I study have little religious heterogeneity. I have focused on class and socioeconomic status only insofar as I have studied policies targeted at poor women. The dynamics of how economic and gender hierarchies interact to produce political hierarchies merits further investigation.

Exploring the challenges that women collectively face in navigating the process of political empowerment has, however, strengthened our understanding of Indian politics more generally. The micro-dynamics of how women navigate political decision-making reveals how men organize their political behavior – and how this ultimately shapes systems of politics and governance more broadly. The dominance of patriarchy – which creates the incentives and capacities for the coercion of women in the household – highlights that identity politics in India has, in many respects, been built on women's exclusion and cooperation. Systems of political exchange have formed in response to the way in which gendered power structures are constructed. While this book has focused on women, it is an account of power and politics. We owe much to the women in this book who, in their pursuit of political inclusion, have improved our understanding of how political power in rural India is built.

Appendices

A1   Appendix to Chapter 1

Table A1.1 compares socioeconomic and demographic characteristics in the sample of districts and villages studied in Madhya Pradesh alongside other relevant geographic regions. While on some socioeconomic indicators, such as literacy, the study sample is broadly similar to the rest of India, the sample is not representative of the ethnic composition and employment characteristics of the rest of the country. The sample of districts and villages in this study was selected for their participation in various welfare programs offered by the NGO PRADAN (as described in Chapters 6 and 7). These programs target regions of India with the highest levels of poverty and aim to particularly support tribal populations. As a result, it is not surprising that this sample includes both greater agricultural employment and higher shares of the population from Scheduled Tribes.

TABLE A1.1 *Demographic comparison of the study sample*

	India	BIMARU States	Madhya Pradesh	Madhya Pradesh Study Districts	Madhya Pradesh Study Village
Number of Villages	602,000	318,018	54,922	5,889	376
Total Population	1,120,000,000	513,000,000	72,600,000	6,277,839	346,924
Rural Population Share	69%	79%	72%	82%	100%
Female Population Share	49%	48%	48%	50%	50%
Scheduled Tribe Population Share	11%	10%	27%	43%	62%
Scheduled Caste Population Share	18%	19%	16%	8%	6%
Literacy Rate	58%	53%	54%	59%	54%
Female Literacy Rate	50%	43%	44%	50%	47%
Male Literacy Rate	66%	62%	63%	67%	62%
Employment Rate	41%	39%	47%	53%	55%
Female Employment Rate	29%	27%	39%	48%	51%
Male Employment Rate	53%	49%	54%	58%	58%
Agricultural Employment Rate	9%	8%	12%	13%	13%
Female Agricultural Employment Rate	6%	5%	10%	12%	12%
Male Agricultural Employment Rate	11%	10%	14%	15%	14%

Note: Data are from the 2011 Indian census, and statistics are author's own calculation. BIMARU states include Bihar, Chhattisgarh, Jharkhand, Madhya Pradesh, Rajasthan, and Uttar Pradesh. All demographic statistics subset to populations residing in rural villages.

A2 Appendix to Chapter 2

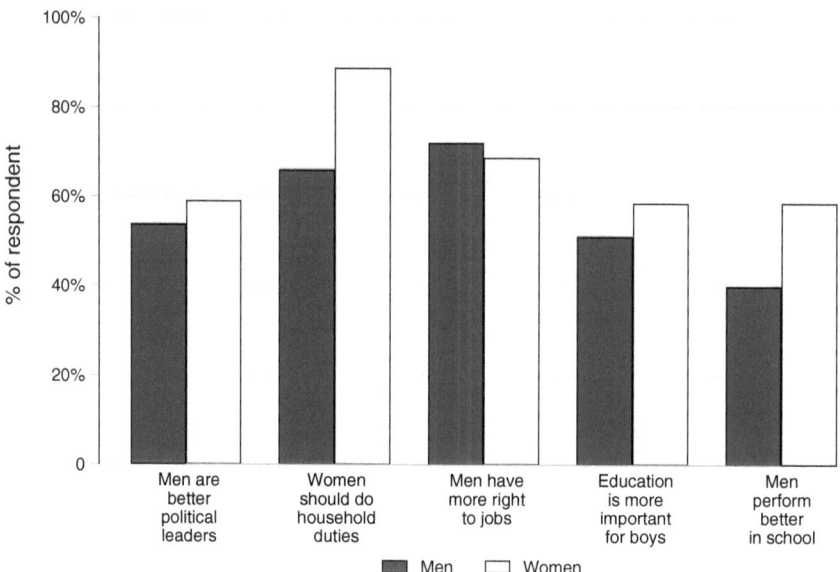

FIGURE A2.1 Women and men report pro-male gender attitudes in Madhya Pradesh

Note: The figure plots the average share of men and women who report agreement with a series of statements about attitudes toward gender. Data are from the 2016 sample survey administered in seventy-six villages in five districts of Madhya Pradesh.[1] The sample of villages includes only those that did not have PRADAN SHGs. This includes data from 1,106 women and 512 men, all of whom are married pairs. Data reflect average affirmative responses to questions regarding each attitude; responses of somewhat agree and strongly agree are coded as affirmative.

---

[1] While this survey collected data from 376 villages in Madhya Pradesh, I subset to the 76 villages that had not received any social programs implemented by the NGO PRADAN, since I show in subsequent chapters that these programs significantly affected women's political participation. Therefore, to accurately describe a priori attitudes and behaviors, I include only villages without such interventions. Women from these seventy-six villages were randomly sampled from census lists of married women over eighteen. In total, this includes a sample of 1,106 women (around 15 per village). Half of the husbands of the female respondents were also surveyed, generating a sample of 512 men. ST women were significantly overrepresented in this survey, so caste-wise differences are provided throughout.

(a) By caste category

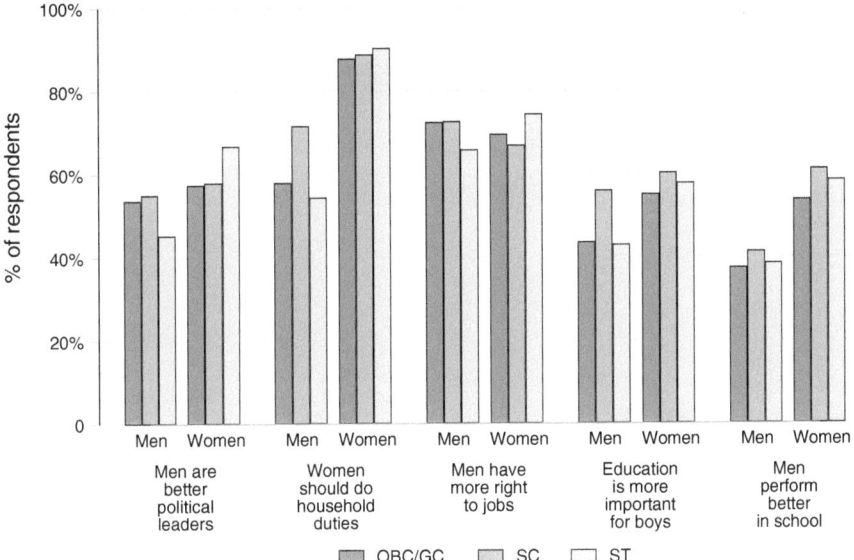

(b) By age group

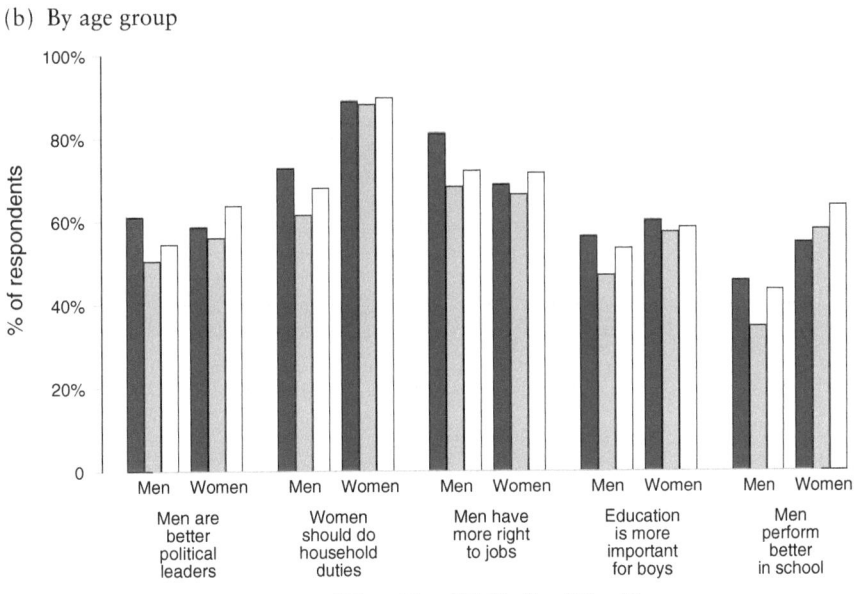

FIGURE A2.2 Reported gender attitudes in Madhya Pradesh do not vary by caste category and age group

Note: The figure plots the average share of men and women, by caste category and age group, that report agreement with a series of statements about attitudes toward gender. Data are from the 2016 sample survey in seventy-six villages in five districts of Madhya Pradesh. The sample of villages includes only those villages that did not have PRADAN SHGs. This includes data from 1,106 women and 512 men, all of whom are married pairs. Data reflect average affirmative responses to questions regarding each attitude with responses of either somewhat agree or strongly agree coded as affirmative.

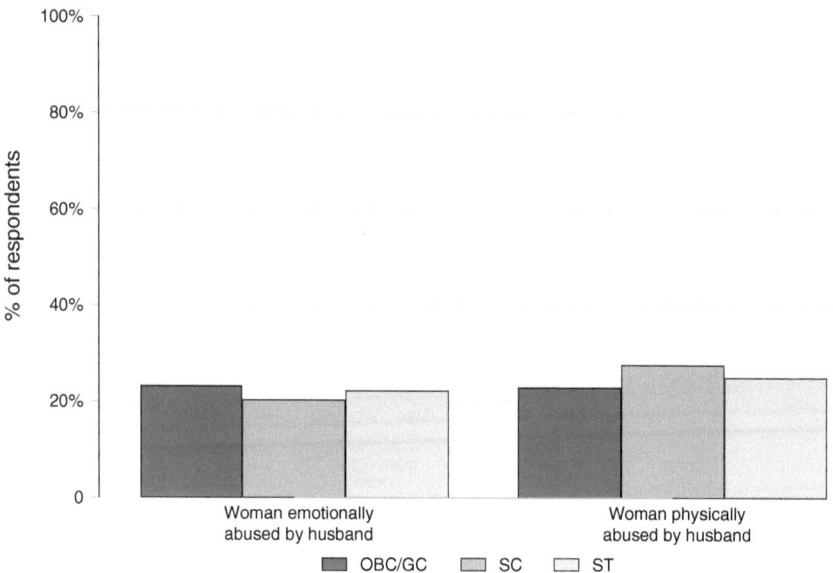

FIGURE A2.3 One-fourth of women report experiences of domestic violence in Madhya Pradesh

Note: The figure plots the average share of women who report having experienced any of two indicators of intimate partner abuse. Data are from the 2016 sample survey in seventy-six villages in five districts of Madhya Pradesh. The sample of villages includes only those villages that did not have PRADAN SHGs. This includes data from 1,106 women. Experience of emotional abuse is determined by affirmative responses to any of the following questions: Does your husband ever say or do something to humiliate you in front of others? Does your husband ever threaten to hurt or harm you or someone close to you? Does your husband ever insult you or make you feel bad about yourself? Experience of physical abuse is determined by affirmative statements that the respondent's husband had done any of the following: push or slap you; pull your hair, punch you with his fist or other item, or kick you; physically force you to have sexual intercourse with him even when you did not want to.

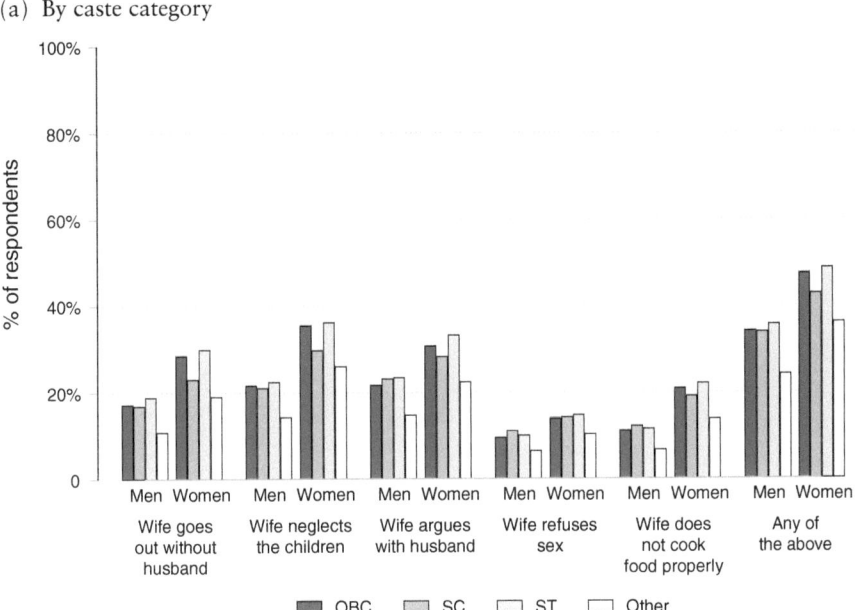

(a) By caste category

(b) By age group

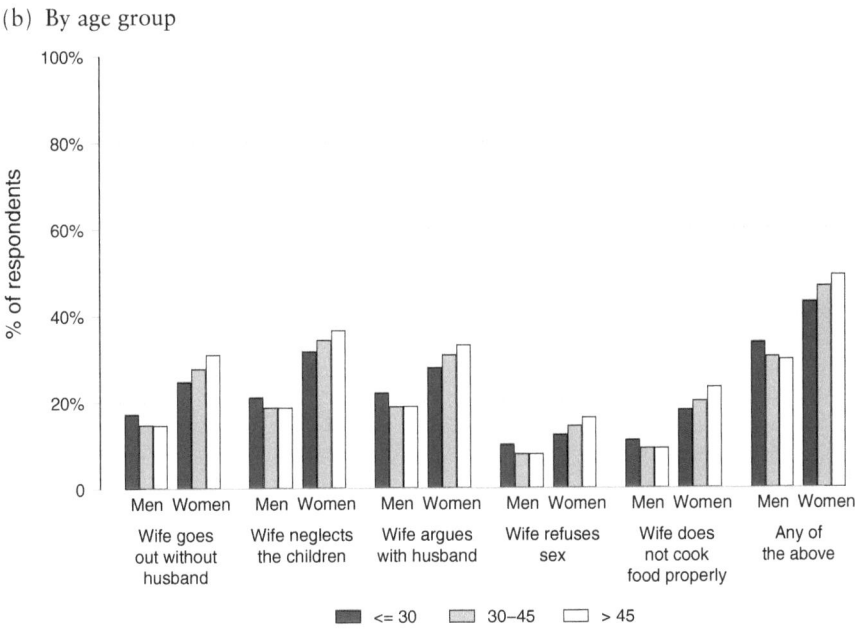

FIGURE A2.4 Acceptability of domestic violence does not vary by caste category or gender across India

Note: The figure plots the average share of men and women that state that a husband beating his wife is acceptable under each of five conditions. Data are from the 2015–16 National Family Health Survey (IIPS 2017). Average responses to the question "in your opinion, is a husband justified in hitting or beating his wife in the following situations" are reported, with responses of don't know coded as missing. Responses are weighted by the survey weight provided. The sample includes 111,188 men and 121,651 women.

A4 Appendix to Chapter 4

TABLE A4.1 *Demographic characteristics and public goods provision according to the 2011 census in Villages A and B*

	Village A	Village B
Female Population %	48%	50%
Scheduled Tribe Population %	50%	78%
Scheduled Caste Population %	2%	1%
Literate Population %	51%	41%
Literate Female Population %	43%	33%
Working Population %	53%	48%
Working Female Population %	44%	45%
Distance to Town	17	36
Geographic Area (Hectares)	521	597
Forest Land (Hectares)	20	85
Sown Land (Hectares)	404	45
Non-cultivable Land (Hectares)	4	0
On Major District Road	No	Yes
Has Access via Paved Road	Yes	Yes
Has Tap Water	Yes	No
Has Water Pump	Yes	Yes
Has Domestic Power Supply	Yes	Yes
Has Primary Health Center	No	No
Has Primary School	Yes	Yes
Has Middle School	Yes	Yes
Has Secondary School	Yes	No
Has Anganwadi	Yes	Yes
Has ASHA	Yes	Yes
Has Community Toilet Complex	No	No
Has Polling Booth Station	Yes	Yes

TABLE A4.2 *Survey compliance and nonresponse reason in Villages A and B*

	N	%
Surveyed	1,725	93.3%
Refused Survey	3	.2%
Unable to Contact	19	1%
Sick or Unable to Respond	41	2.2%
Temporary Migrant	43	2.3%
Unspecified	17	1%
Total	1,848	

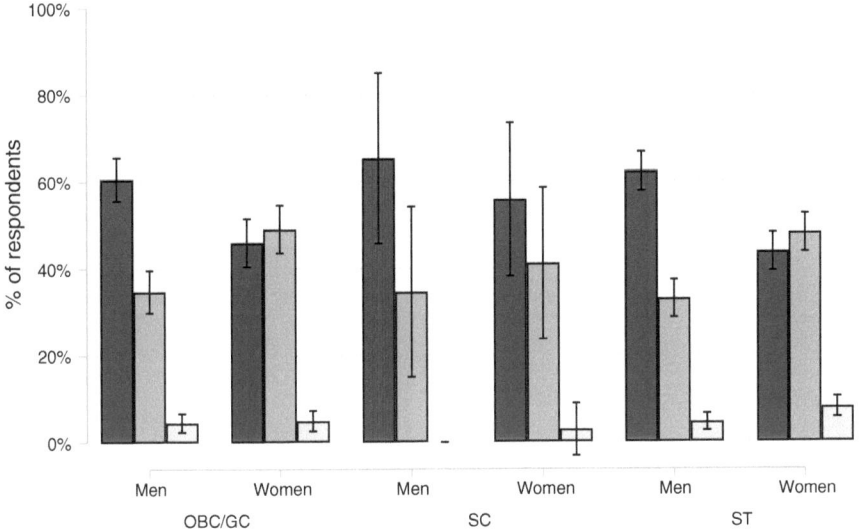

Who has the most say over vote choice?: ■ I do ▢ Male family member(s) ▢ Female family member(s)

FIGURE A4.1 Vote autonomy does not vary by caste category
Note: Data are from the census survey conducted in Villages A and B. Error bars denote 95 percent confidence intervals around the reported means.

A5 Appendix to Chapter 5

TABLE A5.1 *Within-household predictors of non-electoral participation are similar for women and men*

	Vote in National Election	Any Non-electoral Political Participation	Has Most Say Over Vote
	(1)	(2)	(3)
Female	−0.082	−0.260	0.470
	(0.143)	(0.202)	(0.210)**
Proportion of Political Network from Outside the Household	−0.008	0.058	0.318
	(0.086)	(0.142)	(0.149)**
Female X Prop. of Pol. Network from Outside the Household	0.051	0.014	−0.254
	(0.091)	(0.148)	(0.157)
Size of Political Discussion Network (Out-degree)	0.001	0.043	−0.007
	(0.007)	(0.011)***	(0.013)
Female X Size of Pol. Network	0.005	−0.006	−0.013
	(0.011)	(0.018)	(0.019)
Years of Education	0.002	0.017	−0.008
	(0.003)	(0.004)***	(0.005)
Female X Years of Education	−0.007	−0.008	0.010
	(0.004)*	(0.005)	(0.006)
Political Knowledge Index	0.022	0.096	−0.001
	(0.014)	(0.021)***	(0.022)
	−0.023	−0.026	0.057

(continued)

TABLE A5.1 (*continued*)

	Vote in National Election	Any Non-electoral Political Participation	Has Most Say Over Vote
	(1)	(2)	(3)
Female X Political Knowledge Index	(0.021)	(0.030)	(0.032)*
Personal Income (10,000s Rs.)	−0.002	−0.017	0.011
	(0.006)	(0.009)*	(0.009)
Female X Personal Income	0.017	0.032	−0.022
	(0.008)**	(0.013)**	(0.014)
Perceived Share of Population Politically Gender Biased	0.000	−0.001	0.001
	(0.001)	(0.001)	(0.001)
Female X Perceived Share of Pop. Gender Biased	−0.001	−0.000	−0.000
	(0.001)	(0.001)	(0.001)
Interested in Politics	0.027	0.113	0.058
	(0.023)	(0.039)***	(0.040)
Female X Interested in Politics	0.076	−0.088	−0.108
	(0.035)**	(0.051)*	(0.055)*
Bargaining Power Index	−0.001	0.048	0.027
	(0.012)	(0.019)**	(0.021)
Female X Bargaining Power Index	0.026	−0.019	0.020
	(0.021)	(0.027)	(0.030)
Age	0.003	0.002	0.010
	(0.001)***	(0.001)	(0.001)***
Female X Age	0.002	0.002	−0.005
	(0.001)**	(0.002)	(0.002)***
Married	0.262	0.118	0.119
	(0.038)***	(0.048)**	(0.051)**
Female X Married	−0.094	−0.088	−0.177
	(0.053)*	(0.064)	(0.067)***
N	1,721	1,725	1,721
Dependent Variable Mean	0.89	0.48	0.53
Fixed Effects	HH	HH	HH

Note: ***, **, * indicates significance at the 1 percent, 5 percent, and 10 percent levels, respectively. Robust standard errors are reported. Data are from the census survey conducted in Villages A and B. All models include fixed effects as specified.

TABLE A5.2 *Within-village predictors of political participation are similar across caste categories*

	Vote in National Election		Any Non-electoral Political Participation	
	Men	Women	Men	Women
	(1)	(2)	(3)	(4)
SC	−0.492	0.914	−6.650	0.079
	(1.460)	(0.397)**	(4.937)	(0.409)
ST	−0.212	−0.141	−0.087	−0.106
	(0.223)	(0.183)	(0.305)	(0.215)
Proportion of Political Network	0.110	−0.010	0.091	0.029
from Outside the Household	(0.162)	(0.055)	(0.177)	(0.080)
SC X Prop. of Pol. Network from	1.127	−0.408	6.572	−0.464
Outside the Household	(1.712)	(0.274)	(5.280)	(0.231)**
ST X Prop. of Pol. Network from	−0.124	0.034	−0.101	0.128
Outside the Household	(0.182)	(0.068)	(0.243)	(0.095)
Size of Political Discussion	0.008	−0.011	0.036	0.053
Network (Out-degree)	(0.008)	(0.014)	(0.013)***	(0.020)***
SC X Size of Pol. Network	−0.020	0.161	−0.025	0.174
	(0.021)	(0.055)***	(0.063)	(0.081)**
ST X Size of Pol. Network	−0.007	0.031	0.010	−0.023
	(0.010)	(0.018)*	(0.019)	(0.025)
Years of Education	0.006	0.001	0.008	−0.001
	(0.003)*	(0.004)	(0.005)	(0.007)
SC X Years of Education	−0.000	−0.016	0.010	−0.005
	(0.007)	(0.012)	(0.018)	(0.011)
ST X Years of Education	0.001	−0.002	0.009	0.006
	(0.005)	(0.007)	(0.007)	(0.009)
Political Knowledge Index	−0.010	−0.045	0.106	0.106
	(0.018)	(0.030)	(0.027)***	(0.034)***
SC X Political Knowledge Index	−0.051	−0.250	−0.065	0.041
	(0.050)	(0.109)**	(0.029)	(0.076)
ST X Political Knowledge Index	0.039	0.077	−0.034	−0.037
	(0.022)*	(0.034)**	(0.036)	(0.043)
Personal Income (10,000s Rs.)	−0.002	0.018	−0.012	0.015
	(0.006)	(0.008)**	(0.010)	(0.016)
SC X Personal Income	0.014	0.014	−0.004	0.041
	(0.014)	(0.028)	(0.033)	(0.035)
ST X Personal Income	0.005	−0.013	0.008	−0.007
	(0.009)	(0.011)	(0.015)	(0.020)
Perceived Share of Population	−0.001	−0.001	0.000	0.000
Politically Gender Biased	(0.001)	(0.001)	(0.001)	(0.001)
SC X Perceived Share of Pop.	−0.001	−0.005	0.001	−0.005
Gender Biased	(0.002)	(0.003)*	(0.005)	(0.002)**

(continued)

TABLE A5.2 (*continued*)

	Vote in National Election		Any Non-electoral Political Participation	
	Men	Women	Men	Women
	(1)	(2)	(3)	(4)
ST X Perceived Share of Pop. Gender Biased	0.001 (0.001)	0.000 (0.001)	−0.002 (0.002)	−0.000 (0.002)
Interested in Politics	0.018 (0.033)	0.053 (0.040)	0.146 (0.051)***	0.042 (0.055)
SC X Interested in Politics	−0.064 (0.071)	−0.058 (0.107)	0.002 (0.181)	0.126 (0.124)
ST X Interested in Politics	0.002 (0.041)	0.031 (0.048)	−0.059 (0.069)	0.027 (0.067)
Bargaining Power Index	0.018 (0.014)	0.015 (0.030)	0.005 (0.024)	0.033 (0.035)
SC X Bargaining Power Index	−0.053 (0.035)	0.132 (0.065)**	−0.103 (0.093)	0.183 (0.076)**
ST X Bargaining Power Index	−0.009 (0.020)	0.010 (0.035)	0.053 (0.034)	−0.005 (0.042)
HH Member with Most Bargaining Power Gender Biased	−0.015 (0.027)	−0.054 (0.038)	−0.021 (0.045)	−0.100 (0.048)**
SC X HH Member with Most Bargaining Power Gender Biased	0.131 (0.097)	0.149 (0.105)	−0.095 (0.179)	0.108 (0.114)
ST X HH Member with Most Bargaining Power Gender Biased	0.004 (0.036)	0.067 (0.047)	0.051 (0.060)	0.065 (0.060)
Age	0.003 (0.001)***	0.007 (0.002)***	−0.000 (0.002)	0.003 (0.002)
SC X Age	−0.007 (0.004)*	−0.010 (0.004)**	0.005 (0.007)	−0.002 (0.005)
ST X Age	0.002 (0.001)	0.001 (0.002)	0.003 (0.002)	−0.001 (0.003)
Married	0.149 (0.052)***	0.162 (0.057)***	0.078 (0.061)	−0.087 (0.064)
SC X Married	−0.060 (0.088)	−0.043 (0.117)	0.148 (0.298)	0.344 (0.170)**
ST X Married	0.167 (0.078)**	−0.023 (0.074)	0.051 (0.088)	0.123 (0.083)
N	853	868	853	872
Dependent Variable Mean	0.92	0.86	0.73	0.24
Fixed Effects	Village	Village	Village	Village

Note: ***, **, * indicates significance at the 1 percent, 5 percent, and 10 percent levels, respectively. Robust standard errors are reported. Data are from the census survey conducted in Villages A and B. All models include fixed effects as specified.

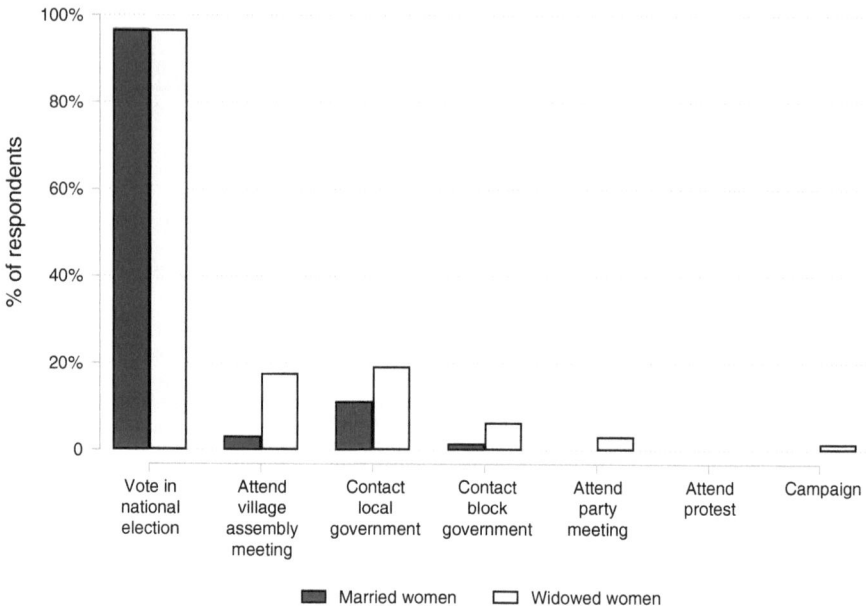

FIGURE A5.1 Widowed women are significantly more likely to attend village assembly meetings than similarly aged married women

Note: The figure plots the share of widowed and married women who report participating in each political activity. Data are from the census survey conducted in Villages A and B. In total, there were sixty-two widows in these villages. To account for the correlation between age and being a widow, sixty-two married women were randomly sampled to match the age distribution of the widows. The figure reports the shares of these sixty-two widows and sixty-two sampled married women participating in each form of politics.

A6 Appendix to Chapter 6

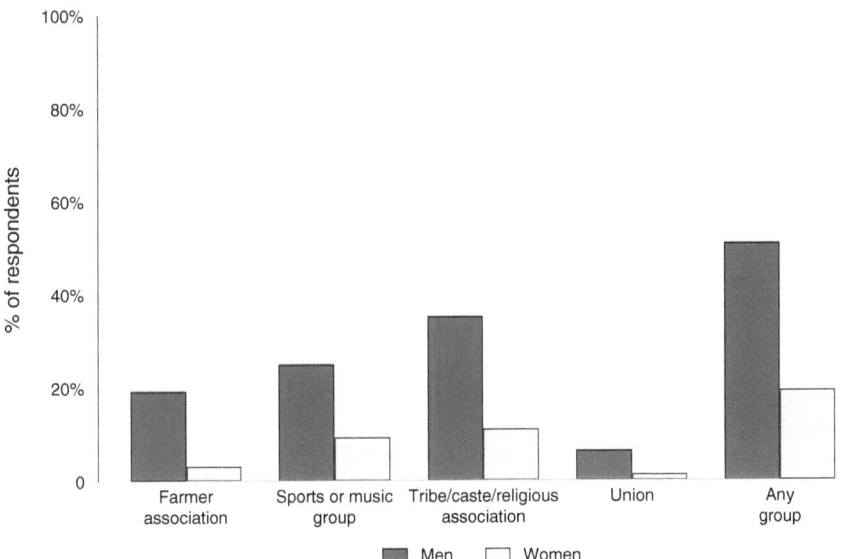

FIGURE A6.1 Men are more likely to be in a civil society group than women
Note: The figures plot the average share of men and women who are members in each type of civil
society group. Data are from the census survey conducted in Villages A and B.

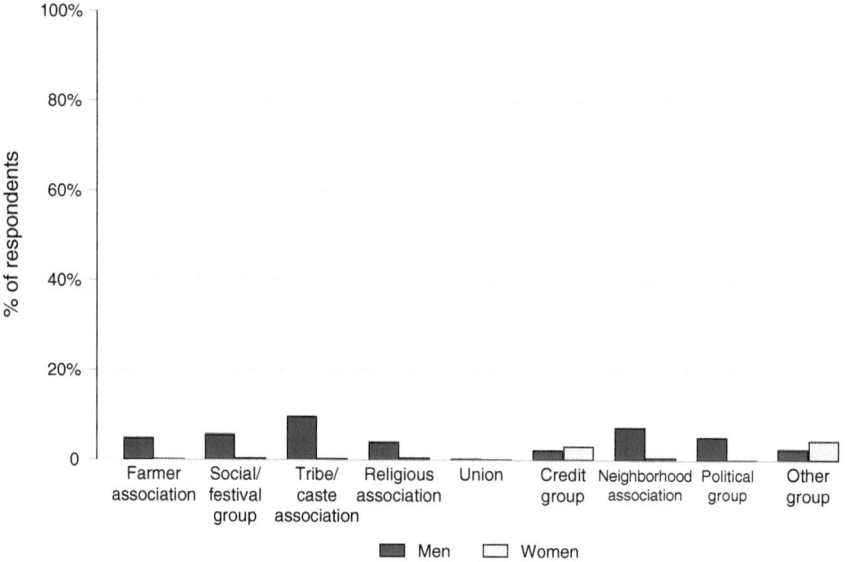

FIGURE A6.2 Husbands are more likely to be in a civil society group than their wives
Note: The figures plot the average share of men and women who are members in each type of civil society group. Data for this figure come from the survey of spouses in seventy-six villages in Madhya Pradesh. As a result, these gender disparities show that associational membership is distributed unequally among men and women *within* the household.

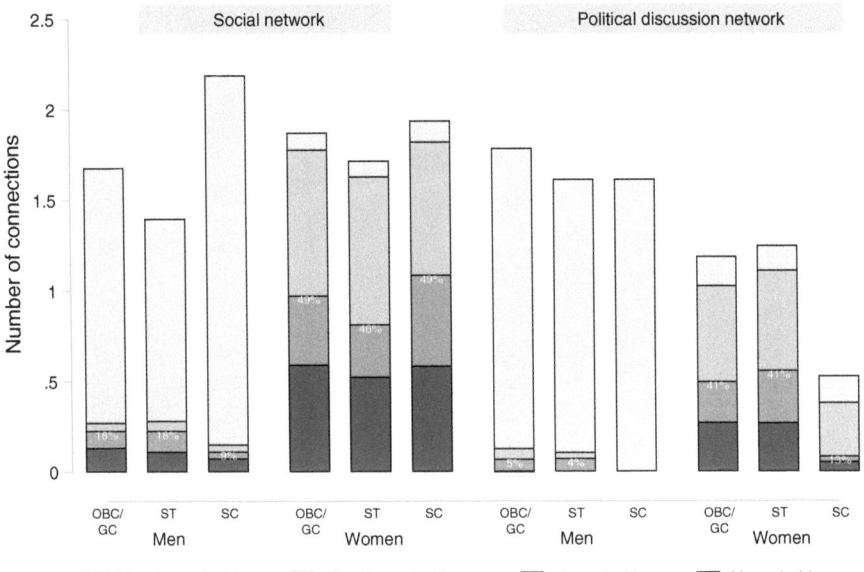

FIGURE A6.3 The household comprises a significantly larger share of women's networks as compared to men's across all caste groups

Note: The figure plots the average network size for men and women by caste group across networks of people with whom they socialize and discuss politics. Shades differentiate the gender and household composition of these networks. Data are from the census survey conducted in Villages A and B. Only 3.4 percent of the sample (n = 180) is from an SC; 38.8 percent (n = 2,007) is from either general categories or OBC, and 57.7 percent (n = 2,998) is from an ST.

A7 Appendix to Chapter 7

A7.1 BALANCE TABLES

TABLE A7.1.1 *Balance in village-level measures across treated and control villages*

Dependent Variable:	RDD Specification		Matched Pair Fixed Effects
	Full Sample	< 10 km of Boundary	Full Sample
Population	-11.987	187.734	-34.947
	(117.944)	(161.103)	(57.223)
Female Population %	-0.001	-0.005	-0.001
	(0.003)	(0.005)	(0.003)
Scheduled Tribe Population %	0.002	-0.048	0.012
	(0.038)	(0.059)	(0.013)
Literate Population %	-0.028	-0.007	-0.037*
	(0.018)	(0.023)	(0.016)
Literate Female Population %	-0.043*	-0.016	-0.05*
	(0.018)	(0.023)	(0.016)
Working Female Population %	0.03	-0.022	0.01
	(0.023)	(0.031)	(0.025)
Distance to Town	8.52	4.797	10.171
	(5.921)	(3.168)	(5.764)
Area	30.56	43.419	22.434
	(44.385)	(69.902)	(28.948)
Forest Land	6.233	19.646	7.908
	(19.956)	(30.501)	(18.644)

(continued)

TABLE A7.1.1 *(continued)*

Dependent Variable:	RDD Specification		Matched Pair Fixed Effects
	Full Sample	< 10 km of Boundary	Full Sample
Non-cultivable Land	−7.786	−17.295	−8.934
	(12.717)	(22.268)	(12.755)
Access via Paved Road	0.049	0.243*	0.026
	(0.08)	(0.114)	(0.07)
Access via Mud Road	−0.114	−0.294*	−0.079
	(0.065)	(0.092)	(0.059)
Has Education Facility	0.027	0.101	0.026
	(0.041)	(0.057)	(0.032)
# Primary Health Center	−0.016	−0.037	−0.013
	(0.016)	(0.032)	(0.023)
Has Drinking Water	−0.014		−0.013
	(0.014)		(0.013)
Has Power Supply	0.045	0.028	0.053
	(0.047)	(0.064)	(0.041)
N Villages	152	78	152

Note: Village-clustered standard errors in parentheses. * significant at $p < 0.05$. Each row is a dependent variable, and each column is a different model specification. Each cell is the estimated coefficient on the treatment indicator. All models include person-level covariates. Regression discontinuity design (RDD) models include village-level covariates and district fixed effects. Matched pair models include pair-matched fixed effects. Some coefficients are missing for boundary models due to perfect singularity. Data are from the 2011 census.

TABLE A7.1.2 *Balance in individual-level measures across treated and control villages*

Dependent Variable:	Original Sample			Selection Resample	
	RDD Specification		Matched Pair Fixed Effects	Matched Pair Fixed Effects	
	Full Sample	< 10 km of Boundary	Full Sample	Local ITT	Local CATE
Age	−0.889	−1.168	−1.168[*]	−0.503	−1.313
	(0.541)	(0.677)	(0.364)	(0.696)	(1.818)
Years of Education	0.417	0.612	0.34[*]	−0.529[*]	−1.382[*]
	(0.231)	(0.313)	(0.145)	(0.2)	(0.526)
Married	0.009	0.003	0.01	0.041[*]	0.108[*]
	(0.016)	(0.024)	(0.012)	(0.018)	(0.048)
Hindu	−0.006	0	−0.006	0.001	0.003
	(0.006)	(0.009)	(0.005)	(0.006)	(0.016)
Scheduled Tribe	0.023	0.023	0.053[*]	−0.061[*]	−0.161[*]
	(0.04)	(0.054)	(0.021)	(0.027)	(0.072)
Scheduled Caste	0.003	−0.024	−0.01	0.096[*]	0.251[*]
	(0.022)	(0.028)	(0.017)	(0.023)	(0.065)
Years Living in Village	−0.493	−1.634	−0.993	0.763	1.993
	(0.836)	(1.069)	(0.65)	(0.864)	(2.261)
Amount of Land	0.422	0.321	0.616	34.862	91.112
	(0.483)	(0.261)	(0.358)	(47.688)	(124.874)
Number of Children	0.165	0.069	0.16	0.754[*]	1.97[*]
	(0.11)	(0.134)	(0.088)	(0.136)	(0.373)
N Respondents	1796	958	1796	1332	1332
N Villages	152	78	152	62	62

Note: Village-clustered standard errors in parentheses. * significant at $p < 0.05$. Each row is a dependent variable, and each column is a different model specification. Each cell is the estimated coefficient on the treatment indicator. All models include person-level covariates. RDD models include village-level covariates and district fixed effects. Matched-pair models include match-pair fixed effects. Data are from the 2016 sample survey.

TABLE A7.1.3 *Balance across treated and untreated villages within PRADAN's implementation boundary*

	Sampled Mean	Not Sampled Mean	Difference in Means	P-Value
Population	877.92	697.30	180.62	0.00
Female Population %	0.50	0.50	0.00	0.69
Scheduled Tribe Population %	0.70	0.72	−0.02	0.38
Literate Population %	0.51	0.51	−0.00	0.79
Literate Female Population %	0.43	0.43	0.01	0.55
Working Female Population %	0.55	0.55	−0.00	0.83

Note: Data are from the 2011 census.

A7.2 DEALING WITH SELECTION CONCERNS

Since only treated women were originally sampled in treated villages, there are concerns about selection bias. The main concern is that the women who selected into treatment are more participatory than the sampled women in control villages. In addition to the resample using identical selection procedures, I address selection bias concerns in two ways. First, I conduct a placebo test in Figure A7.2.1 to evaluate the effect of the treatment on husbands. These results indicate that men in treated households are not inherently more participatory than those in control households. If we assume husband's and wives' political behavior is correlated, then this provides suggestive evidence that the households that opted into the intervention were no more participatory than those that did not. Second, I conduct a placebo test in Figure A7.2.2 to evaluate the effect of the treatment on untreated women in treated villages. These results suggest that treated villages are not inherently more participatory than control villages and suggest that spillover effects within treated villages were minimal.

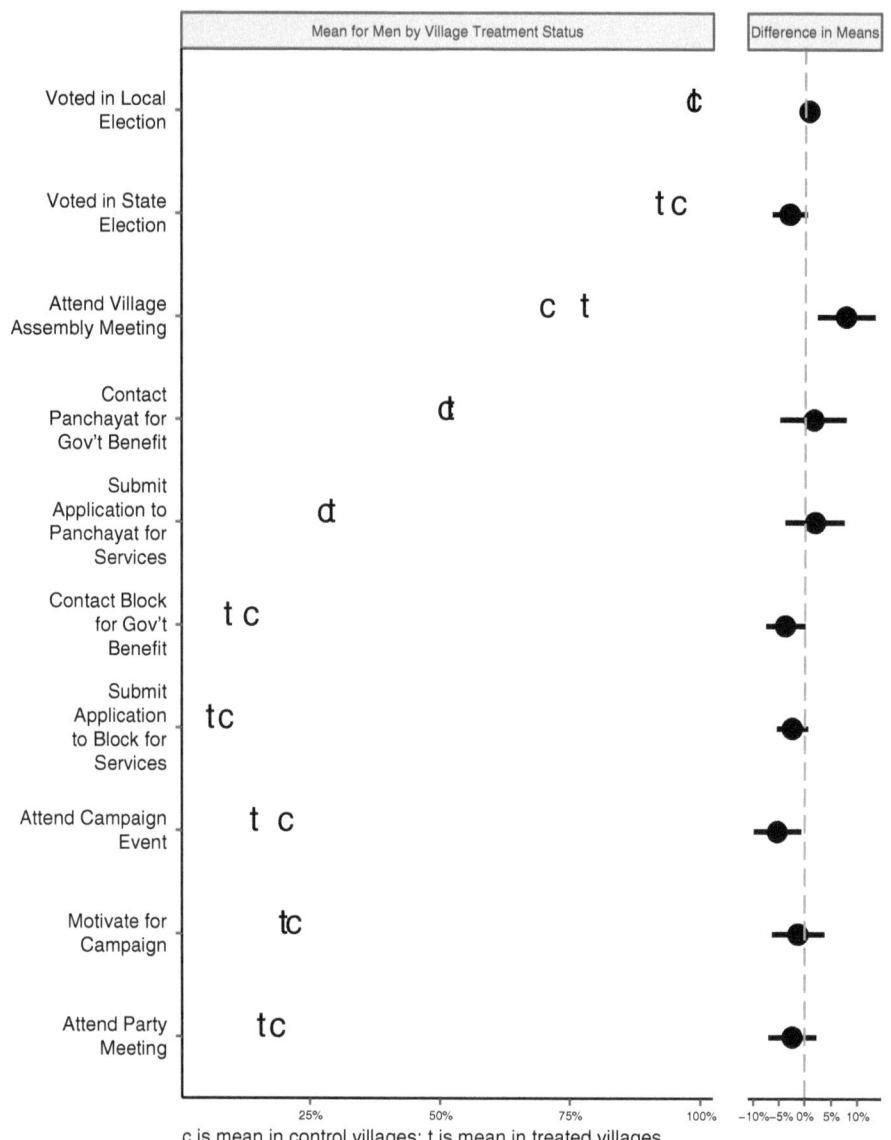

FIGURE A7.2.1 Husbands of respondents in treated villages are no more likely to participate in politics than husbands of respondents in control villages

Note: The figure plots the average levels of political participation of husbands in treated and control villages along with the difference in means and a 95 percent confidence interval around that difference. Data are from the 2016 sample re-survey in sixty-two villages in five districts of Madhya Pradesh.

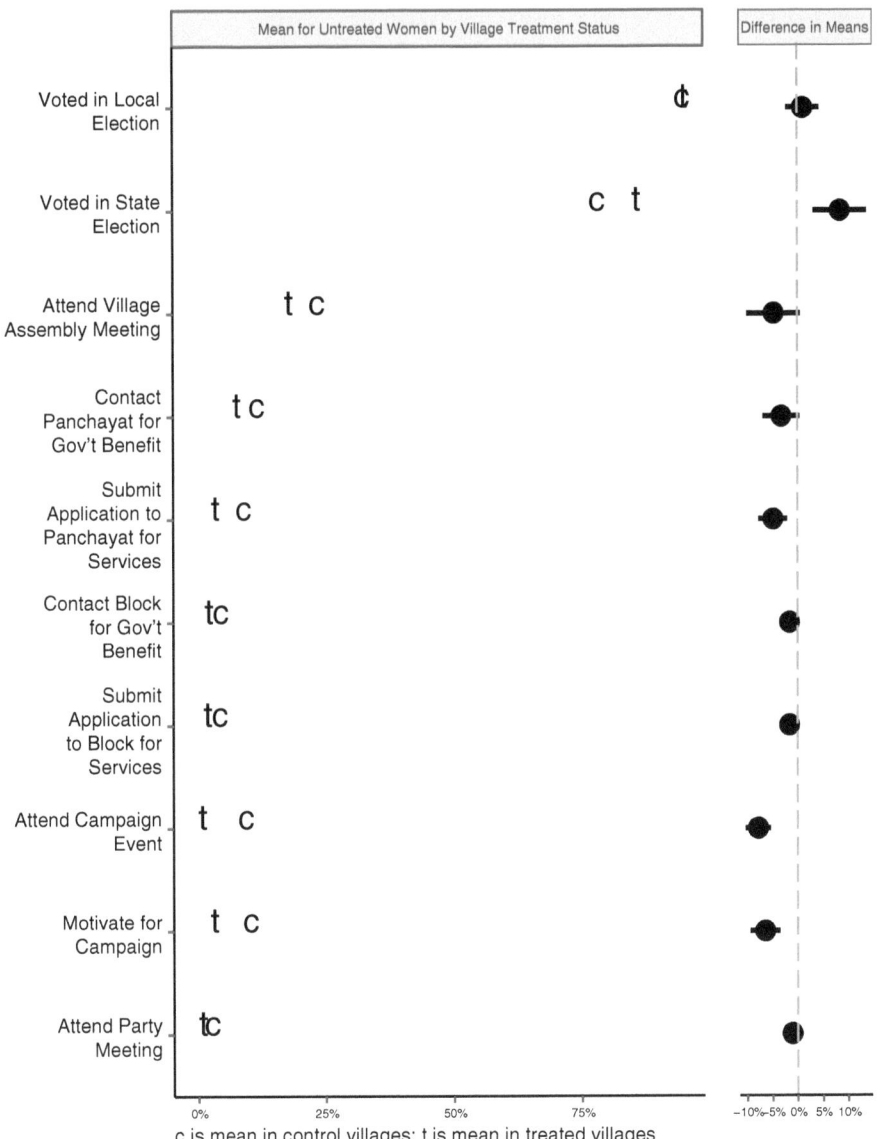

FIGURE A7.2.2 Untreated women in control and treated villages have similar political behavior

Note: The figure plots the average levels of political participation of untreated women in treated and control villages along with the difference in means and a 95 percent confidence interval around that difference. Data are from the 2016 sample re-survey in sixty-two villages in five districts of Madhya Pradesh.

A7.3 GEOGRAPHIC REGRESSION DISCONTINUITY
SPECIFICATION

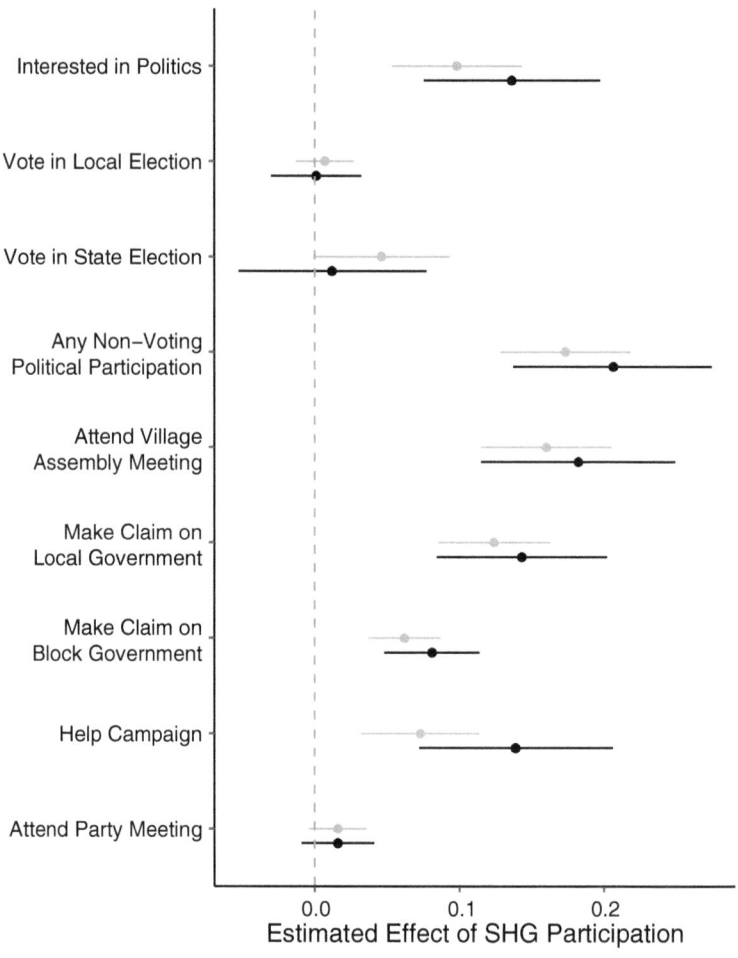

Model: ○ GRD   ● GRD <10km

FIGURE A7.3.1 The effect of the SHG intervention on women's political participation
estimated with controls for latitude and longitude in cubic functional form
Note: Estimated effects from two models with different bandwidths are shown along with
corresponding 95 percent confidence intervals. Each variable on the y-axis is a distinct dependent
variable, and point estimates are the effect of the SHG treatment on each outcome. Underlying
models include village pair-matched fixed effects and individual covariates, and standard errors are
clustered at the village level. Data are from the 2016 sample survey in 152 villages in five districts of
Madhya Pradesh.

A7.4 THE RELATIONSHIP BETWEEN SHGS AND WOMEN'S PARTICIPATION ACROSS INDIA

TABLE A7.4.1 *SHG membership correlates with women's political participation across India*

	Attend Village Assembly Meeting
SHG Member	0.109 (0.015)***
Member of non-SHG Associational Group	0.224 (0.020)***
Years of Education	0.002 (0.001)***
Worked in Last Year	0.024 (0.006)***
Household Income in Last Year	−0.000 (0.000)
Below Poverty Line	0.011 (0.004)**
Household Consumption Index	0.004 (0.002)
Household Asset Index	−0.000 (0.000)
Personally Owns Land	0.034 (0.010)***
Personally Has Cash on Hand	0.018 (0.009)**
Personally Has Bank Account	0.022 (0.007)***
Lives in Natal Village	0.007 (0.007)
Age	0.001 (0.000)***
Married	−0.007 (0.017)
Widowed	0.011 (0.018)
Hindu	0.005 (0.008)
Scheduled Tribe	0.011 (0.008)
Scheduled Caste	0.016 (0.006)***
N	24269
R-squared	0.28
Mean	0.61

Note: ***, **, * indicate significance at the 1 percent, 5 percent, and 10 percent levels, respectively. District fixed effects are included, and district-clustered standard errors are reported. Income is measured in thousands of rupees and has been winsorized to remove outliers. Data are from the 2011–2012 Indian Human Development Survey and include only women residing in rural villages.

A7.5 EFFECT OF SHG PARTICIPATION ON WOMEN'S POLITICAL PARTICIPATION BY AGE AND LAND OWNERSHIP

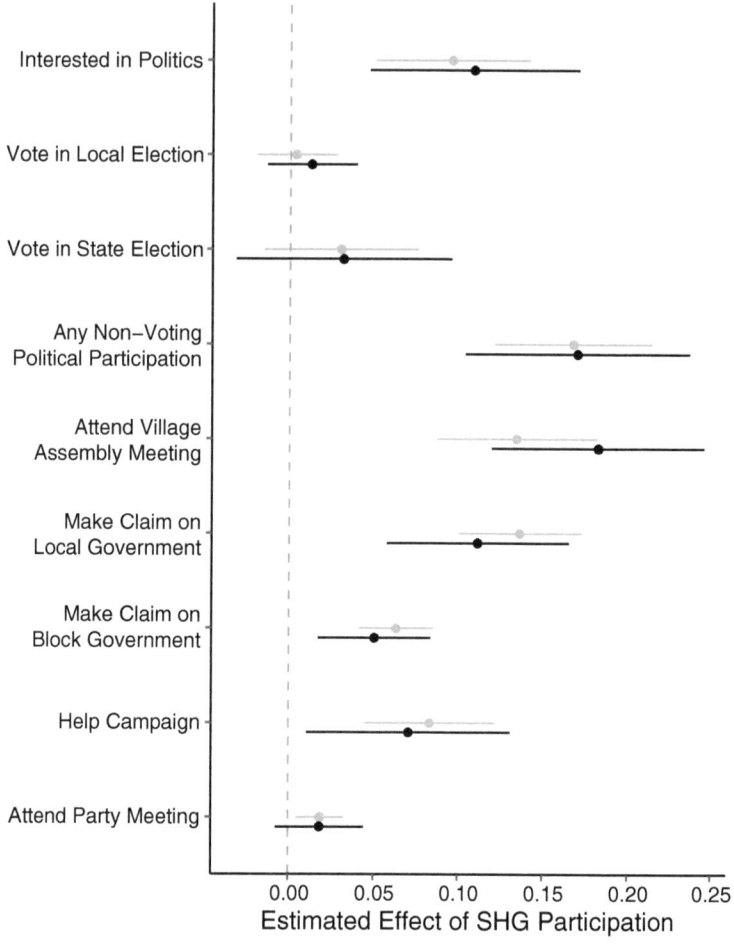

Age group: ○ <= 40   ● > 40

FIGURE A7.5.1 The effect of the SHG intervention on women's political participation does not vary by age

Note: Estimated effects reflect the marginal effect of the SHG intervention from an interaction model that interacts treatment status with caste group along with corresponding 95 percent confidence intervals. Reported effects are only for the model with the full sample of villages and denote the average effects for those in SHGs. Each variable on the y-axis is a distinct dependent variable, and point estimates are the marginal effect of the SHG treatment on each outcome. Underlying models include village pair-matched fixed effects and individual covariates; standard errors are clustered at the village level. Data are from the 2016 sample survey in 152 villages in five districts of Madhya Pradesh.

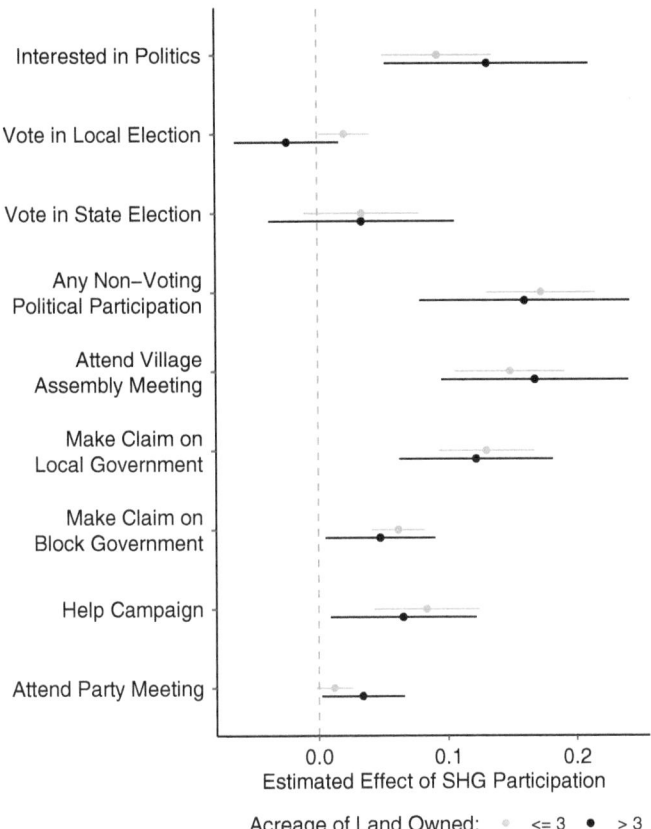

FIGURE A7.5.2 The effect of the SHG intervention on women's political participation does not vary by land ownership

Note: Estimated effects reflect the marginal effect of the SHG intervention from an interaction model that interacts treatment status with caste group along with corresponding 95 percent confidence intervals. Reported effects are only for the model with the full sample of villages and denote the average effects for those in SHGs. Each variable on the y-axis is a distinct dependent variable, and point estimates are the marginal effect of the SHG treatment on each outcome. Underlying models include village pair-matched fixed effects and individual covariates; standard errors are clustered at the village level. Data are from the 2016 sample survey in 152 villages in five districts of Madhya Pradesh.

A7.6 PREFERENCE DIFFERENCES BETWEEN SHG AND NON-SHG WOMEN

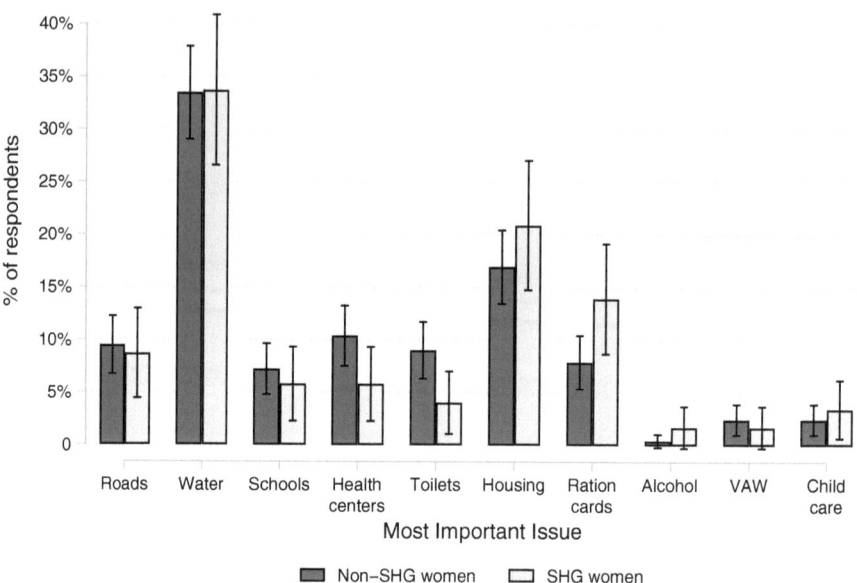

FIGURE A7.6.1 SHG members and non-SHG members show marginally different political preferences
Note: This figure depicts women's most important problem in the village, by SHG membership. Data are from the census survey conducted in Villages C and D.

A8   Appendix to Chapter 8

The Kamal/Kamali activity involves the narration of a story of two sisters-in-law who married into the same family on the same day, got pregnant around the same time, and gave birth to two infants – one boy and one girl – around the same time. Two participants enter the room role-playing the two cousins. The aim of the activity is to highlight patterns of socialization as they begin from birth. Through a series of questions posed to the group, step-by-step, the facilitator peels off the layers of social life throughout the life cycle. Group participants are asked to represent society guiding the infants through what to do and what not to do. With every positive experience for Kamali and Kamal, they would take a step forward, and with every negative experience, each would take a step back. Afterward, the positions of Kamal and Kamali are assessed and discussed.

The participants are asked the following questions during the activity:

○   from birth to 6 months of age:
  ▪ What would be the most common reaction in the family at the news of the birth of Kamal and Kamali?
  ▪ How would the ceremonies of having the first solid food by Kamal be celebrated? What would be the ceremony for Kamali?
  ▪ During this time, how would the mothers of Kamal and Kamali be treated?
○   from 6 months to 8 years old:
  ▪ Since Kamal and Kamali are growing up in the same family with the same family members, what would their childhood look like? Would there be any differences? If yes, what?

- Which kinds of toys would the family members bring for Kamal? And what kinds of toys would Kamali get?
- Which kind of school would be chosen for Kamal? Which school would be chosen for Kamali?
- What would Kamal do before leaving for school and after returning home? What would Kamali do before she leaves for school and after she returns?

○ from 9 years old to 18 years old:
- Who gets the tuition first, Kamal or Kamali?
- On whose education would the family spend its money?
- What kinds of physiological changes happen for Kamal and Kamali? Are these changes similar, or not? If not, what are the differences?
- What are the most common dos and don'ts for Kamal and Kamali around this time of life? Would the attitude/behavior of family members change toward Kamal and Kamali?

○ from 19 years old to 25 years old:
- What changes will be seen during these years of life for Kamal and Kamali?
- While seeking a marital contact, how would Kamal and Kamali be approached for their consent in marriage?
- What changes would Kamal and Kamali go through after their marriages?
- What responsibilities for their in-laws would Kamal and Kamali generally shoulder in daily life?

○ in middle age:
- What differences are generally seen in the typical days of the lives of Kamal and Kamali?

○ In old age until death:
- What would typical days for Kamal and Kamali look like? Would there be any differences in their conditions in the household? If yes, please describe.
- How does the family's behavior toward them change around this stage of their lives?
- Would the last rites of Kamal and Kamali be performed in the same way?
- After Kamal's death, what would be the status of Kamal's widow in the family? After Kamali's death, what would be the status of her widower in the family?

A8.2 FALSIFICATION TESTS

The key identifying assumption for estimating treatment effects under matching is unconfoundedness conditional on matched covariates. Figure A8.2.1

compares the balance in village-level pretreatment measures from the 2011 census and individual-level pretreatment measures captured in the 2016 sample survey. The figure displays the impacts of the gender program using the same specifications as the main analysis. Village- and individual-level

(a) Village-level characteristics

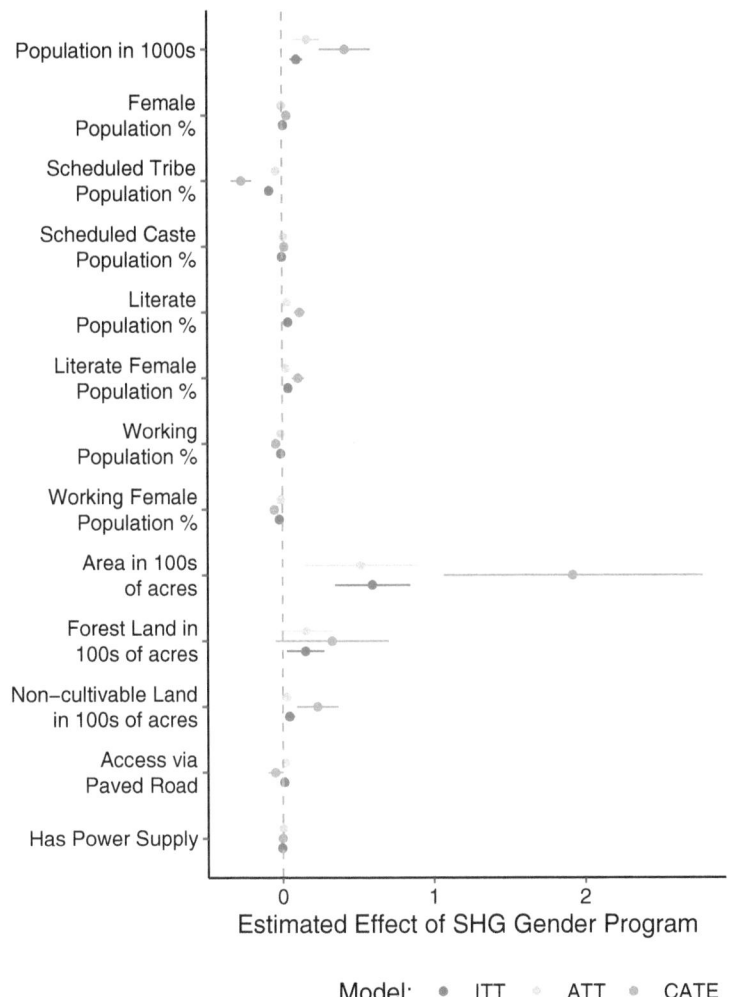

FIGURE A8.2.1 Balance across matched treated and control villages on village and individual characteristics

Note: Village-level analysis utilizes data from the 2011 census. The individual-level analysis utilizes data from the 2016 sample survey.

(b) Person-level characteristics

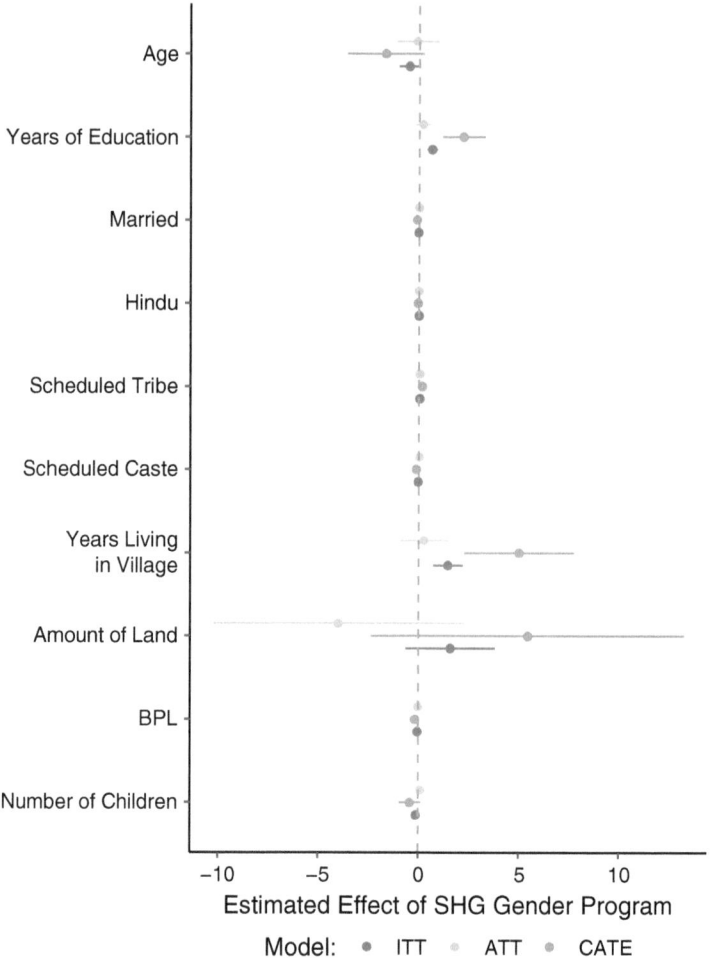

FIGURE A8.2.1 (*cont.*)

covariates are largely statistically identical across treated and control villages. Treated villages are slightly larger, have larger populations, and marginally higher literacy rates. At the individual level, estimates are quite noisy, but SHG members in treated villages are somewhat better educated and may have been residing in their villages longer. For most indicators, the reported balance demonstrates that there are no significant differences in the characteristics of SHG members across treated and control villages.

A8.3 EFFECTS OF THE GENDER PROGRAM ON MEN'S POLITICAL BEHAVIOR

There are reasons to believe that the villages that received the gender program may be different from those that did not. To reduce concerns around village selection, I conducted a placebo test comparing the behavior of men in treated and control villages. Since men were not allowed to participate in the gender trainings, we would not expect the treatment to directly affect their political behavior. It is possible, however, that the treatment could have indirectly influenced their behavior in response to women's behavioral changes. This chapter has demonstrated that women experienced substantial backlash to participating in the gender program. One method of resistance is for men to become more political. Figure A8.3.1 reports the estimates of the effect of the treatment on men's political participation.

Figure A8.3.1 provides some confidence that treated villages may be similar to control villages in terms of baseline participation. Overall, the effect of the gender program on men's political behavior is quite noisy, and for many measures, such as interest in politics, there is no difference. While there is a significant positive relationship between the treatment and some measures of men's political participation, it is not entirely surprising. If my theory is correct, then women's political mobilization will increase political competition. Men will therefore respond with increased campaigning and electoral mobilization. Alternatively, if men see women's political mobilization as a threat to either the social order or their political interests, they may respond by becoming more politically active. It is difficult on the basis of this evidence to rule out the possibility that the gender program entailed some amount of selection bias, as men's behavior may also change in response to the treatment. The noisiness in these estimates provides some minimally suggestive evidence that treated and control villages may have had similar levels of political participation prior to the treatment.

(a) Men's political participation

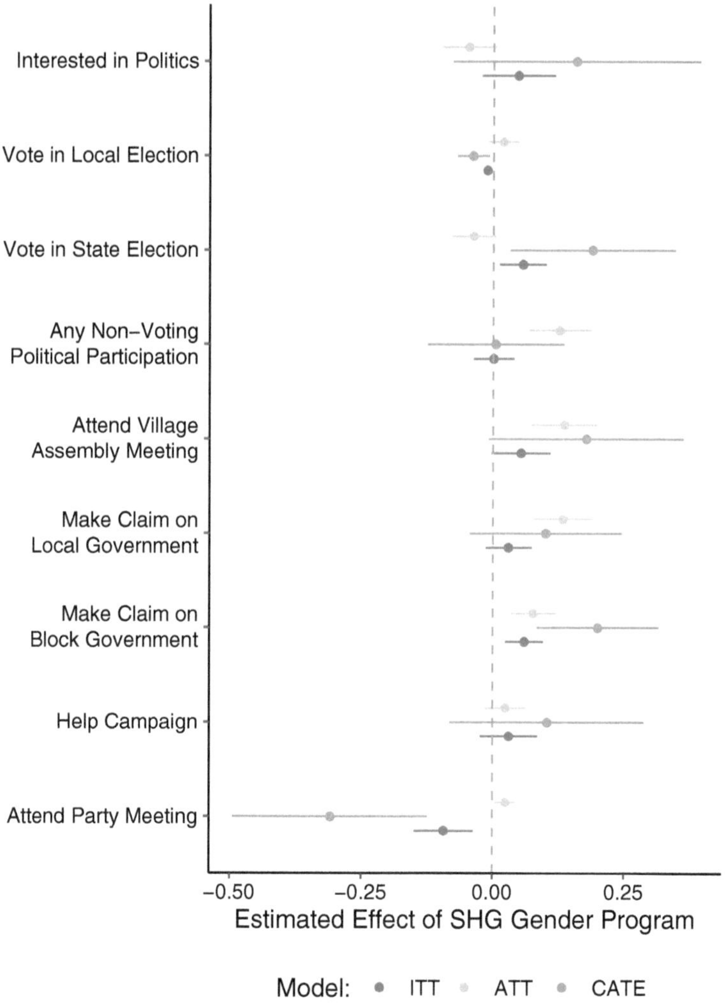

FIGURE A8.3.1 The effect of the SHG gender training program on men's political participation

Note: Estimated effects are shown along with corresponding 95 percent confidence intervals. Each variable on the y-axis is a distinct dependent variable, and point estimates indicate the effect of the gender training treatment on each outcome.

(b) Men's attitudes toward gender equality

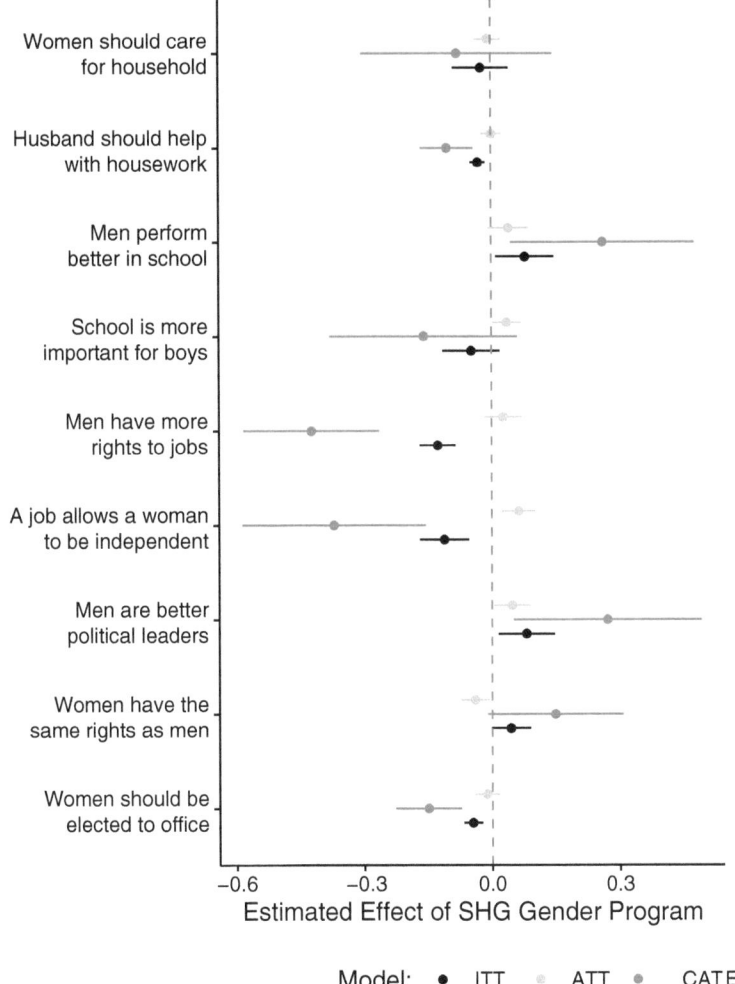

FIGURE A8.3.1 *(cont.)*

A8.4 EFFECTS OF THE GENDER PROGRAM ON WOMEN'S POLITICAL BEHAVIOR USING GENETIC MATCHING

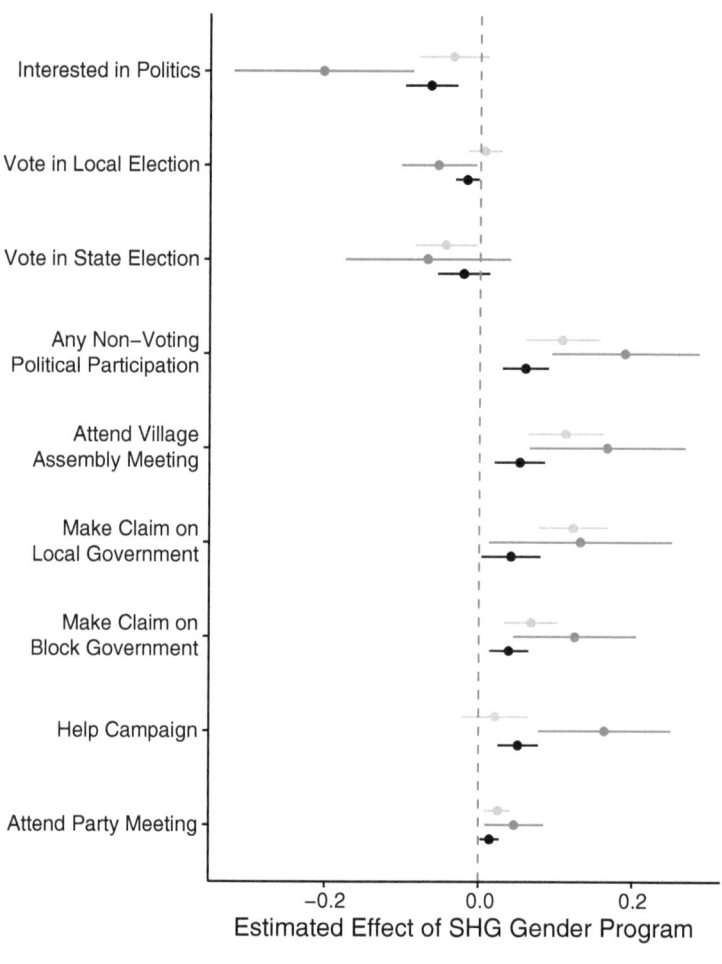

FIGURE A8.4.1 The effect of the SHG gender training program on women's political participation using genetic matching

Note: Estimated effects are shown along with corresponding 95 percent confidence intervals. Each variable on the y-axis is a distinct dependent variable, and point estimates indicate the effect of the gender training treatment on each outcome.

References

Abadie, Alberto, and Guido W. Imbens. "Large sample properties of matching estimators for average treatment effects." *Econometrica* 74.1 (2006): 235–267.

Abrams, Samuel, Torben Iversen, and David Soskice. "Informal social networks and rational voting." *British Journal of Political Science* 41.2 (2011): 229–257.

Acemoglu, Daron, and James A. Robinson. "Why did the West extend the franchise? Democracy, inequality, and growth in historical perspective." *The Quarterly Journal of Economics* 115.4 (2000): 1167–1199.

"Weak, despotic, or inclusive? How state type emerges from state versus civil society Competition." *American Political Science Review* 117 (2022): 1–14.

Acemoglu, Daron, and Alexander Wolitzky. "The economics of labor coercion." *Econometrica* 79.2 (2011): 555–600.

Afridi, Farzana, et al. "Women's work, social norms and the marriage market." (2023).

Afzal, Uzma, et al. "Intrahousehold consumption allocation and demand for agency: A triple experimental investigation." *American Economic Journal: Applied Economics* 14.3 (2022): 400–444.

Agarwal, Bina. *A field of one's own: Gender and land rights in South Asia.* Vol. 58. Cambridge University Press, 1994.

"'Bargaining' and gender relations: Within and beyond the household." *Feminist Economics* 3.1 (1997): 1–51.

"Livelihoods in COVID times: Gendered perils and new pathways in India." *World Development* 139 (2021): 105312.

Ahuja, Amit. *Mobilizing the marginalized: Ethnic parties without ethnic movements.* Modern South Asia, 2019.

Aidt, Toke S., and Bianca Dallal. "Female voting power: The contribution of women's suffrage to the growth of social spending in Western Europe (1869–1960)." *Public Choice* 134 (2008): 391–417.

Akerlof, George. "The economics of caste and of the rat race and other woeful tales." *The Quarterly Journal of Economics* 90 (1976): 599–617.

Alatas, Vivi, et al. "Network structure and the aggregation of information: Theory and evidence from Indonesia." *American Economic Review* 106.7 (2016): 1663–1704.

Alesina, Alberto, and Eliana La Ferrara. "Participation in heterogeneous communities." *The Quarterly Journal of Economics* 115.3 (2000): 847–904.

Alesina, Alberto, Paola Giuliano, and Nathan Nunn. "On the origins of gender roles: Women and the plough." *The Quarterly Journal of Economics* 128.2 (2013): 469–530.

Allie, Feyaad. "The representation trap: How and why Muslims struggle to maintain power in India." Unpublished manuscript (2023).

Allport, Gordon Willard, Kenneth Clark, and Thomas Pettigrew. *The nature of prejudice*. Addison-Wesley, 1954.

Alvarez, Sonia E. *Engendering democracy in Brazil: Women's movements in transition politics*. Princeton University Press, 1990.

Ameerudheen, T. A. "Sabarimala: As BJP observes yet another hartal in Kerala, it is accused of exploiting man's suicide." *Scroll.in*, December 15, 2018, https://scroll.in/article/905743/sabarimala-as-bjp-observes-yet-another-hartal-in-kerala-it-is-accused-of-exploiting-mans-suicide.

Ananthpur, Kripa, Kabir Malik, and Vijayendra Rao. *The anatomy of failure: An ethnography of a randomized trial to deepen democracy in rural India*. The World Bank, 2014.

Anderberg, Dan, and Helmut Rainer. "Economic abuse: A theory of intrahousehold sabotage." *Journal of Public Economics* 97 (2013): 282–295.

Anderson, Siwan, Patrick Francois, and Ashok Kotwal. "Clientelism in Indian villages." *American Economic Review* 105.6 (2015): 1780–1816.

Anukriti, S., Catalina Herrera-Almanza, and Praveen Pathak. "Curse of the Mummy-ji: The influence of mothers-in-Law on women's social networks, mobility, and reproductive health in India." No. 2317-2019-4794. 2019.

Asher, Sam, and Paul Novosad. "Politics and local economic growth: Evidence from India." *American Economic Journal: Applied Economics* 9.1 (2017): 229–273.

Atkeson, Lonna Rae. "Not all cues are created equal: The conditional impact of female candidates on political engagement." *The Journal of Politics* 65.4 (2003): 1040–1061.

Auerbach, Adam Michael. "Clients and communities: The political economy of party network organization and development in India's urban slums." *World Politics* 68.1 (2016): 111–148.

"Neighborhood associations and the urban poor: India's slum development committees." *World Development* 96 (2017): 119–135.

Demanding development: The politics of public goods provision in India's urban slums. Cambridge University Press, 2019.

Auerbach, Adam Michael, and Gabrielle Kruks-Wisner. "The geography of citizenship practice: How the poor engage the state in rural and urban India." *Perspectives on Politics* 18 (2020): 1–17.

Auerbach, Adam Michael, and Tariq Thachil. "How clients select brokers: Competition and choice in India's slums." *American Political Science Review* 112.4 (2018): 775–791.

Auerbach, Adam Michael, et al. "Rethinking the study of electoral politics in the developing world: Reflections on the Indian case." *Perspectives on Politics* 20.1 (2022): 250–264.

Badrinathan, Sumitra, et al. "Partisan disagreement: The role of media, personal networks and gender in forming political preferences." *Urbanisation* 6.1(suppl) (2021): S141–S157.

Balagopal, K. "Slaying of a spirituous Demon." *Economic and Political Weekly* 27 (1992): 2457–2461.

Baldassarri, Delia. "Cooperative networks: Altruism, group solidarity, reciprocity, and sanctioning in Ugandan producer organizations." *American Journal of Sociology* 121.2 (2015): 355–395.

Baldez, Lisa. *Why women protest: Women's movements in Chile.* Cambridge University Press, 2002.

Ban, Radu, and Vijayendra Rao. "Tokenism or agency? The impact of women's reservations on village democracies in South India." *Economic Development and Cultural Change* 56.3 (2008): 501–530.

Ban, Radu, Saumitra Jha, and Vijayendra Rao. "Who has voice in a deliberative democracy? Evidence from transcripts of village parliaments in south India." *Journal of Development Economics* 99.2 (2012): 428–438.

Banerjee, Abhijit Vinayak. "Microcredit under the microscope: What have we learned in the past two decades, and what do we need to know?" *Annual Review of Economics* 5.1 (2013): 487–519.

Banerjee, Abhijit, et al. "The diffusion of microfinance." *Science* 341.6144 (2013): 1236498.

"Marry for what? Caste and mate selection in modern India." *American Economic Journal: Microeconomics* 5.2 (2013): 33–72.

Bardhan, Pranab, and Dilip Mookherjee. "Political clientelism and capture: Theory and evidence from West Bengal, India." No. 2012/97. WIDER Working Paper, 2012.

Barnes, Tiffany D., and Stephanie M. Burchard. "'Engendering' politics: The impact of descriptive representation on women's political engagement in Sub-Saharan Africa." *Comparative Political Studies* 46.7 (2013): 767–790.

Basu, Amrita. *Two faces of protest.* University of California Press, 1992.

Basu, Moni. "The girl whose rape changed a country." *CNN News*, November 2013, www.cnn.com/interactive/2013/11/world/india-rape/.

Basu, Srimati. "Gathering steam: Organising strategies of the Indian Men's Rights Movement." *Economic and Political Weekly* 50 (2015): 67–75.

"Looking through misogyny: Indian men's rights activists, law, and challenges for feminism." *Canadian Journal of Women and the Law* 28.1 (2016): 45–68.

Bates, Robert. "Violence and prosperity: The political economy of development." (2000).

Batliwala Srilatha. "Empowerment of Women in South Asia: Concepts and Practices." Asian-South Pacific Bureau of Adult Education: Mumbai, 1993.

Batliwala, Srilatha. "The meaning of women's empowerment: New concepts from action." In *Population policies reconsidered: Health, empowerment, and rights,* Sen, G, Germain, A, Chen, LC (eds). Harvard Center for Population and Development Studies, 1994.

Beaman, Lori, et al. "Powerful women: Does exposure reduce bias?" *The Quarterly Journal of Economics* 124.4 (2009): 1497–1540.

"Female leadership raises aspirations and educational attainment for girls: A policy experiment in India." *Science* 335.6068 (2012): 582–586.

Beath, Andrew, Fotini Christia, and Ruben Enikolopov. "Empowering women through development aid: Evidence from a field experiment in Afghanistan." *American Political Science Review* 107 (2013): 540–557.

Becker, Gary S. "A theory of social interactions." *Journal of Political Economy* 82.6 (1974): 1063–1093.

A treatise on the family. Harvard University Press, 1981.

"Human capital, effort, and the sexual division of labor." *Journal of Labor Economics* 3.1, Part 2 (1985): S33–S58.

Beckwith, Karen. "Interests, issues, and preferences: Women's interests and epiphenomena of activism." *Politics & Gender* 7.3 (2011): 424–429.

"Gender, class, and the structure of intersectionality: Working-class women and the Pittston Coal strike." *Politics, Groups, and Identities* 2.1 (2014): 17–34.

Benstead, Lindsay J. "Why quotas are needed to improve women's access to services in clientelistic regimes." *Governance* 29.2 (2016): 185–205.

Berenschot, Ward. "Everyday mediation: The politics of public service delivery in Gujarat, India." *Development and Change* 41.5 (2010): 883–905.

Berman, Sheri. "Civil society and the collapse of the Weimar Republic." *World Politics* 49.3 (1997): 401–429.

Bertocchi, Graziella, and Michael Spagat. "The politics of co-optation." *Journal of Comparative Economics* 29.4 (2001): 591–607.

Besley, Timothy, and Stephen Coate. "Group lending, repayment incentives and social collateral." *Journal of Development Economics* 46.1 (1995): 1–18.

Besley, Timothy, Rohini Pande, and Vijayendra Rao. "Just rewards? Local politics and public resource allocation in South India." *The World Bank Economic Review* 26.2 (2012): 191–216.

Bevir, Mark. "Foucault and critique: Deploying agency against autonomy." *Political Theory* 27.1 (1999): 65–84.

Bhalotra, Sonia, Irma Clots-Figueras, and Lakshmi Iyer. "Pathbreakers? Women's electoral success and future political participation." *The Economic Journal* 128.613 (2018): 1844–1878.

Bhatnagar, Rahul. "Take five: 'Elected women representatives are key agents for transformational economic, environmental and social change in India.'" *UnWomen*, July 18, 2019, www.unwomen.org/en/news/stories/2019/7/take-five-rahul-bhatnagar-india

Bhattacharya, Deya. "Domestic violence: Supreme Court verdict on Section 498A puts family honour over women's rights." *Firstpost*, July 29, 2017, www.firstpost.com/india/domestic-violence-supreme-court-verdict-on-section-498a-puts-family-honour-over-womens-rights-3870627.html.

Bhavnani, Rikhil R. "Do electoral quotas work after they are withdrawn? Evidence from a natural experiment in India." *American Political Science Review* 103.1 (2009): 23–35.

Bicchieri, Cristina. *Norms in the wild: How to diagnose, measure, and change social norms*. Oxford University Press, 2016.

Bittman, Michael, et al. "When does gender trump money? Bargaining and time in household work." *American Journal of Sociology* 109.1 (2003): 186–214.

Blackman, Alexandra Domike, and Marlette Jackson. "Gender stereotypes, political leadership, and voting behavior in Tunisia." *Political Behavior* 43 (2021): 1–30.

Blais, André. *To vote or not to vote?: The merits and limits of rational choice theory*. University of Pittsburgh Press, 2000.

Blaydes, Lisa, and Drew A. Linzer. "The political economy of women's support for fundamentalist Islam." *World Politics* 60.4 (2008): 576–609.

Bloch, Francis, and Vijayendra Rao. "Terror as a bargaining instrument: A case study of dowry violence in rural India." *American Economic Review* 92.4 (2002): 1029–1043.

Bohlken, Anjali Thomas. *Democratization from above: The logic of local democracy in the developing world*. Cambridge University Press, 2016.

Bourdieu, Pierre. "The field of cultural production, or: The economic world reversed." *Poetics* 12.4–5 (1983): 311–356.

Brady, Henry E., Sidney Verba, and Kay Lehman Schlozman. "Beyond SES: A resource model of political participation." *American Political Science Review* 89.2 (1995): 271–294.

Bratton, Michael, et al. "The effects of civic education on political culture: evidence from Zambia." *World Development* 27.5 (1999): 807–824.

Braunstein, Elissa, and Nancy Folbre. "To honor and obey: Efficiency, inequality, and patriarchal property rights." *Feminist Economics* 7.1 (2001): 25–44.

Breeding, Mary E. "The micro-politics of vote banks in Karnataka." *Economic and Political Weekly* 46 (2011): 71–77.

Brehm, John, and Wendy Rahn. "Individual-level evidence for the causes and consequences of social capital." *American Journal of Political Science* 41 (1997): 999–1023.

Brody, Carinne, et al. "Economic self-help group programs for improving women's empowerment: A systematic review." *Campbell Systematic Reviews* 11.1 (2015): 1–182.

Browning, Martin, and Pierre-André Chiappori. "Efficient intra-household allocations: A general characterization and empirical tests." *Econometrica* 66 (1998): 1241–1278.

Brulé, Rachel, and Nikhar Gaikwad. "Culture, capital and the political economy gender gap: Evidence from Meghalaya's matrilineal tribes." *The Journal of Politics* 83 (2021) 834–850.

Brulé, Rachel E. "Reform, representation, and resistance: The politics of property rights' enforcement." *The Journal of Politics* 82.4 (2020a): 1390–1405.

  Women, power, and property: The paradox of gender equality laws in India. Cambridge University Press, 2020b.

Brusco, Valeria, Marcelo Nazareno, and Susan C. Stokes. "Vote buying in Argentina." *Latin American Research Review* 39 (2004): 66–88.

Burns, Nancy, Kay Lehman Schlozman, and Sidney Verba. *The private roots of public action*. Harvard University Press, 2001.

Bursztyn, Leonardo, Alessandra L. González, and David Yanagizawa-Drott. "Misperceived social norms: Women working outside the home in Saudi Arabia." *American Economic Review* 110.10 (2020): 2997–3029.

Bussell, Jennifer. *Clients and constituents: Political responsiveness in patronage democracies*. Modern South Asia, 2019.

Calman, Leslie J. *Toward empowerment: Women and movement politics in India*. Routledge, 1992.

Cammett, Melani. "Using proxy interviewing to address sensitive topics." *Interview Research in Political Science* (2013): 125–143.

Campbell, Colin. "Distinguishing the power of agency from agentic power: A note on Weber and the 'black box' of personal agency." *Sociological Theory* 27.4 (2009): 407–418.

Carpena, Fenella, and Francesca R. Jensenius. "Age of marriage and women's political engagement: Evidence from India." *The Journal of Politics* 83.4 (2021): 1823–1828.

Carranza, Eliana. "Soil endowments, female labor force participation, and the demographic deficit of women in India." *American Economic Journal: Applied Economics* 6.4 (2014): 197–225.

Carruthers, Celeste K., and Marianne H. Wanamaker. "Municipal housekeeping: The impact of women's suffrage on the provision of public education." *Journal of Human Resources* 50 (2014) 837–872.

Chandra, Kanchan. *Why ethnic parties succeed: Patronage and ethnic head counts in India.* Cambridge University Press, 2004.

"Counting Heads: A theory of voter and elite behavior in patronage democracies." *Patrons, clients, and policies: Patterns of democratic accountability and political competition* (2007): 84–109.

Chattopadhyay, Raghabendra, and Esther Duflo. "Women as policy makers: Evidence from a randomized policy experiment in India." *Econometrica* 72.5 (2004): 1409–1443.

Chauchard, Simon. *Why representation matters: The meaning of ethnic quotas in rural India.* Cambridge University Press, 2017.

Chaudhary, Ruchika. "Working or not: What determines women's labour force participation in India." (2021). *Unpublished manuscript.*

Cheema, Ali, et al. "Canvassing the gatekeepers: A field experiment to increase women voters' turnout in Pakistan." *American Political Science Review* 117 (2021): 1–21.

Chhibber, Pradeep K. *Democracy without associations: Transformation of the party system and social cleavages in India.* University of Michigan Press, 2001.

Chhibber, Pradeep. "Why are some women politically active? The household, public space, and political participation in India." *International Journal of Comparative Sociology* 43.3–5 (2002): 409–429.

Chhibber, Pradeep K., and Rahul Verma. *Ideology and identity: The changing party systems of India.* Oxford University Press, 2018.

Chowdhury, Anirvan. "Religiously Conservative Parties and Women's Political Mobilization." Manuscript in progress (2023).

Chowdhury, Romit. "Conditions of emergence: The formation of men's rights groups in contemporary India." *Indian Journal of Gender Studies* 21.1 (2014): 27–53.

Clayton, Amanda. "Electoral gender quotas and attitudes toward traditional leaders: A policy experiment in Lesotho." *Journal of Policy Analysis and Management* 33.4 (2014): 1007–1026.

"Women's political engagement under quota-mandated female representation: Evidence from a randomized policy experiment." *Comparative Political Studies* 48.3 (2015): 333–369.

"How do electoral gender quotas affect policy?." *Annual Review of Political Science* 24 (2021): 235–252.

Clayton, Amanda, and Pär Zetterberg. "Quota shocks: Electoral gender quotas and government spending priorities worldwide." *The Journal of Politics* 80.3 (2018): 916–932.

Clayton, Amanda, et al. "In whose interest? Gender and mass–elite priority congruence in Sub-Saharan Africa." *Comparative Political Studies* 52.1 (2019): 69–101.

Clots-Figueras, Irma. "Women in politics: Evidence from the Indian States." *Journal of Public Economics* 95.7–8 (2011): 664–690.

Coase, R. H. "The problem of social cost." *Journal of Law and Economics* 3 (1960): 1–44.

Coleman, James S. "Social theory, social research, and a theory of action." *American Journal of Sociology* 91.6 (1986): 1309–1335.

"Social capital in the creation of human capital." *American Journal of Sociology* 94 (1988): S95–S120.

Conover, Pamela Johnston. "Feminists and the gender gap." *The Journal of Politics* 50.4 (1988): 985–1010.

Conover, Pamela Johnston, and Virginia Gray. *Feminism and the new right: Conflict over the American family.* Praeger Publishers, 1983.

Cools, Sara, and Andreas Kotsadam. "Resources and intimate partner violence in Sub-Saharan Africa." *World Development* 95 (2017): 211–230.

Corder, J. Kevin, and Christina Wolbrecht. *Counting women's ballots.* Cambridge University Press, 2016.

Corntassel, Jeff. "Partnership in action? Indigenous political mobilization and co-optation during the first UN Indigenous Decade (1995–2004)." *Human Rights Quarterly* 29 (2007): 137–166.

Cornwall, Andrea. "Women's empowerment: What works?" *Journal of International Development* 28.3 (2016): 342–359.

Cox, Gary W., Frances M. Rosenbluth, and Michael F. Thies. "Mobilization, social networks, and turnout: Evidence from Japan." *World Politics* 50.3 (1998): 447–474.

Crenshaw, Kimberlé. "Mapping the margins: Intersectionality, identity politics, and violence against women of color." *Stanford Law Review* 43 (1990): 1241.

Cruz, Cesi. "Social networks and the targeting of vote buying." *Comparative Political Studies* 52.3 (2019): 382–411.

Cruz, Cesi, and Charis Tolentino. "Gender, social recognition, and political influence." *Manuscript in progress* (2019).

Daby, Mariela. "The gender gap in political clientelism: problem-solving networks and the division of political work in Argentina." *Comparative Political Studies* 54.2 (2021): 215–244.

Dahl, Robert Alan. *Polyarchy: Participation and opposition.* Yale University Press, 1971.

Dahlerup, Drude. "From a small to a large minority: Women in Scandinavian politics." *Scandinavian Political Studies* 11.4 (1988): 275–298.

Daly, Mary. "Gender mainstreaming in theory and practice." *Social Politics: International Studies in Gender, State & Society* 12.3 (2005): 433–450.

Das, Maitreyi. *The women's development program in Rajasthan.* Working Paper. World Bank, 1992.

De Alwis, Rangita de Silva, and Indira Jaising. "The role of personal laws in creating a second sex." *NYUJ International Law and Politics* 48 (2015): 1085.

Deendayal Antyodaya Yojanaj – NRLM. https://aajeevika.gov.in/en/content/mission. Accessed October 28, 2021.

Dell, Melissa. "The persistent effects of Peru's mining mita." *Econometrica* 78.6 (2010): 1863–1903.

Desai, Sonalde, and Reeve Vanneman. *India Human Development Survey-II (IHDS-II), 2011–12.* Inter-university Consortium for Political and Social Research, 2015.

Desposato, Scott, and Barbara Norrander. "The gender gap in Latin America: Contextual and individual influences on gender and political participation." *British Journal of Political Science* 39 (2009): 141–162.

Devika, J. "The 'Kudumbashree woman' and the Kerala model woman: Women and politics in contemporary Kerala." *Indian Journal of Gender Studies* 23.3 (2016): 393–414.

Dhar, Diva, Tarun Jain, and Seema Jayachandran. *Reshaping adolescents' gender attitudes: Evidence from a school-based experiment in India.* No. w25331. National Bureau of Economic Research, 2018.

Diaz-Cayeros, Alberto, Federico Estévez, and Beatriz Magaloni. *The political logic of poverty relief: Electoral strategies and social policy in Mexico.* Cambridge University Press, 2016.

Diekman, Amanda B., and Monica C. Schneider. "A social role theory perspective on gender gaps in political attitudes." *Psychology of Women Quarterly* 34.4 (2010): 486–497.

Dobbin, Frank, and Alexandra Kalev. "The promise and peril of sexual harassment programs." *Proceedings of the National Academy of Sciences* 116.25 (2019): 12255–12260.

Doepke, Matthias, and Michele Tertilt. "Women's liberation: What's in it for men?." *The Quarterly Journal of Economics* 124.4 (2009): 1541–1591.

Doepke, M., and M. Tertilt. "Does female empowerment promote economic development? IZA Discussion Papers 5637." *Institute for the Study of Labor (IZA)* (2011).

Duflo, Esther. "Women empowerment and economic development." *Journal of Economic Literature* 50.4 (2012): 1051–1079

Dunning, Thad, and Janhavi Nilekani. "Ethnic quotas and political mobilization: Caste, parties, and distribution in Indian village councils." *American Political Science Review* 107.1 (2013): 35–56.

Durkheim, Emile. *Le suicide: Étude de sociologie.* Alcan, 1897.

Dwyer, Daisy Hilse, and J. Bince. "A home divided: Women and income in the Third World." (1988).

Edlund, Lena, and Rohini Pande. "Why have women become left-wing? The political gender gap and the decline in marriage." *The Quarterly Journal of Economics* 117.3 (2002): 917–961.

Emirbayer, Mustafa. "Manifesto for a relational sociology." *American Journal of Sociology* 103.2 (1997): 281–317.

Express News Service. "Kerala BJP admits it orchestrated Sabarimala agitation as part of its 'agenda'." *The New Indian Express*, November 5, 2018, www .newindianexpress.com/states/kerala/2018/nov/05/kerala-bjp-admits-it-orches trated-sabarimala-agitation-as-part-of-its-agenda-1894559.html.

Fearon, James D., and David D. Laitin. "Explaining interethnic cooperation." *American Political Science Review* 90.4 (1996): 715–735.

Fearon, James D., and Macartan Humphreys. "Why do women co-operate more in women's groups?." *Towards Gender Equity in Development* (2018): 217.

Feddersen, Timothy J. "Rational choice theory and the paradox of not voting." *Journal of Economic Perspectives* 18.1 (2004): 99–112.

Feigenberg, Benjamin, Erica M. Field, and Rohini Pande. *Building social capital through microfinance*. No. w16018. National Bureau of Economic Research, 2010.

Feigenberg, Benjamin, Erica Field, and Rohini Pande. "The economic returns to social interaction: Experimental evidence from microfinance." *Review of Economic Studies* 80.4 (2013): 1459–1483.

Feigenberg, Benjamin, et al. "Do group dynamics influence social capital gains among microfinance clients? Evidence from a randomized experiment in urban India." *Journal of Policy Analysis and Management* 33.4 (2014): 932–949.

Finkel, Steven E. "Civic education and the mobilization of political participation in developing democracies." *Journal of Politics* 64.4 (2002): 994–1020.

Finkel, Steven E., and Howard R. Ernst. "Civic education in post-apartheid South Africa: Alternative paths to the development of political knowledge and democratic values." *Political Psychology* 26.3 (2005): 333–364.

Fletcher, Erin, Rohini Pande, and Charity Maria Troyer Moore. "Women and work in India: Descriptive evidence and a review of potential policies." (2017).

Folbre, Nancy. *Who pays for the kids?: Gender and the structures of constraint*. Routledge, 1994.

The rise and decline of patriarchal systems: An intersectional political economy. Verso Books, 2021.

Foos, Florian, and Eline A. De Rooij. "All in the family: Partisan disagreement and electoral mobilization in intimate networks – A spillover experiment." *American Journal of Political Science* 61.2 (2017): 289–304.

Franceschet, Susan, and Jennifer M. Piscopo. "Gender quotas and women's substantive representation: Lessons from Argentina." *Politics & Gender* 4.3 (2008): 393–425.

Frese, H. "Women's power: The anti-arrack movement in Andhra Pradesh." *Südasien-Chronik–South Asia Chronicle* 2 (2012) 219–234.

Gandhi, M.K. "Women and the Vote." *Young India* (1920).

Gelb, Joyce, and Marian Lief Palley. *Women and public policies: Reassessing gender politics*. University of Virginia Press, 1996.

Ghatak, Maitreesh. "Group lending, local information and peer selection." *Journal of Development Economics* 60.1 (1999): 27–50.

Gilardi, Fabrizio. "The temporary importance of role models for women's political representation." *American Journal of Political Science* 59.4 (2015): 957–970.

Gine, Xavier, and Ghazala Mansuri. *Together we will: Experimental evidence on female voting behavior in Pakistan*. The World Bank, 2011.

Glaser, William A. "The family and voting turnout." *Public Opinion Quarterly* 23.4 (1959): 563–570.

Gleason, Christy. "Presence, perspectives and power: Gender and the rationale differences in the debate over the violence against women act." *Women's Rights Law Reporter* 23 (2001): 1.

Glynn, Adam N., and Maya Sen. "Identifying judicial empathy: Does having daughters cause judges to rule for women's issues?" *American Journal of Political Science* 59.1 (2015): 37–54.

Gochhayat, Artatrana. "Political participation of women in Gram Panchayat elections in Odisha: A case study of Hindol block in Dhenkanal district." *International Journal of Rural Studies* 20.2 (2013): 1–7.

Goetz, Anne Marie, and Rina Sen Gupta. "Who takes the credit? Gender, power, and control over loan use in rural credit programs in Bangladesh." *World Development* 24.1 (1996): 45–63.

Goetz, Anne Marie, and Rob Jenkins. "Feminist activism and the politics of reform: When and why do states respond to demands for gender equality policies?" *Development and Change* 49.3 (2018): 714–734.

Goldin, Claudia. "The quiet revolution that transformed women's employment, education, and family." *American Economic Review* 96.2 (2006): 1–21.

Gottlieb, Jessica. "Greater expectations: A field experiment to improve accountability in Mali." *American Journal of Political Science* 60.1 (2016a): 143–157.

"Why might information exacerbate the gender gap in civic participation? Evidence from Mali." *World Development* 86 (2016b): 95–110.

Gottlieb, Jessica, Guy Grossman, and Amanda Lea Robinson. "Do men and women have different policy preferences in Africa? Determinants and implications of gender gaps in policy prioritization." *British Journal of Political Science* 48.3 (2016): 611–636.

Goyal, Tanushree. "How women mobilize women into politics: A natural experiment in India." *Available at SSRN 3583693* (2019).

"Local female representation as a pathway to power: A natural experiment in India." *Available at SSRN 3590118* (2020).

Granovetter, Mark S. "The strength of weak ties." *American Journal of Sociology* 78.6 (1973): 1360–1380.

Gray, Jeffrey S. "Divorce-law changes, household bargaining, and married women's labor supply." *The American Economic Review* 88.3 (1998): 628–642.

Green, Donald P., and Alan S. Gerber. "Introduction to social pressure and voting: New experimental evidence." *Political Behavior* 32.3 (2010): 331–336.

Gugerty, Mary Kay, Pierre Biscaye, and C. Leigh Anderson. "Delivering development? Evidence on self-help groups as development intermediaries in South Asia and Africa." *Development Policy Review* 37.1 (2019): 129–151.

Guha, Ramachandra. "Adivasis, naxalites and Indian democracy." *Economic and Political Weekly* 42 (2007): 3305–3312.

Gulzar, Saad, Nicholas Haas, and Benjamin Pasquale. "Does political affirmative action work, and for whom? Theory and evidence on India's scheduled areas." *American Political Science Review* 114.4 (2020): 1230–1246.

Gulzar, Saad, Muhammad Yasir Khan, and Luke Sonnet. "Pessimistic beliefs of norms: Descriptive findings on women's political participation in Pakistan." *Manuscript in progress* (2020).

Hassim, Shireen. *Women's organizations and democracy in South Africa: Contesting authority.* Univ of Wisconsin Press, 2006.

Herbst, Jeffrey. *States and power in Africa: Comparative lessons in authority and control.* Vol. 149. Princeton University Press, 2014.

Heyer, Judith. "The role of dowries and daughters' marriages in the accumulation and distribution of capital in a South Indian community." *Journal of International Development* 4.4 (1992): 419–436.

Ho, Daniel E., et al. "Matching as nonparametric preprocessing for reducing model dependence in parametric causal inference." *Political Analysis* 15.3 (2007): 199–236.

Holden, Jenny, et al. *Evaluation of the Madhya Pradesh Safe Cities Initiative*. DFID Endline Report, (2016).

Htun, Mala, and S. Laurel Weldon. "The civic origins of progressive policy change: Combating violence against women in global perspective, 1975–2005." *American Political Science Review* 106 (2012): 548–569.

The logics of gender justice: State action on women's rights around the world. Cambridge University Press, 2018.

Huber, John D., and Pavithra Suryanarayan. "Ethnic inequality and the ethnification of political parties: Evidence from India." *World Politics* 68.1 (2016): 149–188.

Huckfeldt, R. Robert. "Political participation and the neighborhood social context." *American Journal of Political Science* 23 (1979): 579–592.

Huckfeldt, Robert. "Information, persuasion, and political communication networks." In *The Oxford handbook of political behavior*, Dalton, Russell J, Hans-Dieter Klingemann (eds). Oxford Handbooks, 2007, 100.

Huckfeldt, Robert, and John Sprague. "Networks in context: The social flow of political information." *The American Political Science Review* 81 (1987): 1197–1216.

"Political parties and electoral mobilization: Political structure, social structure, and the party canvass." *The American Political Science Review* 86 (1992): 70–86.

Huckfeldt, Robert, Eric Plutzer, and John Sprague. "Alternative contexts of political behavior: Churches, neighborhoods, and individuals." *The Journal of Politics* 55.2 (1993): 365–381.

Hunnicutt, Gwen. "Varieties of patriarchy and violence against women: Resurrecting "patriarchy" as a theoretical tool." *Violence against Women* 15.5 (2009): 553–573.

International Institute for Population Sciences (IIPS) and ICF. 2017. *National Family Health Survey (NFHS-4), 2015-16: India*. IIPS.

International Labour Organization. "Labour force participation rate by sex and age (%) – Annual." *ILOSTAT database*, https://ilostat.ilo.org/data. Accessed September 18, 2021.

Imbens, Guido W., and Jeffrey M. Wooldridge. "Recent developments in the econometrics of program evaluation." *Journal of Economic Literature* 47.1 (2009): 5–86.

Inglehart, R., C. Haerpfer, A. Moreno, C. Welzel, K. Kizilova, J. Diez-Medrano, M. Lagos, P. Norris, E. Ponarin & B. Puranen et al., eds. 2014. World Values Survey: All Rounds – Country-Pooled Datafile Version: www.worldvaluessurvey.org/WVSDocumentationWVL.jsp. Madrid: JD Systems Institute.

Inglehart, Ronald, and Pippa Norris. "The developmental theory of the gender gap: Women's and men's voting behavior in global perspective." *International Political Science Review* 21.4 (2000): 441–463.

Rising tide: Gender equality and cultural change around the world. Cambridge University Press, 2003.

Inkeles, Alex. "Making men modern: On the causes and consequences of individual change in six developing countries." *American Journal of Sociology* 75.2 (1969): 208–225.

International Institute for Population Sciences (IIPS) and ICF. *National Family Health Survey (NFHS-4), 2015-16: India*. IIPS, 2017.

Inter-Parliamentary Union. *Country ranking of women in national parliaments*. Geneva, Switzerland, 2022. Web. January 4, 2023, http://archive.ipu.org/wmn-e/classif-arc .htm

Isaksson, Ann-Sofie, Andreas Kotsadam, and Måns Nerman. "The gender gap in African political participation: Testing theories of individual and contextual determinants." *Journal of Development Studies* 50.2 (2014): 302–318.

Iversen, Torben, and Frances Rosenbluth. "The political economy of gender: Explaining cross-national variation in the gender division of labor and the gender voting gap." *American Journal of Political Science* 50.1 (2006): 1–19.

"Work and power: The connection between female labor force participation and female political representation." *Annual Review Political Science* 11 (2008): 479–495.

Women, work, and politics: The political economy of gender inequality. Yale University Press, 2010.

Iyer, Lakshmi, et al. "The power of political voice: Women's political representation and crime in India." *American Economic Journal: Applied Economics* 4.4 (2012): 165–193.

Jackson, Matthew O., Tomas Rodriguez-Barraquer, and Xu Tan. "Social capital and social quilts: Network patterns of favor exchange." *American Economic Review* 102.5 (2012): 1857–1897.

Jaffrelot, Christophe. *Religion, caste, and politics in India.* Primus Books, 2010.

Jain, Shruti. "Self-help group women as COVID-19 warriors." *Observer Research Foundation*, April 27, 2020, www.orfonline.org/expert-speak/self-help-group-women-covid19-warriors-65220/.

Javaid, Maham. "Pakistan's feminists say will persevere amid increased threats." *Al Jazeera*, March 22, 2021, www.aljazeera.com/features/2021/3/22/pakistans-feminists-say-will-persevere-amid-increased-threats.

Jayachandran, Seema. "The roots of gender inequality in developing countries." *Annual Review of Economics* 7.1 (2015): 63–88.

Social norms as a barrier to women's employment in developing countries. No. w27449. National Bureau of Economic Research, 2020.

Jayachandran, Seema, and Rohini Pande. "Why are Indian children so short? The role of birth order and son preference." *American Economic Review* 107.9 (2017): 2600–2629.

Jensenius, Francesca R. *Social justice through inclusion: The consequences of electoral quotas in India.* Oxford University Press, 2017.

Johnson, Allan G. *The gender knot: Unraveling our patriarchal legacy.* Temple University Press, 1997.

Jost, John T., and Mahzarin R. Banaji. "The role of stereotyping in system-justification and the production of false consciousness." *British Journal of Social Psychology* 33.1 (1994): 1–27.

Kabeer, Naila. *Reversed realities: Gender hierarchies in development thought.* Verso, 1994.

"Resources, agency, achievements: Reflections on the measurement of women's empowerment." *Development and Change* 30.3 (1999): 435–464.

"Is microfinance a 'magic bullet' for women's empowerment? Analysis of findings from South Asia." Economic and Political Weekly 40 (2005): 4709–4718.

"Empowerment, citizenship and gender justice: A contribution to locally grounded theories of change in women's lives." *Ethics and Social Welfare* 6.3 (2012): 216–232.

Kabeer, Naila, et al. "Group rights and gender justice: Exploring tensions within an indigenous community in India." (2019).

Kalmijn, Matthijs. "Intermarriage and homogamy: Causes, patterns, trends." *Annual Review of Sociology* 24.1 (1998): 395–421.

Kandiyoti, Deniz. "Bargaining with patriarchy." *Gender & Society* 2.3 (1988): 274–290.

Kandpal, Eeshani, and Kathy Baylis. "Expanding horizons: Can women's support groups diversify peer networks in rural India?" *American Journal of Agricultural Economics* 95.2 (2013): 360–367.

The social lives of married women: Peer effects in female autonomy and investments in children. The World Bank, 2019.

Kanter, Rosabeth Moss. "Men and women of the corporation." (1977).

Kapur, Devesh. "Why does the Indian state both fail and succeed?." *Journal of Economic Perspectives* 34.1 (2020): 31–54.

Karekurve-Ramachandra, Varun. "Gender quotas and upward political mobility in India." *Manuscript in progress* (2021).

Karekurve-Ramachandra, Varun and Alexander Lee. "Can gender quotas improve public service provision? Evidence from Indian Local Government." *Manuscript in progress* (2021).

Karim, Nafis I., Alexandru Maries, and Chandralekha Singh. "Do evidence-based active-engagement courses reduce the gender gap in introductory physics?" *European Journal of Physics* 39.2 (2018): 025701.

Kapadia, Karin. "Impure women, virtuous men: Religion, resistance, and gender." *South Asia Research* 1.14 (1994): 2.

Siva and her sisters: Gender, caste, and class in rural South India. Routledge, 1995.

Karpowitz, Christopher F., and Tali Mendelberg. *The silent sex: Gender, deliberation, and institutions.* Princeton University Press, 2014.

Karpowitz, Christopher F., Tali Mendelberg, and Lee Shaker. "Gender inequality in deliberative participation." *American Political Science Review* 106.3 (2012): 533–547.

Keele, Luke J., and Rocio Titiunik. "Geographic boundaries as regression discontinuities." *Political Analysis* 23.1 (2015): 127–155.

Kelly, Caroline, and Sara Breinlinger. *The social psychology of collective action: Identity, injustice and gender.* Taylor & Francis US, 1996.

Kitschelt, Herbert, and Steven I. Wilkinson, eds. *Patrons, clients and policies: Patterns of democratic accountability and political competition.* Cambridge University Press, 2007.

Khan, Aleena. "Pakistan: A rising women's movement confronts a New Backlash." *United States Institute of Peace* (2021).

Khan, Sarah. "Count Me Out: Gendered Preference Expression in Pakistan." *Unpublished manuscript* (2021).

Kittilson, Miki Caul, and Leslie Schwindt-Bayer. "Engaging citizens: The role of power-sharing institutions." *The Journal of Politics* 72.4 (2010): 990–1002.

Kittilson, Miki Caul, and Leslie A. Schwindt-Bayer. *The gendered effects of electoral institutions: Political engagement and participation.* Oxford University Press, 2012.

Klasen, Stephan, and Janneke Pieters. "What explains the stagnation of female labor force participation in urban India?." *The World Bank Economic Review* 29.3 (2015): 449–478.

Klein, Ethel. *Gender politics: From consciousness to mass politics.* Harvard University Press, 1986.

Knight, Jack. *Institutions and social conflict.* Cambridge University Press, 1992.

Knight, Jack, and Jean Ensminger. "Conflict over changing social norms: Bargaining, ideology, and enforcement." In *The New Institutionalism in Sociology*, Brinton, MC, Nee, V. (eds). Russell Sage Foundation, 1998, 105–126.

Knoke, David. "Networks of political action: Toward theory construction." *Social Forces* 68.4 (1990): 1041–1063.

Political networks: The structural perspective. Vol. 4. Cambridge University Press, 1994.

Kochar, Anjini, et al. "Impact evaluation of the National Rural Livelihoods Project." Impact Evaluation Report 128 (2020).

Kothari, Rajni. "The congress 'system' in India." *Asian Survey* 4 (1964): 1161–1173.

Krishna, Anirudh. *Active social capital: Tracing the roots of development and democracy*. Columbia University Press, 2002a.

"Enhancing political participation in democracies: What is the role of social capital?." *Comparative Political Studies* 35.4 (2002b): 437–460.

Krishnakumar, Akshaya, and Shankey Verma. "Understanding domestic violence in India during COVID-19: A routine activity approach." *Asian Journal of Criminology* 16.1 (2021): 19–35.

Krook, Mona Lena. "Reforming representation: The diffusion of candidate gender quotas worldwide." *Politics & Gender* 2.3 (2006): 303.

"Violence against women in politics." In *How gender can transform the social sciences*. Palgrave Pivot, Springer Nature, 2020, 57–64.

Krook, Mona Lena, and Diana Z. O'Brien. "The politics of group representation: Quotas for women and minorities worldwide." *Comparative Politics* 42.3 (2010): 253–272.

Krook, Mona Lena, and Juliana Restrepo Sanín. "The cost of doing politics? Analyzing violence and harassment against female politicians." *Perspectives on Politics* 18.3 (2020): 740–755.

Kruks-Wisner, Gabrielle. "Seeking the local state: Gender, caste, and the pursuit of public services in post-tsunami India." *World Development* 39.7 (2011): 1143–1154.

Claiming the state: Active citizenship and social welfare in rural India. Cambridge University Press, 2018.

Kulkarni, Purushottam M. *Sex ratio at birth in India: Recent trends and patterns*. United Nations Population Fund (UNFPA), 2020.

Kumar, Neha, et al. "Social networks, mobility, and political participation: The potential for women's self-help groups to improve access and use of public entitlement schemes in India." *World Development* 114 (2019): 28–41.

Kumar, Nitish. "While implementing prohibition in Bihar, there will be no half measures, writes Nitish Kumar." *The Hindustan Times*, June 31, 2018, www.hindustantimes.com/analysis/while-implementing-prohibition-in-bihar-there-will-be-no-half-measures-writes-nitish-kumar/story-RLMqz09mSKtzcZ8lkqpTIJ.html

Kumar, Rithika. "Left behind or left ahead?." (2022). *Manuscript in progress*.

Laitin, David D., and James T. Watkins IV. *Identity in formation: The Russian-speaking populations in the near abroad*. Cornell University Press, 1998.

Lake, Ronald La Due, and Robert Huckfeldt. "Social capital, social networks, and political participation." *Political Psychology* 19.3 (1998): 567–584.

Larreguy, Horacio, John Marshall, and Pablo Querubín. "Parties, brokers, and voter mobilization: How turnout buying depends upon the party's capacity to monitor brokers." *American Political Science Review* 110.1 (2016): 160–179.

Larson, Jennifer M., and Janet I. Lewis. "Ethnic networks." *American Journal of Political Science* 61.2 (2017): 350–364.

Lee, Alexander. *From hierarchy to ethnicity: The politics of caste in twentieth-century India*. Cambridge University Press, 2020.

Lehne, Jonathan, Jacob N. Shapiro, and Oliver Vanden Eynde. "Building connections: Political corruption and road construction in India." *Journal of Development Economics* 131 (2018): 62–78.

Leighley, Jan E. "Social interaction and contextual influences on political participation." *American Politics Quarterly* 18.4 (1990): 459–475.

Li, Lixing, and Xiaoyu Wu. "Gender of children, bargaining power, and intrahousehold resource allocation in China." *Journal of Human Resources* 46.2 (2011): 295–316.

Liaqat, Asad. "No representation without information: Politician responsiveness to citizen preferences." (2019).

Lipset, Seymour Martin. "Some social requisites of democracy: Economic development and political legitimacy1." *American Political Science Review* 53.1 (1959): 69–105.

Lizzeri, Alessandro, and Nicola Persico. "Why did the elites extend the suffrage? Democracy and the scope of government, with an application to Britain's 'Age of Reform'." *The Quarterly Journal of Economics* 119.2 (2004): 707–765.

Lott, Jr, John R., and Lawrence W. Kenny. "Did women's suffrage change the size and scope of government?" *Journal of Political Economy* 107.6 (1999): 1163–1198.

Lowes, Sara. "Matrilineal kinship and spousal cooperation: Evidence from the matrilineal belt." *Unpublished manuscript. URL:* https://scholar.harvard.edu/files/slowes/files/lowes_matrilineal.pdf (2017).

Lukes, Steven. *Power: A radical view*. Macmillan International Higher Education, 1974.

Lundberg, Shelly, and Robert A. Pollak. "Separate spheres bargaining and the marriage market." *Journal of Political Economy* 101.6 (1993): 988–1010.

"Noncooperative bargaining models of marriage." *The American Economic Review* 84.2 (1994): 132–137.

Mabsout, Ramzi, and Irene Van Staveren. "Disentangling bargaining power from individual and household level to institutions: Evidence on women's position in Ethiopia." *World Development* 38.5 (2010): 783–796.

MacKinnon, Catharine A.. *Toward a feminist theory of the state*. Harvard University Press. 1989.

Madan, Kamlesh, and Martijn H. Breuning. "Impact of prenatal technologies on the sex ratio in India: An overview." *Genetics in Medicine* 16.6 (2014): 425–432.

Madan, Preeti. "Self-help groups rise to Covid challenge." *The Tribune*, April 14, 2020, www.tribuneindia.com/news/comment/self-help-groups-rise-to-covid-challenge-70719.

Malapit, Hazel Jean L. "Why do spouses hide income?" *The Journal of Socio-Economics* 41.5 (2012): 584–593.

Mansbridge, Jane. "Should blacks represent blacks and women represent women? A contingent 'yes'." *The Journal of Politics* 61.3 (1999): 628–657.

Mansbridge, Jane, and Shauna L. Shames. "Toward a theory of backlash: Dynamic resistance and the central role of power." *Politics & Gender* 4.4 (2008): 623–634.

Manser, Marilyn, and Murray Brown. "Marriage and household decision-making: A bargaining analysis." *International Economic Review* 21 (1980): 31–44.

Mansuri, Ghazala, and Vijayendra Rao. "Community-based and-driven development: A critical review." *The World Bank Research Observer* 19.1 (2004): 1–39. *Localizing development: Does participation work?* The World Bank, 2012.

Marshall, Monty G. and Ted Robert Gurr. *Polity 5: Political regime characteristics and transitions, 1800–2018.* Center for Systemic Peace, 2021.

McAdam, Doug. *Political process and the development of black insurgency, 1930–1970.* University of Chicago Press, 1999.

McAdam, Doug, and Ronnelle Paulsen. "Specifying the relationship between social ties and activism." *American Journal of Sociology* 99.3 (1993): 640–667.

McAdam, John. "Joint action learning: A collective collaborative paradigm for the management of change in unionized organizations." *Journal of Managerial Psychology* 10 (1995): 31–40.

McClurg, Scott D. "Social networks and political participation: The role of social interaction in explaining political participation." *Political Research Quarterly* 56.4 (2003): 449–464.

McElroy, Marjorie B., and Mary Jean Horney. "Nash-bargained household decisions: Toward a generalization of the theory of demand." *International Economic Review* 22 (1981): 333–349.

Mehra, Rekha, and Geeta Rao Gupta. "Gender mainstreaming: Making it happen." *International Center for Research on Women (ICRW)* (2006).

Mehta, Soumya Kappor. "How women are shaping political fortunes in India." *The Hindustan Times*, May 7, 2021, www.hindustantimes.com/opinion/how-women-are-shaping-political-fortunes-in-india-101620398460498.html.

Miguel, Edward, and Mary Kay Gugerty. "Ethnic diversity, social sanctions, and public goods in Kenya." *Journal of Public Economics* 89.11–12 (2005): 2325–2368.

Mill, John Stuart. *The subjection of women.* Routledge, 2018.

Miller, Grant. "Women's suffrage, political responsiveness, and child survival in American history." *The Quarterly Journal of Economics* 123.3 (2008): 1287–1327.

Milgrom, Paul R., Douglass C. North, and Barry R. Weingast. "The role of institutions in the revival of trade: The law merchant, private judges, and the champagne fairs." *Economics & Politics* 2.1 (1990): 1–23.

Mohmand, Shandana Khan. *Crafty oligarchs, savvy voters: Democracy under inequality in rural Pakistan.* Vol. 8. Cambridge University Press, 2019.

Molyneux, Maxine. "Mobilization without emancipation? Women's interests, the state, and revolution in Nicaragua." *Feminist Studies* 11.2 (1985): 227–254.

"Analysing women's movements." *Development and change* 29.2 (1998): 219–245.

Moore, Charity Troyer, Rohini Pande, and Soledad Artiz Prillaman. "Diversifying opportunity, closing gender gaps: State-led recruitment to vocational training." Working paper (2021).

Morgan-Collins, Mona. "The electoral impact of newly enfranchised groups: The case of women's suffrage in the United States." *The Journal of Politics* 83.1 (2021): 150–165.

Morgan-Collins, Mona, and Grace Natusch. "At the intersection of gender and class: How were newly enfranchised women voters mobilized in Sweden?" *Comparative Political Studies* 55 (2021): 1063–1094.

Morris, Sharon. *Approaches to civic education: Lessons learned.* Office of Democracy and Governance, Bureau for Democracy, Conflict, and Humanitarian Assistance, USAID, 2002.

Morton, Rebecca B. "Groups in rational turnout models." *American Journal of Political Science* 35 (1991): 758–776.

Munshi, Kaivan, and Mark Rosenzweig. "Traditional institutions meet the modern world: Caste, gender, and schooling choice in a globalizing economy." *American Economic Review* 96.4 (2006): 1225–1252.

Narayan, Uma. *Dislocating cultures: Identities, traditions, and third world feminism.* Routledge, 1997.

"Minds of their own: Choices, autonomy, cultural practices, and other women." In *A mind of one's own*, Antony, Louise (ed). Routledge, 2018, 418–432.

Narayanan, Sudha, and Upasak Das. "Women participation and rationing in the employment guarantee scheme." *Economic and Political Weekly* 49 (2014): 46–53.

National Crime Records Bureau. "Crime in India 2020." *Government report*, 2020.

Nayak, Prateep K., and Fikret Berkes. "Politics of co-optation: Community forest management versus joint forest management in Orissa, India." *Environmental Management* 41.5 (2008): 707–718.

Nichols, Carly. "Self-help groups as platforms for development: The role of social capital." *World Development* 146 (2021): 105575.

Nichter, Simeon. "Vote buying or turnout buying? Machine politics and the secret ballot." *American Political Science Review* 102 (2008): 19–31.

Norris, Pippa, and Ronald Inglehart. "Women and democracy: Cultural obstacles to equal representation." *Journal of Democracy* 12.3 (2001): 126–140.

Nussbaum, Martha C. *Women and human development: The capabilities approach.* Vol. 3. Cambridge University Press, 2000.

O'Brien, Diana Z., and Johanna Rickne. "Gender quotas and women's political leadership." *American Political Science Review* 110.1 (2016): 112–126.

O'Neill, Brenda, and Elisabeth Gidengil, eds. *Gender and social capital.* Routledge, 2013.

Olken, Benjamin A. "Direct democracy and local public goods: Evidence from a field experiment in Indonesia." *American Political Science Review* 104 (2010): 243–267.

Olson, Mancur. *The logic of collective action: Public goods and the theory of groups,* second printing with a new preface and appendix. Vol. 124. Harvard University Press, 1965.

Okin, Susan Moller. "Women and the making of the sentimental family." *Philosophy & Public Affairs* 11 (1982): 65–88.

Okin, Susan Moller. *Justice, gender, and the family.* Vol. 171. Basic Books, 1989.

Olson, Mancur. *The logic of collective action: Public goods and the theory of groups.* Harvard University Press, 1965.

Ostrom, Elinor. "6. Constituting social capital and collective action." *Journal of Theoretical Politics* 6.4 (1994): 527–562.

Pal, Poulomi. "The Indian Women's Movement Today: The challenges of addressing gender-based violence." In *Women's movements in the global era*, Amrita Basu (ed). Routledge, 2018, 129–154.

Palaniswamy, Nethra, Ramya Parthasarathy, and Vijayendra Rao. "Unheard voices: The challenge of inducing women's civic speech." *World Development* 115 (2019): 64–77.

Paluck, Elizabeth Levy. "Reducing intergroup prejudice and conflict using the media: A field experiment in Rwanda." *Journal of Personality and Social Psychology* 96.3 (2009): 574.

Panda, Pradeep, and Bina Agarwal. "Marital violence, human development and women's property status in India." *World Development* 33.5 (2005): 823–850.

Pande, Rekha. "From anti-arrack to total prohibition: The women's movement in Andhra Pradesh, India." *Gender, Technology and Development* 4.1 (2000): 131–144.

Pande, Rohini. "Can mandated political representation increase policy influence for disadvantaged minorities? Theory and evidence from India." *American Economic Review* 93.4 (2003): 1132–1151.

Pande, Rohini, and Deanna Ford. "Gender s and female leadership." (2012).

Pankaj, Ashok, and Rukmini Tankha. "Empowerment effects of the NREGS on women workers: A study in four states." *Economic and Political Weekly* 45 (2010): 45–55.

Parthasarathy, Ramya, Vijayendra Rao, and Nethra Palaniswamy. "Deliberative democracy in an unequal world: A text-as-data study of South India's Village Assemblies." *The American Political Science Review* 113.3 (2019): 623–640.

Pateman, Carole. *The sexual contract*. Stanford University Press, 1988.

Patherya, Kaamila. "Domestic violence and the Indian Women's movement: A short history." *Inquiries Journal* 9.11 (2017): 1.

Pew Research Center, March 2, 2022, "How Indians view gender roles in families and society."

Piliavsky, Anastasia, ed. *Patronage as politics in South Asia*. Cambridge University Press, 2014.

Pitt, Mark M., Mark R. Rosenzweig, and Mohammad Nazmul Hassan. "Human capital investment and the gender division of labor in a brawn-based economy." *American Economic Review* 102.7 (2012): 3531–3560.

Pollak, Robert A. "Bargaining power in marriage: Earnings, wage rates and household production." (2005).

Posner, Daniel N. "The political salience of cultural difference: Why Chewas and Tumbukas are allies in Zambia and adversaries in Malawi." *American Political Science Review* 98 (2004): 529–545.

Institutions and ethnic politics in Africa. Cambridge University Press, 2005.

Poteete, Amy R., and Elinor Ostrom. "Heterogeneity, group size and collective action: The role of institutions in forest management." *Development and Change* 35.3 (2004): 435–461.

PRADAN and Jagori. "Transforming Development Practice: Taking a gender equality approach to support rural women in advancing their social, economic and political rights." *UN Women Report* (2016).

Prillaman, Soledad Artiz. "Strength in numbers: How women's groups close India's political gender gap." *American Journal of Political Science* 67 (2021): 390–410.

Prillaman, Soledad Artiz, et al. What constrains young Indian women's labor force participation? Evidence from a survey of vocational trainees. Technical Report. Cambridge, MA: J-PAL and Evidence for Policy Design, Harvard University.

https://epod.cid.harvard.edu/sites/default/files/2018-05/pandeprillamanmoore singh_skillspolicybrief.pdf, 2017.

Putnam, Robert D. "Bowling alone: America's declining social capital." In *Culture and politics*, Lane, Crothers, Charles, Lockhart (eds). Palgrave Macmillan, 2000. 223–234. P. 67.

Putnam, Robert D., Robert Leonardi, and Raffaella Y. Nanetti. *Making democracy work: Civic traditions in modern Italy.* Princeton University Press, 1992.

Qian, Nancy. "Missing women and the price of tea in China: The effect of sex-specific earnings on sex imbalance." *The Quarterly Journal of Economics* 123.3 (2008): 1251–1285.

Ragavan, Maya, and Kirti Iyengar. "Violence perpetrated by mothers-in-law in northern India: Perceived frequency, acceptability, and options for survivors." *Journal of Interpersonal Violence* 35.17–18 (2020): 3308–3330.

Rahman, Aminur. *Women and microcredit in rural Bangladesh: Anthropological study of the rhetoric and realities of Grameen Bank lending.* Routledge, 2019.

Raleigh, C., Linke, A., Hegre, H., and Karlsen, J. (2010). "Introducing ACLED: An armed conflict location and event dataset: Special data feature". *Journal of Peace Research*, 47(5), 651–660. https://doi.org/10.1177/0022343310378914

Raman, Sita Anantha. *Women in India: A social and cultural history: A social and cultural history.* ABC-CLIO, 2009.

Rao, Vijayendra. "Wife-beating in rural South India: A qualitative and econometric analysis." *Social Science & Medicine* 44.8 (1997): 1169–1180.

Rautry, Samanwaya. "Supreme Court modifies its order on dowry harassment." *The Economic Times*, September 15, 2018, https://economictimes.indiatimes.com/news/politics-and-nation/supreme-court-modifies-its-order-on-dowry-harassment/article show/65806068.cms.

Rawlings, Laura B., and Gloria M. Rubio. "Evaluating the impact of conditional cash transfer programs." *The World Bank Research Observer* 20.1 (2005): 29–55.

Ray, Raka. *Fields of protest: Women's movements in India.* University of Minnesota Press, 2000.

Reddy, D. Narasimha, and Arun Patnaik. "Anti-arrack agitation of women in Andhra Pradesh." *Economic and Political Weekly* 28 (1993): 1059–1066.

Reuters. "BJP's Kerala president calls for protests as women enter Sabarimala temple." *Reuters*, January 1, 2019, www.reuters.com/article/india-temple-idINKCN1OW0AH.

Reynolds, Andrew. "Women in the legislatures and executives of the world: Knocking at the highest glass ceiling." *World Politics* 51.4 (1999): 547–572.

Robinson, Amanda Lea, and Jessica Gottlieb. "How to close the gender gap in political participation: Lessons from matrilineal societies in Africa." *British Journal of Political Science* 51 (2019): 1–25.

Robinson, Marguerite. *The microfinance revolution: Sustainable finance for the poor.* World Bank Publications, 2001.

Ronconi, Lucas, and Rodrigo Zarazaga. "Household-based clientelism: Brokers' allocation of temporary public works programs in Argentina." *Studies in Comparative International Development* 54.3 (2019): 365–380.

Rosenstone, Steven J., and John Mark Hansen. *Mobilization, participation, and democracy in America.* Longman Publishing Group, 1993.

Roychowdhury, Poulami. ""The Delhi gang rape": The making of international causes." *Feminist Studies* 39.1 (2013): 282–292.

Capable women, incapable states: Negotiating violence and rights in India. Oxford University Press, 2020.

Rueda, David. "Insider-outsider politics in industrialized democracies: The challenge to social democratic parties." *American Political Science Review* 99 (2005): 61–74.

Samuelson, Paul A. "Social indifference curves." *The Quarterly Journal of Economics* 70.1 (1956): 1–22.

Sanyal, Paromita. "From credit to collective action: The role of microfinance in promoting women's social capital and normative influence." *American Sociological Review* 74.4 (2009): 529–550.

Credit to capabilities: A sociological study of microcredit groups in India. Cambridge University Press, 2014.

Sanyal, Paromita, Vijayendra Rao, and Shruti Majumdar. *Recasting culture to undo gender: A sociological analysis of Jeevika in Rural Bihar, India.* The World Bank, 2015.

Sapiro, Virginia. "Research frontier essay: When are interests interesting? The problem of political representation of women." *The American Political Science Review* 75 (1981): 701–716.

The political integration of women: Roles, socialization, and politics. University of Illinois Press, 1983.

Sarachild, Kathie. *Consciousness raising: A radical weapon.* Na, 1978.

Schlozman, Kay Lehman, Nancy Burns, and Sidney Verba. "Gender and the pathways to participation: The role of resources." *The Journal of Politics* 56.4 (1994): 963–990.

Schlozman, Kay Lehman, et al. "Gender and citizen participation: Is there a different voice?" *American Journal of Political Science* (1995): 267–293.

Schwartz, Matthew S. "Protests erupt in southern India after women defy centuries-old temple ban." *NPR*, January 2, 2019, www.npr.org/2019/01/02/681544151/pro tests-erupt-in-southern-india-after-women-defy-centuries-old-temple-ban.

Schwindt-Bayer, Leslie A., and William Mishler. "An integrated model of women's representation." *The Journal of Politics* 67.2 (2005): 407–428.

Sen, Amartya. "More than a hundred million women are missing." *New York Review of Books* 20 (1990): 61–66.

"Well-being, agency and freedom: The Dewey lectures 1984." *The Journal of Philosophy* 82.4 (1985): 169–221.

"Gender and cooperative conflicts." (1987).

Inequality reexamined. Harvard University Press, 1995.

Development as freedom. Alfred A. Knopf, 1999.

Sen, Gita. "Empowerment as an approach to poverty." Working Paper Series 97.07 (1997), background paper for the UNDP Human Development Report, New York: UNDP.

Sen, Samita. *Toward a feminist politics?: The Indian Women's Movement in historical perspective.* World Bank, Development Research Group/Poverty Reduction and Economic Management Network, 2000.

Sharma, Aradhana. *Logics of empowerment: Development, gender, and governance in neoliberal India.* University of Minnesota Press, 2008.

Shapiro, Robert Y., and Harpreet Mahajan. "Gender differences in policy preferences: A summary of trends from the 1960s to the 1980s." *Public Opinion Quarterly* 50.1 (1986): 42–61.

Sherwin, Susan. *The politics of women's health: Exploring agency and autonomy.* Temple University Press, 1998.

Sheth, Surili, Nivedita Narain, Arundhita Bhanjdeo, and Michael Walton. "Seeing like a state or seeing the state? A qualitative study of a government program to support women's self-help groups in Madhya Pradesh, India." *Manuscript in progress* (2021).

Shingles, Richard D. "Black consciousness and political participation: The missing link." *The American Political Science Review* 75 (1981): 76–91.

Sinclair, Betsy. *The social citizen: Peer networks and political behavior.* University of Chicago Press, 2012.

Singh, Anubha. "The PRADAN-Jagori Collaboration for Gender Equality." *NewsReach* (2014).

Singh, Prerna. *How solidarity works for welfare: Subnationalism and social development in India.* Cambridge University Press, 2015.

Skorge, Øyvind. "Mobilizing the underrepresented: Electoral systems and gender inequality in political participation." *American Journal of Political Science* (2021).

Solijonov, Abdurashid. "Voter turnout trends around the world." Institute for Democracy and Electoral Assistance (2016).

Soss, Joe. *Unwanted claims: The politics of participation in the US welfare system.* University of Michigan Press, 2002.

Srinivas, M. N. "The Indian road to equality." *Economic Weekly* 12 (1960): 867–872.

Spary, Carole. "Women candidates, women voters, and the gender politics of India's 2019 parliamentary election." *Contemporary South Asia* 28 (2020): 1–19.

Stevenson, Betsey, and Justin Wolfers. "Bargaining in the shadow of the law: Divorce laws and family distress." *The Quarterly Journal of Economics* 121.1 (2006): 267–288.

Stoker, Laura, and M. Kent Jennings. "Life-cycle transitions and political participation: The case of marriage." *American Political Science Review* 89 (1995): 421–433.

Stokes, Susan C. "Perverse accountability: A formal model of machine politics with evidence from Argentina." *American Political Science Review* 99 (2005): 315–325.

Stokes, Susan C., et al. *Brokers, voters, and clientelism: The puzzle of distributive politics.* Cambridge University Press, 2013.

Sundström, Aksel, et al. "Women's political empowerment: A new global index, 1900–2012." *World Development* 94 (2017): 321–335.

Suryanarayan, Pavithra, and Steven White. "Slavery, reconstruction, and bureaucratic capacity in the American south." *American Political Science Review* 115.2 (2021): 568–584.

Szymanski, Dawn M., Susan Kashubeck-West, and Jill Meyer. "Internalized heterosexism: A historical and theoretical overview." *The Counseling Psychologist* 36.4 (2008): 510–524.

Tankard, Margaret E., and Elizabeth Levy Paluck. "Norm perception as a vehicle for social change." *Social Issues and Policy Review* 10.1 (2016): 181–211.

Teele, Dawn Langan. *Forging the franchise: The political origins of the women's vote.* Princeton University Press, 2018.

Teele, Dawn Langan, Joshua Kalla, and Frances Rosenbluth. "The ties that double bind: Social roles and women's underrepresentation in politics." *The American Political Science Review* 112.3 (2018): 525–541.

Tewari, Ruhi. "Rural livelihoods plan in focus ahead of 2019 as BJP looks to gain from welfare push." *The Pint*, June 7, 2018, https://theprint.in/india/governance/bjp-hopes-to-gain-from-push-for-rural-livelihoods-in-election-year/67161/.

"TCPD-IED: TCPD Indian Elections Data 1.0", Trivedi Centre for Political Data, Ashoka University. 2021.

Thachil, Tariq. *Elite parties, poor voters: How social services win votes in India.* Cambridge University Press, 2014.

The Indian Express. "The rise of the female voting bloc." *The Indian Express*, May 10, 2021, https://indianexpress.com/article/opinion/the-rise-of-the-female-voting-bloc-elections-7309796/.

The Times of India. "Women's Wall highlights: Massive turnout in Kerala for equal rights." *The Times of India*, January 1, 2019, https://timesofindia.indiatimes.com/city/thiruvananthapuram/womens-wall-live-updates-massive-turnout-in-kerala-for-equal-rights/articleshow/67335718.cms.

The Times of India. "PM Modi to interact with woman self-help groups on Thursday." *The Times of India*, August 11, 2021, https://timesofindia.indiatimes.com/india/pm-modi-to-interact-with-woman-self-help-groups-on-thursday/articleshow/85237062.cms.

Thiagarajan, Kamala. "Millions of women in India join hands to form a 385-mile wall of protest." *NPR*, January 4, 2019, www.npr.org/sections/goatsandsoda/2019/01/04/681988452/millions-of-women-in-india-join-hands-to-form-a-385-mile-wall-of-protest.

Tong, James. "The gender gap in political culture and participation in China." *Communist and Post-Communist Studies* 36.2 (2003): 131–150.

Tripp, Aili Mari. "Women's movements, customary law, and land rights in Africa: The case of Uganda." *African Studies Quarterly* 7.4 (2004): 1–19.

Tripp, Aili Mari, and Alice Kang. "The global impact of quotas: On the fast track to increased female legislative representation." *Comparative Political Studies* 41.3 (2008): 338–361.

Tripp, Aili Mari, et al. *African women's movements: Transforming political landscapes.* Cambridge University Press, 2008.

Uhlaner, Carole J. "Rational turnout: The neglected role of groups." *American Journal of Political Science* 33 (1989): 390–422.

UN Women. "Violence against women and girls: The shadow pandemic." Retrieved November 8 (2020): 2020.

UNESCO Institute for Statistics (UIS). http://uis.unesco.org/en/country/in. September 18, 2020.

United Nations. *Gender Mainstreaming.* Report of the economic and social council (1997).

Unnithan, P. S. Gopikrishnan. "Sabarimala protests bring BJP, Congress on same side in Kerala." *India Today*, November 20, 2018, www.indiatoday.in/india/story/sabarimala-protests-bring-bjp-congress-on-same-side-in-kerala-1392598-2018-11-20.

Urbinati, Nadia, and Mark E. Warren. "The concept of representation in contemporary democratic theory.' *Annual Review of Political Science*, 11 (2008): 387.

Vaishnav, Milan. "Indian women are voting more than ever. Will they change Indian society?" *Carnegie Endowment for International Peace*, November 8, 2018.

Vaishnav, Milan and Jamie Hintston. "Will women decide India's 2019 elections?" *Carnegie Endowment for International Peace*, November 12, 2018.

Van der Windt, Peter, Macartan Humphreys, and Raul Sanchez de la Sierra. "Gender quotas in development programming: Null results from a field experiment in Congo." *Journal of Development Economics* 133 (2018): 326–345.

Van Zomeren, Martijn, Tom Postmes, and Russell Spears. "Toward an integrative social identity model of collective action: A quantitative research synthesis of three socio-psychological perspectives." *Psychological Bulletin* 134.4 (2008): 504.

Varshney, Ashutosh. "Ethnic conflict and civil society: India and beyond." *World Politics* 53 (2001): 362–398.

Ethnicity and ethnic conflict. Oxford University Press, 2009.

Verba, Sidney, Norman H. Nie, and Jae-on Kim. *Participation and political equality: A seven-nation comparison.* Cambridge University Press Archive, 1978.

Verba, Sidney, Kay Lehman Schlozman, and Henry E. Brady. *Voice and equality: Civic voluntarism in American politics.* Harvard University Press, 1995.

Verba, Sidney, Nancy Burns, and Kay Lehman Schlozman. "Knowing and caring about politics: Gender and political engagement." *The Journal of Politics* 59.4 (1997): 1051–1072.

"Unequal at the starting line: Creating participatory inequalities across generations and among groups." *The American Sociologist* 34.1–2 (2003): 45–69.

Verma, Rahul and Ankita Barthwal. "How women voters are altering India's electoral politics, in five charts." *Live Mint*, March 8, 2021, www.livemint.com/news/india/how-women-voters-are-altering-india-s-electoral-politics-in-five-charts-1161518449640 7.html.

Vicente, Pedro C., and Leonard Wantchekon. "Clientelism and vote buying: Lessons from field experiments in African elections." *Oxford Review of Economic Policy* 25.2 (2009): 292–305.

Walby, Sylvia. "Gender mainstreaming: Productive tensions in theory and practice." *Social Politics: International Studies in Gender, State & Society* 12.3 (2005): 321–343.

Wantchekon, Leonard. "Clientelism and voting behavior: Evidence from a field experiment in Benin." *World Politics* 55.3 (2003): 399–422.

Ward, Michael D., Katherine Stovel, and Audrey Sacks. "Network analysis and political science." *Annual Review of Political Science* 14 (2011): 245–264.

Washington, Ebonya L. "Female socialization: How daughters affect their legislator fathers." *American Economic Review* 98.1 (2008): 311–32.

Waylen, Georgina, and Vicky Randall, eds. *Gender, politics and the state.* Routledge, 1998.

Weeks, Ana Catalano. *Quotas matter: The impact of gender quota laws on work-family policies.* Mimeo, 2019.

Making gender salient: From gender quota laws to policy. Cambridge University Press, 2022.

Weeks, Ana Catalano, et al. "When do Männerparteien elect women? Radical right populist parties and strategic descriptive representation." *American Political Science Review* 117 (2023): 1–18.

Weldon, S. Laurel. *Protest, policy, and the problem of violence against women: A cross-national comparison.* University of Pittsburgh Press, 2002.

Weston, Cynthia, et al. "Analyzing interview data: The development and evolution of a coding system." *Qualitative Sociology* 24.3 (2001): 381–400.

Wilkinson, Steven. *Votes and violence: Electoral competition and ethnic riots in India.* Cambridge University Press, 2006.

Wilkinson, Steven I. "The politics of infrastructural spending in India." *Department of Political Science, University of Chicago, mimeo* 31 (2006).

World Bank. "In India, women's self-help groups combat the COVID-19 (Coronavirus) pandemic." *World Bank*, April 11, 2020, www.worldbank.org/en/news/feature/2020/04/11/women-self-help-groups-combat-covid19-coronavirus-pandemic-india

World Health Organization, Department of Reproductive Health and Research, London School of Hygiene and Tropical Medicine, South African Medical Research Council (2013). Global and regional estimates of violence against women: Prevalence and health effects of intimate partner violence and non-partner sexual violence, p. 2.

World Health Organization. "Violence against women prevalence estimates, 2018: Global, regional and national prevalence estimates for intimate partner violence against women and global and regional prevalence estimates for non-partner sexual violence against women." (2021).

Ziegfeld, Adam. *Why regional parties?* Cambridge University Press, 2016.

Zimmermann, Laura. "It's a boy! Women and decision-making benefits from a son in India." *World Development* 104 (2018): 326–335.

Ziparo, Roberta. "Why do spouses communicate? Love or interest? A model and some evidence from Cameroon." Unpublished manuscript (2014).

Index

Other Books in the Series (continued from page iii)

For EU product safety concerns, contact us at Calle de José Abascal, 56–1°, 28003 Madrid, Spain or eugpsr@cambridge.org.

www.ingramcontent.com/pod-product-compliance
Ingram Content Group UK Ltd.
Pitfield, Milton Keynes, MK11 3LW, UK
UKHW040621240426
470322UK00011B/247